THE JEW IN A
GENTILE WORLD

THE MACMILLAN COMPANY
NEW YORK · CHICAGO
DALLAS · ATLANTA · SAN FRANCISCO
LONDON · MANILA

IN CANADA
BRETT-MACMILLAN LTD.
GALT, ONTARIO

An Anthology of Writings
About Jews, by Non-Jews

THE JEW IN A
GENTILE WORLD

Edited by
ARNOLD A. ROGOW

With an Introduction by
C. P. SNOW
and an Epilogue by
HAROLD D. LASSWELL

New York
The Macmillan Company
1961

First Printing

The Macmillan Company, New York
Brett-Macmillan Ltd., Galt, Ontario

Printed in the United States of America

Library of Congress catalog card number: 61-10338

To the memory of my parents,
Morris Rogow and Mary Hilelson Rogow;
And for Sadie Rogow Simon.

PREFACE

The justification for this book, insofar as it needs one, is that non-Jews have been interested in Jews for several thousands of years. The ancient world saw the Jews as separate and unique, and the sense of separateness and uniqueness, whether or not based on any reality, has been characteristic of the Gentile view of the Jew throughout history. But there has never been agreement on the particular qualities that make Jews "different." The responses or reactions engendered in non-Jews by these alleged qualities are almost infinite.

In the selections that follow, covering a period of almost twenty-five centuries, Jews are loved and hated, accepted and rejected, held in esteem and held in contempt. The authors of these selections reflect the whole range of feeling about Jews, from an extreme anti-Semitism threatening, and in some cases accomplishing, wholesale extermination of Jews, to an extreme philo-Semitism tending toward self-identification with Jews. Certain writers, it will become evident, began as philo-Semites, and ended as anti-Semites, and there are even a few who reversed this direction. Perhaps it is true, as Edmund Wilson suggests, that an obsessive pro-Semitism is capable of a sudden transformation into a neurotic anti-Semitism. It may also be argued that the "democrat" who insists that Jews are "like other people" and the anti-Semite, to the extent that they *both* deny the right of the Jew to be a Jew, that is, different, are joined in an endeavor to annihilate his essential Jewishness. Indeed history records that the Jew has been accepted (or rejected) as a man but not as a Jew almost as frequently as he has been accepted (or rejected) as a Jew but not as a man.

Nevertheless, it is difficult to look back upon twenty-five centuries of Gentile-Jewish relations and avoid the conclusion that every Jew is entitled to say, with Stephen Dedalus in Joyce's *Ulysses*, that "History is a nightmare from which I am trying to awake." During most of history, the Jews have suffered not too much but too little at the hands of philo-Semites, pro-Semites, and "democrats." Jew-baiters and anti-Semites of one variety or the other—Greek, Roman, and Christian—have largely dominated the Gentile world, and as a result that world has been one in which the Jew has always had to move cautiously and, more often than not, live dangerously. Although the rise of the democratic state has been accompanied by increased toleration of Jews and other minorities, it is worth recalling that the full political and civil emancipation of Jews dates only to 1791 in France and to 1860 in England. Nor should grants of emancipation be confused with the absence of anti-Semitism. In the modern world no less than in earlier times, anti-Semites have had, and continue to have, their say—or, as was the case in Nazi Germany, their day.

It may be hoped, however, that the present volume will serve to clarify not merely the historical record, but certain issues and problems of contemporary Gentile-Jewish relations. Non-Jews, in reading the selections, may find themselves questioning or modifying their own attitudes toward Jews. If, for example, they are "democrats," are they fully reconciled to the elimination of whatever contribution Jews, as Jews, can make to their world? And if they believe that Jews are and should continue to be "different," can they accept Jewish "difference," live with it, perhaps cherish it? Finally, they may be inclined to ask themselves the question: What is it, or who is it, that I should like the Jew to be? Am I capable of admiring him or liking him if he is, or becomes—simply himself?

Jewish readers, confronting the diverse images of themselves in the following pages, may also find much to ponder. While, for most Gentiles, the Jews have always been "different," the "difference" imputed to Jews has changed over time. What is the significance of these shifts of emphasis, Jews may want to ask, for an understanding of Gentile-Jewish relations in the past, present, and future? More specifically, does the history of these relations argue for the survival of the Jew as a member of a distinct religion and culture, or does it promote a choice between two kinds of extinction: assimilation or physical liquidation? And for the Jew, as for the Gentile, there is a form of the question asked above: What is it, or who is it, that I should like to be? In the depths of my consciousness, am I proud or ashamed of being a Jew in a Gentile world?

The task of selecting materials for this anthology has not been easy, and no doubt some explanations, or even justifications, are in order. Since the book is concerned with Gentile attitudes toward Jews, I have not included Jewish writings with the exception of a few documents that provide important background for understanding particular selections (as in the cases of Peter Stuyvesant, U. S. Grant, and others), or that constitute the only source of such selections (for example, the anti-Semitic views of Apion, a Greek grammarian of the first century A.D., are known to us only through the work of the Jewish historian Flavius Josephus). Although portrayals of Jews abound in fiction, poetry, and drama, I have excluded most of these sources for a variety of reasons. To begin with, novels, poems, and plays that deal with Jews—for instance, *The Merchant of Venice*—are much better known than nonfiction writings about Jews. Second, the Jew in literature has been treated extensively [in such books as M. J. Landa, *The Jew in Drama* (London, 1926); Montagu Frank Modder, *The Jew in the Literature of England* (Philadelphia, 1939); and Edgar Rosenberg, *From Shylock to Svengali* (Stanford, 1960)]. Finally—and this with reference to the omission of certain nonfiction selections as well—space limitations have necessitated a rigorous pruning of available materials. It simply has not been possible to include in one volume everything that has been written about Jews over a period of twenty-five centuries.

I am indebted to a large number of writers and publishers for permission to reprint portions of their works. I am especially grateful to the American Jewish Historical Society, the Jewish Publication Society of America, and the Union of American Hebrew Congregations for permission to draw on their publications. Jacob R. Marcus, Adolf S. Ochs Professor of American Jewish History at Hebrew Union College and Director of the American Jewish Archives, kindly permitted me to reprint certain documents from his *The Jew in the Medieval World/ A Source Book: 315–1791* (copyright 1938 by Union of American Hebrew Congregations, reprinted 1960 by Meridian Books, Inc., and the Jewish Publication Society of America).

I am deeply appreciative of the assistance provided by a number of individuals. My research assistants, Miss Sandra Levinson and Mr. James Kerr, gave me indispensable aid. Miss Levinson helped in the preparation of the historical and biographical notes. Mr.

Kerr assisted me in locating materials from which the selections are taken. Thus they both deserve a measure of credit for whatever merit the anthology may possess.

My debt is very great to my friends, C. P. Snow and Harold D. Lasswell. I am grateful to them for contributing the Introduction and Epilogue, respectively.

I should like to thank Mrs. Mary Prendergast for her expert secretarial services. Mrs. Prendergast typed the final draft of the manuscript, and relieved me of a variety of other chores connected with its publication.

Finally, I owe a good deal to my wife, Patricia Evans Rogow. Had she not protected the study from frequent invasions by small and large persons (who here shall be nameless) at considerable sacrifice of her own time and energy, the entire venture would have suffered from an extended neglect. And beyond that, she has contributed much to these pages and to me that can be neither repaid nor adequately acknowledged.

ARNOLD A. ROGOW

Stanford, Calif.
June 1, 1961.

CONTENTS

PART III
THE JEW IN THE MIDDLE AGES
1186–1588

PART IV
THE JEW IN MODERN EUROPE
1621–1959

INTRODUCTION

C. P. Snow

When I was very poor and very young, I was taken up by one of the rich patrician Anglo-Jewish families. It was a startling experience. I was a Gentile, and I had never seen the inside of a Jewish family before. What impressed me more at the time, I had never been inside an influential family before. This was my first contact with the easy, interconnected, confident world of the English ruling classes. Up to that time, cabinet ministers, high court judges, bosses of the civil service were, for me, people one read about in newspapers. At my friends' houses I met these people: in fact, my friends' relatives occupied just such jobs. It was a slightly off-beat introduction to a layer of English society which later on I happened to get to know quite well. The introduction was off-beat, of course, because my friends' family, in ninety-nine ways out of one hundred indistinguishable from an upper-class English family, in one way was not. They were, after all, Jewish: and the younger ones, my own generation, were conscious of it. When I got fascinated by the argumentativeness, the brilliance, the vivacity of the great family parties, my friends were anxious, pressingly anxious, that I should not take them at a false valuation. "You seem to think," they used to say, "that Jews are more intelligent than anyone else. You must get it into perspective. We can produce Jews for you who are much stupider and much duller than anyone you can possibly believe. You just have a look at Cousin X and Aunt Y."

My friends' desire was to prove that everyone is much the same, which is a very praiseworthy thing to do. Also they didn't want me to be beglamoured. I suppose I was a bit beglamoured then. To an extent I have remained so ever since. It is very difficult, and pretty disreputable intellectually, to make generalizations about large groups of people whose main connection is that they are called by the same label. But I should have thought that, if one were going to play that game at all, Jews have—to a slight but significant extent —thrown out more ability in relation to their numbers than any other group on earth.

It is worth remembering that, when one estimates how many Jews have ever lived, the number is quite small. Yet the amount of Jewish genius and talent in almost every high level of activity can bear comparison, not in relative but in absolute terms, with that of far larger groups such as the Russians or the English or the French, who themselves have a creditable record.

It is a bit of a mystery why this should be so. Part of it must be owing to the genes, and the Jews, who have not been lucky in much, have obviously been lucky in the genes. Where has this wonderful gene pool come from? No one has given me an answer which seems remotely satisfactory. If the marriage laws had been kept, all the genes would date back to before the Babylonian captivity. But with all respect to tradition, I just do not believe that is true. You have only got to look at Jews from different parts of the world to see that the structure of the gene pool is more complicated than that. It would be of the deepest interest to see a genetic reconstruction of the Jewish "race" from the diaspora onward.

Then, as well as the genetic inheritance, there is environment. You can't persecute a group of people for nearly two thousand years, keep them out of various sorts of jobs, set them apart and cause them to set themselves apart, without producing certain minimum effects. Some of these effects, of course, inhibited the emergence of Jewish talents. For instance, it must have been difficult for a Jew to show his athletic prowess in Western Europe in the Middle Ages, or almost up to the time of the emergence of the great Jewish boxers in the eighteenth century. But some talents, particularly the intellectual talents, based on the belief that the mind is a good and private thing, the centuries of persecution probably reinforced.

In any case, the result is on the table. As I said before, in almost every sphere of human activity, the Jews have made a contribution utterly out of proportion to their numbers. I have often heard this contribution undervalued, even in England, which, of the countries I know well, is probably the least anti-Semitic. The technique is always the same. It consists of praising the Jewish talent for one kind of activity, in order to disparise it for another, which for the purposes of argument is regarded as more significant. Thus: Jews have done pretty well in mathematics, or theoretical physics, or idea-spinning, but have never really been any good at experimental science, at really plucking out the secrets of nature. I used to hear that thirty years ago. It sounds very silly now. Of the last dozen Nobel Prize winners for experimental physics, three have been Jewish. Only the other day I heard one of these ranked by his peers as the greatest experimental physicist alive. In exactly the same way, it used to be said that in literature Jews produced some of the best critics, but not the first-class creative artists. This was still being said in England in the thirties after Proust's great book, after Svevo, after heaven knows how many others. Now I think it would take some nerve to say it. Try writing down the ten most interesting creative artists in prose fiction in the United States at the present day under the age of fifty. Most of us will include five or six Jewish names. In productive industry one hears the same dismal trick. Jews are all right in the City, or Wall Street, as the case may be, but are no use at making the hardware. Yet, from H. R. Ricardo down increasingly to the present day, American and British industry employs in the highest ranks of engineers about five times as many Jews as is statistically reasonable.

I am sick and tired of all this special pleading, of all these attempts to prove that one group of people, for the moment disapproved of, Jews or Russians or Japanese, are in some subtle way less creative than our own. These attempts are nonsense and, consciously or unconsciously, dishonest nonsense. This is specially true when applied to the Jewish talent. The only point about the Jewish talent that ought to matter deeply to the world is that there is a lot of it.

My first Jewish friends were, of course, right when they didn't want me to see or think of Jews as a collective entity. It is an outrage to human dignity to think of someone first as a label and then as a man. That is why all class structures and all "race" structures degrade, in an unnecessary and trivial fashion, the human condition. Yet we are still living, let us hope temporarily, in just such structures. Ilya Ehrenburg, in a speech on his seventieth birthday, recently said that he liked to think of himself first and foremost as a man, but that while there is a single anti-Semite alive, he is proud to be a Jew. Perhaps our Jewish friends will forgive us if we, who are not Jews, say much the same thing. While there is a single anti-Semite alive, we are proud to be on the other side.

I

THE JEW IN THE
ANCIENT WORLD

419 B.C.—*First Century* A.D.

HISTORICAL NOTE

The Jew, according to Biblical tradition, can trace his ancestry to Abraham, the son of Terah, who lived more than fifteen hundred years before the birth of Christ. Abraham's descendents, along with the Assyrians and Arameans, are regarded by the Bible as having a common ancestor in Shem, the son of Noah. The Canaanites, who spoke a language rather similar to Hebrew, and the Egyptians, on the other hand, are placed in the line of descent from Shem's brother, Ham. But all these ancient peoples spoke related languages, commonly referred to as Semitic (Shemitic), and it is clear that there was a good deal of cultural interchange. History suggests that the ancestry of the modern Children of Israel was, in fact, a mixed one.

When Abraham left his father's home in Ur of the Chaldees for the Land of Canaan (called by the Romans Palestine, and by the Jews Land of Israel), he was accompanied by Lot, his brother's son and the father of Moab and Ammon. We are told in Isaiah (51:2) that Abraham was "called" by God to Palestine, where he was to establish, in a foreign land, a separate and independent nation. The Children of Israel, under this Covenant, were to worship the one true God, *Yahweh,* and they were to be His chosen people. The Land of Israel (Palestine) was promised by God to the Jews, and they were to hold it forever.

Although the early Hebrews were a nomadic people, by the sixteenth century before the Christian era the Israelites, divided into twelve tribes, had established settlements throughout Palestine. Refusing to intermarry with the native tribes, the Israelites largely led a life apart. They abominated the religious polytheism of the Canaanites, and regarded their cities as dens of iniquity. Canaanite practices—idol worship, sorcery and magic, self-immolation during certain religious rites, sexual promiscuity—horrified them, and relations with their Canaanite neighbors were mainly confined to transactions affecting the ownership of land. For the most part, these transactions were peaceful, but occasionally land or water rights were acquired by force.

The several centuries preceding the birth of Moses were characterized by some dissension among the twelve tribes, and by persecution at the hands of the Egyptian overlords of Palestine. It is to this period that the Biblical story of Joseph belongs, and the long period of bondage under a succession of Egyptian kings. The epochal event of the exodus from Egypt in 1220, led by Moses, is too well known to be narrated here. The religious birth of Israel, and in significant measure the origin of the Western religious tradition, can be dated to that momentous occasion when Moses received from God the two stone tablets on which were graven the Ten Words.

The years after Moses' death were followed by intermittent warfare with Canaanites, Moabites, Midianites, and Philistines. In an effort to strengthen themselves, especially against the Philistines, the tribes of Israel established a limited monarchy *circa* 1100 with Saul, of the tribe of Benjamin, upon the throne. Saul was succeeded by David, of the tribe of Judah, who founded a long dynasty. Under King David nomadic culture gradually began to give way to urban society, and the process of urbanization was continued during the reign of David's son, Solomon. Solomon transferred the centers of Jewish life from rural settlements to the towns and cities, and his elaborate court and ambitious building program created a large class of religious and civic officials.

Even in Solomon's time, however, there was much popular discontent occasioned by the high taxes necessary for the maintenance of his court and the Temple in Jerusalem. Thus when Solomon was followed by his son, the unpopular Rehoboam, the ten tribes of Israel revolted and renounced the union with Judah. The secession of Northern Israel from the united monarchy in 937 was followed by more than two centuries of war and internal upheaval. In 720 the divided and weakened Israelites were conquered by Sargon II of Assyria. When Nebuchadnezzar, King of Babylon, destroyed the Kingdom of Judah and its capital, Jerusalem, in 586, the population was forced into captivity in Babylonia.

The relatively short period of the Babylonian exile (586–538) was terminated by the Persian conquest of Babylonia. Although the Persians permitted the Jews to return to Palestine, many chose to remain in Babylonia where, on the whole, they were fairly treated. Indeed, the two centuries of Persian supremacy (538–332) were marked by a relative peace that permitted the Jews to devote themselves to spiritual and religious concerns. The Jews who returned to Jerusalem, for example, received permission from King Cyrus of Persia to rebuild the Temple. The Temple, a visible symbol of the religious tradition, was completed during the reign of Darius I in 515. The years after saw the consolidation of religious beliefs and practices that could be traced back to the time of

Moses, and they also constituted a period of intellectual activity and ferment.

Meanwhile the influence of Hellenistic civilization was slowly advancing from the West. The culminating event was the triumph over Persia of Alexander the Great in 332, a victory that brought the whole of Western Asia under Greek dominion. Alexander's generals divided the conquered territory among themselves: the Ptolemies ruled in Egypt, and the Seleucids gained control of Syria. Under the Ptolemies, who treated the Jews with some benevolence, Jewish settlements rapidly expanded in Egypt, especially in Alexandria. And even when the Seleucids occupied Egypt in 202, the constitutional position of Palestine remained unaffected. Hellenism, moreover, enjoyed considerable support within the Jewish community. But when the Temple at Jerusalem was dedicated to Jupiter in 168, sympathizers with Hellenism were overwhelmed by fierce protestations which led to the insurrection of the Maccabees.

In 165, following the Maccabean revolt which was national as well as religious in scope, the Temple was rededicated by Judah, the Maccabee. Although Syria intervened and ultimately gained control, the Maccabeans, in a period of twenty-six years (168–142) succeeded in establishing religious and political independence for Judea. The Syrians did not attempt to interfere with Jewish religious practices and institutions.

The period of Greek ascendancy was followed by Roman mastery of the Eastern and Western worlds, and toward the close of the second century B.C. Judea was governed as a Roman feudal principality. In 139 the Jews were expelled from Rome itself, but in the same year the Roman Senate gave formal recognition to the independence of Judea. Relations between the Romans and the Jews, however, were far from easy. The conquest of Jerusalem by the Roman general Pompey, in 63, was followed by a massacre of gigantic proportions; many of the survivors were sent to Rome, as slaves. Thirty years after Pompey's triumph, Herod the Great was named Prefect of Galilee. Known as a magnificent builder and patron of the arts, Herod (who ruled 37–4) filled Judea with public buildings in the Roman style. He also rebuilt the Temple in magnificent splendor, and was friendly to the Pharisees, one of the three major Jewish sects (the other two were the Sadducees and the Essenes) that had come into existence since the Maccabean insurrection.

Herod's successor, his son, was disliked by the Jews, and their complaints to Rome were finally responsible for his removal. Ultimately, effective power in Palestine passed to the Roman procurators, one of whom, Pontius Pilate, will be remembered until the end of time. It was during his procuratorship (A.D. 26–36) that John the Baptist was executed (29), and Jesus crucified (30).

Pontius Pilate was disliked by the Jews, and initially there was much rejoicing when Caligula became emperor in 37. Agrippa, the grandson of Herod, was friendly with the emperor, and it was thought that the friendship would be beneficial to Roman-Jewish relations. The Jews, however, refused to accept Caligula's claims to divinity, with the result that angry mobs in Alexandria and elsewhere rioted against the Jews and placed statues of the emperor in the synagogues.

Again with Claudius, who succeeded Caligula, there were hopes of an improvement in relations with Rome. Nor were these hopes frustrated at the outset. Claudius appointed Agrippa ruler of the entire area governed by his grandfather. Agrippa proved to be a popular monarch but his reign was short. His death in 44 restored the procurators to power, and the years that followed were characterized by increasing misunderstanding and ill will between Romans and Jews. Finally, pressed beyond endurance by heavy taxes, punitive exactions, and mockery of their religious practices, the Jews revolted against Roman rule. During the first phase of the rebellion, Roman forces were expelled from Jerusalem, and a revolutionary government established. But in 66, Roman brigades vastly superior to the Jewish army, laid siege to the city. In 70 the Temple was burned, and with its destruction the Jewish state ceased to exist.

YEDONIAH:

"If it please our lord,
take thought of this temple
to rebuild it, since they
do not let us rebuild it."
(407 B.C.)

The following documents, which date to the early fifth century B.C., relate to the Jewish military colony in Elephantine, an island in the Nile
River. The first document, known as the "Passover Papyrus" (419 B.C.)
authorizes the Jewish Garrison of Elephantine to commemorate the Feast
of Passover. The second document, in the form of a petition to the Governors of Judea and Samaria, concerns the destruction in the year 410 B.C.
of the Jewish Temple at Elephantine by a group of Egyptian priests.
Yedoniah, one of the military commanders of the Garrison, is petitioning
the Persian official Bagoas (or Bagohi), Governor of Judea, to have the
Temple rebuilt. As the third document (407 B.C.) records, Yedoniah's
petition was received with favor.

The Darius referred to is Darius II, who ruled Persia 424–404 B.C.

"The Passover Papyrus" (419 B.C.)

[To] my [brethren Yedo]niah and his colleagues the [J]ewish gar-
[rison], your brother Hanan[iah]. The welfare of my brothers may
God [seek at all times]. Now, this year, the fifth year of King Darius,

The selections from Yedoniah are translated by H. L. Ginsberg, in James B.
Pritchard, editor, *Ancient Near Eastern Texts Relating to the Old Testament*
(Princeton, New Jersey: Princeton University Press, 1950), pp. 491–492. Copy-
right 1950, Princeton University Press.

word was sent from the king to Arsa[mes saying, *"Authorize a festival of unleavened bread* for the Jew]ish [garrison]." So do you count fou[rteen days of the month of Nisan and] obs[erve *the passover*], and from the 15th to the 21st day of [Nisan observe the festival of unleavened bread]. Be (ritually) clean and take heed. [Do n]o work [on the 15th or the 21st day, no]r drink [beer, nor eat] anything [in] which the[re is] leaven [from the 14th at] sundown until the 21st of Nis[an. For seven days it shall not be seen among you. Do not br]ing it into your dwellings but seal (it) up between these date[s. *By order of King Darius.* To] my brethren Yedoniah and the Jewish garrison, your brother Hanani[ah].

"Petition for Authorization to Rebuild the Temple of Yaho" (*407* B.C.)

To our Lord Bagoas, governor of Judah, your servants Yedoniah and his colleagues, the priests who are in the fortress of Elephantine. May the God of Heaven seek after the welfare of our lord exceedingly at all times and give you favor before King Darius and the nobles a thousand times more than now. May you be happy and healthy at all times. Now, your servant Yedoniah and his colleagues depose as follows: In the month of Tammuz in the 14th year of King Darius, when Arsames departed and went to the king, the priests of the god Khnub, who is in the fortress of Elephantine, conspired with Vidaranag, who was commander-in-chief here, to wipe out the temple of the god Yaho from the fortress of Elephantine. So that wretch Vidaranag sent to his son Nefayan, who was in command of the garrison of the fortress of Syene, this order, "The temple of the god Yaho in the fortress of Yeb is to be destroyed." Nefayan thereupon led the Egyptians with the other troops. Coming with their weapons to the fortress of Elephantine, they entered that temple and razed it to the ground. The stone pillars that were there they smashed. Five "great" gateways built with hewn blocks of stone which were in that temple they demolished, but their doors *are standing*, and the hinges of those doors are of bronze; and *their* roof of cedarwood, all of it, with the . . . and whatever else was there, everything they burnt with fire. As for the basins of gold and silver and other articles that were in that temple, they carried all of them off and made them their own.—Now, our forefathers built this temple in the fortress of Elephantine back in the days of the kingdom of Egypt, and when Cambyses came to Egypt he found it built. They knocked down all the

temples of the gods of Egypt, but no one did any damage to this
temple. But when this happened, we and our wives and our children
wore sackcloth, and fasted, and prayed to Yaho the Lord of Heaven,
who has let us see our desire upon that Vidaranag. The dogs took
the fetter out of his feet, and any property he had gained was lost;
and any men who have sought to do evil to this temple have all been
killed and we have seen our desire upon them.—We have also sent a
letter before now, when this evil was done to us, [to] our lord and
to the high priest Johanan and his colleagues the priests in Jerusalem and to Ostanes the brother of Anani and the nobles of the Jews.
Never a letter have they sent to us. Also, from the month of Tammuz, year 14 of King Darius, to this day, we have been wearing
sackcloth and fasting, making our wives as widows, not anointing
ourselves with oil or drinking wine. Also, from then to now, in the
year 17 of King Darius, no meal-offering, in[cen]se, nor burnt offering have been offered in this temple. Now your servants Yedoniah,
and his colleagues, and the Jews, the citizens of Elephantine, all say
thus: if it please our lord, take thought of this temple to rebuild it,
since they do not let us rebuild it. Look to your well-wishers and
friends here in Egypt. Let a letter be sent from you to them concerning the temple of the god Yaho to build it in the fortress of Elephantine as it was built before; and the meal-offering, incense, and
burnt offering will be offered in your name, and we shall pray for
you at all times, we, and our wives, and our children, and the Jews
who are here, all of them, if you do thus, so that that temple is
rebuilt. And you shall have a merit before Yaho the God of Heaven
more than a man who offers to him burnt offering and sacrifices
worth a thousand talents of silver and [because of] gold. Because
of this we have written to inform you. We have also set the whole
matter forth in a letter in our name to Delaiah and Shelemiah, the
sons of Sanballat the governor of Samaria. Also, Arsames knew nothing of all that was done to us. On the 20th of Marheshwan, year 17
of King Darius.

*"Advice of the Governors of Judah and Samaria to the Jews of
Elephantine"* (*407* B.C.)

Memorandum of what Bagoas and Delaiah said to me: Let this be
an instruction to you in Egypt to say before Arsames about the
house of offering of the God of Heaven which had been in existence

in the fortress of Elephantine since ancient times, before Cambyses, and was destroyed by that wretch Vidaranag in the year 14 of King Darius: to rebuild it on its site as it was before, and the meal-offering and incense to be made on that altar as it used to be.

MARCUS TULLIUS CICERO:

"While Jerusalem was flourishing,
and while the Jews were in a peaceful state,
still the religious ceremonies and
observances of that people were very much at
variance with the splendor of this empire."
(55 B.C.?)

Marcus Tullius Cicero (106–43 B.C.), one of the greatest of Roman orators, was also a statesman, jurist, and author. Although he rendered distinguished service in a variety of positions, including that of consul, Cicero was banished from Rome by the First Triumvirate composed of Gaius Julius Caesar, Pompey, and Marcus Lincinius Grassus. He made few speeches during the period of Caesar's dictatorship, and the death of Caesar in March, 44 B.C., aroused hopes in Cicero that the Senate would become the foremost agency of Roman government. These hopes, however, were short-lived. Upon the formation of the Second Triumvirate of Antony, Octavianus, and Lepidus, Cicero's name was placed upon the proscribed list, and shortly thereafter he was assassinated at his villa.

Lucius Valerius Flaccus, whom Cicero defended against charges of misgovernment in Asia, had been a praetor during Cicero's consulship. Cicero's speech in his defense, from which the following is reprinted, deals in part with the accusation that Lucius Flaccus, as praetor, had prohibited the Jews of his province from collecting gold annually for the temple in Jerusalem. While the gold seized from the Jews was recommitted to Rome, and not reserved for the praetor's personal use, Lucius Flaccus was charged by his enemies with having departed from well established customs and traditions. Thus in defending Lucius Flaccus, Cicero is inclined to be critical of the Jews as such, in addition to stressing the virtues of his friend and client, the former praetor.

From Marcus Tullius Cicero, "In Defense of Lucius Flaccus," *The Orations of Marcus Tullius Cicero,* translated by C. D. Yonge (London: George Bell & Sons, 1880), Vol. II, 454–455.

The next thing is that charge about the Jewish gold. And this, forsooth, is the reason why this cause is pleaded near the steps of Aurelius. It is on account of this charge, O Lælius, that this place and that mob has been selected by you. You know how numerous that crowd is, how great is its unanimity, and of what weight it is in the popular assemblies. I will speak in a low voice, just so as to let the judges hear me. For men are not wanting who would be glad to excite that people against me and against every eminent man; and I will not assist them and enable them to do so more easily. As gold, under pretence of being given to the Jews, was accustomed every year to be exported out of Italy and all the provinces to Jerusalem, Flaccus issued an edict establishing a law that it should not be lawful for gold to be exported out of Asia. And who is there, O judges, who cannot honestly praise this measure? The senate had often decided, and when I was consul it came to a most solemn resolution that gold ought not to be exported. But to resist this barbarous superstition were an act of dignity, to despise the multitude of Jews, which at times was most unruly in the assemblies in defence of the interests of the republic, was an act of the greatest wisdom. "But Cnæus Pompeius, after he had taken Jerusalem, though he was a conqueror, touched nothing which was in that temple." In the first place, he acted wisely, as he did in many other instances, in leaving no room for his detractors to say anything against him, in a city so prone to suspicion and to evil speaking. For I do not suppose that the religion of the Jews, our enemies, was any obstacle to that most illustrious general, but that he was hindered by his own modesty. Where then is the guilt? Since you nowhere impute any theft to us, since you approve of the edict, and confess that it was passed in due form, and do not deny that the gold was openly sought for and produced, the facts of the case themselves show that the business was executed by the instrumentality of men of the highest character. There was a hundredweight of gold, more or less, openly seized at Apamea, and weighed out in the forum at the feet of the praetor, by Sextus Cæsius, a Roman knight, a most excellent and upright man; twenty pounds weight or a little more were seized at Laodicea, by Lucius Peducæus, who is here in court, one of our judges; some was seized also at Adramyttium, by Cnæus Domitius, the lieutenant, and a small quantity at Pergamus. The amount of the gold is known; the gold is in the treasury; no theft is imputed to him; but it is attempted to render him unpopular. The speaker turns away from the judges, and addresses himself to the surrounding multitude. Each city, O Lælius, has its own peculiar religion; we have ours. While Jerusalem was flourishing, and while the Jews were in a peaceful state, still the religious ceremonies and observances of that people were very much at variance with the splendour of this empire, and the dignity of our name, and the institutions of our ancestors. And they are the more odious to us now, because that nation has shown by arms what were its feelings towards our supremacy. How dear it was to the immortal gods is proved by its having been defeated, by its revenues having been farmed out to our contractors, by its being reduced to a state of subjection.

DIODORUS OF SICILY:

" . . . among the Jews
Moyses referred his laws to
the god who is invoked
as Iao."
(*49* B.C.)

Diodorus of Sicily was a Greek historian who lived during the first century B.C. A contemporary of Julius Caesar and Augustus, Diodorus traveled in the Middle East and spent some time in Rome and Egypt. Thirty years of his life, which ended before the Christian era, were spent in compiling his massive *Library of History,* consisting of forty books, divided into three parts. The forty books, a number of which do not survive, dealt with the histories of ancient Egypt, Ethiopia, Arabia, India, Spain, Gaul, Sicily, Sardinia, and Corsica. Diodorus also concerned himself with science and religion, and, as the following excerpt demonstrates, Diodorus made one of the earliest efforts to approach religion comparatively and, to a limited extent, in psychological terms.

We must speak also of the lawgivers who have arisen in Egypt and who instituted customs unusual and strange. After the estab-

From *Diodorus of Sicily,* translated by C. H. Oldfather. Reprinted by permission of Harvard University Press from Loeb Classical Library edition, Vol. I, 91, 319–321.

lishment of settled life in Egypt in early times, which took place, according to the mythical account, in the period of the gods and heroes, the first, they say, to persuade the multitudes to use written laws was Mneves, a man not only great of soul but also in his life the most public-spirited of all lawgivers whose names are recorded. According to the tradition he claimed that Hermes had given the laws to him, with the assurance that they would be the cause of great blessings, just as among the Greeks, they say, Minos did in Crete and Lycurgus among the Lacedaemonians, the former saying that he received his laws from Zeus and the latter his from Apollo. Also among several other peoples tradition says that this kind of a device was used and was the cause of much good to such as believed it. Thus it is recorded that among the Arians Zathraustes claimed that the Good Spirit gave him his laws, among the people known as the Getae who represent themselves to be immortal Zalmoxis asserted the same of their common goddess Hestia, and among the Jews Moyses referred his laws to the god who is invoked as Iao. They all did this either because they believed that a conception which would help humanity was marvelous and wholly divine, or because they held that the common crowd would be more likely to obey the laws if their gaze were directed towards the majesty and power of those to whom their laws were ascribed.

Now the Egyptians say that also after these events a great number of colonies were spread from Egypt over all the inhabited world. To Babylon, for instance, colonists were led by Belus, who was held to be the son of Poseidon and Libya; and after establishing himself on the Euphrates river he appointed priests, called Chaldaeans by the Babylonians, who were exempt from taxation and free from every kind of service to the state, as are the priests of Egypt; and they also make observations of the stars, following the example of the Egyptian priests, physicists, and astrologers. They say also that those who set forth with Danaus, likewise from Egypt, settled what is practically the oldest city of Greece, Argos, and that the nation of the Colchi in Pontus and that of the Jews, which lies between Arabia and Syria, were founded as colonies by certain emigrants from their country; and this is the reason why it is a long-established institution among these two peoples to circumcise their male children, the custom having been brought over from Egypt.

STRABO:

"Moses . . . was one of the Aegyptian priests, and held a part of Lower Aegypt, as it is called, but he went away from there to Judaea, since he was displeased with the state of affairs there, and was accompanied by many people who worshipped the Divine Being."
(*First century* A.D.)

Strabo, the Greek geographer, was born in Pontus about the year 63 B.C. Not much is known about his early life, but his *Geography* is one of the most important works on that subject which survives from antiquity. It is probable that Strabo, although he traveled much, depended heavily upon records and documents that were available in the library at Alexandria. For the most part, Strabo made use of Greek authorities, and paid comparatively little attention to Roman sources.

Strabo apparently made at least one trip to Egypt, accompanying the Prefect of Egypt on an expedition to the upper portion of that country circa 25 B.C. The portion of the *Geography* here reprinted contains one of the earliest Greek accounts of the Jewish exodus from Egypt, and it also provides us with a contemporary Greek view of Jewish religious beliefs and practices.

Moses, . . . was one of the Aegyptian priests, and held a part of Lower Aegypt, as it is called, but he went away from there to Judaea, since he was displeased with the state of affairs there, and was accompanied by many people who worshipped the Divine Being. For he said, and taught, that the Aegyptians were mistaken in representing the Divine Being by the images of beasts and cattle, as were also the Libyans; and that the Greeks were also wrong in modelling gods in human form; for, according to him, God is this one thing alone that encompasses us all and encompasses land and

From *The Geography of Strabo*, translated by Horace Leonard Jones. Reprinted by permission of Harvard University Press from Loeb Classical Library, Vol. VII, 283–285.

sea—the thing which we call heaven, or universe, or the nature of all that exists. What man, then, if he has sense, could be bold enough to fabricate an image of God resembling any creature amongst us? Nay, people should leave off all image-carving, and, setting apart a sacred precinct and a worthy sanctuary, should worship God without an image; and people who have good dreams should sleep in the sanctuary, not only themselves on their own behalf, but also others for the rest of the people; and those who live self-restrained and righteous lives should always expect some blessing or gift or sign from God, but no other should expect them.

Now Moses, saying things of this kind, persuaded not a few thoughtful men and led them away to this place where the settlement of Jerusalem now is; and he easily took possession of the place, since it was not a place that would be looked on with envy, nor yet one for which anyone would make a serious fight; for it is rocky, and, although it itself is well supplied with water, its surrounding territory is barren and waterless, and the part of the territory within a radius of sixty stadia is also rocky beneath the surface. At the same time Moses, instead of using arms, put forward as defence his sacrifices and his Divine Being, being resolved to seek a seat of worship for Him and promising to deliver to the people a kind of worship and a kind of ritual which would not oppress those who adopted them either with expenses or with divine obsessions or with other absurd troubles. Now Moses enjoyed fair repute with these people, and organised no ordinary kind of government, since the peoples all round, one and all, came over to him, because of his dealings with them and of the prospects he held out to them.

His successors for some time abided by the same course, acting righteously and being truly pious toward God; but afterwards, in the first place, superstitious men were appointed to the priesthood, and then tyrannical people; and from superstition arose abstinence from flesh, from which it is their custom to abstain even to-day, and circumcisions and excisions and other observances of the kind. And from the tyrannies arose the bands of robbers; for some revolted and harassed the country, both their own country and that of their neighbours, whereas others, co-operating with the rulers, seized the property of others and subdued much of Syria and Phoenicia. But still they had respect for their acropolis, since they did not loathe it as the seat of tyranny, but honoured and revered it as a holy place.

APION:

"After a six days' march, they [the Jews] developed tumors in the groin, and that was why . . . they rested on the seventh day, and called that day sabbaton, *preserving the Egyptian terminology; for disease of the groin in Egypt is called* sabbo."

(*First century* A.D.)

Apion, Greek grammarian, commentator, and arch anti-Semite, was born in Libya. He taught rhetoric in Alexandria and Rome, and in the year A.D. 38 led a deputation of Alexandrians sent to Caligula to lodge complaints against the Jews. Apion apparently believed that the Jews drank the blood of Christian children, and were capable of casting evil spells upon Christians.

Ironically, Apion is known to us chiefly through the work, *Against Apion,* written by the Jewish historian and military commander, Flavius Josephus (A.D. 37–95?). Although Josephus led Jewish troops against the Romans during the rebellion in A.D. 66, he found favor with the Roman General Vespasian by predicting that Vespasian would become Emperor. When the prophecy was fulfilled, Josephus was made a Roman citizen and assumed the name of Flavius, the family name of Vespasian. He was also awarded a pension, and received an estate in Judea.

In the selection that follows, Josephus is mainly concerned to refute the charges against the Jews made by Apion. But he also deals with a number of other writers and commentators, notably Aristotle (384–322 B.C.), Clearchus (*circa* 401 B.C.), Hecataeus (fourth and third centuries B.C.), Agatharcides (second century B.C.), Posidonius (135–151 B.C.), and Apollonius Molon (first century, B.C.).

Not only did the Greeks know the Jews, but they admired any of their number whom they happened to meet. This statement applies

    Jewish history, religion, and character according to Aristotle, Clearchus, Hecataeus, Agatharcides, Posidonius, Apollonius Melon, Apion, and others, as quoted and referred to in Josephus, *Against Apion,* translated by H. St. J. Thackeray. Reprinted by permission of Harvard University Press from Loeb Classical Library edition, Vol. I, 233–248, 293–305, 325–337.

not to the lowest class of Greeks, but to those with the highest reputation for wisdom, and can easily be proved. Clearchus, a disciple
of Aristotle, and in the very first rank of peripatetic philosophers,
relates, in his first book on Sleep, the following anecdote told of a
certain Jew by his master. He puts the words into the mouth of
Aristotle himself. I quote the text:

"It would take too long to repeat the whole story, but there were features in that man's character, at once strangely marvellous and philosophical, which merit description. I warn you, Hyperochides," he said,
"that what I am about to say will seem to you as wonderful as a dream."
Hyperochides respectfully replied, "That is the very reason why we are
all anxious to hear it." "Well," said Aristotle, "in accordance with the
precepts of rhetoric, let us begin by describing his race, in order to keep
to the rules of our masters in the art of narration." "Tell the story as you
please," said Hyperochides. "Well," he replied, "the man was a Jew of
Coele-Syria. These people are descended from the Indian philosophers.
The philosophers, they say, are in India called Calani, in Syria by the
territorial name of Jews; for the district which they inhabit is known as
Judaea. Their city has a remarkably odd name: they call it Hierusaleme.
Now this man, who was entertained by a large circle of friends and was
on his way down from the interior to the coast, not only spoke Greek,
but had the soul of a Greek. During my stay in Asia, he visited the same
places as I did, and came to converse with me and some other scholars,
to test our learning. But as one who had been intimate with many cultivated persons, it was rather he who imparted to us something of his own."

These are the words of Aristotle as reported by Clearchus, and he
went on to speak of the great and astonishing endurance and sobriety displayed by this Jew in his manner of life. Further information can be obtained, if desired, from the book itself; I forbear to
quote more than is necessary.

This allusion of Aristotle to us is mentioned parenthetically by
Clearchus, who was dealing with another subject. Of a different
nature is the evidence of Hecataeus of Abdera, at once a philosopher
and a highly competent man of affairs, who rose to fame under
King Alexander, and was afterwards associated with Ptolemy, son
of Lagus. He makes no mere passing allusion to us, but wrote a
book entirely about the Jews, from which I propose briefly to touch
on some passages. I will begin with fixing his date. He mentions
the battle near Gaza between Ptolemy and Demetrius, which, as
Castor narrates, was fought eleven years after the death of Alex-

ander, in the 117th Olympiad. For under the head of this Olympiad he says:

In this period Ptolemy, son of Lagus, defeated in a battle at Gaza Demetrius, son of Antigonus, surnamed Poliorcetes.

And all agree that Alexander died in the 114th Olympiad. It is evident, therefore, that our race was flourishing both under Ptolemy and under Alexander.

Hecataeus goes on to say that after the battle of Gaza Ptolemy became master of Syria, and that many of the inhabitants, hearing of his kindliness and humanity, desired to accompany him to Egypt and to associate themselves with his realm.

Among these (he says) was Ezechias, a chief priest of the Jews, a man of about sixty-six years of age, highly esteemed by his countrymen, intellectual, and moreover an able speaker and unsurpassed as a man of business. Yet (he adds) the total number of Jewish priests who receive a tithe of the revenue and administer public affairs is about fifteen hundred.

Reverting to Ezechias, he says:

This man, after obtaining this honour and having been closely in touch with us, assembled some of his friends and read to them [a statement showing] all the advantages [of emigration]; for he had in writing the conditions attaching to their settlement and political status.

In another passage Hecataeus mentions our regard for our laws, and how we deliberately choose and hold it a point of honour to endure anything rather than transgress them.

And so (he says), neither the slander of their neighbours and of foreign visitors, to which as a nation they are exposed, nor the frequent outrages of Persian kings and satraps can shake their determination; for these laws, naked and defenceless, they face tortures and death in its most terrible form, rather than repudiate the faith of their forefathers.

Of this obstinacy in defence of their laws he furnishes several instances. He tells how on one occasion Alexander, when he was at

Babylon and had undertaken to restore the ruined temple of Bel, gave orders to all his soldiers, without distinction, to bring materials for the earthworks; and how the Jews alone refused to obey, and even submitted to severe chastisement and heavy fines, until the king pardoned them and exempted them from this task. Again, when temples and altars were erected in the country by its invaders, the Jews razed them all to the ground, paying in some cases a fine to the satraps, and in others obtaining pardon. For such conduct, he adds, they deserve admiration. Then he goes on to speak of our vast population, stating that, though many myriads of our race had already been deported to Babylon by the Persians, yet after Alexander's death myriads more migrated to Egypt and Phoenicia in consequence of the disturbed condition of Syria.

The same writer has referred to the extent and beauty of the country which we inhabit in the following words:

They occupy almost three million *arourae* of the most excellent and fertile soil, productive of every variety of fruits. Such is the extent of Judea.

Again, here is his description of Jerusalem itself, the city which we have inhabited from remote ages, of its great beauty and extent, its numerous population, and the temple buildings:

The Jews have many fortresses and villages in different parts of the country, but only one fortified city, which has a circumference of about fifty *stades* and some hundred and twenty thousand inhabitants; they call it Jerusalem. Nearly in the centre of the city stands a stone wall, enclosing an area about five *plethra* long and a hundred cubits broad, approached by a pair of gates. Within this enclosure is a square altar, built of heaped up stones, unhewn and unwrought; each side is twenty cubits long and the height ten cubits. Beside it stands a great edifice, containing an altar and a lampstand, both made of gold, and weighing two talents; upon these is a light which is never extinguished by night or day. There is not a single statue or votive offering, no trace of a plant, in the form of a sacred grove or the like. Here priests pass their nights and days performing certain rites of purification, and abstaining altogether from wine while in the temple.

The author further attests the share which the Jews took in the campaigns both of King Alexander and of his successors. One incident on the march in which a Jewish soldier was concerned, he states that he witnessed himself. I will give the story in his own words:

When I was on the march towards the Red Sea, among the escort of Jewish cavalry which accompanied us was one named Mosollamus, a very intelligent man, robust, and, by common consent, the very best of bowmen, whether Greek or barbarian. This man, observing that a number of men were going to and fro on the route and that the whole force was being held up by a seer who was taking the auspices, inquired why they were halting. The seer pointed out to him the bird he was observing, and told him that if it stayed in that spot it was expedient for them all to halt; if it stirred and flew forward, to advance; if backward, then to retire. The Jew, without saying a word, drew his bow, shot and struck the bird, and killed it. The seer and some others were indignant, and heaped curses upon him. "Why so mad, you poor wretches?" he retorted; and then, taking the bird in his hands, continued, "Pray, how could any sound information about our march be given by this creature, which could not provide for its own safety? Had it been gifted with divination, it would not have come to this spot, for fear of being killed by an arrow of Mosollamus the Jew."

But I have given enough evidence from Hecataeus; any who care to pursue the subject can easily peruse his book. There is another writer whom I shall name without hesitation, although he mentions us only to ridicule our folly, as he regards it—I mean Agatharcides. He is telling the story of Stratonice, how she deserted her husband Demetrius and came from Macedonia to Syria, and how, when Seleucus disappointed her by refusing to marry her, she created a revolution at Antioch while he was starting on a campaign from Babylon; and then how, after the king's return and the capture of Antioch, she fled to Seleucia, and instead of taking sail immediately, as she might have done, let herself be stopped by a dream, was captured and put to death. After telling this story and deriding the superstition of Stratonice, Agatharcides quotes in illustration a tale told about us. The following are his words:

The people known as Jews, who inhabit the most strongly fortified of cities, called by the natives Jerusalem, have a custom of abstaining from work every seventh day; on those occasions they neither bear arms nor take any agricultural operations in hand, nor engage in any other form of public service, but pray with outstretched hands in the temples until the evening. Consequently, because the inhabitants, instead of protecting their city, persevered in their folly, Ptolemy, son of Lagus, was allowed to enter with his army; the country was thus given over to a cruel master, and the defect of a practice enjoined by law was exposed. That experience has taught the whole world, except that nation, the lesson not to resort to dreams and traditional fancies about the law, until its difficulties are such as to baffle human reason.

Agatharcides finds such conduct ridiculous; dispassionate critics will consider it a grand and highly meritorious fact that there are men who consistently care more for the observance of their laws and for their religion than for their own lives and their country's fate.

I am doubtful, indeed, whether the remarks of Apion the grammarian deserve serious refutation. Some of these resemble the allegations made by others, some are very indifferent additions of his own; most of them are pure buffoonery, and, to tell the truth, display the gross ignorance of their author, a man of low character and a charlatan to the end of his days. Yet, since most people are so foolish as to find greater attraction in such compositions than in works of a serious nature, to be charmed by abuse and impatient of praise, I think it incumbent upon me not to pass over without examination even this author, who has written an indictment of us formal enough for a court of law. For I observe, on the other hand, that people in general also have a habit of being intensely delighted when one who has been the first to malign another has his own vices brought home to him. His argument is difficult to summarize and his meaning to grasp. But, so far as the extreme disorder and confusion of his lying statements admit of analysis, one may say that some fall into the same category as those already investigated, relating to the departure of our ancestors from Egypt; others form an indictment of the Jewish residents in Alexandria; while a third class, mixed up with the rest, consists of accusations against our temple rites and our ordinances in general.

That our ancestors neither were Egyptians by race nor were expelled from that country in consequence of contagious diseases or any similar affliction, I think I have already given not merely sufficient, but even superabundant, proof. I propose, however, briefly to mention the details added by Apion. In the third book of his *History of Egypt* he makes the following statement:

Moses, as I have heard from old people in Egypt, was a native of Heliopolis, who, being pledged to the customs of his country, erected prayer-houses, open to the air, in the various precincts of the city, all facing eastwards; such being the orientation also of Heliopolis. In place of obelisks he set up pillars, beneath which was a model of a boat; and the shadow cast on this basin by the statue described a circle corresponding to the course of the sun in the heavens.

Such is the grammarian's amazing statement. Its mendacious character needs no comment; it is exposed by the facts. When Moses built the first tabernacle for God, he neither placed in it himself, nor instructed his successors to make, any graven imagery of this kind. When Solomon, later on, built the temple at Jerusalem, he too refrained from any curiosities of art such as Apion has conceived. He tells us that he heard from "old people" that Moses was a Heliopolitan. Obviously, as a junior, he believed what he was told by men old enough to have known and associated with him! Literary critic as he was, he could not positively have stated what was the birthplace of the poet Homer, or even of Pythagoras, who lived, one may say, but the other day. But when asked about Moses, who preceded them by such a vast number of years, he, on the strength of the old men's report, answers with an assurance which proclaims him a liar.

On the question of the date which he assigns to the exodus of the lepers, the blind and the lame under Moses' leadership, we shall find, I imagine, this accurate grammarian in perfect agreement with previous writers. Well, Manetho states that the departure of the Jews from Egypt occurred in the reign of Tethmosis, 393 years before the flight of Danaus to Argos; Lysimachus says, under King Bocchoris, that is to say, 1700 years ago; Molon and others fix a date to suit themselves. Apion, however, the surest authority of all, precisely dates the exodus in the seventh Olympiad, and in the first year of that Olympiad, the year in which, according to him, the Phoenicians founded Carthage. This mention of Carthage he has doubtless inserted under the belief that it would afford a striking proof of his veracity; he has failed to see that he has thereby brought upon himself his own refutation. For, if the Phoenician chronicles may be trusted, it is there recorded that King Hirom lived more than 150 years before the foundation of Carthage. Evidence from those chronicles to this effect has been given earlier in this work, where I showed that Hirom was a friend of Solomon, who built the Temple at Jerusalem, and that he contributed largely towards its construction. But Solomon himself built the Temple 612 years after the departure of the Jews from Egypt.

After stating that the fugitives numbered 110,000, in which imaginary figure he agrees with Lysimachus, he gives an astonishing and plausible explanation of the etymology of the word "sabbath"!

After a six days' march, he says, they developed tumours in the groin, and that was why, after safely reaching the country now called Judea, they rested on the seventh day, and called that day *sabbaton,* preserving the Egyptian terminology; for disease of the groin in Egypt is called *sabbo.*

One knows not whether to laugh at the nonsense, or rather to be indignant at the impudence, of such language. Clearly all these 110,000 persons were attacked by tumours. But if they were blind and lame and suffering from all kinds of disease, as represented by Apion, they could not have accomplished a single day's march. If, on the contrary, they were capable not only of traversing a vast desert, but of defeating their adversaries in battles in which they all took part, they would not have succumbed in a body to the tumours after six days. For persons on a forced march are not naturally subject to a malady of this kind; myriads of men in armies maintain a regular pace for many days in succession. Nor can one attribute such an accident to chance; that would be the height of absurdity. This astonishing Apion, after stating that they reached Judaea in six days, tells us elsewhere that Moses went up into the mountain called Sinai, which lies between Egypt and Arabia, remained in concealment there for forty days, and then descended and gave the Jews their laws. However could the same body of men stay forty days in a desert and waterless region, and yet cover the whole distance to their destination in six days? The grammarian's distortion of the word "sabbath" betrays either gross impudence or shocking ignorance; there is a wide difference between *sabbo* and *sabbaton. Sabbaton* in the Jews' language denotes cessation from all work, while *sabbo* among the Egyptians signifies, as he states, disease of the groin.

Such are some of the novel features which the Egyptian Apion, improving upon other authors, has introduced into the story of Moses and the departure of the Jews from Egypt. That he should lie about our ancestors and assert that they were Egyptians by race is by no means surprising. He told a lie which was the reverse of this one about himself. Born in the Egyptian oasis, more Egyptian than them all, as one might say, he disowned his true country and falsely claimed to be an Alexandrian, thereby admitting the ignominy of his race. It is therefore natural that he should call persons whom he detests and wishes to abuse Egyptians. Had he not had the meanest opinion of natives of Egypt, he would never have turned his back on his own nation. Patriots are proud to bear their country's name, and denounce those who lay unjust claim to the title of citizens. In their relation to us, Egyptians are swayed by one of two feelings: either they feign to be our kinsmen in order to gain prestige, or else they drag us into their ranks to share their bad reputation. The noble Apion's calumny upon us is apparently designed as a sort of return to the Alexandrians for the rights of citizenship which they bestowed upon him. Knowing their hatred of their Jewish neighbours in Alexandria, he has made it his aim to vilify the latter and has included all the rest of the Jews in his condemnation. In both these attacks he shows himself an impudent liar.

I am no less amazed at the proceedings of the authors who supplied him with his materials, I mean Posidonius and Apollonius. On the one hand they charge us with not worshipping the same gods as other people; on the other, they tell lies and invent absurd calumnies about our temple, without showing any consciousness of impiety. Yet to high-minded men nothing is more disgraceful than a lie, of any description, but above all on the subject of a temple of world-wide fame and commanding sanctity.

Within this sanctuary Apion has the effrontery to assert that the Jews kept an ass's head, worshipping that animal and deeming it worthy of the deepest reverence; the fact was disclosed, he maintains, on the occasion of the spoliation of the temple by Antiochus Epiphanes, when the head, made of gold and worth a high price, was discovered. On this I will first remark that, even if we did possess any such object, an Egyptian should be the last person to reproach us; for an ass is no worse than the cats [?], he-goats, and other creatures which in his country rank as gods. Next, how did it escape him that the facts convict him of telling an incredible lie?

Throughout our history we have kept the same laws, to which we are eternally faithful. Yet notwithstanding the various calamities which our city, like others, has undergone, when the temple was occupied by successive conquerors, [Antiochus] the Pious, Pompey the Great, Licinius Crassus, and most recently Titus Caesar, they found there nothing of the kind, but the purest type of religion, the secrets of which we may not reveal to aliens. That the raid of Antiochus [Epiphanes] on the temple was iniquitous, that it was impecuniosity which drove him to invade it, when he was not an open enemy, that he attacked us, his allies and friends, and that he found there nothing to deserve ridicule; these facts are attested by many sober historians. Polybius of Megalopolis, Strabo the Cappadocian, Nicolas of Damascus, Timagenes, Castor the chronicler, and Apollodorus all assert that it was impecuniosity which induced Antiochus, in violation of his treaties with the Jews, to plunder the temple with its stores of gold and silver. There is the evidence which Apion should have considered, had he not himself been gifted with the mind of an ass and the impudence of the dog, which his countrymen are wont to worship. An outsider can make no sense of his lies. We Jews attribute no honour or virtue to asses, such as is ascribed to crocodiles and asps by Egyptians, who regard persons bitten by a viper or mauled by a crocodile as blessed souls found worthy of God. With us, as with other sensible people, asses are beasts that carry loads on their backs, and if they invade our threshing-floors and eat the corn, or stop short on the road, they are soundly beaten, as humble ministers for labour and agriculture. Either Apion was the greatest blockhead as a writer of fiction, or, to say the least, he could draw no just conclusion from such facts as he had to start from; for every one of his calumnies upon us is a failure.

He adds a second story, of Greek origin, which is a malicious slander upon us from beginning to end. On this it will suffice to remark that persons who venture upon religious topics ought to be aware that there is less profanity in violating the precincts of a temple than in calumniating its priests. But these authors are more concerned to uphold a sacrilegious king than to give a fair and veracious description of our rites and temple. In their anxiety to defend Antiochus and to cover up the perfidy and sacrilege practised upon our nation under pressure of an empty exchequer, they have further invented, to discredit us, the fictitious story which follows. Apion, who is here the spokesman of others, asserts that:—

Antiochus found in the temple a couch, on which a man was reclining, with a table before him laden with a banquet of fish of the sea, beasts of the earth, and birds of the air, at which the poor fellow was gazing in stupefaction. The king's entry was instantly hailed by him with adoration, as about to procure him profound relief; falling at the king's knees, he stretched out his right hand and implored him to set him free. The king reassured him and bade him tell him who he was, why he was living there, what was the meaning of his abundant fare. Thereupon, with sighs and tears, the man, in a pitiful tone, told the tale of his distress. He said that he was a Greek and that, while travelling about the province for his livelihood, he was suddenly kidnapped by men of a foreign race and conveyed to the temple; there he was shut up and seen by nobody, but was fattened on feasts of the most lavish description. At first these unlooked for attentions deceived him and caused him pleasure; suspicion followed, then consternation. Finally, on consulting the attendants who waited upon him, he heard of the unutterable law of the Jews, for the sake of which he was being fed. The practice was repeated annually at a fixed season. They would kidnap a Greek foreigner, fatten him up for a year, and then convey him to a wood, where they slew him, sacrificed his body with their customary ritual, partook of his flesh, and, while immolating the Greek, swore an oath of hostility to the Greeks. The remains of their victim were then thrown into a pit. The man (Apion continues) stated that he had now but a few days left to live, and implored the king, out of respect for the gods of Greece, to defeat this Jewish plot upon his life-blood and to deliver him from his miserable predicament.

A tale of this kind is not merely packed with all the horrors of a tragedy; it is also replete with the cruelty of impudence. It does not, for all that, acquit Antiochus of sacrilege, as its obsequious authors imagined. He suspected nothing of the sort when he invaded the temple; the discovery admittedly surprised him. His iniquity, impiety, and godlessness were, therefore, none the less gratuitous, however many lies may be told about him. These reveal their character on their face. Greeks, as is well known, are not the only people with whom our laws come into conflict; those principally so affected are Egyptians and many others. Is there one of these nations whose citizens have not happened at some time or other to visit our country? Why should Greeks be the only objects of our periodically repeated conspiracy and bloodthirsty assault? Again, how is it conceivable that all Jews should assemble to partake of these victims, and that the flesh of one should suffice for so many thousand participants, as Apion asserts? Why in the world after discovering this man, whoever he was (his name is not given in the story) did not the king convey him in triumph to his country, when by so doing he might have gained a reputation for piety and rare devotion to the Greeks, and encountered Jewish hatred with the powerful support of public opinion? But I refrain to pursue these inquiries; fools must be refuted, not by argument, but by facts.

All who ever saw our temple are aware of the general design of the building, and the inviolable barriers which preserved its sanctity. It had four surrounding courts, each with its special statutory restrictions. The outer court was open to all, foreigners included; women during their impurity were alone refused admission. To the second court all Jews were admitted and, when uncontaminated by any defilement, their wives; to the third male Jews, if clean and purified; to the fourth the priests robed in their priestly vestments. The sanctuary was entered only by the high-priests, clad in the raimant peculiar to themselves. So careful is the provision for all the details of the service, that the priests' entry is timed to certain hours. Their duty was to enter in the morning, when the temple was opened, and to offer the customary sacrifices, and again at mid-day, until the temple was closed. One further point: no vessel whatever might be carried into the temple, the only objects in which were an altar, a table, a censer, and a lampstand, all mentioned in the Law. There was nothing more; no unmentionable mysteries took place, no repast was served within the building. The foregoing statements are attested by the whole community, and conclusively proved by the order of procedure. For, although there are four priestly tribes, each comprising upwards of five thousand members, these officiate by rotation for a fixed period of days; when the term of one party ends, others come to offer the sacrifices in their place, and assembling at mid-day in the temple, take over from the outgoing ministers the keys of the building and all its vessels, duly numbered. Nothing of the nature of food or drink is brought within the temple; objects of this kind may not even be offered on the altar, save those which are prepared for the sacrifices.

Are we then left to conclude that Apion put out this incredible story without any investigation of these facts? But that is disgraceful; as a learned doctor, did he not profess to present an accurate historical picture? No; he knew the pious rites of our temple, but passed them over when he concocted this story of a kidnapped Greek, an unmentionable banquet of the richest and most sumptuous fare, and slaves entering precincts to which even the highest Jewish nobles are not admitted, unless they are priests. Here, then, we have rank impiety at its worst, and a gratuitous lie, designed to mislead persons who do not trouble to investigate the facts. For the one aim of the inventors of the unspeakable horrors to which I have alluded is to bring us into odium.

II

THE JEW IN THE

EARLY CHRISTIAN ERA

First Century A.D.*—750*

HISTORICAL NOTE

The fall of Judea in A.D. 70 marked the beginning of the Jewish *Diaspora,* or Dispersion. With the destruction of the Temple in Jerusalem by the Roman General Titus, the Jews were deprived of their most important tangible symbol of nationality and religious unity. Henceforth they were to be without homeland, or government, or religious center. While, according to legend, the Roman emperor Vespasian permitted a school of Hebrew culture to be established at Jabneh, the major institutions of Jewish life were not permitted to reestablish themselves in the land promised to Abraham. In 135 Jews were forbidden access to Jerusalem, although no such prohibition applied to Christians.

Roman persecution of the Jews in Palestine was designed to destroy the last remaining vestiges of the Jewish national and religious tradition. The study of Talmudic law was banned by edict. Jewish scholars were not allowed to hold classes or to meet with students; for violations of this rule ten outstanding Jewish teachers were martyred during the reign of Hadrian in 135. At the beginning of the fifth century, the Patriarchate was abolished altogether by Roman authorities.

As a result, Palestine declined in importance, and the centers of Jewish life were shifted to areas of Asia Minor and Europe. Babylonia, which was under Persian rule, became the new Eastern Center. There the Jews were relatively free from persecution, and thus were able to devote themselves to religious study and practice. From the sixth to the eighth centuries, the Babylonian Jews even enjoyed a measure of autonomy in their internal affairs. But Jewish revival in Babylonia was limited by the fact that the civilized world had long since begun to move from the

Arabian Gulf to the Mediterranean Sea. Nevertheless, despite the declining political and economic importance of Babylon, Babylonian Jewry made a number of important contributions to Judaism, notably the Babylonian Talmud.

The rise of the Moslems in the seventh century had no immediate effect on Jewish life. But when the Jews rejected Mohammed, he made war upon them and drove them out of Arabia. Although his successors were more lenient, they accorded the Jews in Moslem territory only the status of second-class citizens. They were forced to pay a poll tax, and were not permitted to build synagogues or to worship aloud.

In the West, meanwhile, Jews had begun to settle in the cities of Northern Italy and Sicily. By the beginning of the fourth century Jewish settlements were located in Spain and the Rhineland. The Roman emperor Caracalla conferred full citizenship upon the Jews in 212, and during the reign of Alexander Severus (222–235) the ethnic and religious character of Judaism was formally recognized. Although proselytizing by Jews was prohibited, they were permitted to practice their religion and to live in peace among themselves.

With the conversion of Constantine to Christianity *circa* 312 the position of Jews in the Roman Empire was vastly altered. Despite the fact that Christianity was of Jewish origin, and notwithstanding the relentless persecution of Christians by earlier Roman emperors, especially Nero and Diocletian, the Christianization of the Empire bore harshly on the Jews. The Church policy that was adopted by the state regarded Judaism as a "nefarious" and "sacrilegious" religious movement. The Theodosian and Justinian Codes of the fourth and fifth centuries excluded Jews from positions of authority. Intermarriage between Jews and Christians was strictly forbidden, and Jews were not permitted to hold Christian slaves. Social intercourse with Christians was severely restricted. The construction of synagogues was banned, although established places of worship could be maintained and kept in repair. While the Church was officially opposed to the use of force, anti-Jewish demonstrations and physical aggression against Jews were not unknown in areas under its nominal control. And in the Byzantine Empire, the line between discrimination and oppression was rapidly obliterated.

Although the regulations aimed at Jews were frequently more honored in theory than in practice, the principles upon which they were based were incorporated into Western law and legislation over a period of many centuries. The concept of the Jew as an alien and an outcast within the Gentile community owes much to the early promulgations of the Christian Roman emperors.

Such enactments, however, did not prevent the survival of Jewish life and culture in several areas of Europe. The beginning of the sixth century saw important Jewish communities established in various parts of Italy, Byzantium, France, and Visigothic Spain. The obsessive intolerance of the Church, although it was not as widespread or as violent as it later became, made its first appearance at this time. A wave of forced conversions of Jews spread through Europe, reaching its height under the Catholic Visigoths in Spain. For a time the practice of Judaism was absolutely forbidden. In certain areas of France the treatment of Jews anticipated the more systematic and bloody persecution of subsequent years.

Until the Arab invasion of Spain in 711, the insignificant number and insecure position of Jews precluded the founding in Europe of any major Jewish religious and cultural center. The Mohammedan conquerors of Spain, in contradiction to the earlier teachings of the Prophet, granted the Jews (and Christians) religious freedom, and they were also permitted to live in accordance with their own laws. As a consequence, the Jewish population of Spain grew rapidly. Jewish communal organization was strengthened, and Jewish scholarship and learning underwent rapid development. By the eleventh century, the spiritual leadership of the Jews rested with Spanish Jewry, and the destiny of Judaism was inextricably merged with the future of the West.

TACITUS:

*"To ensure his future hold over the people,
Moses introduced a new cult, which was
the opposite of all other religions. All
that we hold sacred they held profane, and
allowed practices which we abominate."
(First century)*

Tacitus (55?–117?) held a variety of political offices before turning to history and literary pursuits. Married to the daughter of the Roman General Agricola, Tacitus filled several posts during the reigns of Vespasian, Titus, and Domitian. He participated with Pliny, the Younger, in the prosecution for extortion of Marius Priscus, Proconsul of Africa, and earned in that role a reputation for distinguished oratory.

Tacitus' writings on the Jews reflect opinions which were quite common among the Romans of his day.

Early in this same year Titus Caesar had been entrusted by his father with the task of completing the reduction of Judaea. While he and his father were both still private citizens, Titus had distinguished himself as a soldier, and his reputation for efficiency was steadily increasing, while the provinces and armies vied with one another in their enthusiasm for him. Wishing to seem independent of his good fortune, he always showed dignity and energy in the field. His affability called forth devotion. He constantly helped in

Tacitus, *The Histories*, translated with introduction and notes by W. Hamilton Fyfe (Oxford: The Clarendon Press, 1912), Vol. II, 202–208, 211–218.

the trenches and could mingle with his soldiers on the march without compromising his dignity as general. Three legions awaited him in Judaea, the Fifth, Tenth, and Fifteenth, all veterans from his father's army. These were reinforced by the Twelfth from Syria and by detachments of the Twenty-second and the Third, brought over from Alexandria. This force was accompanied by twenty auxiliary cohorts and eight regiments of auxiliary cavalry besides the Kings Agrippa and Sohaemus, King Antiochus' irregulars, a strong force of Arabs, who had a neighbourly hatred for the Jews, and a crowd of persons who had come from Rome and the rest of Italy, each tempted by the hope of securing the first place in the prince's still unoccupied affections. With this force Titus entered the enemy's country at the head of his column, sending out scouts in all directions, and holding himself ready to fight. He pitched his camp not far from Jerusalem.

Since I am coming now to describe the last days of this famous city, it may not seem out of place to recount here its early history. It is said that the Jews are refugees from Crete, who settled on the confines of Libya at the time when Saturn was forcibly deposed by Jupiter. The evidence for this is sought in the name. Ida is a famous mountain in Crete inhabited by the Idaei, whose name became lengthened into the foreign form Judaei. Others say that in the reign of Isis the superfluous population of Egypt, under the leadership of Hierosolymus and Juda, discharged itself upon the neighbouring districts, while there are many who think the Jews an Ethiopian stock, driven to migrate by their fear and dislike of King Cepheus. Another tradition makes them Assyrian refugees, who, lacking lands of their own, occupied a district of Egypt, and later took to building cities of their own and tilling Hebrew territory and the frontierland of Syria. Yet another version assigns to the Jews an illustrious origin as the descendants of the Solymi—a tribe famous in Homer—who founded the city and called it Hiero*solyma* after their own name.

Most authorities agree that a foul and disfiguring disease once broke out in Egypt, and that King Bocchoris, on approaching the oracle of Ammon and inquiring for a remedy, was told to purge his kingdom of the plague and to transport all who suffered from it into some other country, for they had earned the disfavour of Heaven. A motley crowd was thus collected and abandoned in the desert.

While all the other outcasts lay idly lamenting, one of them, named Moses, advised them not to look for help to gods or men, since both had deserted them, but to trust rather in themselves and accept as divine the guidance of the first being by whose aid they should get out of their present plight. They agreed, and set out blindly to march wherever chance might lead them. Their worst distress came from lack of water. When they were already at death's door and lying prostrate all over the plain, it so happened that a drove of wild asses moved away from their pasture to a rock densely covered with trees. Guessing the truth from the grassy nature of the ground, Moses followed and disclosed an ample flow of water. This saved them. Continuing their march for six successive days, on the seventh they routed the natives and gained possession of the country. There they consecrated their city and their temple.

To ensure his future hold over the people, Moses introduced a new cult, which was the opposite of all other religions. All that we hold sacred they held profane, and allowed practices which we abominate. They dedicated in a shrine an image of the animal whose guidance had put an end to their wandering and thirst. They killed a ram, apparently as an insult to Ammon, and also sacrificed a bull, because the Egyptians worship the bull Apis. Pigs are subject to leprosy; so they abstain from pork in memory of their misfortune and the foul plague with which they were once infected. Their frequent fasts bear witness to the long famine they once endured, and, in token of the corn they carried off, Jewish bread is to this day made without leaven. They are said to have devoted the seventh day to rest, because that day brought an end to their troubles. Later, finding idleness alluring, they gave up the seventh year as well to sloth. Others maintain that they do this in honour of Saturn; either because their religious principles are derived from the Idaei, who are supposed to have been driven out with Saturn and become the ancestors of the Jewish people; or else because, of the seven constellations which govern the lives of men, the star of Saturn moves in the topmost orbit and exercises peculiar influence, and also because most of the heavenly bodies move round their courses in multiples of seven.

Whatever their origin, these rites are sanctioned by their antiquity. Their other customs are impious and abominable, and owe their prevalence to their depravity. For all the most worthless rascals, renouncing their national cults, were always sending money to swell the sum of offerings and tribute. This is one cause of Jewish prosperity. Another is that they are obstinately loyal to each other, and always ready to show compassion, whereas they feel nothing but hatred and enmity for the rest of the world. They eat and sleep separately. Though immoderate in sexual indulgence, they refrain from all intercourse with foreign women: among themselves anything is allowed. They have introduced circumcision to distinguish themselves from other people. Those who are converted to their customs adopt the same practice, and the first lessons they learn are to despise the gods, to renounce their country, and to think nothing of their parents, children, and brethren. However, they take steps to increase their numbers. They count it a crime to kill any of their later-born children, and they believe that the souls of those who die in battle or under persecution are immortal. Thus they think much of having children and nothing of facing death. They prefer to bury and not burn their dead. In this, as in their burial rites, and in their belief in an underworld, they conform to Egyptian custom. Their ideas of heaven are quite different. The Egyptians worship most of their gods as animals, or in shapes half animal and half human. The Jews acknowledge one god only, of whom they have a purely spiritual conception. They think it impious to make images of gods in human shape out of perishable materials. Their god is almighty and inimitable, without beginning and without end. They therefore set up no statues in their temples, nor even in their cities, refusing this homage both to their own kings and to the Roman emperors. However, the fact that their priests intoned to the flute and cymbals and wore wreaths of ivy, and that a golden vine was found in their temple has led some people to think that they worship Bacchus, who has so enthralled the East. But their cult would be most inappropriate. Bacchus instituted gay and cheerful rites, but the Jewish ritual is preposterous and morbid.

The greater part of the population live in scattered villages but they also have towns. Jerusalem is the Jewish capital, and contained the temple, which was enormously wealthy. A first line of fortifications guarded the city, another the palace, and an innermost line enclosed the temple. None but a Jew was allowed as far as the doors: none but the priests might cross the threshold. When the East was in the hands of the Assyrians, Medes and Persians, they

regarded the Jews as the meanest of their slaves. During the Mace-
donian ascendancy King Antiochus endeavoured to abolish their
superstitions and to introduce Greek manners and customs. But
Arsaces at that moment rebelled, and the Parthian war prevented
him from effecting any improvement in the character of this grim
people. Then, when Macedon waned, as the Parthian power was
not yet ripe and Rome was still far away, they took kings of their
own. The mob were fickle and drove them out. However, they recov-
ered their throne by force; banished their countrymen, sacked cities,
slew their brothers, wives, and parents, and committed all the usual
kingly crimes. But this only fostered the hold of the Jewish religion,
since the kings had strengthened their authority by assuming the
priesthood.

Cnaeus Pompeius was the first Roman to subdue the Jews and
set foot in their temple by right of conquest. It was then first realized that the temple contained no image of any god: their sanctuary
was empty, their mysteries meaningless. The walls of Jerusalem
were destroyed, but the temple was left standing. Later, during the
Roman civil wars, when the eastern provinces had come under the
control of Mark Antony, the Parthian Prince Pacorus seized Judaea,
and was killed by Publius Ventidius. The Parthians were driven
back over the Euphrates, and Caius Sosius subdued the Jews. Antony
gave the kingdom to Herod, and Augustus, after his victory, enlarged it. After Herod's death, somebody called Simon, without
awaiting the emperor's decision, forcibly assumed the title of king.
He was executed by Quintilius Varus, who was Governor of Syria;
the Jews were repressed and the kingdom divided between three of
Herod's sons. Under Tiberius all was quiet. Caligula ordered them
to put up his statue in the temple. They preferred war to that. But
Caligula's death put an end to the rising. In Claudius' reign the
kings had all either died or lost most of their territory. The emperor
therefore made Judaea a province to be governed by Roman knights
or freedmen. One of these, Antonius Felix, indulged in every kind
of cruelty and immorality, wielding a king's authority with all the
instincts of a slave. He had married Drusilla, a granddaughter of
Antony and Cleopatra, so that he was Antony's grandson-in-law,
while Claudius was Antony's grandson.

The Jews endured such oppression patiently until the time of
Gessius Florus, under whom war broke out. Cestius Gallus, the

Governor of Syria, tried to crush it, but met with more reverses than victories. He died, either in the natural course or perhaps of disgust, and Nero sent out Vespasian, who, in a couple of campaigns, thanks to his reputation, good fortune, and able subordinates, had the whole of the country districts and all the towns except Jerusalem under the heel of his victorious army. The next year was taken up with civil war, and passed quietly enough as far as the Jews were concerned. But peace once restored in Italy, foreign troubles began again with feelings embittered on our side by the thought that the Jews were the only people who had not given in. At the same time it seemed best to leave Titus at the head of the army to meet the eventualities of the new reign, whether good or bad.

Thus, as we have already seen, Titus pitched his camp before the walls of Jerusalem and proceeded to display his legions in battle order. The Jews formed up at the foot of their own walls, ready, if successful, to venture further, but assured of their retreat in case of reverse. A body of cavalry and some light-armed foot were sent forward, and fought an indecisive engagement, from which the enemy eventually retired. During the next few days a series of skirmishes took place in front of the gates, and at last continual losses drove the Jews behind their walls. The Romans then determined to take it by storm. It seemed undignified to sit and wait for the enemy to starve, and the men all clamoured for the risks, some being really brave, while many others were wild and greedy for plunder. Titus himself had the vision of Rome with all her wealth and pleasures before his eyes, and felt that their enjoyment was postponed unless Jerusalem fell at once. The city, however, stands high and is fortified with works strong enough to protect a city standing on the plain. Two enormous hills were surrounded by walls ingeniously built so as to project or slope inwards and thus leave the flanks of an attacking party exposed to fire. The rocks were jagged at the top. The towers, where the rising ground helped, were sixty feet high, and in the hollows as much as a hundred and twenty. They are a wonderful sight and seem from a distance to be all of equal height. Within this runs another line of fortification surrounding the palace, and on a conspicuous height stands the Antonia, a castle named by Herod in honour of Mark Antony.

The temple was built like a citadel with walls of its own, on which more care and labour had been spent than on any of the others.

Even the cloisters surrounding the temple formed a splendid rampart. There was a never-failing spring of water, catacombs hollowed out of the hills, and pools or cisterns for holding the rain-water. Its original builders had foreseen that the peculiarities of Jewish life would lead to frequent wars, consequently everything was ready for the longest of sieges. Besides this, when Pompey took the city, bitter experience taught them several lessons, and in the days of Claudius they had taken advantage of his avarice to buy rights of fortification, and built walls in peace-time as though war were imminent. Their numbers were now swelled by floods of human refuse and unfortunate refugees from other towns. All the most desperate characters in the country had taken refuge there, which did not conduce to unity. They had three armies, each with its own general. The outermost and largest line of wall was held by Simon; the central city by John, and the temple by Eleazar. John and Simon were stronger than Eleazar in numbers and equipment, but he had the advantage of a strong position. Their relations mainly consisted of fighting, treachery, and arson: a large quantity of corn was burnt. Eventually, under pretext of offering a sacrifice, John sent a party of men to massacre Eleazar and his troops, and by this means gained possession of the temple. Thus Jerusalem was divided into two hostile parties, but on the approach of the Romans the necessities of foreign warfare reconciled their differences.

Various portents had occurred at this time, but so sunk in superstition are the Jews and so opposed to all religious practices that they think it wicked to avert the threatened evil by sacrifices or vows. Embattled armies were seen to meet in the sky with flashing arms, and the temple shone with sudden fire from heaven. The doors of the shrine suddenly opened, a supernatural voice was heard calling the gods out, and at once there began a mighty movement of departure. Few took alarm at all this. Most people held the belief that, according to the ancient priestly writings, this was the moment at which the East was fated to prevail; they would now start forth from Judaea and conquer the world. This enigmatic prophecy really applied to Vespasian and Titus. But men are blinded by their hopes. The Jews took to themselves the promised destiny, and even defeat could not convince them of the truth. The number of the besieged, men and women of every age, is stated to have reached six hundred thousand. There were arms for all who could carry them, and far more were ready to fight than would be expected from their total numbers. The women were as determined as the men: if they were forced to leave their homes they had more to fear in life than in death.

Such was the city and such the people with which Titus was faced. As the nature of the ground forbade a sudden assault, he determined to employ siege-works and penthouse shelters. The work was accordingly divided among the legions, and there was a truce to fighting until they had got ready every means of storming a town that had ever been devised by experience or inventive ingenuity.

PLUTARCH:

". . . the time and manner of the greatest
and most holy solemnity of the Jews is
exactly agreeable to the holy rites of
Bacchus; for that which they call the Fast
they celebrate in the midst of the
vintage, furnishing their tables with all
sorts of fruits, while they sit under
tabernacles made of vines and ivy;
and the day which immediately goes before
this they call the day of Tabernacles."
(First and second centuries)

Plutarch (46–120), Greek biographer, was educated in Athens. For a time he lived in Rome, where he was involved in the education of Hadrian (who ultimately appointed him Procurator of Greece). Plutarch's fame rests on his authorship of the *Parallel Lives*, a collection of biographies which compares and contrasts Greek statesmen, generals, and orators with their Roman counterparts.

Plutarch's initiation into the cult of Dionysus is reflected in several portions of the *Symposiacs*, from which the following treatment of the Jews is reprinted.

From the *Symposiacs* of Plutarch, in *Plutarch's Morals*, corrected and revised by William W. Goodwin (Boston: Little, Brown, and Company, 1870), Vol. III, 307–312.

WHETHER THE JEWS ABSTAINED FROM SWINE'S FLESH BECAUSE THEY
WORSHIPPED THAT CREATURE, OR BECAUSE THEY HAD AN ANTIPATHY
AGAINST IT

Callistratus, Polycrates, Lamprias

1. After these things were spoken, and some in the company
were minded to say something in defence of the contrary opinion,
Callistratus interrupted their discourse and said: Sirs, what do you
think of that which was spoken against the Jews, that they abstain
from the most lawful flesh? Very well said, quoth Polycrates, for
that is a thing I very much question, whether it was that the Jews
abstained from swine's flesh because they conferred divine honor
upon that creature, or because they had a natural aversion to it.
For whatever we find in their own writings seems to be altogether
fabulous, except they have some more solid reasons which they have
no mind to discover.

2. Hence it is, says Callistratus, that I am of an opinion that this
nation has that creature in some veneration; and though it be
granted that the hog is an ugly and filthy creature, yet it is not quite
so vile nor naturally stupid as a beetle, griffin, crocodile, or cat, most
of which are worshipped as the most sacred things by some priests
amongst the Egyptians. But the reason why the hog is had in so
much honor and veneration amongst them is, because, as the report
goes, that creature breaking up the earth with its snout showed
the way to tillage, and taught them how to use the ploughshare,
which instrument for that very reason, as some say, was called
hynis from ῦς, *a swine*. Now the Egyptians inhabiting a country
situated low, and whose soil is naturally soft, have no need of the
plough; but after the river Nile hath retired from the grounds it
overflowed, they presently let all their hogs into the fields, and they
with their feet and snouts break up the ground, and cover the sown
seed. Nor ought this to seem strange to any one, that there are in
the world those who abstain from swine's flesh upon such an account as this; when it is evident that among barbarous nations there
are other animals had in greater honor and veneration for lesser,
if not altogether ridiculous, reasons. For the field-mouse only for
its blindness was worshipped as a God among the Egyptians, because they were of an opinion that darkness was before light, and
that the latter had its birth from mice about the fifth generation at

the new moon; and moreover that the liver of this creature diminishes in the wane of the moon. But they consecrate the lion to the sun, because the lioness alone, of all clawed quadrupeds, brings forth her young with their eyesight; for they sleep a moment, and when they are asleep their eyes sparkle. Besides, they place gaping lions' heads for the spouts of their fountains, because Nilus overflows the Egyptian fields when the sign is Leo: they give it out that their bird ibis, as soon as hatched, weighs two drachms, which are of the same weight with the heart of a new-born infant; and that its legs being spread with the bill make an exact equilateral triangle. And yet who can find fault with the Egyptians for these trifles, when it is left upon record that the Pythagoreans worshipped a white cock, and of sea creatures abstained especially from the mullet and urtic. The Magi that descended from Zoroaster adored the land hedgehog above other creatures, but had a deadly spite against water-rats, and thought that man was dear in the eyes of the Gods who destroyed most of them. But I should think that if the Jews had such an antipathy against a hog, they would kill it as the magicians do mice; when, on the contrary, they are by their religion as much prohibited to kill as to eat it. And perhaps there may be some reason given for this; for as the ass is worshipped by them as the first discoverer of fountains, so perhaps the hog may be had in like veneration, which first taught them to sow and plough. Nay, some say that the Jews also abstain from hares, as abominable and unclean.

3. They have reason for that, said Lamprias, because a hare is so like an ass which they detest; for in its color, ears, and the sparkling of its eyes, it is so like an ass, that I do not know any little creature that represents a great one so much as a hare doth an ass; unless in this likewise they imitate the Egyptians, and suppose that there is something of divinity in the swiftness of this creature, as also in its quickness of sense; for the eyes of hares are so unwearied that they sleep with them open. Besides they seem to excel all other creatures in quickness of hearing; whence it was that the Egyptians painted the ear of a hare amongst their other hieroglyphics, as an emblem of hearing. But the Jews do hate swine's flesh, because all the barbarians are naturally fearful of a scab and leprosy, which they presume comes by eating such kind of flesh. For we may observe that all pigs under the belly are overspread with a leprosy and scab; which may be supposed to proceed from an ill disposition

of body and corruption within, which breaks out through the skin. Besides swine's feeding is commonly so nasty and filthy, that it must of necessity cause corruptions and vicious humors; for, setting aside those creatures that are bred from and live upon dung, there is no other creature that takes so much delight to wallow in the mire, and in other unclean and stinking places. Hogs' eyes are said to be so flattened and fixed upon the ground, that they see nothing above them, nor ever look up to the sky, except when forced upon their back they turn their eyes to the sun against nature. Therefore this creature, at other times most clamorous, when laid upon his back, is still, as astonished at the unusual sight of the heavens; while the greatness of the fear he is in (as it is supposed) is the cause of his silence. And if it be lawful to intermix our discourse with fables, it is said that Adonis was slain by a boar. Now Adonis is supposed to be the same with Bacchus; and there are a great many rites in both their sacrifices which confirm this opinion. Others will have Adonis to be Bacchus's paramour; and Phanocles an amorous love-poet writes thus,

> Bacchus on hills the fair Adonis saw,
> And ravished him, and reaped a wondrous joy.

WHAT GOD IS WORSHIPPED BY THE JEWS?

Symmachus, Lamprias, Moeragenes

1. Here Symmachus, greatly wondering at what was spoken, says: What, Lamprias, will you permit our tutelar God, called Evius, the inciter of women, famous for the honors he has conferred upon him by madmen, to be inscribed and enrolled in the mysteries of the Jews? Or is there any solid reason that can be given to prove Adonis to be the same with Bacchus? Here Moeragenes interposing, said: Do not be so fierce upon him, for I who am an Athenian answer you, and tell you, in short, that these two are the very same. And no man is able or fit to hear the chief confirmation of this truth, but those amongst us who are initiated and skilled in the triennial . . . , or great mysteries of the God. But what no religion forbids to speak of among friends, especially over wine, the gift of Bacchus, I am ready at the command of these gentlemen to disclose.

2. When all the company requested and earnestly begged it of him; first of all (says he), the time and manner of the greatest and most holy solemnity of the Jews is exactly agreeable to the holy rites of Bacchus; for that which they call the Fast they celebrate in the midst of the vintage, furnishing their tables with all sorts of fruits, while they sit under tabernacles made of vines and ivy; and the day which immediately goes before this they call the day of Tabernacles. Within a few days after they celebrate another feast, not darkly but openly, dedicated to Bacchus, for they have a feast amongst them called Kradephoria, from carrying palmtrees, and Thyrsophoria, when they enter into the temple carrying thyrsi. What they do within I know not; but it is very probable that they perform the rites of Bacchus. First they have little trumpets, such as the Grecians used to have at their Bacchanalia to call upon their Gods withal. Others go before them playing upon harps, which they call Levites, whether so named from Lusius or Evius,—either word agrees with Bacchus. And I suppose that their Sabbaths have some relation to Bacchus; for even at this day many call the Bacchi by the name of Sabbi, and they make use of that word at the celebration of Bacchus's orgies. And this may be made appear out of Demosthenes and Menander. Nor would it be absurd, were any one to say that the name Sabbath was imposed upon this feast from the agitation and excitement which the priests of Bacchus indulged in. The Jews themselves testify no less; for when they keep the Sabbath, they invite one another to drink till they are drunk; or if they chance to be hindered by some more weighty business, it is the fashion at least to taste the wine. Some perhaps may surmise that these are mere conjectures. But there are other arguments which will clearly evince the truth of what I assert. The first may be drawn from their High-priest, who on holidays enters their temple with his mitre on, arrayed in a skin of a hind embroidered with gold, wearing buskins, and a coat hanging down to his ankles; besides, he has a great many little bells hanging at his garment which make a noise as he walks the streets. So in the nightly ceremonies of Bacchus (as the fashion is amongst us), they make use of musical instruments, and call the God's nurses . . . High up on the wall of their temple is a representation of the thyrsus and timbrels, which surely can belong to no other God than Bacchus. Moreover they are forbidden the use of honey in their sacrifices, because they

suppose that a mixture of honey corrupts and deadens the wine. And honey was used for sacrificing in former days, and with it the ancients were wont to make themselves drunk, before the vine was known. And at this day barbarous people who want wine drink metheglin, allaying the sweetness of the honey by bitter roots, much of the taste of our wine. The Greeks offered to their Gods these sober offerings or honey-offerings, as they called them, because that honey was of a nature quite contrary to wine. But this is no inconsiderable argument that Bacchus was worshipped by the Jews, in that, amongst other kinds of punishment, that was most remarkably odious by which malefactors were forbid the use of wine for so long a time as the judge was pleased to prescribe.

MINUCIUS FELIX:

"You will understand that they [the Jews] deserted God before He deserted them."
(End of second century)

Marcus Minucius Felix was a Christian spokesman during the second century of the Christian era. Unfriendly to Judaism and Paganism, Minucius Felix was representative of the intellectual and professional stratum of Roman society, and his *Octavius,* which is his only surviving work, is revealing of the social and religious opinion held by the upper-class Romans of his day. The *Octavius,* from which the following account is extracted, is in the form of a dialogue between the pagan Q. Caecilus Natalis and the Christian Octavius Januarius, a lawyer and friend of Minucius Felix. The selection here reprinted originated with Octavius.

"But what did it profit the Jews that they too, with reverence the most scrupulous, worshipped one God with altars and with tem-

From Minucius Felix, *Octavius,* translated by Gerald H. Rendall (Cambridge, Mass.: Harvard University Press, and London: William Heinemann Ltd., 1953), p. 417. Reprinted by permission of Harvard University Press from Loeb Classical Library editions.

ples?" There you are betrayed into ignorance, if you forget or ignore their earlier history, and remember only the later; the Jews, so long as they worshipped our God—one God, the same for all—in purity and innocence and holiness—so long as they obeyed his precepts of salvation, grew from a small people to a numberless, from being poor to rich, from being slaves to kings; few in numbers and unarmed they overwhelmed armed hosts, and at the command of God with the assistance of the elements pursued them in their flight. Read their own writings; or omitting the ancients, turn to Flavius Josephus; or, if you prefer Romans, consult Antonius Julianus on the Jews, and you will see that it was their own wickedness which brought them to misfortune, and that nothing happened to them which was not predicted in advance, if they persisted in rebelliousness. You will understand that they deserted God before he deserted them, and that they were not—as you profanely say—led captive with their God, but were handed over by God as deserters from his disciplines.

PHILOSTRATUS (EUPHRATES):

". . . the Jews have long been in revolt not only against the Romans, but against humanity; and a race that has made its own a life apart and irreconcilable . . . are separated from ourselves by a greater gulf than divides us from Susa or Bactra or the more distant Indies." (217?)

Philostratus, "The Athenian" (170–245), studied and taught in Athens, but spent most of his adult life in Rome. His *Life of Apollonius of Tyana,* from which the following is reprinted, is less a biography of Apollonius than a collection of impressions and largely fictional episodes.

From Philostratus, *The Life of Apollonius of Tyana,* translated by F. C. Conybeare (London: William Heinemann, and New York: The Macmillan Company, 1912), Vol. I, 539–541. Reprinted by permission of Harvard University Press from Loeb Classical Library editions.

Apollonius of Tyana, a Greek philosopher, was born a few years before the dawn of the Christian era. Widely traveled throughout Europe and Asia, he was influenced by Oriental mysticism and occult practice, and even enjoyed some reputation as a miracle-worker. He himself claimed the power to foretell the future, and it was believed by some that he could restore life to dead bodies. For reasons which have never been clear, he was accused of treason by both Nero and Domitian, but he apparently was able to escape trial.

Euphrates, to whom the speech against Apollonius is attributed, was a stoic philosopher who spent a good part of his life in Syria. A close friend of Pliny, the Younger, Euphrates for a time enjoyed the confidence of Apollonius, but the relationship was neither stable nor permanent. At an advanced age, and out of favor, Euphrates fell victim to an incurable disease, and in accordance with principles sanctioned by Stoic philosophy, took his own life.

From the speech of Euphrates to Apollonius

How escape the reproach of having been afraid of Nero, the most cowardly and supine of rulers? Look at the revolt against him planned by Vindex, you surely were the man of the hour, its natural leader, and not he! For you had an army at your back, and the forces you were leading against the Jews, would they not have been more suitably employed in chastising Nero? For the Jews have long been in revolt not only against the Romans, but against humanity; and a race that has made its own a life apart and irreconcilable, that cannot share with the rest of mankind in the pleasures of the table nor join in their libations or prayers or sacrifices, are separated from ourselves by a greater gulf than divides us from Susa or Bactra or the more distant Indies. What sense then or reason was there in chastising them for revolting from us whom we had better have never annexed? As for Nero, who would not have prayed with his own hand to slay a man well-nigh drunk with human blood, singing as he sat amidst the hecatombs of his victims? I confess that I ever pricked up my ears when any messenger from yonder brought tidings of yourself, and told us how in one battle you had slain thirty thousand Jews and in the next fifty thousand. In such cases I would take the courier aside and quietly ask him: "But what of the great man? Will he not rise to higher things than this?"

TERTULLIAN:

*"The Jews knew that Christ was to come,
of course, for it was to them that the
prophets spoke. Even now the Jews look
for his coming, nor is there any greater
cause of clash between us than that they
do not believe he has come."*
(Third century)

Tertullian (155?–222?), the earliest and, except for Augustine, the greatest of the ancient interpreters of Christianity, was born in Carthage. Educated in the classics and in law, Tertullian was converted to Christianity sometime between 190 and 195. Tertullian's writings attempted to harmonize Christian and Stoic doctrines, and his works evidence an increasing hostility to Judaism, Gnosticism, and Catholicism. Unable to reconcile himself to the secularization of the Catholic Church and its emergence as a political organization, Tertullian broke with the Church at Rome, and became the most important representative of Montanism in the West.

But now that we have stated that this school[1] rests on the very ancient books of the Jews—this school which most people know to be rather modern, as dating from the reign of Tiberius—a fact we ourselves admit—perhaps some question may be raised as to the standing of the school, on the ground that, under cover of a very famous religion (and one certainly permitted by law), the school insinuates quietly certain claims of its own; because (waiving all question as to age) as regards forbidden food, sacred days, the bodily "seal,"[2] or common designation, we have nothing to do with the Jews, as should surely be the case, if we were servants of the same God. But by now even the common people know the name of

From Tertullian, *Apology*, translated by T. R. Glover (Cambridge, Mass.: Harvard University Press, and London: William Heinemann Ltd., 1953), pp. 103–105, 109–115.

[1] *Secta*, the common word for a philosophic school, is adopted by Tertullian to describe the Christian community united in thought learnt from a great Teacher.

[2] *I.e.*, circumcision.

Christ, taking him to be some man (as the Jews also thought), so that it is easier for anybody to think of us as worshippers of a man. But we neither blush for Christ (for it is our delight to be reckoned under His name and under it to be condemned) nor do we differ in our idea of God [from the Jews]. We must then say a few words about Christ as God.

Of old the Jews had favour with God; such was the outstanding righteousness and faith of the original founders of their race; and thence followed for them a nation's greatness, a kingdom's splendour, such prosperity (in short) that by God's own words (the source of their training) they were warned to deserve God's care and not to offend Him. But what sin they committed; how proud confidence in their origin led to their decline; and how they turned from what they had been taught into ungodly ways—even if they did not confess it themselves, the outcome of it all for them to-day would prove it. Scattered, wanderers, exiles from their own soil and sky, they stray the world over, without man or God for their king; they are not permitted even as foreigners to greet their native land, with so much as a footfall. Of this those holy voices warned them beforehand, and insisted at the same time (every one of them always, and in unison) that the day should come when in the last courses of time God would from every race, people and place gather Himself worshippers far more faithful, to whom He would transfer his favour, and that in fuller measure, because they would be able to bear an ampler discipline.

The Jews knew that Christ was to come, of course, for it was to them that the prophets spoke. Even now the Jews look for his coming, nor is there any other greater cause of clash between us than that they do not believe he has come. Two comings were predicted for him; in the first (which is already fulfilled) he should come in the lowliness of human form; in the second, which impends for the ending of the world, it should be in the majesty of deity displayed. But the Jews misunderstood the first coming; and the second, which was more clearly foretold and for which they hope, they took to be the only one. As for the first coming—they would have believed, if they had understood, and they would have won salvation if they had believed—but what prevented them from believing was the result of their sin. They themselves read it written in scripture that they have been deprived of wisdom and understanding, of the fruits of eye and ear.

From his lowly guise they took him to be merely a man; so it followed that, confronted by his power, they counted him a magician. For with a word he drove devils out of men, he gave light again to the blind, he cleansed the lepers, he braced up the paralytic, and to crown all he restored the dead to life by his word; he made the very elements his servants, he controlled the storm, he walked on the sea—showing that he is the *Logos* of God, that is the Word, original and first-begotten, attended by Power and Reason, upheld by Spirit, the same Being who by his word still made as he had made all things. His teaching, with its refutation of the instructors and chief men of the Jews, so incensed them (chiefly because of the vast multitudes it turned to him) that at last they brought him to Pontius Pilate, at that time Roman procurator of Syria, and by the fury of their suffrages extorted it from Pilate that Jesus should be handed over to them to be crucified. He himself had foretold that they would do this. If that be not enough, so had the prophets long before. Yet, nailed to the cross he showed many signs by which his death was distinguished from others. For with a word, of his own will, he dismissed his spirit—forestalling the work of the executioner. At that very moment though the sun was in mid sky, day was withdrawn. An eclipse, of course, they supposed it, who did not know that this too was predicted of Christ; yet that cosmic event you have in your archives; it is told there. He was taken down from the cross and laid in a tomb; the Jews with supreme care surrounded it with a great military guard, lest, since he had foretold his rising from death on the third day, his disciples by stealth should get the dead body away and trick them for all their suspicions. But, look you! on the third day, there was a sudden earthquake; the structure that blocked the tomb was shaken down; the guard was scattered in terror; but though no disciples appeared on the scene, nothing was found in the tomb but the cloths in which he was buried. None the less, the chief men of the Jews—it was to their interest to tell a false tale and to recapture from the faith a people to pay them tribute and yield them service; so they spread the story about that the disciples had stolen him. For he did not display himself to the common gaze, lest the wicked should be set free from their misjudgement; and that faith, with that supreme prize set before it, should not be too easy. With certain disciples he spent forty days in Galilee, a region of Judaea, teaching them what they should teach. Then he appointed them to the duty of preaching throughout the world, and, with a cloud cast about him, he was caught up to heaven—far more truly than any Romulus of yours in the tale of Proculus.

This whole story of Christ was reported to Caesar (at that time it was Tiberius) by Pilate, himself in his secret heart already a Christian. Yes, and the Caesars also would have believed on Christ, if Caesars had not been necessary for the world, or if the Caesars, too, could have been Christians. His disciples, also, were scattered through the world, in obedience to the precept of God their teacher; they suffered much from Jewish persecution—but gladly enough because of their faith in the truth; finally at Rome, through the cruelty of Nero, they sowed the seed of Christian blood.

CONSTANTINE THE GREAT:

". . . if any one of the population
should join their [the Jews'] abominable
sect and attend their meetings, he will bear
with them the deserved penalties." (315)

CONSTANTIUS:

"This prohibition is to be preserved for
the future lest the Jews induce Christian
women to share their shameful lives." (339)

THEODOSIUS II:

". . . we forbid that any synagogue shall
rise as a new building." (439)

Constantine the Great (280?–337), Emperor of Rome during the early fourth century of the Christian era, was converted to Christianity circa 312. During his reign the capitol of the Empire was moved from Rome

Reprinted from Jacob R. Marcus, editor, *The Jew in the Medieval World* (Cincinnati, Ohio: The Union of American Hebrew Congregations, 1938), pp. 4–6; Copyright 1938 by Union of American Hebrew Congregations; reprinted 1960 by the Jewish Publication Society of America, Philadelphia, Pa.

to a city on the Bosporus which, in 330, was renamed Constantinople and dedicated with a mixture of Christian and pagan ceremonies. Constantine's conversion may have been motivated more by political reasons than theological convictions, but, whatever the motivation, Constantine's conversion gave Christianity the status of an official state religion in the vast territory ruled by Constantine and his successors.

Constantius II (317–361), second son of Constantine, was beset by revolts throughout the Empire, including revolts by the Jews. The latter were put down with special severity, and centers of Jewish culture and learning throughout the Empire were largely destroyed or forced into dissolution.

Theodosius II (408–450) minimally tolerated the Jewish religion, but under his reign the Jews were subjected to a large variety of restrictions and discriminations. Conversion to Judaism, intermarriage between Jews and Christians, the ownership by Jews of Christian slaves, and Jewish tenure of public office were prohibited. Finally, when the Jewish patriarchal office in Palestine fell vacant, Theodosius abolished it. With that action, the only remaining symbol of Jewish unity and organization, maintained in Palestine for more than three centuries, was destroyed.

The laws of Constantine, Constantius, and Theodosius, here reprinted, reflect the conditions under which Jews lived, or survived, not merely during the fourth and fifth centuries, but for many centuries thereafter.

A Law of Constantine the Great, October 18, 315

We wish to make it known to the Jews and their elders and their patriarchs that if, after the enactment of this law, any one of them dares to attack with stones or some other manifestation of anger another who has fled their dangerous sect and attached himself to the worship of God [Christianity], he must speedily be given to the flames and burnt together with all his accomplices.

Moreover, if any one of the population should join their abominable sect and attend their meetings, he will bear with them the deserved penalties.

A Law of Constantius, August 13, 339

This pertains to women, who live in our weaving factories and whom Jews, in their foulness, take in marriage. It is decreed that these women are to be restored to the weaving factories.

This prohibition is to be preserved for the future lest the Jews induce Christian women to share their shameful lives. If they do this they will subject themselves to a sentence of death.

If any one among the Jews has purchased a slave of another sect or nation, that slave shall at once be appropriated for the imperial treasury.

If, indeed, he shall have circumcised the slave whom he has purchased, he will not only be fined for the damage done to that slave but he will also receive capital punishment.

If, indeed, a Jew does not hesitate to purchase slaves—those who are members of the faith that is worthy of respect—then all these slaves who are found in his possession shall at once be removed. No delay shall be occasioned, but he is to be deprived of the possession of those men who are Christians.

A Law of Theodosius II, January 31, 439

Wherefore, although according to an old saying "no cure is to be applied in desperate sicknesses," nevertheless, in order that these dangerous sects which are unmindful of our times may not spread into life the more freely, in indiscriminate disorder as it were, we ordain by this law to be valid for all time:

No Jew—or no Samaritan who subscribes to neither religion—shall obtain offices and dignities; to none shall the administration of city service be permitted; nor shall any one exercise the office of a defender of the city. Indeed, we believe it sinful that the enemies of the heavenly majesty and of the Roman laws should become the executors of our laws—the administration of which they have slyly obtained—and that they, fortified by the authority of the acquired rank, should have the power to judge or decide as they wish against Christians, yes, frequently even over bishops of our holy religion themselves, and thus, as it were, insult our faith.

Moreover, for the same reason, we forbid that any synagogue shall rise as a new building. However, the propping up of old synagogues which are now threatened with imminent ruin is permitted. To these things we add that he who misleads a slave or a freeman against his will or by punishable advice, from the service of the Christian religion to that of an abominable sect and ritual, is to be punished by loss of property and life.

On the one hand, whoever has built a synagogue must realize that he has worked to the advantage of the Catholic church; on the other hand, whoever has already secured the badge of office shall not hold the dignities he has acquired. On the contrary, he who worms himself into office must remain, as before, in the lowest rank even though he will have already earned an honorary office. And as for him who begins the building of a synagogue and is not moved by the desire of repairing it, he shall be punished by a fine of fifty pounds gold for his daring. Moreover, if he will have prevailed with his evil teachings over the faith of another, he shall see his wealth confiscated and himself soon subjected to a death sentence.

And since it behooves the imperial majesty to consider everything with such foresight that the general welfare does not suffer in the least, we ordain that the tax-paying office-holders of all towns as well as the provincial civil servants—who are obligated to employ their wealth and to make public gifts as part of their burdensome and diverse official and military duties—shall remain in their own classes no matter what sect they belong to. Let it not appear as if we have accorded the benefit of exemption to those men, detestable in their insolent maneuvering, whom we wish to condemn by the authority of this law.

This further limitation is to be observed, namely, that these public servants from these above mentioned sects shall never, as far as private affairs are concerned, carry out judicial sentences, nor be wardens of the jail. This is done in order that Christians, as it sometimes happens, may not be hidden away and suffer a double imprisonment through the hatred of the guards. And furthermore it may be doubted that they have been justly imprisoned.

JULIAN:

*"But that from the beginning God cared
only for the Jews and that He chose them
out as his portion, has been clearly
asserted not only by Moses and Jesus
but by Paul as well." (361–363)*

The Emperor Julian (331–363) was born in Constantinople. Following the death of his uncle, Constantine the Great, in 337, Julian's entire family was murdered, except for himself and his half brother Gallus, to ensure the succession of the throne to Constantine's sons. Although Gallus was banished, Julian was allowed to remain in Constantinople where he pursued his studies under the supervision of family tutors. The death of Gallus in 354, after a short period as emperor, left Constantius and Julian as the sole surviving male descendants of Constantine. In 361 Julian became emperor, but his reign lasted only two years. Mortally wounded in a battle against the Persians on June 26, 363, Julian died in his tent on the evening of the engagement. A recurrent story that he was murdered by a Christian has never been authenticated.

Julian was raised in the Christian faith, but apparently never abandoned an early attachment to paganism and Hellenic philosophy. The tolerant polytheism of his own religious convictions led Julian to regard Christianity as a deviant movement that substituted persecution for faith and reason. The very model of a Philosopher King, Julian combined Neoplatonist philosophy and pagan ideals with considerable skill in the arts of war and statecraft. His short reign did not allow time for a revival of the older customs and traditions, but it is interesting to speculate what effect a longer emperorship might have had on the future of Christianity and the Roman Empire.

Julian's partiality to the Jews, reflected in the documents here reprinted, is one of many factors that makes him unique among Roman emperors both before and after Constantine.

To the community of the Jews

In times past, by far the most burdensome thing in the yoke of your slavery has been the fact that you were subjected to unauthorised

From *The Works of the Emperor Julian,* translated by Wilmer Cave Wright. Reprinted by permission of Harvard University Press from Loeb Classical Library, Vol. III, 177–181, 341–345.

ordinances and had to contribute an untold amount of money to the accounts of the treasury. Of this I used to see many instances with my own eyes, and I have learned of more, by finding the records which are preserved against you. Moreover, when a tax was about to be levied on you again I prevented it, and compelled the impiety of such obloquy to cease here; and I threw into the fire the records against you that were stored in my desks; so that it is no longer possible for anyone to aim at you such a reproach of impiety. My brother Constantius of honoured memory was not so much responsible for these wrongs of yours as were the men who used to frequent his table, barbarians in mind, godless in soul. These I seized with my own hands and put them to death by thrusting them into the pit, that not even any memory of their destruction might still linger amongst us. And since I wish that you should prosper yet more, I have admonished my brother Iulus, your most venerable patriarch, that the levy which is said to exist among you should be prohibited, and that no one is any longer to have the power to oppress the masses of your people by such exactions; so that everywhere, during my reign, you may have security of mind, and in the enjoyment of peace may offer more fervid prayers for my reign to the Most High God, the Creator, who has deigned to crown me with his own immaculate right hand. For it is natural that men who are distracted by any anxiety should be hampered in spirit, and should not have so much confidence in raising their hands to pray; but that those who are in all respects free from care should rejoice with their whole hearts and offer their suppliant prayers on behalf of my imperial office to Mighty God, even to him who is able to direct my reign to the noblest ends, according to my purpose. This you ought to do, in order that, when I have successfully concluded the war with Persia, I may rebuild by my own efforts the sacred city of Jerusalem, which for so many years you have longed to see inhabited, and may bring settlers there, and, together with you, may glorify the Most High God therein.

Against the Galilaeans

Moses says that the creator of the universe chose out the Hebrew nation, that to that nation alone did he pay heed and cared for it, and he gives him charge of it alone. But how and by what sort of gods the other nations are governed he has said not a word—unless indeed one should concede that he did assign to them the sun and moon. However of this I shall speak a little later. Now I will only point out that Moses himself and the prophets who came after him and Jesus the Nazarene, yes and Paul also, who surpassed all the magicians and charlatans of every place and every time, assert that he is the God of Israel alone and of Judaea, and that the Jews are his chosen people. Listen to their own words, and first to the words of Moses: "And thou shalt say unto Pharaoh, Israel is my son, my firstborn. And I have said to thee, Let my people go that they may serve me. But thou didst refuse to let them go." And a little later, "And they say unto him, The God of the Hebrews hath summoned us; we will go therefore three days' journey into the desert, that we may sacrifice unto the Lord our God." And soon he speaks again in the same way, "The Lord the God of the Hebrews hath sent me unto thee, saying, Let my people go that they may serve me in the wilderness."

But that from the beginning God cared only for the Jews and that He chose them out as his portion, has been clearly asserted not only by Moses and Jesus but by Paul as well; though in Paul's case this is strange. For according to circumstances he keeps changing his views about God, as the polypus changes its colours to match the rocks, and now he insists that the Jews alone are God's portion, and then again, when he is trying to persuade the Hellenes to take sides with him, he says: "Do not think that he is the God of Jews only, but also of Gentiles: yea of Gentiles also." Therefore it is fair to ask of Paul why God, if he was not the God of the Jews only but also of the Gentiles, sent the blessed gift of prophecy to the Jews in abundance and gave them Moses and the oil of anointing, and the prophets and the law and the incredible and monstrous elements in their myths? For you hear them crying aloud: "Man did eat angels' food." And finally God sent unto them Jesus also, but unto us no prophet, no oil of anointing, no teacher, no herald to announce his love for man which should one day, though late, reach even unto us also. Nay he even looked on for myriads, or if you prefer, for thousands of years, while men in extreme ignorance served idols, as you call them, from where the sun rises to where he sets, yes and from North to South, save only that little tribe which less than two thousand years before had settled in one part of Palestine. For if he is the God of all of us alike, and the creator of all, why did he neglect us? Wherefore it is natural to think that the God of the Hebrews was not the begetter of the whole universe with lordship over the whole, but rather, as I said before, that He is confined within limits, and that since His empire has bounds we must conceive of Him as only one of the crowd of other gods. Then are we to pay further heed to you because you or one of your stock imagined the God of the universe, though in any case you attained only to a bare conception of Him? Is not all this partiality? God, you say, is a jealous God. But why is He so jealous, even avenging the sins of the fathers on the children?

SOZOMENUS:

". . . [Julian] gave them public money,
commanded them to rebuild the Temple,
and to practice the cult similar to that
of their ancestors, by sacrificing after the
ancient way. The Jews entered upon
the undertaking, without reflecting that,
according to the prediction of the holy
prophets, it could not be accomplished."
(443–450)

Salamanius Hermias Sozomenus (circa 400–443) was a well known Church historian of the fifth century. Born of a wealthy Palestinian family, Sozomenus was brought up by monks, and as a young man studied law in Beirut. The nine books of his *Ecclesiastical History* dealt with the period from Constantine to the death of Honorius in 423. Sozomenus' account of the failure to rebuild the Temple, which was promised by Julian, was influenced by the fact that as a devout Churchman, Sozomenus was hostile to Julian and the Jews.

From Sozomenus, *Ecclesiastical History* (443–450). Reprinted from Jacob R. Marcus, editor, *The Jew in the Medieval World* (Cincinnati, Ohio: The Union of American Hebrew Congregations, 1938), pp. 9–12; Copyright 1938 by Union of American Hebrew Congregations; reprinted 1960 by the Jewish Publication Society of America, Philadelphia, Pa.

Though the emperor hated and oppressed the Christians, he manifested benevolence and humanity towards the Jews. He wrote to the Jewish patriarchs and leaders, as well as to the people, requesting them to pray for him, and for the prosperity of the empire. In taking this step he was not actuated, I am convinced, by any respect for their religion; for he was aware that it is, so to speak, the mother of the Christian religion, and he knew that both religions rest upon the authority of the patriarchs and the prophets; but he thought to grieve the Christians by favoring the Jews, who are their most inveterate enemies. But perhaps he also calculated upon persuading the Jews to embrace paganism and sacrifices; for they were only acquainted with the mere letter of Scripture, and could not, like the Christians and a few of the wisest among the Hebrews, discern the hidden meaning.

Events proved that this was his real motive; for he sent for some of the chiefs of the race and exhorted them to return to the observance of the laws of Moses and the customs of their fathers. On their replying that because the Temple in Jerusalem was overturned, it was neither lawful nor ancestral to do this in another place than the metropolis out of which they had been cast, he gave them public money, commanded them to rebuild the Temple, and to practice the cult similar to that of their ancestors, by sacrificing after the ancient way. The Jews entered upon the undertaking, without reflecting that, according to the prediction of the holy prophets, it could not be accomplished. They sought for the most skillful artisans, collected materials, cleared the ground, and entered so earnestly upon the task, that even the women carried heaps of earth, and brought their necklaces and other female ornaments towards defraying the expense.

The emperor, the other pagans, and all the Jews, regarded every other undertaking as secondary in importance to this. Although the pagans were not well-disposed towards the Jews, yet they assisted them in this enterprise, because they reckoned upon its ultimate success, and hoped by this means to falsify the prophecies of Christ. Besides this motive, the Jews themselves were impelled by the consideration that the time had arrived for rebuilding their Temple.

When they had removed the ruins of the former building, they dug up the ground and cleared away its foundation; it is said that on the following day when they were about to lay the first foundation, a great earthquake occurred, and by the violent agitation of the earth, stones were thrown up from the depths, by which those of the Jews who were engaged in the work were wounded, as likewise those who were merely looking on. The houses and public porticos, near the site of the Temple, in which they had diverted themselves, were suddenly thrown down; many were caught thereby, some perished immediately, others were found half dead and mutilated of hands or legs, others were injured in other parts of the body.

When God caused the earthquake to cease, the workmen who survived again returned to their task, partly because such was the edict of the emperor, and partly because they were themselves interested in the undertaking. Men often, in endeavoring to gratify their own passions, seek what is injurious to them, reject what would be truly advantageous, and are deluded by the idea that nothing is really useful except what is agreeable to them. When once led astray by this error, they are no longer able to act in a manner conducive to their own interests, or to take warning by the calamities which are visited upon them.

The Jews, I believe, were just in this state; for, instead of regarding this unexpected earthquake as a manifest indication that God was opposed to the reerection of their Temple, they proceeded to recommence the work. But all parties relate that they had scarcely returned to the undertaking, when fire burst suddenly from the foundations of the Temple, and consumed several of the workmen.

This fact is fearlessly stated, and believed by all; the only discrepancy in the narrative is that some maintained that flame burst from the interior of the Temple, as the workmen were striving to force an entrance, while others say that the fire proceeded directly from the earth. In whichever way the phenomenon might have occurred, it is equally wonderful.

A more tangible and still more extraordinary miracle ensued; suddenly the sign of the cross appeared spontaneously on the garments of the persons engaged in the undertaking. These crosses looked like stars, and appeared the work of art. Many were hence led to confess that Christ is God, and that the rebuilding of the Temple was not pleasing to Him; others presented themselves in the church, were initiated, and besought Christ, with hymns and supplications, to pardon their transgression. If any one does not feel disposed to believe my narrative, let him go and be convinced by those who heard the facts I have related from the eyewitnesses of them, for they are still alive. Let him inquire, also, of the Jews and pagans who left the work in an incomplete state, or who, to speak more accurately, were unable to commence it.

SAINT AUGUSTINE:

"Nor do I think the Jews themselves dare
contend that no one has belonged to
God except the Israelites, since the
increase of Israel began on the rejection
of his elder brother." (413–426)

Saint Augustine (354–430), one of the greatest of Catholic theologians, was a pagan in his youth, much given to loose living and dissipation. In 386, at the age of thirty-two, Augustine was converted to Christianity. Nine years later he was appointed Bishop of Hippo (the ancient name of the port city of Buna, Algeria), and he spent the remainder of his life expounding the doctrines of the Roman Catholic Church. His most famous work, *The City of God*, which consisted of twenty-two books, was begun in 413 and completed in 426.

The City of God was designed to refute paganism and establish the basis of Christian life and belief. Augustine's exposition of the heavenly city, or City of God, drew on Hellenism, Neoplatonism, and, to a lesser extent, the Old Testament. According to Augustine, the heavenly city was populated by those, living and dead, whose lives were dedicated to God; more narrowly, the heavenly city was the community of the Church. The earthly city, on the other hand, was the "society of the impious"; its members included angels fallen from grace, non-believers, sinners, and those who lived "after the flesh." Eternal salvation awaited the citizens of the heavenly city. Humans who rejected the true faith would find eternal punishment in the kingdom ruled by the devil.

Although Augustine was in no sense an enemy of the Jews, he was critical of the Jews with respect to their interpretation of the Old Testament, and their rejection of the Messianic character of Jesus. The coming of Jesus, he argued, had been predicted in certain of the Old Testament Psalms, and the dispersal of the Jews foretold in certain chapters of

From Saint Augustine, *The City of God*, translated by Marcus Dods (New York: Random House, The Modern Library, 1950), pp. 656–659.

Isaiah. Despite these views, Augustine's teachings in certain respects were similar to rabbinical doctrines and interpretations. His concept of the heavenly city and his doctrine of predestination, for example, had some resemblance to ideas advanced in the Old Testament and in Talmudic writings.

The following selection is taken from Augustine's *The City of God.*

While Herod, therefore, reigned in Judea, and Caesar Augustus was emperor at Rome, the state of the republic being already changed, and the world being set at peace by him, Christ was born in Bethlehem of Judah, man manifest out of a human virgin, God hidden out of God the Father. For so had the prophet foretold: "Behold, a virgin shall conceive in the womb, and bring forth a Son, and they shall call His name Immanuel, which, being interpreted, is, God with us." He did many miracles that He might commend God in Himself, some of which, even as many as seemed sufficient to proclaim Him, are contained in the evangelic Scripture. The first of these is, that He was so wonderfully born, and the last, that with His body raised up again from the dead He ascended into heaven. But the Jews who slew Him, and would not believe in Him, because it behoved Him to die and rise again, were yet more miserably wasted by the Romans, and utterly rooted out from their kingdom, where aliens had already ruled over them, and were dispersed through the lands (so that indeed there is no place where they are not), and are thus by their own Scriptures a testimony to us that we have not forged the prophecies about Christ. And very many of them, considering this, even before His passion, but chiefly after His resurrection, believed on Him, of whom it was predicted, "Though the number of the children of Israel be as the sand of the sea, the remnant shall be saved." But the rest are blinded, of whom it was predicted, "Let their table be made before them a trap, and a retribution, and a stumbling-block. Let their eyes be darkened lest they see, and bow down their back alway." Therefore, when they do not believe our Scriptures, their own, which they blindly read, are fulfilled in them, lest perchance any one should say that the Christians have forged these prophecies about Christ which are quoted under the name of the sibyl, or of others, if such there be, who do not belong to the Jewish people. For us, indeed, those suffice which are

quoted from the books of our enemies, to whom we make our
acknowledgment, on account of this testimony, which, in spite of
themselves, they contribute by their possession of these books, while
they themselves are dispersed among all nations, wherever the Church
of Christ is spread abroad. For a prophecy about this thing was sent
before in the Psalms, which they also read, where it is written, "My
God, His mercy shall prevent me. My God hath shown me concerning mine enemies, that Thou shalt not slay them, lest they should
at last forget Thy law: disperse them in Thy might." Therefore God
has shown the Church in her enemies the Jews the grace of His
compassion, since, as saith the apostle, "their offence is the salvation
of the Gentiles." And therefore He has not slain them, that is, He
has not let the knowledge that they are Jews be lost in them, although they have been conquered by the Romans, lest they should
forget the law of God, and their testimony should be of no avail in
this matter of which we treat. But it was not enough that he should
say, "Slay them not, lest they should at last forget Thy law," unless
he had also added, "Disperse them"; because if they had only been
in their own land with that testimony of the Scriptures, and not
everywhere, certainly the Church which is everywhere could not
have had them as witnesses among all nations to the prophecies
which were sent before concerning Christ.

Wherefore if we read of any foreigner—that is, one neither born
of Israel nor received by that people into the canon of the sacred
books—having prophesied something about Christ, if it has come or
shall come to our knowledge, we can refer to it over and above;
not that this is necessary, even if wanting, but because it is not in-
congruous to believe that even in other nations there may have been
men to whom this mystery was revealed, and who were also impelled to proclaim it, whether they were partakers of the same grace
or had no experience of it, but were taught by bad angels, who, as
we know, even confessed the present Christ, whom the Jews did not
acknowledge. Nor do I think the Jews themselves dare contend that
no one has belonged to God except the Israelites, since the increase
of Israel began on the rejection of his elder brother. For in very
deed there was no other people who were specially called the people of God; but they cannot deny that there have been certain men
even of other nations who belonged, not by earthly but heavenly
fellowship, to the true Israelites, the citizens of the country that is

above. Because, if they deny this, they can be most easily confuted by the case of the holy and wonderful man Job, who was neither a native nor a proselyte, that is, a stranger joining the people of Israel, but, being bred of the Idumean race, arose there and died there too, and who is so praised by the divine oracle, that no man of his times is put on a level with him as regards justice and piety. And although we do not find his date in the chronicles, yet from his book, which for its merit the Israelites have received as of canonical authority, we gather that he was in the third generation after Israel. And I doubt not it was divinely provided, that from this one case we might know that among other nations also there might be men pertaining to the spiritual Jerusalem who have lived according to God and have pleased Him. And it is not to be supposed that this was granted to any one, unless the one Mediator between God and men, the Man Christ Jesus, was divinely revealed to him; who was pre-announced to the saints of old as yet to come in the flesh, even as He is announced to us as having come, that the self-same faith through Him may lead all to God who are predestinated to be the city of God, the house of God, and the temple of God. But whatever prophecies concerning the grace of God through Christ Jesus are quoted, they may be thought to have been forged by the Christians. So that there is nothing of more weight for confuting all sorts of aliens, if they contend about this matter, and for supporting our friends, if they are truly wise, than to quote those divine predictions about Christ which are written in the books of the Jews, who have been torn from their native abode and dispersed over the whole world in order to bear this testimony, so that the Church of Christ has everywhere increased.

RUTILIUS CLAUDIUS NAMATIANUS:

"For a sour Jew was guardian of the spot,
An animal that spurns at human food.
He charges for the shrubs disturbed, the
wrack
Struck with our sticks, and clamours that
his loss
Is grievous in the water that we drink."
(Fifth century)

Rutilius Claudius Namatianus, Roman poet, was born in Gaul. A member of a distinguished imperial family, the poet also served for a time as a secretary of state and *praefactus urbi*. Sympathetic to paganism, Rutilius Claudius Namatianus was antagonistic to Jews, monks, and others, all of whom served as targets for his poetry. Like his predecessor, the Roman satirical poet Juvenal, Namatianus was a critic of certain real or imagined Jewish beliefs and characteristics: dietary laws, circumcision, observance of the Sabbath, acquisitiveness, and zeal for proselytizing. The Jewish religion he regarded, like Horace before him, as mainly based on superstition.

Landing, we seek the town and roam the wood;
The ponds delight us, sweet, with shoals begirt.
The waters, spread within the enclosed flood,
Allow the sportive fish amid the pools
To dart and play. But he who leased the spot,
A harsher landlord than Antiphates,
Made this reposeful loveliness pay dear.
For a sour Jew was guardian of the spot,
An animal that spurns at human food.
He charges for the shrubs disturbed, the wrack
Struck with our sticks, and clamours that his loss
Is grievous in the water that we drink.
We fling fit answer to the filthy race

From Charles Haines Keene, editor, *The Homecoming of Rutilius Claudius Namatianus from Rome to Gaul in the Year 416* A.D., translated by George F. Savage-Armstrong (London: George Bell & Sons, 1907), p. 141.

That circumcision shamelessly upholds—
Dire folly's root; cold sabbaths charm their heart;
And yet their heart is colder than their creed.
Each seventh day to shameful sloth's condemned,
Effeminate picture of a wearied god!
Their other fancies from the mart of lies
Methinks not even all boys could believe.
Would that Judea ne'er had been subdued
By Pompey's wars and under Titus' sway!
The plague's contagion all the wider spreads;
The conquered presses on the conquering race.

THE "SECRET JEWS":

*". . . whereas the perfidy born of our
obstinacy and the antipathy resulting from
our ancestral errors influenced us to such
an extent that we did not then truly
believe in Our Lord Jesus Christ . . .
henceforth we will observe no Jewish
customs or rites whatever, and will not
associate, or have any intercourse with any
unbaptized Jews." (654)*

In a number of European countries, from the sixth to the sixteenth centuries, Jews could practice their religion only under pain of death or banishment. Many of them accepted the alternative of baptism in the Catholic faith, and thereby obstensibly became Christians. But it was well known that a large number of converts continued secretly to practice Judaism; these were known as "Judaizing Christians" or "Secret Jews." Converts discovered to be practicing, or suspected of practicing, their traditional faith were frequently tortured, killed, or exiled. In an effort to avoid such punishment, the "Secret Jews" often sent declarations of faith and loyalty to their Catholic rulers, sometimes accompanied by gifts of money and jewelry.

From Jacob R. Marcus, editor, *The Jew in the Medieval World* (Cincinnati, Ohio: The Union of American Hebrew Congregations, 1938), pp. 20–22; Copyright 1938 by Union of American Hebrew Congregations; reprinted 1960 by the Jewish Publication Society of America, Philadelphia, Pa.

One such declaration is reprinted below. It was sent to King Recceswinth of Spain in 654 by the "Judaizing Christians" of Toledo.

To our most pious and noble lord and master, King Recceswinth: We, Jews of the city of Toledo, who have hereto attached our signatures or seals, call your attention to the fact that formerly we were compelled to present a memorial to King Chintila, of holy memory, by which we bound ourselves to uphold the Catholic faith, as, in like manner, we do now.

But, whereas the perfidy born of our obstinacy and the antipathy resulting from our ancestral errors influenced us to such an extent that we did not then truly believe in our Lord Jesus Christ and did not sincerely embrace the Catholic faith, therefore now, freely and voluntarily, we promise Your Majesty for ourselves, our wives, and our children, by this, our memorial, that henceforth we will observe no Jewish customs or rites whatever, and will not associate, or have any intercourse with any unbaptized Jews.

Nor will we marry any person related to us by blood, within the sixth degree, which union has been declared to be incestuous and wicked. Nor will we, or our children, or any of our posterity, at any time hereafter, contract marriage outside our sect; and both sexes shall hereafter be united in marriage according to Christian rites. We will not practice the operation of circumcision. We will not celebrate the Passover, Sabbath, and other festival days, as enjoined by the Jewish ritual. We will not make any distinction in food, according to our ancient usages. We will not observe, in any way, ceremonies prescribed by the abominable practices and habits of the Hebrews.

But, with sincere faith, grateful hearts, and perfect devotion, we believe that Christ is the son of the living God, as declared by ecclesiastical and evangelical tradition; and we hereby acknowledge Him to be such, and venerate Him accordingly. Moreover, all the ceremonies enjoined by the Christian religion—whether said ceremonies relate to festivals, or to marriage and food—we will truly and exactly observe; and we will maintain the same with sincerity, without any objection or opposition thereto; and without any subterfuge on our part, by means of which we might hereafter deny our acts, return to what has been prohibited, or not completely fulfill all that we have promised.

With regard to the flesh of animals which we consider unclean, if we should be unable to eat the same on account of our ancient prejudices, nevertheless, when it is cooked along with other food, we hereby promise to partake of the latter with no manifestation of disgust or horror.

And if, at any time, we should be found to have transgressed, and to have violated any of the promises hereinbefore specified; or should presume to act contrary to the doctrines of the Christian faith; or if we should, in word or deed, neglect to fulfill the obligations to which we have bound ourselves, as being acceptable to the Catholic religion; we hereby swear by the Father, Son and Holy Spirit, who form one God in the Trinity, that, in case a single transgressor should be found among our people, he shall be burned, or stoned to death, either by ourselves, or by our sons. And should Your Majesty graciously grant such culprit his life, he shall at once be deprived of his freedom, so that Your Majesty may deliver him to be forever a slave to anyone whom Your Majesty may select; and Your Majesty shall have full authority to make whatever disposition of him and his property as may seem expedient; not only on account of the power attached to your royal office, but also by the authority granted by this our memorial. Made in the name of God, at Toledo, on the Kalends of March, in the sixth year of Your Majesty's happy reign [March 1, 654].

SAINT JOHN OF DAMASCUS:

"For though to this day they [the Jews]
worship the One Omnipotent God, yet it is
not according unto knowledge; for they
deny Christ the Son of God, and are
like the heathen. . . ." (Circa 750 A.D.)

Saint John of Damascus (676?–754?) was a distinguished theologian of the Eastern (Greek) Church. Born in Damascus, of Christian ancestry, John for a time held high office in the Court of Damascus. In 726, he

From St. John Damascene, *Barlaam and Ioasaph,* translated by G. R. Woodward (London: William Heinemann, and New York: The Macmillan Company, 1914), pp. 419–421.

became embroiled in the Iconoclastic controversy, during the course of which he wrote several treatises defending image worship. A few years later he asked, and received permission from, the Caliph to be relieved of his official duties. He then disposed of his worldly goods and retired to a monastery near Jerusalem. Eventually he was ordained Priest of the church of Jerusalem, in which capacity he revised the prayer books used in Greek religious services. Although at one time out of favor with Eastern Church authorities—accusations against him included that of favoring the Saracens—John ultimately came to be regarded as one of the Fathers of the Greek Church.

Saint John, like the majority of Western theologians, could never forgive the Jews for rejecting Christ, and in his writings he held them responsible for Christ's death. From his point of view, the sufferings and dispersal of the Jews were their punishment for refusing to accept the Son of God.

The following selection is from Saint John's *Barlaam and Ioasaph*.

Come we now, O king, to the Jews, that we may see what they also think concerning God. The Jews are the descendants of Abraham, Isaac and Jacob, and went once to sojourn in Egypt. From thence God brought them out with a mighty hand and stretched out arm by Moses their lawgiver; and with many miracles and signs made he known unto them his power. But, like the rest, these proved ungrateful and unprofitable, and often worshipped images of the heathen, and killed the prophets and righteous men that were sent unto them. Then, when it pleased the Son of God to come on earth, they did shamefully entreat him and deliver him to Pilate the Roman governor, and condemn him to the Cross, regardless of his benefits, and the countless miracles that he had worked amongst them. Wherefore by their own lawlessness they perished. For though to this day they worship the One Omnipotent God, yet it is not according unto knowledge; for they deny Christ the Son of God, and are like the heathen, although they seem to approach the truth from which they have estranged themselves. So much for the Jews.

III

THE JEW IN THE
MIDDLE AGES
1186–1588

HISTORICAL NOTE

For almost half a millennium, culminating in the "Golden Age" of Jewish history from the eleventh to the early thirteenth centuries, the Jews of Spain, under Mohammedan rule, enjoyed a freedom that was unparalleled in any of the Christian countries of Europe. The amalgamation of the Jewish and Arabic cultures was stimulating to both, and indeed produced more lasting and significant results than the earlier blending of Judaic culture and Hellenism. For the first time in centuries, the Jews were able to engage in a variety of careers. The study of the Talmud and Hebraic lore was combined with the study of medicine, mathematics, physics, and astronomy.

The privileged position of Spanish Jewry was not shared by the Jews of Christian Europe. Constantly exposed to persecution, they were largely isolated, and therefore all the more vulnerable to discrimination, in the Gentile community. The crusades, beginning in 1096, were a clear demonstration, especially to the Jews of France and Germany, of what could be expected from crusading Christians: the First Crusade (1096–1099) was accompanied by wholesale butchery and frequent Jewish suicides.

The Third and Fourth Lateran Councils (1179 and 1215), believing that Jews were partly responsible for the heretical Albigensian movement, renewed the older restrictions that applied to Jews, and imposed some additional ones. The Fourth Council declared that Jews were outcasts with whom there was to be no intermarriage or social mingling. Jews were not to employ Christian servants, or hold public office, and they were to remain in their homes during Easter Week. Since Jews were infidels, the Council ordered that henceforth they were to wear a special badge of identification—a round patch of yellow cloth—on the upper garment. Although these restrictions were not enforced everywhere in Catholic Europe, they were frequently invoked by religious and secular authorities during the next several centuries. Indeed they achieved some prominence in the sixteenth century, as a consequence of the Protestant Reformation, regarded by many Catholics as a Jewish conspiracy against the Church.

But everywhere in Europe the Middle Ages constituted a long Jewish martyrdom. England, the last country to be settled by Jews, who arrived there at the time of the Norman Conquest in 1066, was also the first to expel them, in 1290. The French Jews, after a series of massacres, extortions, and partial banishments, were expelled in 1394. In Germany, the Jews were designated *servi camerae*, or serfs of the state; as such, they were heavily taxed and confined to petty trades, such as usury and peddling.

Even the Spanish Jews were not exempt from persecution. In the early thirteenth century the Arabs were forced out of the Iberian Peninsula, and power passed to the Catholic rulers of Castile and Aragon. Incited by clerical propaganda, the people of Spain turned savagely on the Jews. The fourteenth century witnessed a number of anti-Jewish riots that culminated, in 1391, with the massacre of thousands of Jews at Seville. The Seville incident led many Jews to embrace Catholicism outwardly, while, in secret, they continued to practice Judaism. Until 1492, when the Jews were expelled from Spain, the ostensible converts, the *Marranos,* were incessantly harassed by the Inquisition, which was established in 1480 by Ferdinand and Isabella.

With the expulsion of Jews from Portugal, Navarre, and Provence at the close of the fifteenth century, most of Western Europe was closed to the Jews. The majority of Jewish refugees found asylum in Moslem areas and in Turkey (Sultan Bajazet of Turkey, hearing that the Jews had been banished from Spain, is supposed to have exclaimed: "How can you call Ferdinand of Aragon a wise king, the same Ferdinand who has made his land poor and enriched ours?"). Important Jewish communities were beginning to develop in Poland and Lithuania. From 1500 to 1650 the Jewish population in these countries increased from fifty thousand to more than half a million.

The Protestant Reformation in Germany and elsewhere did little to alleviate the situation of the Jews. Luther himself indulged in bigotry, and the religious wars arising from the Reformation fanned the fires of intolerance. In certain countries, notably Spain and Italy, the Jews were the favored scapegoats of increased Papal fanaticism. Pope Paul IV in 1555 enforced the perpetual wearing of the Jewish badge of identity. He also created the ghetto by requiring Jews to live apart from Christians, and excluded the Jews from all honorable positions and occupations.

Although the Papacy was opposed to the Spanish Inquisition and, on occasion, treated the Jews with more leniency than they were accorded by secular rulers, it remains true that the Church bore a heavy responsibility for medieval intolerance. Its obsession with infidels and heretics permitted, and in numerous cases encouraged anti-Jewish feeling in areas under its religious control. Ultimately, the effects of much Papal legislation were to promote persecution and discrimination, and the expulsion of Jews from Catholic countries owed much to Papal influence. It should not be forgotten, however, that until the nineteenth century Protestant sects were hardly less intolerant of Jews than the Roman Catholic Church.

RIGORD (PHILIP AUGUSTUS):

*"The Jews who dwelt in Paris were wont
every year on Easter Day, or during the
sacred week of Our Lord's Passion, to go
down secretly into underground vaults
and kill a Christian as a sort of sacrifice in
contempt of the Christian religion."*
(Circa *1186*)

Philip Augustus (1165–1223), unlike some of his predecessors, had no
difficulty believing that the Jews indulged in ritual murder, and he was
also aware that persecution of the Jews was useful, up to a point, in
providing revenue for the Royal Treasury. In 1180, not long after his
coronation, all Jews were arrested in their Synagogues and forced to pay
a ransom of some 15,000 silver marks. Philip also declared null and void
all debts owed to Jews by Christians. Finally, in 1182, an Edict forced
the emigration of all Jews who resided in the Royal domains. The emigrants were allowed three months in which to dispose of their personal
property; all other property, such as land and buildings, was confiscated
by the King.

In 1198, however, the Jews were allowed to return. Although a special
tax was levied on Jewish trade and commerce, the Jews were permitted
to engage in money-lending operations and to determine the interest rates
charged. The reversal of policy was apparently due to a belated recognition by Philip of the importance of Jews in banking and related business
enterprises. But another theory credits the change to Philip's defiance of
Pope Innocent III, who had excommunicated him following the renunciation of his marriage.

The account here reprinted deals with the expulsion of the Jews in
1182. It was written by the Catholic Monk, Rigord, and is taken from
his *Gesta Philippi Augusti*, a contemporary history begun sometime
after 1186.

Reprinted from Jacob R. Marcus, editor, *The Jew in the Medieval World*
(Cincinnati, Ohio: The Union of American Hebrew Congregations, 1938), pp.
24–27; Copyright 1938 by Union of American Hebrew Congregations; reprinted
1960 by the Jewish Publications Society of America, Philadelphia, Pa.

[T]he Jews who dwelt in Paris were wont every year on Easter
day, or during the sacred week of our Lord's Passion, to go down
secretly into underground vaults and kill a Christian as a sort of
sacrifice in contempt of the Christian religion. For a long time they
had persisted in this wickedness, inspired by the devil, and in
Philip's father's time, many of them had been seized and burned
with fire. St. Richard, whose body rests in the church of the Holy
Innocents-in-the-Fields in Paris, was thus put to death and crucified
by the Jews, and through martyrdom went in blessedness to God.
Wherefore many miracles have been wrought by the hand of God
through the prayers and intercessions of St. Richard, to the glory of
God, as we have heard.

And because the most Christian King Philip inquired diligently,
and came to know full well these and many other iniquities of the
Jews in his forefathers' days, therefore he burned with zeal, and in
the same year in which he was invested at Rheims with the holy
governance of the kingdom of the French, upon a Sabbath, the sixteenth of February, by his command, the Jews throughout all France
were seized in their synagogues and then despoiled of their gold
and silver and garments, as the Jews themselves had spoiled the
Egyptians at their exodus from Egypt. This was a harbinger of their
expulsion, which by God's will soon followed. . . .

At this time a great multitude of Jews had been dwelling in
France for a long time past, for they had flocked thither from divers
parts of the world, because peace abode among the French, and
liberality; for the Jews had heard how the kings of the French were
prompt to act against their enemies, and were very merciful toward
their subjects. And therefore their elders and men wise in the law
of Moses, who were called by the Jews *didascali*, made resolve to
come to Paris.

When they had made a long sojourn there, they grew so rich that
they claimed as their own almost half of the whole city, and had
Christians in their houses as menservants and maidservants, who
were open backsliders from the faith of Jesus Christ, and *judaized*
with the Jews. And this was contrary to the decree of God and the
law of the Church. And whereas the Lord had said by the mouth of
Moses in Deuteronomy, "Thou shalt not lend upon usury to thy
brother," but "to a stranger," the Jews in their wickedness understood by "stranger" every Christian, and they took from the Chris-

tians their money at usury. And so heavily burdened in this wise were citizens and soldiers and peasants in the suburbs, and in the various towns and villages, that many of them were constrained to part with their possessions. Others were bound under oath in houses of the Jews in Paris, held as if captives in prison.

The most Christian King Philip heard of these things, and compassion was stirred within him. He took counsel with a certain hermit, Bernard by name, a holy and religious man, who at that time dwelt in the forest of Vincennes, and asked him what he should do. By his advice the King released all Christians of his kingdom from their debts to the Jews, and kept a fifth part of the whole amount for himself.

Finally came the culmination of their wickedness. Certain ecclesiastical vessels consecrated to God—the chalices and crosses of gold and silver bearing the image of our Lord Jesus Christ crucified—had been pledged to the Jews by way of security when the need of the churches was pressing. These they used so vilely, in their impiety and scorn of the Christian religion, that from the cups in which the body and blood of our Lord Jesus Christ was consecrated they gave their children cakes soaked in wine. . . .

In the year of our Lord's Incarnation 1182, in the month of April, which is called by the Jews Nisan, an edict went forth from the most serene king, Philip Augustus, that all the Jews of his kingdom should be prepared to go forth by the coming feast of St. John the Baptist. And then the King gave them leave to sell each his movable goods before the time fixed, that is, the feast of St. John the Baptist. But their real estate, that is, houses, fields, vineyards, barns, winepresses, and such like, he reserved for himself and his successors, the kings of the French.

When the faithless Jews heard this edict some of them were born again of water and the Holy Spirit and converted to the Lord, remaining steadfast in the faith of our Lord Jesus Christ. To them the King, out of regard for the Christian religion, restored all their possessions in their entirety, and gave them perpetual liberty.

Others were blinded by their ancient error and persisted in their perfidy; and they sought to win with gifts and golden promises the great of the land—counts, barons, archbishops, bishops—that through their influence and advice, and through the promise of infinite wealth, they might turn the King's mind from his firm intention.

But the merciful and compassionate God, who does not forsake those who put their hope in Him and who doth humble those who glory in their strength . . . so fortified the illustrious King that he could not be moved by prayers nor promises of temporal things. . . .

The infidel Jews, perceiving that the great of the land, through whom they had been accustomed easily to bend the King's predecessors to their will, had suffered repulse, and astonished and stupefied by the strength of mind of Philip the King and his constancy in the Lord, exclaimed with a certain admiration "Shema Israel!" and prepared to sell all their household goods. The time was now at hand when the King had ordered them to leave France altogether, and it could not be in any way prolonged. Then did the Jews sell all their movable possessions in great haste, while their landed property reverted to the crown. Thus the Jews, having sold their goods and taken the price for the expenses of their journey, departed with their wives and children and all their households in the aforesaid year of the Lord 1182.

FREDERICK II:

*". . . if a Christian raises his hand in
violence against a Jewess, we order that the
hand of that person be cut off." (1244)*

Frederick II (1211–1246), better known as Frederick the Belligerent, was ruler of Austria in the early thirteenth century. Truculent and quarrelsome by nature, Frederick was unpopular with his subjects and with the rulers of neighboring kingdoms; his relatively short reign was characterized by a succession of military campaigns and domestic troubles. At the age of thirty-five, he died in battle, leading his troops against Bela IV of Hungary.

Unlike most of his contemporaries, Frederick viewed the Jews of Austria with some favor. Two Jews were placed in charge of the state's finances, and various statutes gave the Jews legal status and a consider-

Reprinted from Jacob R. Marcus, editor, *The Jew in the Medieval World* (Cincinnati, Ohio: The Union of American Hebrew Congregations, 1938), pp. 28–32; Copyright 1938 by Union of American Hebrew Congregations; reprinted 1960 by the Jewish Publication Society of America, Philadelphia, Pa.

able measure of equality with other citizens. Indeed the position of Austrian Jews under Frederick was superior to that enjoyed by Jews in most of the other countries of Europe.

The selection here reprinted, "The Charter of the Jews of the Duchy of Austria," dates to July 1, 1244.

Frederick, by the grace of God Duke of Austria and Styria and lord of Carniola, offers greetings at all times to all who will read this letter in the future. Inasmuch as we desire that men of all classes dwelling in our land should share our favor and good will, we do therefore decree that these laws, devised for all Jews found in the land of Austria, shall be observed by them without violation.

I. We decree, therefore, first, that in cases involving money, or immovable property, or a criminal complaint touching the person or property of a Jew, no Christian shall be admitted as a witness against a Jew unless there is a Jewish witness together with the Christian.

II. Likewise, if a Christian should bring suit against a Jew, asserting that he had pawned his pledges with him and the Jew should deny this, and then if the Christian should not wish to accord any belief in the mere statement of the Jew, the Jew may prove his contention by taking an oath upon an object equivalent in value to that which was brought to him, and shall then go forth free.

III. Likewise, if a Jew says that he returned the Christian's pledge as a loan to the Christian, without, however, the presence of witnesses, and if the Christian deny this, then the Christian is able to clear himself in this matter through the oath of himself alone.

IV. Likewise, if a Christian has deposited a pledge with a Jew, stating that he had left it with the Jew for a smaller sum than the Jew admits, the Jew shall then take an oath upon the pledge pawned with him, and the Christian must not refuse to pay the amount that the Jew has proved through his oath.

V. Likewise, a Jew is allowed to receive all things as pledges which may be pawned with him—no matter what they are called—without making any investigation about them, except bloody and wet clothes which he shall under no circumstances accept.

VI. Likewise, if a Christian charges that the pledge which a Jew has, was taken from him by theft or robbery, the Jew must swear on that pledge that when he received it he did not know that it had been removed by theft or robbery. In this oath the amount for which the pledge was pawned to him shall also be included. Then, inasmuch as the Jew has brought his proof, the Christian shall pay him the capital and the interest that has accrued in the meantime.

VII. Likewise, if a Jew, through the accident of fire or through theft or violence, should lose his goods, together with the pledges pawned with him, and this is established, yet the Christian who has pledged something with him nevertheless brings suit against him, the Jew may free himself merely by his own oath.

VIII. Likewise, if the Jews engage in quarreling or actually fight among themselves, the judge of our city shall claim no jurisdiction over them; only the Duke alone or the chief official of his land shall exercise jurisdiction. If, however, the accusation touches the person, this case shall be reserved for the Duke alone for judgment.

IX. Likewise, if a Christian should inflict any sort of a wound upon a Jew, the accused shall pay to the Duke twelve marks of gold which are to be turned in to the treasury. He must also pay, to the person who has been injured, twelve marks of silver and the expenses incurred for the medicine needed in his cure.

X. Likewise, if a Christian should kill a Jew he shall be punished with the proper sentence, death, and all his movable and immovable property shall pass into the power of the Duke.

XI. Likewise, if a Christian strikes a Jew, without, however, having spilt his blood, he shall pay to the Duke four marks of gold, and to the man he struck four marks of silver. If he has no money, he shall offer satisfaction for the crime committed by the loss of his hand.

XII. Likewise, wherever a Jew shall pass through our territory no one shall offer any hindrance to him or molest or trouble him. If, however, he should be carrying any goods or other things for which he must pay duty at all custom offices, he shall pay only the prescribed duty which a citizen of that town, in which the Jew is then dwelling, pays.

XIII. Likewise, if the Jews, as is their custom, should transport any of their dead either from city to city, or from province to province, or from one Austrian land into another, we do not wish anything to be demanded of them by our customs officers. If, however, a customs officer should extort anything, then he is to be punished for *praedatio mortui,* which means, in common language, robbery of the dead.

XIV. Likewise, if a Christian, moved by insolence, shall break into or devastate the cemetery of the Jews, he shall die, as the court determines, and all his property, whatever it may be, shall be forfeited to the treasury of the Duke.

XV. Likewise, if any one wickedly throw something at the synagogues of the Jews we order that he pay two talents to the judge of the Jews.

XVI. Likewise, if a Jew be condemned by his judge to a money penalty, which is called *wandel* ("fine"), he shall pay only twelve dinars to him.

XVII. Likewise, if a Jew is summoned to court by order of his judge, but does not come the first or second time, he must pay the judge four dinars for each time. If he does not come at the third summons he shall pay thirty-six dinars to the judge mentioned.

XVIII. Likewise, if a Jew has wounded another Jew he may not refuse to pay a penalty of two talents, which is called *wandel,* to his judge.

XIX. Likewise, we decree that no Jew shall take an oath on the Torah unless he has been summoned to our [the Duke's] presence.

XX. Likewise, if a Jew was secretly murdered, and if through the testimony it cannot be determined by his friends who murdered him, yet if after an investigation has been made the Jews begin to suspect some one, we are willing to supply the Jews with a champion against this suspect.

XXI. Likewise, if a Christian raises his hand in violence against a Jewess, we order that the hand of that person be cut off.

XXII. Likewise, the judge of the Jews shall bring no case that has arisen among the Jews before his court, unless he be invited due to a complaint.

XXIII. Likewise, if a Christian has redeemed his pledge from a Jew but has not paid the interest, the interest due shall become compounded if it is not paid within a month.

XXIV. Likewise, we do not wish any one to seek quarters in a Jewish house.

XXV. Likewise, if a Jew has lent money to a magnate of the country on his possessions or on a note and proves this documentarily, we will assign the pledged possessions to the Jew and defend them for him against violence.

XXVI. Likewise, if any man or woman should kidnap a Jewish child we wish that he be punished as a thief.

XXVII. Likewise, if a Jew has held in his possession, for a year, a pledge received from a Christian, and if the value of the pledge does not exceed the money lent together with the interest, the Jew may show the pledge to his judge and shall then have the right to sell it. If any pledge shall remain for a "year and a day" with a Jew, he shall not have to account for it afterwards to any one.

XXVIII. Likewise, whatever Christian shall take his pledge away from a Jew by force or shall exercise violence in the Jew's home shall be severely punished as a plunderer of our treasury.

XXIX. Likewise, one shall in no place proceed in judgment against a Jew except in front of his synagogues, saving ourselves who have the power to summon them to our presence.

XXX. Likewise, we decree that Jews shall indeed receive only eight dinars a week interest on the talent. . . .

> Given at Starkenberg, in the year of the incarnation of the Lord, 1244, on the first of July.

ALPHONSO X:

"Jews should pass their lives among
Christians quietly and without disorder,
practicing their own religious rites, and not
speaking ill of the faith of Our Lord Jesus
Christ, which Christians acknowledge."
(1265)

Alphonso X (1221–1284), also known as "El Sabio" or "The Learned," was one of the more intelligent, if less capable, Spanish kings of the Middle Ages. Interested in astronomy and jurisprudence, he endeavored

Reprinted from Jacob R. Marcus, editor, *The Jew in the Medieval World* (Cincinnati, Ohio: The Union of American Hebrew Congregations, 1938), pp. 34–40; Copyright 1938 by Union of American Hebrew Congregations; reprinted 1960 by the Jewish Publication Society of America, Philadelphia, Pa.

to advance the arts and sciences in Spain, and he also attempted to provide his kingdom with a systematic and reliable code of laws. But he had little ability in financial matters, and a long period of economic distress during his rule gradually undermined his position. When he tried to unite the nation against the Moors, one of his own sons and a large section of the nobility turned against him. Although his situation had begun to improve by 1280, he had been defeated and deserted by many of his former allies and associates when he died at Seville in 1284.

Making allowance for his time and place, Alphonso was humane and even benevolent in his relations with the Jews. The Spanish Jews were allowed to practice their religion, and a number of Jews held high office during Alphonso's reign. Jewish scientists were regarded with particular favor, and Alphonso employed several of them as translators of texts in astronomy and astrology from Arabic to Spanish.

Nevertheless, as the following selection demonstrates, Jews were strictly regulated in their religious practices and in their relations with Christians. *Las siete partidas*, or *The Seven-Part Code*, drawn up in 1265 under Alphonso's supervision, incorporated laws, many of them hostile to Jews, which had originated in the Roman and Early Christian eras. For centuries after Alphonso, *The Seven-Part Code*, a portion of which is here reprinted, governed the Jews not only in Spain but in all Spanish possessions, including Puerto Rico, Florida, and Louisiana.

TITLE XXIV

CONCERNING THE JEWS

Jews are a people, who, although they do not believe in the religion of Our Lord Jesus Christ, yet, the great Christian sovereigns have always permitted them to live among them. . . .

LAW I. WHAT THE WORD JEW MEANS, AND WHENCE THIS TERM IS DERIVED

A party who believes in, and adheres to the law of Moses is called a Jew, according to the strict signification of the term, as one who is circumcised, and observes the other precepts commanded by his religion. This name is derived from the tribe of Judah which was nobler and more powerful than the others, and, also possessed another advantage, because the king of the Jews had to be selected from that tribe, and its members always received the first wounds in battle. The reason that the church, emperors, kings and princes, permitted the Jews to dwell among them and with Christians, is because they always lived, as it were, in captivity, as it was constantly in the minds of men that they were descended from those who crucified Our Lord Jesus Christ.

LAW II. IN WHAT WAY JEWS SHOULD PASS THEIR LIVES AMONG CHRISTIANS; WHAT THINGS THEY SHOULD NOT MAKE USE OF OR PRACTICE, ACCORDING TO OUR RELIGION; AND WHAT PENALTY THOSE DESERVE WHO ACT CONTRARY TO ITS ORDINANCES

Jews should pass their lives among Christians quietly and without disorder, practicing their own religious rites, and not speaking ill of the faith of Our Lord Jesus Christ, which Christians acknowledge. Moreover, a Jew should be very careful to avoid preaching to, or converting any Christian, to the end that he may become a Jew, by exalting his own belief and disparaging ours. Whoever violates this law shall be put to death and lose all his property. And because we have heard it said that in some places Jews celebrated, and still celebrate Good Friday, which commemorates the Passion of Our Lord Jesus Christ, by way of contempt: stealing children and fastening them to crosses, and making images of wax and crucifying them, when they cannot obtain children; we order that, hereafter, if in any part of our dominions anything like this is done, and can be proved, all persons who were present when the act was committed shall be seized, arrested and brought before the king; and after the king ascertains that they are guilty, he shall cause them to be put to death in a disgraceful manner, no matter how many there may be.

We also forbid any Jew to dare to leave his house or his quarter on Good Friday, but they must all remain shut up until Saturday morning; and if they violate this regulation, we decree that they shall not be entitled to reparation for any injury or dishonor inflicted upon them by Christians.

LAW III. NO JEW CAN HOLD ANY OFFICE OR EMPLOYMENT BY WHICH HE MAY BE ABLE TO OPPRESS CHRISTIANS

Jews were formerly highly honored, and enjoyed privileges above all other races, for they alone were called the People of God. But for the reason that they disowned Him who had honored them and given them privileges; and instead of showing Him reverence humiliated Him, by shamefully putting Him to death on the cross; it was proper and just that, on account of the great crime and wickedness which they committed, they should forfeit the honors and privileges which they enjoyed; and therefore from the day when they crucified Our Lord Jesus Christ they never had either king or priests among themselves, as they formerly did. The emperors who in former times were lords of all the world, considered it fitting and right that, on account of the treason which they committed in killing their lord, they should lose all said honors and privileges, so that no Jew could ever afterwards hold an honorable position, or a public office by means of which he might, in any way, oppress a Christian.

LAW IV. HOW JEWS CAN HAVE A SYNAGOGUE AMONG CHRISTIANS

A synagogue is a place where the Jews pray, and a new building of this kind cannot be erected in any part of our dominions, except by our order. Where, however, those which formerly existed there are torn down, they can be built in the same spot where they originally stood; but they cannot be made any larger or raised to any greater height, or be painted. A synagogue constructed in any other manner shall be lost by the Jews, and shall belong to the principal church of the locality where it is built. And for the reason that a synagogue is a place where the name of God is praised, we forbid any Christian to deface it, or remove anything from it, or take anything out of it by force; except where some malefactor takes refuge there; for they have a right to remove him by force in order to bring him before the judge. Moreover, we forbid Christians to put any animal into a synagogue, or loiter in it, or place any hindrance in the way of the Jews while they are there performing their devotions according to their religion.

LAW V. NO COMPULSION SHALL BE BROUGHT TO BEAR UPON THE JEWS ON SATURDAY, AND WHAT JEWS CAN BE SUBJECT TO COMPULSION

Saturday is the day on which Jews perform their devotions, and remain quiet in their lodgings, and do not make contracts or transact any business; and for the reason that they are obliged by their religion to keep it, no one should on that day summon them or bring them into court. Wherefore we order that no judge shall employ force or any constraint upon Jews on Saturday, in order to bring them into court on account of their debts; or arrest them; or cause them any other annoyance; for the remaining days of the week are sufficient for the purpose of employing compulsion against them, and for making demands for things which can be demanded of them according to law. Jews are not bound to obey a summons served upon them on that day; and, moreover, we decree that any decision rendered against them on Saturday shall not be valid; but if a Jew should wound, kill, rob, steal, or commit any other offense like these for which he can be punished in person and property, then the judge can arrest him on Saturday.

We also decree that all claims that Christians have against Jews, and Jews against Christians, shall be decided and determined by our judges in the district where they reside, and not by their old men. And as we forbid Christians to bring Jews into court or annoy them on Saturday; so we also decree that Jews, neither in person, nor by their attorneys, shall have the right to bring Christians into court, or annoy them on this day. And in addition to this, we forbid any Christian, on his own responsibility, to arrest or wrong any Jew either in his person or property, but where he has any complaint against him he must bring it before our judges; and if anyone should be so bold as to use violence against the Jews, or rob them of anything, he shall return them double the value of the same.

LAW VI. JEWS WHO BECOME CHRISTIANS SHALL NOT BE SUBJECT TO
    COMPULSION: WHAT ADVANTAGE A JEW HAS WHO BECOMES A
    CHRISTIAN; AND WHAT PENALTY OTHER JEWS DESERVE WHO
    DO HIM HARM

No force or compulsion shall be employed in any way against a Jew to induce him to become a Christian; but Christians should convert him to the faith of Our Lord Jesus Christ by means of the texts of the Holy Scriptures, and by kind words, for no one can love or appreciate a service which is done him by compulsion. We also decree that if any Jew or Jewess should voluntarily desire to become a Christian, the other Jews shall not interfere with this in any way, and if they stone, wound, or kill any such person, because he wishes to become a Christian, or after he has been baptized, and this can be proved, we order that all the murderers, or the abettors of said murder or attack, shall be burned. But where the party was not killed, but wounded, or dishonored, we order the judges of the neighborhood where this took place shall compel those guilty of the attack, or who caused the dishonor, to make amends to him for the same; and also that they be punished for the offence which they committed, as they think they deserve; and we also order that, after any Jews become Christians, all persons in our dominions shall honor them; and that no one shall dare to reproach them or their descendants, by way of insult, with having been Jews; and that they shall possess all their property, sharing the same with their brothers, and inheriting it from their fathers and mothers and other relatives, just as if they were Jews; and that they can hold all offices and dignities which other Christians can do.

LAW VII. WHAT PENALTY A CHRISTIAN DESERVES WHO BECOMES A JEW

Where a Christian is so unfortunate as to become a Jew, we order that he shall be put to death just as if he had become a heretic; and we decree that his property shall be disposed of in the same way that we stated should be done with that of heretics.

LAW VIII. NO CHRISTIAN, MAN OR WOMAN, SHALL LIVE WITH A JEW

We forbid any Jew to keep Christian men or women in his house, to be served by them; although he may have them to cultivate and take care of his lands, or protect him on the way when he is compelled to go to some dangerous place. Moreover, we forbid any Christian man or woman to invite a Jew or a Jewess, or to accept an invitation from them, to eat or drink together, or to drink any wine made by their hands. We also order that no Jews shall dare to bathe in company with Christians, and that no Christian shall take any medicine or cathartic made by a Jew; but he can take it by the advice of some intelligent person, only where it is made by a Christian, who knows and is familiar with its ingredients.

LAW IX. WHAT PENALTY A JEW DESERVES WHO HAS INTERCOURSE WITH A CHRISTIAN WOMAN

Jews who live with Christian women are guilty of great insolence and boldness, for which reason we decree that all Jews who, hereafter, may be convicted of having done such a thing shall be put to death. For if Christians who commit adultery with married women deserve death on that account, much more do Jews who have sexual intercourse with Christian women, who are spiritually the wives of Our Lord Jesus Christ because of the faith and the baptism which they receive in His name; nor do we consider it proper that a Christian woman who commits an offense of this kind shall escape without punishment. Wherefore we order that, whether she be a virgin, a married woman, a widow, or a common prostitute who gives herself to all men, she shall suffer the same penalty which we mentioned in the last law in the Title concerning the Moors, to which a Christian woman is liable who has carnal intercourse with a Moor.

LAW X. WHAT PENALTY JEWS DESERVE WHO HOLD CHRISTIANS AS SLAVES

A Jew shall not purchase, or keep as a slave a Christian man or woman, and if anyone violates this law the Christian shall be restored to freedom and shall not pay any portion of the price given for him although the Jew may not have been aware when he bought him, that he was a Christian; but if he knew that he was such when he purchased him, and makes use of him afterwards as a slave, he shall be put to death for doing so. Moreover, we forbid any Jew to convert a captive to his religion, even though said captive may be a Moor, or belong to some other barbarous race. If anyone violates this law we order that the said slave who has become a Jew shall be set at liberty, and removed from the control of the party to whom he or she belonged. If any Moors who are the captives of Jews become Christians, they shall at once be freed, as is explained in the Fourth Partida of this book, in the Title concerning Liberty, in the laws which treat of this subject.

LAW XI. JEWS SHALL BEAR CERTAIN MARKS IN ORDER THAT THEY MAY BE KNOWN

Many crimes and outrageous things occur between Christians and Jews because they live together in cities, and dress alike; and in order to avoid the offenses and evils which take place for this reason, we deem it proper, and we order that all Jews, male and female, living in our dominions shall bear some distinguishing mark upon their heads so that people may plainly recognize a Jew, or a Jewess; and any Jew who does not bear such a mark, shall pay for each time he is found without it ten maravedis of gold; and if he has not the means to do this he shall receive ten lashes for his offense.

LOUIS IX:

*" And I tell you that no one, unless he be
a very learned clerk, should dispute
with them [the Jews] . . . unless it be
with his sword. . . ." (Before 1270)*

Louis IX (1214–1270), or Saint Louis, was one of the most accomplished rulers of France during the Middle Ages. Coming to the throne in 1236 following the death of his father, Louis took a personal interest in the administration of justice, education (he founded the Sorbonne), and in recruiting men of learning for the governmental service. A skilled military commander, he defeated the English in 1243, but was less successful in leading crusades against the infidels in the Holy Land. The first of these efforts ended with the capture of Louis and his army by the Saracens, necessitating the payment of a large ransom in land and money. In 1270, he undertook an expedition against Tunis, and died during the course of the crusade. Devout, loyal to the Church, and ascetic in private life, Louis was canonized by Pope Boniface VIII in 1297.

As the following selection testifies, Saint Louis was hostile to the Jews. Like his father before him, Louis VIII, Saint Louis remitted the interest on Christian debts to Jews, and even permitted his subjects to cancel one-third of the principal of such debts. Jewish converts to Christianity were in great favor with the king, and he occasionally managed to be present at their baptisms.

The anecdote here reprinted was first published in a book about Saint Louis written by Jean, Sire de Joinville (1224–1318). Jean was an intimate friend of the king.

Reprinted from Jacob R. Marcus, editor, *The Jew in the Medieval World* (Cincinnati, Ohio: The Union of American Hebrew Congregations, 1938), pp. 41–42; Copyright 1938 by Union of American Hebrew Congregations; reprinted 1960 by the Jewish Publication Society of America, Philadelphia, Pa.

He [Saint Louis] told me that there was once a great disputation between clergy and Jews at the monastery of Cluny. And there was at Cluny a poor knight to whom the abbot gave bread at that place for the love of God; and this knight asked the abbot to suffer him to speak the first words, and they suffered him, not without doubt. So he rose, and leant upon his crutch, and asked that they should bring to him the greatest clerk and most learned master among the Jews; and they did so. Then he asked the Jew a question, which was this: "Master," said the knight, "I ask you if you believe that the Virgin Mary, who bore God in her body and in her arms, was a virgin mother, and is the mother of God?"

And the Jew replied that of all this he believed nothing. Then the knight answered that the Jew had acted like a fool when—neither believing in her, nor loving her—he had yet entered into her monastery and house. "And verily," said the knight, "you shall pay for it!" Whereupon he lifted his crutch and smote the Jew near the ear, and beat him to the earth. Then the Jews turned to flight, and bore away their master, sore wounded. And so ended the disputation.

The abbot came to the knight and told him he had committed a deed of very great folly. But the knight replied that the abbot committed a deed of greater folly in gathering people together for such a disputation; for there were a great many good Christians there who, before the disputation came to an end, would have gone away misbelievers through not fully understanding the Jews. "And I tell you," said the king, "that no one, unless he be a very learned clerk, should dispute with them; but a layman, when he hears the Christian law mis-said, should not defend the Christian law, unless it be with his sword, and with that he should pierce the missayer in the midriff, so far as the sword will enter."

POPE GREGORY X:

". . . most falsely do these Christians claim
that the Jews have secretly and
furtively carried away these children and
killed them." (1272)

Gregory X (1210?–1276), was the Papal successor to Clement IV. Although he had served as archdeacon of Liège, Gregory was neither a cardinal nor a priest when he was elected Pope in 1271. He received word of his elevation to the highest Church office while embarked on a crusade. The selection of Gregory required some thirty-four months of debate in the College of Cardinals, divided between the French and Italian factions.

Gregory's *Bull* of 1272, here reprinted, was one of a series of Papal declarations designed to restrain anti-Semitic extremists whose accusations against the Jews included charging them with ritual murder. As early as 1120 and as late as 1762, a number of Papal decrees defended the Jews against allegations that they engaged in the murder of Christian children and used their blood in preparing the unleavened bread for Passover holidays. But while a number of the Popes attempted to refute the charge of ritual murder (which was the cause of frequent murders of the Jews in the Middle Ages), few of them were tolerant of the Jewish religion as such. Gregory, for example, advised the Inquisition to make certain that converted Jews did not revert to Judaism, and to take stern measures against Jews who were urging their reconversion.

A Bull of Pope Gregory X, October 7, 1272

Gregory, bishop, servant of the servants of God, extends greetings, and the apostolic benediction to the beloved sons in Christ, the faithful Christians, to those here now and to those in the future. Even as it is not allowed to the Jews in their assemblies presumptuously to undertake for themselves more than that which is permitted them by law, even so they ought not to suffer any disadvan-

Reprinted from Jacob R. Marcus, editor, *The Jew in the Medieval World* (Cincinnati, Ohio: The Union of American Hebrew Congregations, 1938), pp. 152–154; Copyright 1938 by Union of American Hebrew Congregations; reprinted 1960 by the Jewish Publication Society of America, Philadelphia, Pa.

tage in those which have been granted them. Although they prefer to persist in their stubbornness rather than to recognize the words of their prophets and the mysteries of the Scriptures, and thus to arrive at a knowledge of Christian faith and salvation; nevertheless, inasmuch as they have made an appeal for our protection and help, we therefore admit their petition and offer them the shield of our protection through the clemency of Christian piety. In so doing we follow in the footsteps of our predecessors of blessed memory, the popes of Rome—Calixtus, Eugene, Alexander, Clement, Celestine, Innocent, and Honorius.

We decree moreover that no Christian shall compel them or any one of their group to come to baptism unwillingly. But if any one of them shall take refuge of his own accord with Christians, because of conviction, then, after his intention will have been manifest, he shall be made a Christian without any intrigue. For, indeed, that person who is known to have come to Christian baptism not freely, but unwillingly, is not believed to possess the Christian faith.

Moreover no Christian shall presume to seize, imprison, wound, torture, mutilate, kill, or inflict violence on them; furthermore no one shall presume, except by judicial action of the authorities of the country, to change the good customs in the land where they live for the purpose of taking their money or goods from them or from others.

In addition, no one shall disturb them in any way during the celebration of their festivals, whether by day or by night, with clubs or stones or anything else. Also no one shall exact any compulsory service of them unless it be that which they have been accustomed to render in previous times.

Inasmuch as the Jews are not able to bear witness against the Christians, we decree furthermore that the testimony of Christians against Jews shall not be valid unless there is among these Christians some Jew who is there for the purpose of offering testimony.

Since it happens occasionally that some Christians lose their Christian children, the Jews are accused by their enemies of secretly carrying off and killing these same Christian children and of making sacrifices of the heart and blood of these very children. It happens, too, that the parents of these children or some other Christian enemies of these Jews, secretly hide these very children in order that they may be able to injure these Jews, and in order that they may be able to extort from them a certain amount of money by redeeming them from their straits.

And most falsely do these Christians claim that the Jews have secretly and furtively carried away these children and killed them, and that the Jews offer sacrifice from the heart and the blood of these children, since their law in this matter precisely and expressly forbids Jews to sacrifice, eat, or drink the blood, or to eat the flesh of animals having claws. This has been demonstrated many times at our court by Jews converted to the Christian faith: nevertheless very many Jews are often seized and detained unjustly because of this.

We decree, therefore, that Christians need not be obeyed against Jews in a case or situation of this type, and we order that Jews seized under such a silly pretext be freed from imprisonment, and that they shall not be arrested henceforth on such a miserable pretext, unless—which we do not believe—they be caught in the commission of the crime. We decree that no Christian shall stir up anything new against them, but that they should be maintained in that status and position in which they were in the time of our predecessors, from antiquity till now.

We decree, in order to stop the wickedness and avarice of bad men, that no one shall dare to devastate or to destroy a cemetery of the Jews or to dig up human bodies for the sake of getting money. Moreover, if any one, after having known the content of this decree, should—which we hope will not happen—attempt audaciously to act contrary to it, then let him be punished by the penalty of excommunication, unless he makes amends for his boldness by proper recompense. Moreover, we wish that only those Jews who have not attempted to contrive anything toward the destruction of the Christian faith be fortified by the support of such protection. . . .

Given at Orvieto by the hand of the Magister John Lectator, vice-chancellor of the Holy Roman Church, on the 7th of October, in the first indiction, in the year 1272 of the divine incarnation, in the first year of the pontificate of our master, the Pope Gregory X.

JACOB VON KÖNIGSHOFEN:

"Agimet [the Jew] took this package full of poison and carried it with him to Venice . . . in order to poison the people who use the water of that cistern."
(1348)

During the Middle Ages, plagues, epidemics, and other calamities were often blamed on the Jews. The assumption underlying such accusations was that the Jews were engaged in a conspiracy to destroy Christianity. Those unhappy Jews who were tortured into making confessions were put to death, and frequently entire Jewish communities fell victim to mob violence.

The first of the following selections was occasioned by a plague which killed millions of people in Europe in 1348–1349. The appearance of the plague in what is now Switzerland led to the arrest of a number of Jews living in or near Geneva, by order of Amadeus VI, Count of Savoy. The "confession" under torture of one of the unfortunate Jews arrested, Agimet of Geneva, is here reprinted.

The second selection concerns the treatment accorded the Jews of Strasbourg on St. Valentine's Day in February, 1349. The Black Death, which was spreading throughout Europe, was attributed to the Jews, and while it had not yet reached Strasbourg, a mob formed and succeeded in destroying the Jewish community in that city. Despite this "precaution," the plague ultimately was responsible for the deaths of an estimated sixteen thousand Strasbourgians.

The third selection testifies to the fact that even those Jews forced to embrace Christianity, at least superficially, did not escape blame for the outbreak of plagues and epidemics. The massacre of the "New Christians" of Lisbon, here described, took the lives of some two thousand persons in 1506, but it had the good effect of persuading King Emmanuel of Portugal that the remaining "New Christians" should be permitted to leave the country, if they so desired.

Jacob von Königshofen (1346–1420), the original source of Agimet's "confession," and author of the report concerning the destruction of the Strasbourg Jewish community, was a German historian of Strasbourg. The account of the Lisbon Massacre is based on the work of Geronymo Osorio (1506–1580), a Catholic Bishop of Portugal.

Reprinted from Jacob R. Marcus, editor, *The Jew in the Medieval World* (Cincinnati, Ohio: The Union of American Hebrew Congregations, 1938), pp. 44–47; Copyright 1938 by Union of American Hebrew Congregations; reprinted 1960 by the Jewish Publication Society of America, Philadelphia, Pa.

The Confession of Agimet of Geneva, Châtel, October 10, 1348

On Friday, the 10th of the month of October, at Châtel, in the castle thereof, there occurred the judicial inquiry which was made by order of the court of the illustrious Prince, our lord, Amadeus, Count of Savoy, and his subjects against the Jews of both sexes who were there imprisoned, each one separately. This was done after public rumor had become current and a strong clamor had arisen—because of the poison put by them into the wells, springs, and other things which the Christians use—demanding that they die, that they are able to be found guilty and, therefore, that they should be punished. Hence this their confession made in the presence of a great many trustworthy persons.

Agimet the Jew, who lived at Geneva and was arrested at Châtel, was there put to the torture a little and then he was released from it. And after a long time, having been subjected again to torture a little, he confessed in the presence of a great many trustworthy persons, who are later mentioned. To begin with it is clear that at the Lent just passed Pultus Clesis de Ranz had sent this very Jew to Venice to buy silks and other things for him. When this came to the notice of Rabbi Peyret, a Jew of Chambéry who was a teacher of their law, he sent for this Agimet, for whom he had searched, and when he had come before him he said: "We have been informed that you are going to Venice to buy silk and other wares. Here I am giving you a little package of half a span in size which contains some prepared poison and venom in a thin, sewed leather-bag. Distribute it among the wells, cisterns, and springs about Venice and the other places to which you go, in order to poison the people who use the water of the aforesaid wells that will have been poisoned by you, namely, the wells in which the poison will have been placed."

Agimet took this package full of poison and carried it with him to Venice, and when he came there he threw and scattered a portion of it into the well or cistern of fresh water which was there near the German House, in order to poison the people who use the water of that cistern. And he says that this is the only cistern of sweet water in the city. He also says that the mentioned Rabbi Peyret promised to give him whatever he wanted for his troubles in this business. Of his own accord Agimet confessed further that after this had been done he left at once in order that he should not be captured by the citizens or others, and that he went personally to Calabria and Apulia and threw the above mentioned poison into many wells. He confesses also that he put some of this same poison in the well of the streets of the city of Ballet.

He confesses further that he put some of this poison into the public fountain of the city of Toulouse and in the wells that are near the sea. Asked if at the time that he scattered the venom and poisoned the wells, above mentioned, any people had died, he said that he did not know inasmuch as he had left everyone of the above mentioned places in a hurry. Asked if any of the Jews of those places were guilty in the above mentioned matter, he answered that he did not know. And now by all that which is contained in the five books of Moses and the scroll of the Jews, he declared that this was true, and that he was in no wise lying, no matter what might happen to him.

The Cremation of Strasbourg Jewry on St. Valentine's Day, Feb. 14, 1349

In the year 1349 there occurred the greatest epidemic that ever happened. Death went from one end of the earth to the other, on that side and this side of the sea, and it was greater among the Saracens than among the Christians. In some lands everyone died so that no one was left. Ships were also found on the sea laden with wares; the crew had all died and no one guided the ship. The Bishop of Marseilles and priests and monks and more than half of all the people there died with them. In other kingdoms and cities so many people perished that it would be horrible to describe. The Pope at Avignon stopped all sessions of court, locked himself in a room, allowed no one to approach him and had a fire burning before him all the time. And from what this epidemic came, all wise teachers and physicians could only say that it was God's will. And as the plague was now here, so was it in other places, and lasted more than a whole year. This epidemic also came to Strasbourg in the summer of the above mentioned year, and it is estimated that about sixteen thousand people died.

In the matter of this plague the Jews throughout the world were reviled and accused in all lands of having caused it through the poison which they are said to have put into the water and the wells—that is what they were accused of—and for this reason the Jews were burnt all the way from the Mediterranean into Germany, but not in Avignon, for the pope protected them there.

Nevertheless they tortured a number of Jews in Berne and Zofingen who then admitted that they had put poison into many wells, and they also found the poison in the wells. Thereupon they burnt the Jews in many towns and wrote of this affair to Strasbourg, Freiburg, and Basel in order that they too should burn their Jews. But the leaders in these three cities in whose hands the government lay did not believe that anything ought to be done to the Jews. However in Basel the citizens marched to the city-hall and compelled the council to take an oath that they would burn the Jews, and that they would allow no Jew to enter the city for the next two hundred years. Thereupon the Jews were arrested in all these places and a conference was arranged to meet at Benfeld. The Bishop of Strasbourg, all the feudal lords of Alsace, and representatives of the three above mentioned cities came there. The deputies of the city of Strasbourg were asked what they were going to do with their Jews. They answered and said that they knew no evil of them. Then they asked the Strasbourgers why they had closed the wells and put away the buckets, and there was a great indignation and clamor against the deputies from Strasbourg. So finally the Bishop and the lords and the Imperial Cities agreed to do away with the Jews. The result was that they were burnt in many cities, and wherever they were expelled they were caught by the peasants and stabbed to death or drowned. . . .

On Saturday—that was St. Valentine's Day—they burnt the Jews on a wooden platform in their cemetery. There were about two thousand people of them. Those who wanted to baptize themselves were spared. Many small children were taken out of the fire and baptized against the will of their fathers and mothers. And everything that was owed to the Jews was cancelled, and the Jews had to surrender all pledges and notes that they had taken for debts. The council, however, took the cash that the Jews possessed and divided it among the working-men proportionately. The money was indeed the thing that killed the Jews. If they had been poor and if the feudal lords had not been in debt to them, they would not have been burnt. After this wealth was divided among the artisans some gave their share to the Cathedral or to the Church on the advice of their confessors.

Thus were the Jews burnt at Strasbourg, and in the same year in all the cities of the Rhine, whether Free Cities or Imperial Cities or cities belonging to the lords. In some towns they burnt the Jews after a trial, in others, without a trial. In some cities the Jews themselves set fire to their houses and cremated themselves.

It was decided in Strasbourg that no Jew should enter the city for a hundred years, but before twenty years had passed, the council and magistrates agreed that they ought to admit the Jews again into the city for twenty years. And so the Jews came back again to Strasbourg in the year 1368 after the birth of our Lord.

The Massacre of the "New Christians" of Lisbon, April, 1506*

About the same time there happened a great tumult at Lisbon, raised by the fury and madness of the rabble; in this almost all the Jews, who, as we before observed, had been converted to Christianity, were cruelly massacred.

The affair was as follows: The greatest part of the citizens had left the town because of the plague, and many French, Belgian, and German ships had arrived there at this time. On the 19th of April many of those who remained in the city went to St. Dominic's church to attend divine service. On the left side of this church is Jesus Chapel, much frequented by people at their devotion. Above the altar is placed a representation of Jesus on the cross, and the hole, representing the wound in our Savior's side, had a glass cover. When many people had fixed their eyes and attention on that wound, a lucid brightness shone from it. On this appearance many said it was a miracle and that the divinity testified his presence by a wonderful sign.

Some one of the Jews, who not long before had taken upon him the profession of Christianity, with a loud voice denied it to be a miracle, adding that it was very unlikely that a piece of dry wood should show forth a miracle. Many indeed doubted of the truth

* Reprinted from Jacob R. Marcus, editor, *The Jew in the Medieval World* (Cincinnati, Ohio: The Union of American Hebrew Congregations, 1938), pp. 56–59; Copyright 1938 by Union of American Hebrew Congregations, reprinted 1960 by the Jewish Publication Society of America, Philadelphia, Pa.

thereof; yet considering the time, place, and congregation, it was highly imprudent for any one, especially a Jew, to endeavor to convince people of a mistake, when they were firmly persuaded the thing was true. The populace, naturally headstrong, inconsiderate, and apt to be struck with anything that appears marvelous, upon hearing that a Jew derogated from the credit of the miracle, began to make an uproar. They called him a perfidious, wicked betrayer of religion and an outrageous and malicious enemy of Christ, and declared him worthy of torture and death.

Nay, their fury arose at last to such a degree, that falling on this unhappy wretch, they dragged him by his hair into the market-place before the church, where they tore him to pieces, and making a fire, threw his body into it. All the common people flocked to this tumult, and a certain monk made a speech too well adapted to their humor at the time. In this he excited them with great vehemence to revenge the impiety of the Jew. The mob too apt of their own accord to be outrageous, by this means became the more transported with fury. Two other monks, at the same time holding forth a crucifix, loudly excited the people to slaughter, at every other word calling out: "Heresy, heresy! Avenge the heresy, and extinguish the wicked race!"

The French and Germans quickly came ashore, and having joined the Portuguese, they committed great havoc. This cruel massacre was begun by five hundred, who were at last joined by several others. Transported with madness and boiling with rage, they fell upon the wretched Jews, of whom they killed great numbers, and threw many half alive into the flames. By this time several fires were kindled near the place where the first offender had been burnt, for the canaille about the streets with eagerness and alacrity had brought fuel from all parts, that nothing might be wanting to execute this horrible design. The shrieks and outcries of the women, together with the piteous supplications of the men, might, one would think, have softened the most savage hearts into pity; but the actors in this horrid scene were so divested of humanity that they spared neither sex nor age, but wreaked their fury on all without distinction; so that above five hundred Jews were either killed or burnt that day.

The news of this massacre having reached the country, next day above a thousand men from the villages flocked into the city and joined the murderers, and the slaughter was renewed. The Jews, being under the greatest terror, concealed themselves in their houses; but the blood-thirsty rabble broke open the doors, rushed in upon them, and butchered men, women, and children in a most barbarous manner; they dashed the infants against the walls, and, dragging all out of doors by the feet, threw them into the fire, some quite dead, and others yet breathing life.

Such an insensibility overwhelmed this wretched people that they were scarce able to lament their ruin or deplore their misery; nay, those who lay concealed, though they beheld their parents or children dragged away to torture and death, durst not even utter a mournful groan, for fear of being discovered. In short they became so stupefied with terror that there was little difference betwixt the living and the dead. Their houses were plundered, and the bloody rioters carried off great quantities of gold and silver and several other things of value. The French put their booty aboard their ships, and had it not been for the desire of plunder, many more would have been murdered that day. Several of the Jews, both young and old, fled to the altars for refuge, and taking hold of crosses and the images of saints, in a most suppliant manner implored the divine protection; but the fury of this abandoned rabble proceeded to such a length that without any regard to religion, they broke into the churches, and dragging the Jews from thence, either cruelly butchered or threw them alive into the fire.

Several who had any resemblance of this people in their looks were in great danger and some were actually killed on that suspicion, and others received many wounds and blows on the same account. Some persons took this opportunity to vent their malice upon those against whom they had a pique by asserting they were Jews, and before the falsity could be confuted, satiated their revenge by their blood. The magistrates had not spirit to oppose the fury of the multitude; however, many worthy persons preserved, with the greatest fidelity, such of the Jews as fled to them for shelter and concealed them in places of safety. Yet above a thousand were massacred this day.

The third day those inhuman barbarians returned again to the slaughter; but they scarcely found any to murder, for most of the Jews who survived had either saved themselves by flight or lay safely concealed; yet some slaughter was committed. On these three days above two thousand of the Jewish race were murdered. In the evening Ayres de Sylva and Alvaro de Castro, men of the first distinction, who presided in the courts of judicature, came with guards into the city; their arrival put a stop to the fury of the mob. The French and Germans repaired to their ships with a considerable booty and set sail with all possible expedition.

Emmanuel, having got account of this massacre, immediately dispatched Diogo de Almeida and Diogo Lobo to Lisbon with full power to punish the perpetrators of this horrid villainy. Many now suffered for their madness and cruelty. The monks who had stirred up the people to slaughter, being first in a solemn manner degraded from the priestly office and dignity, were afterwards strangled and burnt. Those who appeared remiss in restraining the popular fury were partly stripped of their honors, and partly fined; and the city was deprived of several privileges.

MARTIN LUTHER:

*"What then shall we Christians do with this
damned, rejected race of Jews? Since
they live among us . . . we cannot
tolerate them if we do not wish to share
in their lies, curses, and blasphemy." (1543)*

Martin Luther (1483–1546) was the great German religious reformer whose teachings were instrumental in precipitating the Protestant Reformation. Although Luther's father intended him to follow a career in law, Luther became an Augustinian monk, and for some years was a distinguished preacher and professor of theology at Wittenberg. Shocked by a number of Church practices, including the remission of sins through the payment of money, Luther became increasingly critical of Roman Catholicism, and as a German he was inclined to regard Italian domination of the Church at Rome as incompatible with German needs and traditions. In 1517, when he was thirty-four years old, Luther nailed his

Reprinted from Jacob R. Marcus, editor, *The Jew in the Medieval World* (Cincinnati, Ohio: The Union of American Hebrew Congregations, 1938), pp. 166–169; Copyright 1938 by Union of American Hebrew Congregations; reprinted 1960 by the Jewish Publication Society of America, Philadelphia, Pa.

famous ninety-five theses against indulgences on the Castle Church door in Wittenberg. With that action, whatever his intentions at the time, he initiated a religious revolution that was to shake Europe for the next several centuries.

At the beginning of his career, Luther was tolerant of Jews, but after 1523 his attitude changed to one of marked and even ferocious hostility. An advocate of the conversion of the Jews to Christianity, Luther apparently hoped that his own teachings would effect the large-scale conversion of Jews to the Christian religion. The failure of these hopes, and his personal experience with certain Jews, were responsible, perhaps, for the militant anti-Semitism of his later writings. By 1543, as one of the following selections indicates, he was advocating that Jewish synagogues and homes be burned, and that, in effect, Jews be required to perform hard labor.

1523

I will therefore show by means of the Bible the causes which induce me to believe that Christ was a Jew born of a virgin. Perhaps I will attract some of the Jews to the Christian faith. For our fools— the popes, bishops, sophists, and monks—the coarse blockheads! have until this time so treated the Jews that to be a good Christian one would have to become a Jew. And if I had been a Jew and had seen such idiots and blockheads ruling and teaching the Christian religion, I would rather have been a sow than a Christian.

For they have dealt with the Jews as if they were dogs and not human beings. They have done nothing for them but curse them and seize their wealth. Whenever they converted them, they did not teach them either Christian law or life but only subjected them to papistry and monkery. When these Jews saw that Judaism had such strong scriptural basis and that Christianity was pure nonsense without Biblical support, how could they quiet their hearts and become real, good Christians? I have myself heard from pious converted Jews that if they had not heard the gospel in our time they would always have remained Jews at heart in spite of their conversion. For they admit that they have never heard anything about Christ from the rulers who have converted them.

I hope that, if the Jews are treated friendly and are instructed kindly through the Bible, many of them will become real Christians and come back to the ancestral faith of the prophets and patriarchs. . . .

I would advise and beg everybody to deal kindly with the Jews and to instruct them in the Scriptures; in such a case we could expect them to come over to us. If, however, we use brute force and slander them, saying that they need the blood of Christians to get rid of their stench and I know not what other nonsense of that kind, and treat them like dogs, what good can we expect of them? Finally, how can we expect them to improve if we forbid them to work among us and to have social intercourse with us, and so force them into usury?

If we wish to make them better, we must deal with them not according to the law of the pope, but according to the law of Christian charity. We must receive them kindly and allow them to compete with us in earning a livelihood, so that they may have a good reason to be with us and among us and an opportunity to witness Christian life and doctrine; and if some remain obstinate, what of it? Not every one of us is a good Christian.

I shall stop here now until I see what the results will be. May God be gracious to us all. Amen.

1543

What then shall we Christians do with this damned, rejected race of Jews? Since they live among us and we know about their lying and blasphemy and cursing, we can not tolerate them if we do not wish to share in their lies, curses, and blasphemy. In this way we cannot quench the inextinguishable fire of divine rage (as the prophets say) nor convert the Jews. We must prayerfully and reverentially practice a merciful severity. Perhaps we may save a few from the fire and the flames. We must not seek vengeance. They are surely being punished a thousand times more than we might wish them. Let me give you my honest advice.

First, their synagogues or churches should be set on fire, and whatever does not burn should be covered or spread over with dirt so that no one may ever be able to see a cinder or stone of it. And this ought to be done for the honor of God and of Christianity in order that God may see that we are Christians, and that we have not wittingly tolerated or approved of such public lying, cursing, and blaspheming of His Son and His Christians. . . .

Secondly, their homes should likewise be broken down and destroyed. For they perpetrate the same things there that they do in their synagogues. For this reason they ought to be put under one roof or in a stable, like gypsies, in order that they may realize that they are not masters in our land, as they boast, but miserable captives, as they complain of us incessantly before God with bitter wailing.

Thirdly, they should be deprived of their prayer-books and Talmuds in which such idolatry, lies, cursing, and blasphemy are taught.

Fourthly, their rabbis must be forbidden under threat of death to teach any more. . . .

Fifthly, passport and traveling privileges should be absolutely forbidden to the Jews. For they have no business in the rural districts since they are not nobles, nor officials, nor merchants, nor the like. Let them stay at home. I have heard that there is a rich Jew riding around the country with a team of twelve horses—he wants to be a Messiah—and he is exploiting princes, nobles, land, and people to such an extent that important people look askance at this. If you princes and nobles do not close the road legally to such exploiters, then some troop ought to ride against them, for they will learn from this pamphlet what the Jews are and how to handle them and that they ought not to be protected. You ought not, you cannot protect them, unless in the eyes of God you want to share all their abomination. . . .

Sixthly, they ought to be stopped from usury. All their cash and valuables of silver and gold ought to be taken from them and put aside for safe keeping. For this reason, as said before, everything that they possess they stole and robbed from us through their usury, for they have no other means of support. This money should be used in the case (and in no other) where a Jew has honestly become a Christian, so that he may get for the time being one or two or three hundred florins, as the person may require. This, in order that he may start a business to support his poor wife and children and the old and feeble. Such evilly acquired money is cursed, unless, with God's blessing, it is put to some good and necessary use. . . .

Seventhly, let the young and strong Jews and Jewesses be given the flail, the ax, the hoe, the spade, the distaff, and spindle, and let them earn their bread by the sweat of their noses as is enjoined upon Adam's children. For it is not proper that they should want us cursed *Goyyim* to work in the sweat of our brow and that they, pious crew, idle away their days at the fireside in laziness, feasting, and display. And in addition to this, they boast impiously that they have become masters of the Christians at our expense. We ought to drive the rascally lazy bones out of our system.

If, however, we are afraid that they might harm us personally, or our wives, children, servants, cattle, etc. when they serve us or work for us—since it is surely to be presumed that such noble lords of the world and poisonous bitter worms are not accustomed to any work and would very unwillingly humble themselves to such a degree among the cursed *Goyyim*—then let us apply the same cleverness as the other nations, such as France, Spain, Bohemia, etc., and settle with them for that which they have extorted usuriously from us, and after having divided it up fairly let us drive them out of the country for all time. For, as has been said, God's rage is so great against them that they only become worse and worse through mild mercy, and not much better through severe mercy. Therefore away with them. . . .

To sum up, dear princes and nobles who have Jews in your domains, if this advice of mine does not suit you, then find a better one so that you and we may all be free of this insufferable devilish burden—the Jews.

THE SPANISH INQUISITION:

"One cord was applied to the arms and twisted and she was admonished to tell the truth but said she had nothing to tell. Then she screamed and said: 'I have done all they say.' "(1568)

The Spanish Holy Office, or Inquisition, was established by the Church to guard against heresy and to protect the morals of Catholics. While it had no authority over Jews as such, the Inquisition was especially vigilant

Reprinted from Jacob R. Marcus, editor, *The Jew in the Medieval World* (Cincinnati, Ohio: The Union of American Hebrew Congregations, 1938), pp. 174–177; Copyright 1938 by Union of American Hebrew Congregations; reprinted 1960 by the Jewish Publication Society of America, Philadelphia, Pa.

with regard to the Spanish Jews converted to Christianity, the so-called *Marranos*. In order to avoid expulsion from Spain in 1492, thousands of Jews became *Marranos*, and were thus subject to surveillance or investigation by the Spanish Holy Office.

The "confession" under torture of Elvira del Campo, one of the *Marranos*, here reprinted, deals with charges that she refused to eat pork and continued to observe a number of Jewish Sabbath practices. Senora del Campo, who was pregnant at the time, was arrested in July, 1567. Her trial was postponed until the birth of the baby, and she underwent her first torture in April, 1568. Although she insisted that she was a good Christian, in which claim she was supported by several character witnesses, Senora del Campo was sentenced to prison for three years, and required to wear a yellow penitential garment bearing two crosses, one in front and one in back. Her property was confiscated, and when she emerged from prison after serving six months (she had already served almost a year by the time of her trial), she found herself not only poor but stigmatized for life.

Senora del Campo's "confession" is from the official report made by the secretary of the Inquisition.

She was carried to the torture-chamber and told to tell the truth, when she said that she had nothing to say. She was ordered to be stripped and again admonished, but was silent. When stripped, she said: "Senores, I have done all that is said of me and I bear false-witness against myself, for I do not want to see myself in such trouble; please God, I have done nothing." She was told not to bring false testimony against herself but to tell the truth. The tying of the arms was commenced; she said: "I have told the truth; what have I to tell?" She was told to tell the truth and replied: "I have told the truth and have nothing to tell." One cord was applied to the arms and twisted and she was admonished to tell the truth but said she had nothing to tell. Then she screamed and said: "I have done all they say."

Told to tell in detail what she had done she replied: "I have already told the truth." Then she screamed and said: "Tell me what you want for I don't know what to say." She was told to tell what she had done, for she was tortured because she had not done so, and another turn of the cord was ordered. She cried: "Loosen me, Senores, and tell me what I have to say: I do not know what I have done. O Lord have mercy on me, a sinner!" Another turn was given and she said: "Loosen me a little that I may remember what I have to tell; I don't know what I have done; I did not eat pork for it made me sick; I have done everything; loosen me and I will tell the truth." Another turn of the cord was ordered, when she said: "Loosen me and I will tell the truth; I don't know what I have to tell—loosen me for the sake of God—tell me what I have to say—I did it, I did it—they hurt me Senor—loosen me, loosen me, and I will tell it."

She was told to tell it and said: "I don't know what I have to tell —Senor I did it—I have nothing to tell—oh my arms! release me and I will tell it." She was asked to tell what she did and said: "I don't know; I did not eat because I did not wish to." She was asked why she did not wish to and replied: "Ay! loosen me, loosen me—take me from here and I will tell it when I am taken away—I say that I did not eat it." She was told to speak and said: "I did not eat it, I don't know why." Another turn was ordered and she said: "Senor I did not eat it because I did not wish to—release me and I will tell it." She was told to tell what she had done contrary to our holy Catholic faith. She said: "Take me from here and tell me what I have to say—they hurt me—Oh my arms, my arms!" which she repeated many times, and went on: "I don't remember—tell me what I have to say—O wretched me!—I will tell all that is wanted, Senores —they are breaking my arms—loosen me a little—I did everything that is said of me."

She was told to tell in detail truly what she did. She said: "What am I wanted to tell? I did everything—loosen me for I don't remember what I have to tell—don't you see what a weak woman I am?— Oh! Oh! my arms are breaking." More turns were ordered and as they were given she cried: "Oh! Oh! loosen me for I don't know what I have to say—Oh my arms!—I don't know what I have to say—if I did, I would tell it." The cords were ordered to be tightened, when she said: "Senores have you no pity on a sinful woman?" She was told, yes, if you would tell the truth. She said: "Senor, tell me, tell me it." The cords were tightened again, and she said: "I have already said that I did it." She was ordered to tell it in detail, to which she said: "I don't know how to tell it, Senor, I don't know." Then the cords were separated and counted, and there were sixteen turns, and in giving the last turn the cord broke.

She was then ordered to be placed on the *potro*. She said:

"Senores, why will you not tell me what I have to say? Senor, put me on the ground—have I not said that I did it all?" She was told to tell it. She said: "I don't remember—take me away— I did what the witnesses say." She was told to tell in detail what the witnesses said. She said: "Senor, as I have told you, I do not know for certain. I have said that I did all that the witnesses say. Senores, release me, for I do not remember it." She was told to tell it. She said: "I do not know it. Oh! Oh! they are tearing me to pieces—I have said that I did it—let me go." She was told to tell it, She said: "Senores, it does not help me to say that I did it and I have admitted that what I have done has brought me to this suffering—Senor, you know the truth—Senores, for God's sake have mercy on me. Oh, Senor, take these things from my arms—Senor, release me, they are killing me."

She was tied on the *potro* with the cords, she was admonished to tell the truth, and the *garrotes* were ordered to be tightened. She said: "Senor, do you not see how these people are killing me? Senor, I did it—for God's sake let me go." She was told to tell it. She said: "Senor, remind me of what I did not know—Senores, have mercy on me—let me go for God's sake—they have no pity on me—I did it— take me from here and I will remember what I cannot here." She was told to tell the truth, or the cords would be tightened. She said: "Remind me of what I have to say for I don't know it—I said that I did not want to eat it——I know only that I did not want to eat it," and this she repeated many times. She was told to tell why she did not want to eat it. She said: "For the reason that the witnesses say— I don't know how to tell it—miserable that I am that I don't know how to tell it—I say I did it and—my God!—how can I tell it?" Then she said that, as she did not do it, how could she tell it—"They will not listen to me—these people want to kill me—release me and I will tell the truth."

She was again admonished to tell the truth. She said: "I did it, I don't know how I did it—I did it for what the witnesses say—let me go—I have lost my senses and I don't know how to tell it—loosen me and I will tell the truth." Then she said: "Senor, I did it, I don't know how I have to tell it, but I tell it as the witnesses say—I wish to tell it—take me from here—Senor, as the witnesses say, so I say and confess it." She was told to declare it. She said: "I don't know how to say it—I have no memory—Lord, you are witness that if I knew how to say anything else I would say it. I know nothing more to say than that I did it." She said many times: "Senores, Senores, nothing helps me. You, Lord, hear that I tell the truth and can say no more—they are tearing out my soul—order them to loosen me." Then she said: "I do not say that I did it—I said no more."

Then she said: "Senor, I did it to observe that Law." She was asked what Law. She said: "The Law that the witnesses say—I declare it all Senor, and don't remember what Law it was—O wretched was the mother that bore me." She was asked what was the Law she meant and what was the Law that she said the witnesses say. This was asked repeatedly, but she was silent and at last said that she did not know. She was told to tell the truth or the *garrotes* would be tightened, but she did not answer. Another turn was ordered on the *garrotes* and she was admonished to say what Law it was. She said: "If I knew what to say I would say it. Oh Senor, I don't know what I have to say—Oh! Oh! they are killing me—if they would tell me what—Oh, Senores! Oh, my heart!" Then she asked why they wished her to tell what she could not tell and cried repeatedly: "O, miserable me!" Then she said: "Lord bear witness that they are killing me without my being able to confess." She was told that if she wished to tell the truth before the water was poured she should do so and discharge her conscience.

She said that she could not speak and that she was a sinner. Then the linen *toca* was placed and she said: "Take it away, I am strangling and am sick in the stomach." A jar of water was then poured down, after which she was told to tell the truth. She clamored for confession, saying she was dying. She was told that the torture would be continued till she told the truth and was admonished to tell it, but though she was questioned repeatedly she remained silent. Then the inquisitor, seeing her exhausted by the torture, ordered it to be suspended.

CHRISTOPHER MARLOWE:

*"I [Barabas, a Jew of Malta] walk
    abroad o' nights
And kill sick people groaning under walls;
Sometimes I go about and poison wells; . . ."*
(1588)

During the Middle Ages, and well into the modern era, Jews were commonly cast as villains in a large number of plays, novels, and other types of literature. The most famous Jew of the stage is, of course, Shylock of Shakespeare's *The Merchant of Venice,* but references to Jews, genrally unfavorable, occur in several of Shakespeare's plays. In *Two Gentlemen of Verona,* Shakespeare has Launce say at one point that ". . . a Jew would have wept to have seen our parting . . ." (Act II, Scene 3). Launce also tells Speed that Speed is "an Hebrew, a Jew" if he does not accompany Launce to the tavern "Because thou hast not so much charity in thee as to go to the ale with a Christian" (Act II, Scene 5). "If I do not love her," declares Benedict in *Much Ado About Nothing,* "I am a Jew" (Act II, Scene 3). In *Macbeth,* the contents of the cauldron, according to the Third Witch, include the "Liver of blaspheming Jew" (Act IV, Scene 1). Comparatively speaking, however, William Shakespeare (1564–1616) was more favorably disposed toward Jews than certain contemporary playwrights and dramatists.

The first of the following selections is part of a speech by the Jew, Barabas, of Christopher Marlowe's *The Jew of Malta* (1588). Barabas, who appeared on the stage at least eight years before Shylock, is portrayed as totally evil, cynical, and avaricious. Despite, or perhaps because of, the characterization of Barabas, *The Jew of Malta* was an outstanding success when first presented, although it was overshadowed later by Shakespeare's more masterful *The Merchant of Venice.*

The Travels of Three English Brothers, a play by John Day, George Wilkins, and William Rowley, was first presented in 1607. The character of Zariph, a Jew, one of whose speeches forms the second selection, is in many respects even less appealing than that of Barabas, not to mention Shylock.

Barabas, a Jew of Malta

I walk abroad o' nights
And kill sick people groaning under walls;

From Christopher Marlowe, *The Jew of Malta* (1588).

Sometimes I go about and poison wells;
And now and then, to cherish Christian thieves,
I am content to lose some of my crowns,
That I may, walking in my gallery,
See 'em go pinioned along by my door.
Being young, I studied physic and began
To practise first upon the Italian;
There I enriched the priest with burials,
And always kept the sexton's arm in ure
With digging graves and ringing dead men's knells:
And after that, was I an engineer,
And in the wars 'twixt France and Germany,
Under pretence of helping Charles the Fifth,
Slew friend and enemy with my stratagems;
Then, after that, was I an usurer,
And with extorting, cozening, forfeiting,
And tricks belonging unto brokery,
I filled the gaols with bankrupts in a year,
And with young orphans planted hospitals;
And every moon made some or other mad,
And now and then one hang himself for grief,
Pinning on his breast a long, great scroll
How I with interest tormented him.
But mark how I am blest for plaguing them;—
I have as much coin as will buy the town. (Act II.)

Zariph, a Jew

A hundred thousand ducats! sweet remembrance,
I'll read it again, a hundred thousand ducats!
Sweeter still! Who owes it? A Christian
Canaan's brood; honey to my joyful soul,
If this sum fail, (my bond unsatisfied),
He's in the Jew's mercy; mercy! Ha, ha!
The lice of Egypt shall devour them all
Ere I show mercy to a Christian:
Unhallowed brats, seed of the bondwoman,
Swine devourers, uncircumcised slaves

From John Day, George Wilkins, and William Rowley, *The Travels of Three English Brothers* (1607).

That scorn our Hebrew sanctimonious writ,
Despise our laws, profane our synagogues,
Old Moses' ceremonies, to whom was left
The marble Decalogue, twice registered
By high Jehovah; lawless wretches!
One I shall gripe, break he but his minute.
Heaven grant he may want money to defray.
Oh, how I'll then embrace my happiness.
Sweet gold, sweet jewel, but the sweetest part
Of a Jew's feast is a Christian's heart.

IV

THE JEW IN

MODERN EUROPE

1621–1959

HISTORICAL NOTE

The opening of the seventeenth century found the Jewish exiles from Spain and Portugal settling in Turkey, Italy, the Netherlands, and, later, England. For a time Holland became the spiritual center, and Amsterdam the world capital of Jewry. But in neither Holland nor Turkey did Jewish religious and cultural life reach the heights attained earlier in Babylonia and Spain. Gradually, with the expansion of the Jewish community in Eastern Europe, German-Polish Jews became prominent in Jewish affairs.

For a century and a half preceding 1648, large numbers of Jewish refugees arrived in Poland, mainly from Germany. As the Jewish community expanded and prospered, under conditions that permitted a considerable measure of autonomy, leadership in Jewish affairs began to pass from the Sephardim (Spanish Jews) to Askenazi (German-Polish) Jewry. In 1648, however, the Cossack revolt against Polish rule undermined the Ashkenazi supremacy. Although the Cossacks butchered Poles and Jews alike, they reserved their worst cruelties for the Jews. By 1660, when the pogroms abated, more than seven hundred Jewish communities had been destroyed. The Polish Jews were never again to regain their former position.

Expelled from many parts of Western and Central Europe by the sixteenth century, and massacred by the hundreds of thousands during the Polish wars of the mid-seventeenth century, the Jews became increasingly immersed in the life of the ghetto. Many Jews sought hope and solace in mysticism, a tendency that reached its peak in Turkey toward the end of the seventeenth century. Others found spiritual security by attaching themselves to messianic pretenders, of whom the most notable was Sabbatai Zevi of Smyrna. In 1648, he proclaimed himself the long-awaited Redeemer, and even his sudden conversion to Islam in 1666 was interpreted by his fanatical following as an effort to prevent the persecution of Turkish Jewry.

During most of the eighteenth century the Jews were confined to ghettos in Germany, Austria, Italy, and wherever else they were settled in any significant number. At best, they were minimally tolerated and subjected to restrictions; in most countries they suffered oppression and humiliation. While the Jews were regulated more by legislation, and less by mob violence, in the eighteenth century, the legislation and edicts affecting Jews were still based on medieval caricatures and stereotypes. Nevertheless, gradually, almost imperceptibly, the situation of European Jewry began to improve. By the end of the eighteenth century, a variety of influences—political, economic, intellectual—had combined to create a movement for Jewish emancipation.

The new era began with the French Revolution. On September 28, 1791, the French National Assembly conferred equal citizenship upon Jews, in accordance with the emphasis of the French Encyclopedists upon natural rights and freedom of religion. The impulse toward emancipation of the Jews was spread through Europe by Napoleon's armies. Although Napoleon had little personal sympathy for Jews, measures promoting Jewish equality were imposed in almost every country that fell to French forces. Despite the long period of reaction, ushered in by the Congress of Vienna and interrupted only briefly by the liberal revolutions of 1830 and 1848, the movement for emancipation was never entirely suppressed.

Jews were readmitted to England in 1655, and granted religious freedom in 1685. The process which ultimately led to full emancipation began in 1753 with a Parliamentary Act that empowered the government to naturalize foreign-born English Jews. The Act was repealed the following year, but eighty years later an effort was again made to secure the complete emancipation of Jews. In 1860, after much agitation by Thomas Babington Macauley and other eminent persons, the effort was finally successful. When Germany, in 1870, emancipated its Jews, almost all of Western and Central European Jewry enjoyed—at least officially—equal rights.

In Eastern Europe, however, the majority of Jews still lived in conditions approximating those of medieval Europe. The world's largest Jewish population, which came under Russian rule following the partition of Poland between 1772 and 1795, was confined in an enormous ghetto, the so-called Pale of Settlement in the Western provinces. From Catherine the Great (1762–1796) to Nicholas II (1894–1918), the treatment of the Jews fluctuated according to the moods and prejudices of the tzars, but on the whole, Russian policy was characterized more by brutality than by toleration. The assassination of Alexander II in 1881 was followed by a period of persecution that continued virtually unabated until

1917. Jews were made the scapegoats for Russia's defeat by Japan and the abortive revolution of 1904–1906.

The years immediately after World War I seemed to mark the dawn of a new epoch for European Jewry. The Treaty of Versailles appeared to guarantee the political, social, and cultural rights of minorities in Central and Eastern Europe. The new Polish republic, at the insistence of the Allies, emancipated the Jews. In 1917, the Balfour Declaration, issued by the British Secretary of State for Foreign Affairs, announced to the world that "His Majesty's Government view with favour the establishment in Palestine of a national home for the Jewish people. . . ."

Unfortunately, and even tragically, the apparent dawn retreated back into darkness. Despite the Versailles Treaty, there were frequent pogroms during the nineteen twenties in Poland, Rumania, and the Ukraine. The nineteen thirties witnessed the triumph in Germany of Adolf Hitler, an event which ultimately brought suffering and death to more than six million Jews. The thirties also saw the final collapse of the League of Nations, which, during its short lifetime, had exerted its influence in behalf of persecuted minorities everywhere. And, finally, the promised Jewish State did not become a fact until thirty years after the Balfour Declaration.

Recent history, although by no means comparable to the 1918–1945 period, has conferred sorrows as well as blessings on European Jewry. For a variety of reasons, Jewish communities of any significance have not reestablished themselves in Germany and Eastern Europe, and it is not likely that these parts of Europe ever again will contain important centers of Jewish life. While there are thousands of Jews in the Soviet Union, their religious and cultural freedom is severely restricted.

In effect, the future history of European Jews is confined to the countries of Western and Southern Europe. Jews are prominent in many areas of British life, and have held high office in government and in the political parties. Two Jews (Leon Blum and Pierre Mendès-France) have served as Premiers of France. Despite the existence of French anti-Semitic and crypto-Fascist organizations, thus far there has been no repetition of the notorious Dreyfus Affair of 1894–1900, notwithstanding opportunities afforded by the defeat in Indo-China and the fall of the Fourth Republic. In Italy, where the ghetto was abolished in 1870, Jews maintain an active religious and cultural life (indeed Rome is the only major European city in which Jews have lived continuously since the first century); and the Dutch Jews have long been included in a tradition of toleration.

For European and world Jewry, the outstanding event since World War II is the establishment of the State of Israel in May, 1948. The new state has already had a profound influence on Jewish life, but its significance goes well beyond that. Henceforth, when their situation anywhere deteriorates, Jews may repair to the Land of Abraham in accordance with the Israeli declaration that "The State of Israel will be open for the immigration of Jews from all the countries of their dispersion." This simple statement, in the context of the two-thousand-year-old *Diaspora*, has given Jews everywhere a new confidence and dignity.

Nevertheless, the foremost loyalties of Jews are attached not to Israel but to the countries where they reside, and in which they have been hospitably received. While the creation of Israel redeemed the hope of twenty centuries, the existence of the Jewish State cannot and will not bring an end to the Dispersion. Indeed Israel, if, in a sense, a response to the innumerable persecutions that have attended the *Diaspora*, is also a symbol of it. For Israel, like the individual Jew, exists in a Gentile world. If it has its powerful friends and allies in the West, it also has its determined enemies in the Arab world, and perhaps also in Asia and the Soviet Union. Thus its future, like the future of the Jew, would appear to be tied to the future of the West, including not only the future of East-West relations and Arab-West relations, but the future as well of Gentile-Jewish relations. Even assuming an amicable settlement between the Arab countries and Israel, the Jewish State will continue to be dependent upon the West for a large measure of political and economic support. Hence, if Gentile-Jewish relations suffer in the West, in which case it is probable that Arab hostility toward Israel will increase, Israel, too, will suffer, and perhaps ultimately cease to exist.

The fate of Israel, then, is linked to the future of Gentile-Jewish relations. Until Gentiles and Jews, in Europe and elsewhere, can confront each other without guilt, suspicion, and envy, in an atmosphere of mutual acceptance and recognition, there will be no real security for either Israel or the Jew.

FRANCISCO SUÁREZ:

". . . Familiarity with Jews
is placed under a general
prohibition." (1621)

Francisco Suárez, S.J., (1548–1617), Spanish theologian and philosopher, was born in Granada. After becoming a Jesuit in 1564, he taught at a variety of universities in Spain and Italy. A moderate Thomist, Suárez' views appealed to Philip II, by whom he was appointed Professor of Theology at Coimbra.

In 1613, Suárez was encouraged by Pope Paul V to write a theological treatise in honor of the Christian kings of Europe. The treatise, titled *Defensio catholicae fidei contra anglicance sectae errores,* was critical of such doctrines as divine right of kings, and attacked the practice of rendering oaths of allegiance to secular rulers. As a result, the work was publicly burned in London by order of James I. Suárez is better known, however, for his *Tractatus de ligibus ac deo legislatore,* which is regarded by scholars as one of the classics of international law.

The following selection from Suárez, first published in 1621, draws heavily on Church teachings regarding Jews, many of which had been official Catholic doctrine for centuries. Certain rules promulgated or reiterated by Suárez are similar to those which appear in the earlier *Seven-Part Code* of the Spanish Alphonso X (pages 80–87).

Finally, there remains for discussion an obvious question connected with the foregoing, a question of which St. Thomas treats,

From Francisco Suárez, S.J., *Disputation XVIII: On the Means Which May Be Used for the Conversion and Coercion of Unbelievers Who Are Not Apostates* (1621), in James Brown Scott, editor, *Selections From Three Works of Francisco Suárez, S.J.,* Vol. II of *The Classics of International Law,* Publications of the Carnegie Endowment for International Peace (Oxford: The Clarendon Press, and London: Humphrey Milford, 1944), 774–776, 784–785, 791–795.

namely: are the rites of unbelievers to be tolerated in the kingdoms of the faithful? From what has been said, it would seem that such rites ought not to be tolerated; for they are superstitious and injurious to God, Whose true worship the princes of those kingdoms are bound to advance.

However, St. Thomas makes a valid distinction between two kinds of rites: those which are contrary to natural reason, and opposed to God as known by the light of nature, for example, idolatry, and so forth; and those others which are indeed superstitions, by comparison with the Christian faith and its precepts, but which are not intrinsically evil or contrary to natural reason, for example, rites of the Jews, and perhaps even many of the rites of the Saracens and of similar infidels who worship only the one true God.

As to the first group, then, the inference stated at the beginning of this section is valid; for the Church ought not to tolerate these among her infidel subjects, a point proved by all the passages which we have cited and by the fact that, in such toleration or permission, there is no advantage either to the unbelievers themselves or to the Christian state. . . .

As to the other rites of unbelievers, those which are opposed only to the faith but not to natural reason, it is a certainty that unbelievers, even though subjects, should not be compelled to abandon them; on the contrary, such rites should be tolerated by the Church. So St. Gregory teaches, especially with respect to the Jews, when he forbids that the latter be deprived of their synagogues, and urges that they be permitted to engage in their ceremonies therein. He likewise teaches that the Jews should be permitted to celebrate their solemn rites.

The reason for such a view is that these rites are not intrinsincally evil according to the natural law, and that therefore, the temporal power of the prince does not *per se* include the authority to prohibit them; since no reason for the prohibition can be given, save that the rites in question are contrary to the faith, and this is not a sufficient reason in the case of those who are not spiritually subject to the power of the Church.

The confirmation of this argument is the fact that such a prohibition would be a coercion to the acceptance of the faith; and this coercion, as we have said, is not permissible. The foregoing argument applies in general to the Saracens and to the other unbelievers who know and worship the one true God, in so far as pertains to those rites which are not contrary to natural reason.

However, the Church has always considered that this tolerance is especially advisable in dealing with the Jews, because the errors of the latter furnish a testimony to the faith in many particulars. In the first place, the Jews admit that the Messiah was promised, and they accept the Scriptures from which we clearly prove that the promise has been fulfilled. Secondly, we see fulfilled in them what the Prophets and Christ foretold regarding their desertion of Him and their hardness of heart. Finally, Augustine has said that the Jews should be preserved and allowed to live in their own sects, in order that they in turn may preserve a testimony to the Scriptures such as the Church received, even from her enemies; and, in this connexion, Augustine quotes the words of Paul, "But by their offence, salvation is come to the Gentiles"; and also a passage from the *Psalms*, "Slay them not, lest at any time my people forget, scatter them by Thy power, &c." Augustine cites similar examples in his first sermon, on *Psalm* xl, near the end.

However, it should be added that the Church has allowed these rites within certain bounds and limitations.

The first and general limitation is that such rites are not to be celebrated to the scandal of the faithful; a fact which one may gather from the *Decretals* and from the *Code*. Among the Laws of Spain, too, there are many of the same sort.

Secondly, and specifically, although the Jews are permitted to retain and to keep in repair their old synagogues, they are nevertheless forbidden to erect new synagogues. On this point, see the *Code* and the *Decretals*.

Thirdly, although it is forbidden that their synagogues should be taken away from them, nevertheless, if these are once so taken, and consecrated as churches, they are not to be restored, and the loss must be made good in some other way; as Gregory indicates in *Letters*.

Fourthly, the Jews are not allowed to do anything which has not been ordained in their law, a limitation which is laid down by Gregory in the same Letter lviii.

Fifthly, they are not allowed to have their synagogues in the neighbourhood of Christian churches, according to the same Gregory.

Sixthly, on the day of the Passover, Jews are forbidden to go out in public; nay more, they are ordered to keep their doors and windows closed, as we read in the *Decretals*. According to this same authority, they are also commanded to wear an outward sign by which they may be externally distinguished from the faithful. And in general, they are to be severely punished if they do anything or make any public manifestation, in opposition to the honour of the Christian religion; a fact which is also brought out in the *Decretals*, and in the civil laws cited above, and in the *Decretum*.

Finally, for the reason already expounded, the ancient rabbinical books which were written sincerely and without any hatred of the Christian religion are tolerated; but the Books of the Hebrews, who later corrupted the Scriptures, are banned, as Cajetan has noted.

We must consider, [whether] unbelievers who are [themselves] subjects of Christian princes [may be deprived of power over Christians]. Under this head those four topics discussed above may be examined and treated.

As to the first point, indeed—that which relates to jurisdiction—the question has no application with respect to a sovereign prince; for we are assuming that these unbelievers are subjects of some Christian sovereign. Therefore, we have only to inquire as to the inferior judges or governors; and on this point it should be stated briefly that the Church can deprive such unbelievers, either directly or indirectly, of all jurisdiction of this kind over Christians, or—what amounts to the same thing—it may determine that in a Christian kingdom the faithful shall not be governed temporally by infidel judges or other infidel officials.

The direct power to do so clearly exists, because it is a Christian prince who has jurisdiction over the subjects in question, and he may require in his judges and officials such qualifications as he deems necessary for honour, or for distributive justice, or for the peace and safety of his state. On this ground, then, it is easily possible to exclude certain persons from the offices mentioned. The existence of the indirect power, on the other hand, is a self-evident fact; for the act in question is highly expedient to the welfare of the faith, an argument which proves the existence, not only of the power, but even of the obligation.

This teaching agrees with the words of Paul, "But brother goeth to law with brother and that before unbelievers," clearly reproving such behaviour as indecorous; at least, in cases in which it can be avoided. To the same effect is his saying elsewhere, "Bear not the yoke with unbelievers." For although there may be other interpretations of this passage, this also is a probable one; or, in any case, the phrase may well be adapted to such an interpretation by a parity of reasoning.

Furthermore the existence of this power may be clearly proved from the application of human laws. For in the *Code* Justinian forbids the Jews to hold public offices affecting Christians. Innocent III makes a similar ruling in the *Decretals,* when he imposes a penalty upon Jews who accept or hold such offices. Moreover, the application of this rule is extended to the pagans, that is, to Saracens, as may be learned from the last chapter of the same title in which Portugal is expressly enjoined to obey this law, with an additional statement to the effect that she may not sell tribute or royal grants to the Jews except when the latter are joined [in partnership] with some Christian, who will take care lest injury be done to believers. A similar law is laid down by the Third Council of Toledo; and in the Fourth Council of Toledo, it has been enacted that those who entrust such offices to Jews should be excommmunicated. The reason given is that, relying on this authority, the Jews take occasion to do injury to the faithful. Finally, the same rule is laid down in the First Council of Macon.

. . . Familiarity with Jews is placed under a general prohibition. On this point, the *Decretals* may be consulted. In fact, it would seem that absolutely all converse and communication with them was forbidden by the Fourth Council of Toledo. However, that prohibition has reference, not to all the faithful, universally, but to those who have been newly converted to the faith from among the ranks of the Jews themselves. To these new Christians, converse with those of their own people who persevere in Judaism is forbidden, because of the peril attending such converse. Therefore, this prohibition should be understood to refer to frequent, or continued converse, which may result in peril. Thomas Sánchez, following St. Thomas, Sylvester, and others, limits this general prohibition in such a way as to exclude its application in the case of those believers who are firm in the faith and with respect to whom there can be no fear of moral peril. However, if the prohibition contained in a law is general, it does not cease to bind in an individual case, even if the purpose of the law does, in a purely negative sense, cease to be realized in the individual case, as I assume from the treatise on laws. I therefore think that there is a limitation to the prohibition in the case of those persons whose care it is to convert such infidels as we speak of, because the purpose of the law then does not simply cease to be realized in a negative sense, but in addition, it ceases by contrariety.

Secondly, living in the same house with Jews is specifically forbidden. The reason for this prohibition is the avoidance of harm.

But the objection may be made that a Christian can own a slave who is an unbeliever, and that consequently, he can live with that unbeliever. The antecedent is supported in the *Decretals.*

Our reply is as follows: either this fact constitutes an exception to the prohibition set forth above; or else it cannot properly be said that the master dwells with the slave, but rather the converse, so that the prohibition in question does not apply to such a master; or, at least, a certain equality of fellowship and familiar intercourse is required for "dwelling together," in the true sense of the phrase, so that the Christian master, in accordance with other laws abovementioned, must avoid also this equal association with an unbelieving slave.

Thirdly, a Christian is forbidden to invite an unbeliever to his banquet table, or to accept such an invitation from the latter; for this also is dangerous association. This prohibition was especially directed against Jews in the Third Council of Orleans, and in the Council of Agde, the special reason being given that Jews discriminate among different sorts of food, a practice which is not permissible to Christians. However, as a special concession, this eating in common is permitted to preachers who are sent forth to convert unbelievers.

Fourthly, in these same laws, and in the Apostolic canons cited above, Christians are specifically forbidden to eat the unleavened bread of the Jews; an act which is evil in itself, if it is understood to involve the consumption of such food as a Jewish rite; but this rule is also interpreted as a prohibition, in order to avoid suspicion and peril [to the faith], against any partaking of the azyme with the Jews themselves or receiving it from them. When there is no danger of scandal, however, and especially if necessity requires, the eating of this food as ordinary bread is not forbidden, as the eating of idolothytes is forbidden in the *Decretum.*

Fifthly, in case of illness, Christians are forbidden to call in Jews; at least they are forbidden to do so for the purpose of [medical] treatment. This rule may have been made not merely because of special peril to the soul, but also to avoid bodily contact. Hence, a further rule has been laid down against receiving medicine from Jews, a prohibition which is chiefly understood to mean medicine is not to be received at their hands and administered by them, lest familiarity and peril result. But these and like prohibitions should be interpreted as applying only when the case is not one of necessity, since necessity knows no law.

Sixthly, Christians are further ordered not to bathe with Jews at the same time at the same public baths, a prohibition which is laid down in . . . Chapter xiii. This rule should be understood as applying only in a general sense, namely, as referring to the act of walking to the baths with them, that is to say, [the act of bathing together] as the result of an intention to do so. For this deliberate practice involves true social intercourse and familiarity, against which, on account of the danger involved therein, all the prohibitions under discussion are especially directed. If a Christian, then, should come accidentally to a public bath where a Jew is bathing at the time, the rule has no application, and it is not necessary that the Christian should on that account forgo what is convenient to him, or postpone it.

Seventhly, it may be especially noted that Christian women are forbidden to act as nurses for Jewish children, a fact which is brought out in the *Decretals.* However, this qualifying phrase is added: "in their homes"—that is, in the homes of the Jews—so that apparently, the rule in question is made solely to guard against the practice of dwelling together. Consequently, the inference may be drawn that a Christian woman is not forbidden to nurse a Jewish child in her own home; since the words of the law do not include such a case and should not be so extended. However, although this is true in so far as the strict letter of the law is concerned, nevertheless, the situation in question should be avoided because of the familiarity and peculiar affection which, as a general rule, result therefrom.

Eighthly, it is forbidden that Christians, in their wills, should name Jews as their heirs and legatees. This is the doctrine of the canonists, and especially of Felinus, the Gloss thereon, and Sylvester. The *Code* may be cited on the same rule; but in the *Code* the prohibition refers only to the Jews as a whole, that is, as a community, and prohibitions expressed in such terms are not usually extended to apply to individuals, as the Gloss thereon indicates. In this case, however, the extended application is allowed in the interests of the faith and of religion. Yet another chapter in the *Decretals* and one in the *Decretum* may be mentioned in this connexion, in which the said prohibition is imposed upon bishops, in particular, while in the *Decretals* it is extended to clerics.

The Doctors, however, apply that rule to all Catholics, either by the same process of reasoning, or at least *a fortiori;* and such should be the practice observed by all Catholics, especially since there exists a general warning lest they render aid and favour of this sort to Jews. This was the ruling of the Fourth Council of Toledo.

One must note, with respect to these and like questions, that the prohibitions involved are grave, both because of their subject-matter and because of the purpose they serve; and that by their nature, and generally speaking, they are binding under pain of mortal sin, although occasionally, when the particular instance happens to be of slight importance, the transgression may become venial.

Moreover, since a prohibition of the sort under discussion is part of the common law [of the Church], dispensations therefrom cannot usually be given by bishops; but when in any given case the necessity is urgent and delay would be dangerous, then, according to the common teaching on law, the granting of such dispensations is within the power of a bishop.

Finally, it may be asked whether the laws in question are to be interpreted as applying universally to all unbelievers, or whether they have reference only to the Jews.

The cause of the doubt is that the laws cited speak expressly of the Jews, so that some persons hold that, the said laws being penal in nature, there should be no extension of their application. A special reason which is customarily given is that, according to the *Decretals*, the Jews are not only subjects but also slaves. Hostiensis holds that the passage in question refers only to one's own purchased slaves, a view which certain of the Summists adopt. However, such a limitation is certainly not contained in the text, where, on the contrary, it is stated that the Jews have indeed inherently merited this slavery, but that in point of fact they are tributaries with the civil status of subordinate subjects, as Panormitanus notes with reference to this point, and as St. Thomas and Soto have also explained. Therefore, the true reason for this discrimination against the Jews is thought to be the fact that intercourse with the Jews involves more peril on account of their greater pertinacity and their hatred of the Christian religion.

Nevertheless, it is my opinion that the prohibitions which we are discussing, apply also to the Saracens—that is, the Mohammedans—both because such an extension of their force is repeatedly indicated in the civil and canon law; and also because there is an analogy in the reasoning applicable to both cases, inasmuch as these [Mohammedan] unbelievers are also enemies of the Christians, and attempt with all their strength to pervert the faithful.

As for other unbelieving pagans, however, they do not seem to have been included in the aforementioned laws, a fact which has been noted by Sánchez, of whose opinion I approve in so far as relates to this matter. Many statements concerning these prohibitions may also be found in the writings of the jurists on the laws in question, in the comments of the Summists, and in the statements of St. Antoninus, as well as in those of Azor and Sánchez, already cited; and these authorities quote many others.

FRANCIS BACON:

"And for the country of Bensalem, this man would make no end of commending it, being desirous by tradition among the Jews there to have it believed that the people thereof were of the generations of Abraham. . . ." (1629)

Francis Bacon (1561–1626), English philosopher, statesman, and writer, was educated at Cambridge University. He became a Member of Parliament in 1584, and held a variety of governmental posts after the succession of James I in 1603. In 1621, however, Bacon was accused of accepting bribes while he was Lord Chancellor. Admitting his guilt, Bacon was fined 40,000 pounds, and sentenced to the Tower. The fine and imprisonment were later remitted, but Bacon spent the remainder of his life in political retirement.

Intellectually well in advance of his times, Bacon's writings stressed the need for the inductive method in science, in contrast to the traditional *a priori* approach of scholasticism. Although he made no important scientific discoveries of his own, Bacon had an immense influence on the development of experimental science in England. He was relatively free of prejudices, and inclined to question or criticize the "common sense" assumptions of his day. He was the first modern writer, for example, to argue for the legitimacy of charging interest on money loaned.

Bacon's *The New Atlantis* (1629), from which the following selection is extracted, was a description of a scientific utopia which he located in or near the present continent of Australia. Unlike other utopias, the country of Bensalem was founded by a King Salomona who identified himself "with that king of the Hebrews (Solomon), which lived many years before him. . . ." Thus Bensalem's laws and customs incorporated Hebrew as well as Christian principles, a religious blending personified in Bacon's description of the character of Joabin, a Jewish merchant of Bensalem.

"There reigned in this island, about 1,900 years ago, a king, whose memory of all others we most adore; not superstitiously, but as a divine instrument, though a mortal man: his name was Salomona; and we esteem him as the lawgiver of our nation. This king had a large heart, inscrutable for good; and was wholly bent to make his kingdom and people happy. He therefore taking into consideration how sufficient and substantive this land was, to maintain itself without any aid at all of the foreigner; being 5,000 miles in circuit, and of rare fertility of soil, in the greatest part thereof; and finding also the shipping of this country might be plentifully set on work, both by fishing and by transportations from port to port, and likewise by sailing unto some small islands that are not far from us, and are under the crown and laws of this state; and recalling into his memory the happy and flourishing estate wherein this land then was, so as it might be a thousand ways altered to the worse, but scarce any one way to the better; though nothing wanted to his noble and heroical intentions, but only (as far as human foresight might reach) to give perpetuity to that which was in his time so happily estab-

lished, therefore amongst his other fundamental laws of this kingdom he did ordain the interdicts and prohibitions which we have
touching entrance of strangers; which at that time (though it was
after the calamity of America) was frequent; doubting novelties and
commixture of manners. It is true, the like law against the admission
of strangers without license is an ancient law in the kingdom of
China, and yet continued in use. But there it is a poor thing; and
hath made them a curious, ignorant, fearful foolish nation. But our
lawgiver made his law of another temper. For first, he hath preserved all points of humanity, in taking order and making provision
for the relief of strangers distressed; whereof you have tasted." At
which speech (as reason was) we all rose up, and bowed ourselves.
He went on: "That king also still desiring to join humanity and
policy together; and thinking it against humanity, to detain strangers
here against their wills; and against policy, that they should return,
and discover their knowledge of this estate, he took this course; he
did ordain, that of the strangers that should be permitted to land,
as many at all times might depart as many as would; but as many
as would stay, should have very good conditions, and means to live
from the state. Wherein he saw so far, that now in so many ages
since the prohibition, we have memory not of one ship that ever
returned, and but of thirteen persons only, at several times, that
chose to return in our bottoms. What those few that returned may
have reported abroad, I know not. But you must think, whatsoever
they have said, could be taken where they came but for a dream.
Now for our travelling from hence into parts abroad, our lawgiver
thought fit altogether to restrain it. So is it not in China. For the
Chinese sail where they will, or can; which showeth, that their law
of keeping out strangers is a law of pusillanimity and fear. But this
restraint of ours hath one only exception, which is admirable; preserving the good which cometh by communicating with strangers,
and avoiding the hurt: and I will now open it to you. And here I
shall seem a little to digress, but you will by-and-by find it pertinent.
Ye shall understand, my dear friends, that amongst the excellent
acts of that king, one above all hath the pre-eminence. It was the
erection and institution of an order, or society, which we call Salo-
mon's House; the noblest foundation, as we think, that ever was
upon the earth, and the lantern of this kingdom. It is dedicated to
the study of the works and creatures of God. Some think it beareth

the founder's name a little corrupted, as if it should be Solomon's House. But the records write it as it is spoken. So as I take it to be denominate of the king of the Hebrews, which is famous with you, and no strangers to us; for we have some parts of his works which with you are lost; namely, that natural history which he wrote of all plants, from the cedar of Libanus to the moss that groweth out of the wall; and of all things that have life and motion. This maketh me think that our king finding himself to symbolize, in many things, with that king of the Hebrews, which lived many years before him, honoured him with the title of this foundation. And I am the rather induced to be of this opinion, for that I find in ancient records, this order or society is sometimes called Solomon's House, and sometimes the College of the Six Days' Works; whereby I am satisfied that our excellent king had learned from the Hebrews that God had created the world, and all that therein is, within six days: and therefore he instituted that house, for the finding out of the true nature of all things, whereby God might have the more glory in the workman-ship of them, and men the more fruit in their use of them, did give it also that second name."

By that time six or seven days were spent, I was fallen into straight acquaintance with a merchant of that city, whose name was Joabin. He was a Jew and circumcised; for they have some few stirps of Jews yet remaining among them, whom they leave to their own religion. Which they may the better do, because they are of a far differing disposition from the Jews in other parts. For whereas they hate the name of Christ, and have a secret inbred rancour against the people amongst whom they live; these, contrariwise, give unto our Saviour many high attributes, and love the nation of Bensalem extremely. Surely this man of whom I speak would ever acknowledge that Christ was born of a Virgin; and that He was more than a man; and he would tell how God made Him ruler of the seraphims, which guard His throne; and they call Him also the Milken Way, and the Eliah of the Messiah, and many other high names, which though they be inferior to His divine majesty, yet they are far from the language of other Jews. And for the country of Bensalem, this man would make no end of commending it, being desirous by tradition among the Jews there to have it believed that the people thereof were of the generations of Abraham, by another son, whom they call Nachoran; and that Moses by a secret cabala ordained the laws of Bensalem which they now use; and that when the Messias should come, and sit in His throne at Hierusalem, the King of Bensalem should sit at His feet, whereas other kings should keep a great distance. But yet setting aside these Jewish dreams, the man was a wise man and learned, and of great policy, and excellently seen in the laws and customs of that nation.

SAMUEL PEPYS:

*"And in the end they [the Jews] had a
prayer for the King . . . in Hebrew. But,
Lord, to see the disorder, laughing, sporting,
and no attention, but confusion in all
their service." (1663)*

Samuel Pepys (1633–1703) was the famous English diarist. Joining the Admiralty office as clerk in 1659, Pepys began his diary the following year. An able and conscientious civil servant, he held a number of honorary positions in the government and in civil life. Pepys was elected to the House of Commons in 1673, and again in 1679. But his career as an officeholder was too much identified with the old order to survive the "Glorious" Revolution of 1688. The advent of William and Mary to the English throne marked the end of his official life.

Pepys's *Diary* was first made public in 1825. Intimate, candid, and perceptive, Pepys's *Diary*, although never intended for publication, succeeded in capturing the spirit of London life during the Restoration. The pages of the *Diary* provide graphic descriptions of the mores and manners of the post-Cromwellian era—not excluding the lice, bedbugs, and intestinal troubles which were the daily afflictions of London citizens of Pepys's day.

The following selections from his *Diary* record a visit Pepys made to a London synagogue in 1663, and, two years later, the expectation of certain Jews that the coming of the Messiah was imminent. The visit to the synagogue apparently took place on *Simhat Torah,* or the "Rejoicing with the Torah," an event which, unfortunately for Pepys's impressions, is usually celebrated in a festival-like fashion. Pepys's report of the attitude of certain Jews toward the Messianic prospect is interesting in view of the fact that some Jews, during the Protectorate, tended to regard Oliver Cromwell as the Messiah. When it became clear that Cromwell was not the Messiah, hope apparently persisted, especially among the Levantine Jews, that the arrival of the true Messiah was not far removed in time.

October 14th [1663]. Up and to my office, where all the morning, and part of it Sir J. Minnes spent, as he do every thing else, like a fool, reading the Anatomy of the body to me, but so sillily as to the making of me understand any thing that I was weary of him, and so I toward the 'Change, and met with Mr. Grant, and he and I to the Coffee-house, where I understand by him that Sir W. Petty and his vessel are coming, and the King intends to go to Portsmouth to meet it. Thence home and after dinner my wife and I, by Mr. Rawlinson's conduct, to the Jewish Synagogue: where the men and boys in their vayles, and the women behind a lattice out of sight; and some things stand up, which I believe is their Law, in a press to which all coming in do bow; and at the putting on their vayles do say something, to which others that hear him do cry Amen, and the party do kiss his vayle. Their service all in a singing way, and in Hebrew. And anon their Laws that they take out of the press are carried by several men, four or five several burthens in all, and they do relieve one another; and whether it is that every one desires to have the carrying of it, I cannot tell, thus they carried it round about the room while such a service is singing. And in the end they had a prayer for the King, which they pronounced his name in Portugall; but the prayer, like the rest, in Hebrew. But, Lord! to see the disorder, laughing, sporting, and no attention, but confusion in all their service, more like brutes than people knowing the true God, would make a man forswear ever seeing them more: and indeed I never did see so much, or could have imagined there had been any religion in the whole world so absurdly performed as this. Away thence with my mind strongly disturbed with them, by coach and set down my wife in Westminster Hall, and I to White Hall. . . .

February 19th [1665]. . . . So at noon by coach to St. Paul's Church-yarde to my Bookseller's, and there bespoke a few more books to bring all I have lately bought to £10. Here I am told for certain, what I have heard once or twice already, of a Jew in town, that in the name of the rest do offer to give any man £10 to be paid

£100, if a certain person now at Smyrna be within these two years owned by all the Princes of the East, and particularly the grand Signor as the King of the world, in the same manner we do the King of England here, and that this man is the true Messiah. One named a friend of his that had received ten pieces in gold upon this score, and says that the Jew hath disposed of £1,100 in this manner, which is very strange; and certainly this year of 1666 will be a year of great action; but what the consequences of it will be, God knows!

FREDERICK WILLIAM:

"Although they are not permitted to have
a synagogue they are allowed to arrange an
assembly in their homes where they may
offer their prayers and perform their
ceremonies, without, however, offering
any offense to the Christians." (1671)

Frederick William (1620–1688), the "Great Elector," was born in Berlin. He became the ruler of Brandenburg and Prussia in December, 1640, and immediately sought to reduce the havoc caused by the Thirty Years' War, then still in progress. An energetic diplomat and soldier, he was able to outwit the Swedes and Poles in maneuvers designed to extend the area of his rule, and the Treaty of Westphalia, signed in 1648, considerably enlarged the territory over which he governed.

His greatest skill, however, was displayed in governmental administration. The civil service, collection of taxes, expenditures for public services including education, the organization of the military establishment—these functions and agencies of government were substantially improved by major reforms. At the time of his death, Prussia enjoyed one of the most modern and centralized state administrations of any country in Europe. But if the "Great Elector" was an effective ruler, he was also an absolute one, and his methods were frequently ruthless if not despotic.

The edict here reprinted deals with the admission of fifty Jewish families, all of them of substantial means, to Brandenburg. Prior to the edict,

"The Readmission of the Jews into Brandenburg" by Frederick William, the Great Elector, May 21, 1671, reprinted in Jacob R. Marcus, editor, *The Jew in the Medieval World* (Cincinnati, Ohio: The Union of American Hebrew Congregations, 1938), pp. 75–79; Copyright 1938 by Union of American Hebrew Congregations; reprinted 1960 by the Jewish Publication Society, Philadelphia, Pa.

there were few if any Jews in most of the three hundred independent German principalities and free cities, and where there were Jews they were usually confined to ghettos and heavily taxed. Nevertheless, following the edict Jews, with and without permits, began to settle in the larger German cities; by 1710, for example, there were at least seventy Jewish families in Berlin alone.

We, Frederick William, by God's grace Margrave of Brandenburg, Chancellor and Elector of the Holy Roman Empire etc., hereby avow publicly and do graciously inform everyone whom it may concern that for special reasons and upon the most humble request of Hirshel Lazarus, Benedict Veit, and Abraham Ries, Jews, and moved particularly by the desire to further business in general, we have been influenced to take and receive graciously into our land of Electoral and March Brandenburg, under our special protection, a few Jewish families, namely, fifty of them, that have left other places. We do this on the following conditions, by virtue of the power vested in us.

1. We admit into our above mentioned land of Electoral and March Brandenburg and also into our Duchy of Krossen and the included areas the above mentioned fifty families. The names, numbers of persons, and locations where each one has settled must be made known to us immediately in a correct and detailed statement. The conditions of their admission are that the right shall be given them to settle in those places and towns where it is most suitable for them, and there to rent, buy, or build rooms, entire houses, dwelling places, or accommodations for themselves. It is to be understood, however, that those which they secure through purchase may be bought back again, and that which they build must be also returned to Christians even after the passing of a certain number of years. They are, however, to be reimbursed for their expenses.

2. These Jewish families shall be permitted to carry on their business activities in accordance with our edicts in this entire land of our Electoral and March Brandenburg, the Duchy of Krossen, and the places included therein. We allow them explicitly to have public shops and booths, to sell and to retail cloth and similar wares by the piece or by the yard, and to keep large and small weights which must not deviate in the least from the town-scales or the large scales used by the city authorities. The Jews must not practice any decep-

tion with their weights in buying or selling. We permit them to trade in new and old clothes, to slaughter meat in their own homes, and to sell that part of the slaughtered animal which they do not require for their own use or which their laws do not allow them to eat. And finally they are allowed to seek their livelihood everywhere—in places where they live, and in other spots too. They are specifically permitted to earn their livelihood by dealing in wool and groceries, just like the other inhabitants of these territories, and they are also allowed to sell their goods at the fairs and markets.

3. Just as we have drawn their attention above to our edicts, even so shall they continue to carry on their business according to the imperial statutes which have been decreed for Jews. They shall accordingly withhold themselves, as far as possible, from all forbidden business, particularly stolen goods. In matters of business they must not molest unfairly the inhabitants of these lands or any one else, nor deliberately defraud them of anything nor harm them, nor practice usury with their moneys. . . .

4. They are to pay, without any fraud, the tolls, the tax on commodities, and the "war levy" just as our other subjects. Because they are settled here in the country they are, however, exempt at our tollhouses from the body-tax which all other Jews who travel through have to pay. However, other Jews who do not belong here shall not pass through under this pretext. Moreover each family must pay eight Reichsthalers annually as protection-money, and whenever a member of a family marries he must pay a gold gulden, without any deduction, just like the Halberstadt Jews. Concerning the other taxes of the country they must arrive at a fair agreement with the authorities of every town. If they will not be able to do this with mutual fairness, they may report to us accordingly, and we will take the necessary measures.

5. Although we have taken the afore-mentioned fifty families under our special protection, nevertheless they shall not refuse in civil cases to be subject to and to expect justice from each town's chief magistrate. This task is specifically assigned to him and he is not to call in the other members of the town council. However, if any one has a complaint to make against any of the Jews, it must always be submitted in writing. In so far as criminal cases occur among them, these must be brought directly to us. The authorities of each town will accordingly bear this, particularly, in mind.

6. Although they are not permitted to have a synagogue they are

allowed to arrange an assembly in their houses where they may offer their prayers and perform their ceremonies, without, however, offering any offense to the Christians. They must particularly refrain from all abuse and blasphemy, under the threat of heavy penalties. They are also herewith allowed to have a ritual slaughterer as well as a schoolteacher for the instruction of their children. The privileges of these are to be the same as those laid down in the law dealing with Halberstadt Jewry.

7. Moreover they should everywhere evidence and show themselves to be decent, peaceful, and considerate, and must take particular care that they do not carry any good coins out of the country and bring worthless ones back in. They must not dispose of their gold and silver coins in other places but must sell them, as is proper, to our mints. In the event that any one should bring our stolen silver to them for sale, or should they otherwise learn where some is to be found, they are expected to report not only the silver but also the persons, and in the meantime to seize the one who may offer it to them for sale.

8. The officials of every town in this our Electoral March of Brandenburg, Duchy of Krossen, and the included territories, where some of the Jews of the already mentioned fifty families want to settle, are herewith graciously and earnestly commanded to accept this privileged Jewry willingly and gladly; to evidence to them all furtherance and good will in accommodating them; and, in our name, to let them have all proper protection and even to appeal to us ourselves. They are also to treat them fairly in the negotiations which they carry on with them about their staying and about the taxes of the land; to allow no one to affront them or molest them; to treat them as their other citizens and inhabitants; and to treat them well in accordance with the content of this, our Letter of Protection. They are particularly enjoined to assign them at once, for a payment, a place for the burial of their dead.

9. If the now oft-mentioned Jewry will act in accordance with that above which has been laid upon them and has been promised by them, then we most graciously promise them our most benign protection and defense in these our territories from this time forth for twenty years, and, after this termination, the continuation thereof by us and our heirs, as we see fit. Failing this, we reserve for ourselves the right, after proper consideration, to recall our protection even before the twenty years have passed.

10. Should the tumult of war—God forbid—rise in our land during these twenty years, the oft-mentioned Jewry, like our other subjects, shall not be forbidden to take refuge in our fortresses with their families, but shall be admitted and tolerated there.

Accordingly we command all our subjects and followers without regard to station and dignity, that from this day forth, for the whole twenty years, they allow the oft-mentioned Jewry to pass about freely and safely everywhere in our entire Electorate and the lands mentioned with it; that they be allowed to visit the public fairs, business centers, and trading towns; and that they be permitted to sell all their wares publicly and to pursue respectable trade and unforbidden business free and unhampered as opportunity presents itself. No one shall lay violent hands upon them. Furthermore, every magistrate and official of the courts shall aid them, at their request, in that to which they are entitled; shall accord them, like others, the right of civic hospitality; and shall not treat them in any other way, if they would avoid our high disfavor—to say nothing of a penalty of fifty golden gulden and even more, according to circumstances.

In witness whereof this patent and Letter of Protection has been signed by our own hand and confirmed by our gracious seal. Potsdam, the 21st of May, 1671.

JOSEPH ADDISON:

"Their firm adherence to their religion is no less remarkable than their numbers and dispersion, especially considering it as persecuted or contemned over the face of the whole earth." (1712)

Joseph Addison (1672–1719), English essayist, poet, and *litterateur*, is chiefly known for his contributions to *The Tatler* and *The Spectator*, two of the most distinguished English periodicals of the early eighteenth century. Like his friend Richard Steele, founder of *The Tatler*, Addison was a critic of the manners, morals, and politics of his time, but his fame rests less on his intellectual powers, or his plays and poems, than on the

Reprinted in Thomas Arnold, ed., *Addison: Selections from Addison's Papers Contributed to* The Spectator (Oxford: The Clarendon Press, 1894).

prose style which he consistently displayed in his essays. Even Samuel Johnson, who did not share Addison's Whig views, was forced to declare that "Whoever wishes to attain an English style must give his days and nights" to reading Addison's published work.

In his travels, which were extensive, Addison made it a point to visit the Jewish quarters in the cities and towns on his itinerary. His tolerant attitude toward Jews is reflected in a number of his essays. One of them, titled "Gratitude," declares that the Jews "set the Christian world an example how they ought to employ this divine talent." Other essays praise Hebrew as a language (Addison apparently had some command of Hebrew), and commend the Jews for their refusal to use the Divine Name in an irreverent fashion.

The following essay, "The Jews," first appeared in *The Spectator*, No. 495, on September 27, 1712.

As I am one, who, by my profession, am obliged to look into all kinds of men, there are none whom I consider with so much pleasure, as those who have anything new or extraordinary in their characters, or ways of living. For this reason I have often amused myself with speculations on the race of people called Jews, many of whom I have met with in most of the considerable towns which I have passed through in the course of my travels. They are, indeed, so disseminated through all the trading parts of the world, that they are become the instruments by which the most distant nations converse with one another, and by which mankind are knit together in a general correspondence: they are like the pegs and nails in a great building, which, though they are but little valued in themselves, are absolutely necessary to keep the whole frame together.

That I may not fall into any common beaten tracks of observation, I shall consider this people in three views: first, with regard to their number; secondly, their dispersion; and, thirdly, their adherence to their religion: and afterwards endeavour to shew, first, what natural reasons, and, secondly, what providential reasons may be assigned for these three remarkable particulars.

The Jews are looked upon by many to be as numerous at present, as they were formerly in the land of Canaan. This is wonderful, considering the dreadful slaughter made of them under some of the Roman emperors, which historians describe by the death of many hundred thousands in a war; and the innumerable massacres and persecutions they have undergone in Turkey, as well as in all Christian nations of the world. The Rabbins, to express the great havoc which has sometimes been made of them, tell us, after their usual manner of hyperbole, that there were such torrents of holy blood shed as carried rocks of an hundred yards in circumference above three miles into the sea.

Their dispersion is the second remarkable particular in this people. They swarm over all the East, and are settled in the remotest parts of China; they are spread through most of the nations of Europe and Africa, and many families of them are established in the West Indies: not to mention whole nations bordering on Prester John's country, and some discovered in the inner parts of America, if we may give any credit to their own writers.

Their firm adherence to their religion is no less remarkable than their numbers and dispersion, especially considering it as persecuted or contemned over the face of the whole earth. This is likewise the more remarkable, if we consider the frequent apostasies of this people when they lived under their kings, in the land of Promise, and within sight of their temple.

If in the next place we examine, what may be the natural reasons for these three particulars which we find in the Jews, and which are not to be found in any other religion or people, I can, in the first place, attribute their numbers to nothing but their constant employment, their abstinence, their exemption from wars, and above all, their frequent marriages; for they look on celibacy as an accursed state, and generally are married before twenty, as hoping the Messiah may descend from them.

The dispersion of the Jews into all the nations of the earth is the second remarkable particular of that people, though not so hard to be accounted for. They were always in rebellions and tumults while they had the temple and holy city in view, for which reason they have often been driven out of their old habitations in the land of Promise. They have as often been banished out of most other places where they have settled, which must very much disperse and scatter a people, and oblige them to seek a livelihood where they can find it. Besides, the whole people is now a race of such merchants as are wanderers by profession, and at the same time are in most, if not all, places incapable of either lands or offices, that might engage them to make any part of the world their home.

This dispersion would probably have lost their religion, had it not been secured by the strength of its constitution: for they are to live all in a body, and generally within the same inclosure; to marry among themselves, and to eat no meats that are not killed or prepared their own way. This shuts them out from all table conversation, and the most agreeable intercourses of life; and, by consequence, excludes them from the most probable means of conversion.

If, in the last place, we consider what providential reason may be assigned for these three particulars, we shall find that their numbers, dispersion, and adherence to their religion, have furnished every age and every nation of the world with the strongest arguments for the Christian faith, not only as these very particulars are foretold of them, but as they themselves are the depositaries of these and all the other prophecies, which tend to their own confusion. Their number furnishes us with a sufficient cloud of witnesses that attest the truth of the old Bible. Their dispersion spreads these witnesses through all parts of the world. The adherence to their religion makes their testimony unquestionable. Had the whole body of the Jews been converted to Christianity, we should certainly have thought all the prophecies of the Old Testament, that relate to the coming and history of our blessed Saviour, forged by Christians, and have looked upon them, with the prophecies of the Sibyls, as made many years after the events they pretended to foretell.

FREDERICK THE GREAT:

"We herewith establish, regulate, and order earnestly that in the future no Jew shall presume to engage in any manual trade."
(1750)

Frederick II (1712–1786), more popularly known as Frederick the Great, was ruler of Prussia from 1740 to 1786. Following a treaty of peace with Maria Theresa of Austria, Frederick turned his attention to domestic

From "The Charter Decreed by Frederick II for the Jews of Prussia, April 17, 1750," reprinted from Jacob R. Marcus, editor, *The Jew in the Medieval World* (Cincinnati, Ohio: The Union of American Hebrew Congregations, 1938), pp. 85–97; Copyright 1938 by Union of American Hebrew Congregations, reprinted 1960 by The Jewish Publication Society, Philadelphia, Pa.

problems, which included, by his definition, the status and rights of the Prussian Jews. In an effort to establish a fixed ratio between Jews and Christians, and indirectly to promote Christian industrial enterprise, Frederick restricted the number of Jews and severely limited the occupations in which they could engage. Jews were not permitted to serve in the Army during the Seven Years' War, or hold state positions. Instead they were heavily taxed, forced to purchase porcelain from the royal factory, and deliver annually certain amounts of silver to the state treasury. Heavy penalties were imposed on Jews engaged in usury, and on all others who violated or disregarded the regulations which are here reprinted.

On the whole, Frederick's treatment of the Jews was much more severe than that accorded them by his predecessor, Frederick William, the Great Elector. In 1771, Frederick himself struck Mendelssohn's name from a list of members proposed for the *Berliner Akademie der Wissenschaften,* and, according to Thomas Carlyle, broke off relations with Voltaire because of Voltaire's transactions with Abraham Hirsch (or Hirschel).

Frederick's *Charter* for the Prussian Jews, although drafted in 1750, was not promulgated until 1756.

We, Frederick, by God's grace, King of Prussia, Margrave of Brandenburg, Chancellor and Electoral Prince of the Holy Roman Empire, sovereign and supreme Duke of Silesia, etc., etc., etc.,

Make known and order to be made known: We have noticed in our kingdom of Prussia . . . and particularly also in this capital various faults and abuses among the licensed and tolerated Jews, and have particularly observed that the rampant increase of these abuses has caused enormous damage and hardship, not only to the public, particularly to the Christian inhabitants and merchants, but also to Jewry itself. For this reason and because of the surreptitious entry of unlicensed Jews: foreigners and those who are all but without any country, many complaints and difficulties have arisen.

We, however, out of a feeling of most gracious paternal provision wish to establish and maintain, as far as possible, the livelihood and trades of each and every loyal subject under our protection, Christians as well as Jews, in a continually good and flourishing state.

For this reason we have found it necessary to make such provision that this, our most gracious purpose, may be attained, so that a proportion may be maintained between Christian and Jewish business opportunities and trades, and especially that neither be injured through a prohibited expansion of Jewish business activity. For this purpose we have again made an exact investigation of the condition, in our kingdom and in the other above mentioned imperial lands, of all Jewry, of their families, their means of subsistence, and their business activity. We have considered certain feasible proposals which have as their basis justice, fairness, and common safety, and have also deemed them useful for the attainment of our ultimate object and the attendant welfare of all inhabitants of the country who live by means of business activity. As a result of these proposals we wish to prepare and to put into effect a special regulation and constitution for all Jewry. Therefore we establish, regulate, and order, herewith and by virtue of this, that:

I. The Former General-Patent And Regulations For Jewry Are To Be Published And Adjusted According To Present Conditions. . . .

II. No Other Jews Are To Be Tolerated Except Those Named In The Lists That Are Attached To The End Of These Regulations. . . .

III. List Of The Tolerated Communal Jewish Officials In Berlin:
The following list of communal officials for the capital here in Berlin has been fixed:

1. One rabbi or a vice-rabbi.
2. Four assistant-judges.
3. A chief and assistant cantor with his basses and his sopranos. These latter must not be married.
4. Four criers, one of whom must report daily to the police office the arrival of foreign Jews.
5. Two employees in the synagogal-school.
6. Six grave diggers who also do other work for the Jewish community.
7. One cemetery guard.
8. Three slaughterers.
9. Three butchers.
10. One secretary of the meat-market and his supervisor.
11. Three bakers and one restaurant-keeper.

12. A communal scribe.
13. Two doorkeepers and one assistant.
14. Two hospital attendants.
15. One physician.
16. One male and one female bath attendant.
17. A fattener of fowl and cattle.
18. Eight attendants for the sick.
19. Two Hebrew printers.
20. Two teachers for girls. Both must be married.

These and no more shall be appointed by the elders of the Jews with the approval, however, of the War and Domains Office. But, as far as possible, native impoverished Jews are to be prepared for, and installed in, these positions. . . .

For the instruction of the Jewish girls two married communal schoolteachers are allowed in Berlin, Königsberg, Halberstadt, Halle, and Frankfort on the Oder, also in Stargard in Pomerania. If in other cities there are more than ten Jewish families, then one married schoolteacher is permitted; the rest of the towns, however, none at all is permitted. . . .

IV. Every Month The Jewish Elders Must Send In To The War And Domains Office A List Of Any Changes That Have Occurred In The Jewish Community. . . .

V. Principles That Are To Be Observed In The Settlement Of Jews

The following principles respecting the settlement of Jews shall be established and observed in the future. . . .

A distinction is to be made between Regular Protected-Jews and Special Protected-Jews who are merely tolerated during their life time. . . .

Only those are to be considered Regular Protected-Jews who have the right to settle a child. . . .

The above mentioned Special Protected-Jews, however, are not authorized to settle a child nor are they to marry off a child by virtue of their privilege. . . .

In accordance with our most graciously issued cabinet-order of

May 23, 1749, the fixed number of Jewish families at present is not to be exceeded except by our royal command. . . .

The Regular Protected-Jews, however, are allowed by virtue of their Letter of Protection to settle one child, a son or daughter, during their life time, but once they have made their decision they will not be authorized to change it in the future. This child may marry if it can first establish its identity legally. . . .

Foreign Jews are not allowed to settle in our lands at all. However, if one should really have a fortune of ten thousand Reichsthalers and bring the same into the country and furnish authentic evidence of the fact, then we are to be asked about this and concerning the fees he is to pay. . . .

In order that in the future all fraud, cheating, and secret and forbidden increase of the number of families may be more carefully avoided, no Jew shall be allowed to marry, nor will he receive permission to settle, in any manner, nor will he be believed, until a careful investigation has been made by the War and Domains Offices together with the aid of the Treasury. . . .

Male and female servants and other domestics, however, are not allowed to marry. Should they attempt to do this they are not to be tolerated any longer. . . .

The children of licensed Jews, whose fathers have died or have become impoverished, or are in such a condition that they, the children, have no right of "settlement," or do not possess the required fortune, are to be tolerated, even as are the widows of such people. However, when they come of age, they shall in no wise dare, under penalty of expulsion, to set up a business for themselves but they must either work for other licensed Jews, or go away and seek to be accepted somewhere else. They may, indeed, prepare themselves so that they take the place of Jewish communal officials who leave. Thus it will not be necessary to accept so many foreigners for this purpose.

VI. The Established Method Of Collection Is To Be Retained With Respect To The Collection Of The Protection-Tax And Other Public Taxes. . . .

VII. No Protected-Jew Can Stay Away From Home For More Than A Year Without Authorization; Otherwise His Place Will Be Given To Another. . . .

VIII. The Jews Must Pay Their Taxes Quarterly And All The Jews Are Responsible As A Body For The Payment Of The Taxes. . . .

IX. What Is To Be Done With Impoverished Jews or Those Facing Bankruptcy. . . .

X. What Action Is To Be Taken When A Jew Deliberately Becomes Bankrupt. . . .

XI. The Jews Must Not Pursue Any Manual Trade. . . .

We herewith establish, regulate, and order earnestly that in the future no Jew shall presume to engage in any manual trade, nor venture upon any except seal-engraving, painting, the grinding of optical glasses, diamonds, and jewels, gold and silver embroidery, fine cloth needlework, the collecting of gold dust by a sieving process, and other similar trades in which vocational associations and privileged guilds are not found. Particularly are they enjoined not to brew beer nor to distill spirits. However, they are allowed to undertake the distilling of spirits for the nobility, government officials, and others, with the understanding that only licensed Jews and their sons are to be taken for this task. . . . However, those Jews who have received or may receive special concessions for the establishment of particular types of factories or for the sale of goods of Christian manufacturers are to be protected in the future as in the past.

XII. Jews Are Forbidden The Smelting Of Gold And Silver. . . .

XIII. The Slaughter Of Meat For Their Own Consumption Is Permitted The Jews If They Kill The Animals In Christian Slaughterhouses. . . .

XIV. The Jews In Berlin Are Not Allowed To Have Dealings In Raw Wool Or Woolen Yarns Or To Manufacture Woolen Goods. . . .

XV. Jews Are Further Allowed To Sell One Another Beer And Spirits. . . . With The Exception Of Kosher Wines They Are Not Allowed To Do Any Business In Wines. . . .

XVI. Jews Are Not Allowed To Deal In Raw Cattle-And-Horse Hides, Plain Or Dyed Leathers, And Foreign Woolen Wares Except Those Which Are Specifically Permitted In The Following [Paragraph XVIII]. . . .

XVII. Under Special Conditions They May Sell Choice Groceries And Spices To Other Jews. . . . The Jews Are Forbidden To Trade In Raw Tobacco, To Manufacture Tobacco, And To Carry A Line Of [Staple] Groceries. . . .

XVIII. Precisely The Kinds of Goods With Which The Protected-Jews Are Allowed To Do Business

In order that all Jews under our protection may be informed and instructed precisely in the business opportunities and trades allowed them, they are allowed to trade and to do business with the following, namely:

With gold-cloth, silver-cloth, fine fabrics and ribbons, native and foreign embroidered goods, domestic gold and silver laces manufactured in the Berlin Royal Gold and Silver Factory, neck bands of lace, Spanish lace, gold and silver thread and purl; likewise with jewels, broken gold and silver, ingots, all sorts of old pocket-watches, and similar things. Furthermore they are permitted to deal in money-exchange and pledges, money-brokerage, and the buying and selling of houses and estates for other people. They are also permitted to do business in all sorts of Brabant, Dutch, Silesian, and Electoral-Saxonian fine cloth and silk textiles, in laces, muslin, and all-white domestic coarse calico linings, domestic linen, white linen thread, and tablecloths of linen and half-linen. They are also specially allowed to deal with domestic silk goods, also with foreign and native undyed, dressed leather, and with domestic velvet. They are also allowed to deal in all sorts of all-wool and half-wool goods and cotton goods—by whatever name they may be called—manufactured here in this country, as well as with cotton and chintz goods made in our lands.

Furthermore they are permitted to deal in horses, in undressed calf and sheep hides, feathers, wigs, hair, also camel and horsehair, tallow, wax, and honey, Polish wares, undressed and unfinished pelts, but not finished furriers' wares in those cities where furriers live, unless they can without hesitation give the name of the furriers from whom they bought the finished product for further sale. They are also allowed to trade in tea, coffee, chocolate, and foreign and domestic manufactured snuff and smoking tobacco. They are also free to trade, exchange, and do business in all sorts of old clothes, old or used furniture, house and kitchen utensils; to sum up, with everything which is not generally and specifically forbidden in the above paragraphs, even though it is neither specified or mentioned in this special paragraph. But all this is permitted them only in their own homes and in those shops and booths that have been regularly assigned them.

However, with respect to foreign and domestic Jewish trade in our Kingdom of Prussia, the special constitution that has been made there will remain in force, inasmuch as the Polish and Russian business there is still dependent on both Christian and Jewish commerce. . . .

XIX. The Jews Must Not Trade In Anything Herein Forbidden Them, Under Threat Of Confiscation Of Their Wares. . . . They May Not Peddle In Cities Except At The Time Of The Fairs. . . .

XX. No Foreign Jews And Jewish Boys Shall Do Business In Berlin. Outside Of Exceptional Cases Herein Specified, Those Who Remain Over Twenty-Four Hours In Berlin Must Pay One Specie-Ducat To The Potsdam Orphan Home. . . .

Now it has been noticed that many Jews and Jewish boys from other cities and provinces that are subject to us have tarried in Berlin, year in and year out, and almost daily, constantly coming and going, and, as it were, relieving one another. Through private and public trading they have done tremendous damage, not only to the entire public, but particularly to the entire Christian and authorized Jewish trade, and have at the same time deceived and duped our treasuries through all sorts of fraud and malicious practices. Therefore, we establish, regulate, and order herewith and by virtue of this, that except for the local fairs no Jew who does not belong to Berlin—whether he is otherwise licensed or non-licensed within our land—shall be allowed to come into the city with any wares except broken gold and silver. Also no foreign Jew, male or female, shall be allowed in except at the time of the fairs. . . .

XXI. All Foreign Jews Who Do Not Arrive With The Post-Carriage Or Their Own Vehicles May Enter Into And Leave Berlin By Only Two Gates. What Is To Be Done In This Matter In Other Large Cities. . . .

XXII. What Is To Be Done With Jewish Beggars

It has already been decreed many times that Jewish beggars are nowhere to be allowed to cross our borders. We not only repeat this, but order that in the event any such Jewish beggars nevertheless reach our capital surreptitiously, they shall be brought at once to the Poor-Jews Home at the Prenzlau Gate. There they are to be given alms and on the following day evicted through the gate without being allowed to enter into the city. . . .

[All foreign beggars, collectors, (German) Jewish peddlers, Polish Jews, jugglers, bear-trainers, and tramps are forbidden access to this country under penalty of a prison sentence. All gypsies caught will be hanged and shot.]

XXIII. How The Foreign Jews Engaged In Business Are To Be Treated By The Excise Office During The Fairs In Berlin. . . . [They Must Pay A Tax On Goods Sold]

XXIV. The Jews Are Allowed To Lend Out Money On Proper Pledges

Inasmuch as the money-business is a particular source of Jewish support, Jews are therefore allowed to lend money on pledges now as in the past. They must not, however, accept pledges from any non-commisioned officer or soldier, or buy anything where they are not sufficiently assured that this is their lawful property and no part of their soldiers' equipment. And in every case they must demand a note from the company commander with respect to these things. Furthermore, the Jews must be very sure in all pawning and selling that the pledges were not stolen, or secretly removed and then pledged, either by young folks from their parents, or by

unfaithful servants from their employers. On each occasion, therefore, the pawnbrokers must make enquiries from the parents or
the employers.

Furthermore, those Jews, their wives, or employees must not
only surrender such pledges to the owner without compensation,
but in case that they knew that the pledge was stolen or secretly
removed, and shall be legally convicted of this, then, in accordance with the edict of January 15, 1747, the possessors of such
pledges shall be regarded just like those who have wittingly purchased stolen goods. Such a pawnbroker shall lose all rights of
protection, not only for himself, but also for his children if some
of them have already been settled in business, for their Letters of
Protection shall be annulled, and he and his family shall be removed from the country. Furthermore, no one else is to be settled
in the vacancy created by that family, and, besides this, the transgressor is to be compelled to pay the full worth of the stolen or
illegally received things to the lawful owner, who, if necessary, will
take an oath as to their value.

If the offender cannot pay this because his Letter of Protection
has been cancelled and his family already expelled, then the entire
Jewry of the town is officially to be held responsible for the payment in cash—and without any protest—to the robbed owner of the
value of the stolen or illegally received things. For this reason the
Jews must watch one another and pay attention carefully when they
find any of their people on the wrong road and immediately report
such a person to the proper authorities. Jewry, therefore, and particularly the elders are required to anticipate any annoyance and
damage by ridding the country of those receivers of stolen goods
and the other rascally crew among them whenever they discover
them. And when they submit their information they will be given
all assistance. . . .

XXV. How Proper Pledges Are To Be Redeemed And Sold. . . .

XXVI. They Must Keep A Correct Pledge-Book. . . .

XXVII. Interest Which The Jews Are Authorized To Take

When a Jew lends money on bills of exchange he is, according
to the edict of December 24, 1725, and until further decree, still

authorized to take twelve percent interest if the bill of exchange is to run for twelve months or less. If it concerns a capital of one hundred Reichsthalers and over, which is to draw interest for more than a year, he must not take more than eight per cent interest, under threat of loss of the capital and all interest. . . .

If a Jew lends money on pledges or mortgages up to one hundred Reichsthalers, he is likewise not allowed to take more than eight per cent interest under threat of the same penalty.

If, however, a Jew lends out money in small sums on pledges, and the amount loaned on the pledge is less than ten thalers, he may take a pfennig on the thaler as interest every week. . . .

In all these cases the common law holds good that no Jew may take interest from accrued interest, or add such interest to the capital, under threat of the loss of the old capital. . . .

XXVIII. In The Future The Jews Shall Not Buy Houses Of Their Own. The Forty Houses Owned By Jews In Berlin Shall Not Be Increased In Number. . . . In Other Cities Where There Are Five Jewish Families Only One Of Them May Buy A House. . . .

After investigation has been made and an order has been received from those in charge of the royal finances, Jews, in those places where they are tolerated, will be allowed to build on desolate and virgin areas. . . .

However, the Jews are nowhere allowed to buy and possess estates.

XXIX. With Respect To The Election Of The Elders And The Rabbi, The Constitution And Organization That Has Been In Effect Till Now Will Be Maintained. . . .

XXX. The Jews Are To Be Protected In Their Religion, Ceremonies, And Synagogue, And That Which Is Related To It.

We have everywhere most graciously and firmly protected all these Jewish families in their religion and in their Jewish customs and ceremonies which they have practiced till now. We also herewith confirm anew the [right to possess the] synagogues which they have built in Berlin, Königsberg, Halberstadt, Halle, and Frankfort

on the Oder, as well as the schools in the other provinces, the cemeteries, and the small houses belonging to the synagogues and the
cemeteries. This, however, on the condition that they must always
refrain, under penalty of death and complete expulsion of the entire Jewry from Berlin and our other cities, from such abuses as
the Jewish prayer which begins *Alenu* etc., as has already been
emphatically decreed in detail in the edicts of 1703 and 1716. They
must refrain likewise from other prayers of the same type, and also
from all improper excesses in their festivals, particularly during
the so-called Haman or Purim festival.

Various Jews here have ventured, in an arbitrary manner, to hold
assemblies and private prayer-meetings, gathering together many
other Jews, old and young in their houses. This, however, runs
counter to our previous decrees and the public welfare, and as such
is very objectionable to the [Jewish] community also, and is very
detrimental to the religious meetings in the synagogue.

Therefore, we apply again the decrees of the 2nd of February,
1745, which were issued for Berlin in this matter: that such private
assemblies for prayers are to be stopped, and are to be allowed to
no one, except him whom we specifically permit. Moreover, there
are not to be more than two such prayer-meetings in Spandau Street,
and one in Jews' Street, for old and sickly people and children, because such people can hardly go to the synagogue in the winter
time.

These prayer-meetings may be held from Michaelmas till Easter
in certain houses designated by the Jewish elders. These prayer-
meetings are to be conducted in such a manner that, on the one
hand, none but worn-out, old and sickly Jews and children under
twelve years of age, together with one or two schoolteachers, shall
assemble there; on the other hand, that no other religious service,
ceremonies, and activities be engaged in except those which are
absolutely necessary in prayer. And at the same time that which
is usually collected in the synagogue for the poor Jews and otherwise may be contributed here also. The assembly is to be held at
all times in a house back from the street, or in such a place where
the neighbors and the public in general will not be inconvenienced
by too much clamor.

If in spite of this any one be found in the future who, in an arbitrary manner and contrary to this decree, holds such prayer-
meetings with others assembled, he shall be subject to a fine of ten

Reichsthalers. He shall not be spared in any wise by the elders but shall be reported immediately to the city authorities.

XXXI. How The Protected-Jews Are To Conduct Themselves In Religious And Church Matters. . . .

Quarrels that occur actually in the synagogue because of Jewish ceremonies and synagogal customs are to be discussed and settled by the rabbi or vice-rabbi and the elders. According to circumstances they themselves may fine the offenders with a moderate money penalty. However they shall not proceed against any one with the ban and money fines that amount to more than five Reichsthalers, without the previous knowledge of the city authorities; such penalties shall not be imposed on any one by the rabbi alone nor even with the elders.

He shall not presumptuously undertake to make any real decision and settlement of a case in matters of secular law, for the rabbi and the elders have no right to real jurisdiction. On the contrary, matters of law must be referred to the proper court of justice. However, in matters in which Jews have to do with Jews and which come within the province of their rites, such as Jewish marriage-contracts and their validity in bankruptcy, determination of the heir in cases of succession to estates, which can only be settled by them through their Mosaic laws, we concede, for the present, some sort of legal jurisdiction to the rabbis and their learned assistant-judges. This also applies to other judicial acts such as wills, inventories, and appointment of guardians. The Jewish jurisdiction, however, is only in the form of arbitration. When the litigants are not satisfied with a decision they always have the privilege of referring their case back to the ordinary judges as a simple judicial case without respect to the statute of limitations. And the rabbis and the assistant-judges are herewith responsible when they do not proceed legally in matters of inventories, divisions of estates, and appointment of guardians. . . .

XXXII. Courts To Which The Protected-Jews Have Recourse In Civil And Criminal Cases. . . . Concerning The Admission Of Jews, Their Marriages, And The Drawing Up Of Their Letters Of Protection, Etc. . . .

XXXIII. Concerning The Observance Of This General-Patent For The Jews

In order that this general-patent for the Jews shall be contravened as little as possible, the War and Domains Offices of their respective Departments and the local commissaries (the tax-councils) shall watch Jewry very carefully in the cities of the provinces and see to it that the said general-patent is everywhere exactly followed. They are particularly to see that the fixed number of families, communal officials, and Jewish-owned homes in every town is not increased, that no one is admitted without our royal concession, and least of all that no unlicensed Jew be tolerated. For this reason nothing is to be undertaken or conceded by the magistrates on their own authority; nor shall any Jew be permitted to live in the rural districts or in open towns where there is no excise office. . . .

Final Injunction For The Right Observance Of These General Regulations For The Jews. . . .

So done and given at Berlin, the 17th of April, 1750.

FREDERICK.

THOMAS BABINGTON MACAULAY:

"[T]he Jewish religion is of all erroneous religions the least mischievous. There is not the slightest chance the Jewish religion will spread. The Jew does not wish to make proselytes." (1833)

Thomas Babington Macaulay (1800–1859) was a distinguished English historian and essayist of the nineteenth century. A precocious youngster, by the time he was eight Macaulay had already written a volume of history and several literary works. In 1818 he attended Trinity College, Cambridge, and afterward became a Fellow of the College. After a short period at the bar, Macaulay entered the House of Commons as member for the "pocket borough" of Calne. He supported the significant Reform Act of 1832, and in the first Reform Parliament, which met in January,

1833, Macaulay sat as one of two members for Leeds. Despite his service in the House and active participation in governmental affairs, Macaulay was able to accomplish a prodigious amount of literary work. In a period of less than two years, between 1831 and 1833, he wrote eight articles for the influential *Edinburgh Review* in addition to other writings and a ballad on the Armada. He is best known, however, for his *History*, the first two volumes of which appeared in December, 1848. Raised to a peerage in 1857, his failing health prevented more than an occasional appearance in the House of Lords. Macaulay's death two years later was greatly mourned by England's most distinguished figures, and he was buried in Westminster Abbey.

Macaulay's speech in favor of Jewish emancipation, here reprinted, was delivered April 17, 1833, in support of a *Bill for the Removal of Jewish Disabilities*. The Bill, in the form of a resolution submitted to the Committee of the Whole House of Commons, declared "That it is the opinion of this Committee that it is expedient to remove all civil disabilities at present existing with respect to His Majesty's subjects professing the Jewish religion, with the like exceptions as are provided with respect to His Majesty's subjects professing the Roman Catholic religion." Although the resolution was passed, it was not until 1860 that the special discriminations affecting Jews were finally removed.

A Speech on Jewish Emancipation

I recollect, and my honourable friend the Member for the University of Oxford will recollect, that when this subject was discussed three years ago, it was remarked, by one whom we both loved and whom we both regret, that the strength of the case of the Jews was a serious inconvenience to their advocate, for that it was hardly possible to make a speech for them without wearying the audience by repeating the truths which were universally admitted. If Sir James Mackintosh felt this difficulty when the question was first brought forward in this House, I may well despair of being able now to offer any arguments which have a pretence to novelty.

My honourable friend, the Member for the University of Oxford, began his speech by declaring that he had no intention of calling in question the principles of religious liberty. He utterly disclaims persecution, that is to say, persecution as defined by himself. It would, in his opinion, be persecution to hang a Jew, or to flay him, or to draw his teeth, or to imprison him, or to fine him; for every man who conducts himself peaceably has a right to his life and his limbs, to his personal liberty and his property. But it is not persecution, says my honourable friend, to exclude any individual or any class from office; for nobody has a right to office: in every country official appointments must be subject to such regulations as the supreme authority may choose to make; nor can any such regulations be reasonably complained of by any member of the society as unjust. He who obtains an office obtains it, not as matter of right, but as matter of favour. He who does not obtain an office is not wronged; he is only in that situation in which the vast majority of every community must necessarily be. There are in the United Kingdom five and twenty million Christians without places; and, if they do not complain, why should five and twenty thousand Jews complain of being in the same case? In this way my honourable friend has convinced himself that, as it would be most absurd in him and me to say that we are wronged because we are not Secretaries of State, so it is most absurd in the Jews to say that they are wronged because they are, as a people, excluded from public employment.

Now, surely my honourable friend cannot have considered to what conclusions his reasoning leads. Those conclusions are so monstrous that he would, I am certain, shrink from them. Does he really mean that it would not be wrong in the legislature to enact that no man should be a judge unless he weighed twelve stone, or that no man should sit in Parliament unless he were six feet high? We are about to bring in a bill for the government of India. Suppose that we were to insert in that bill a clause providing that no graduate of the University of Oxford should be Governor-General or Governor of any Presidency, would not my honourable friend cry out against such a clause as most unjust to the learned body which he represents? And would he think himself sufficiently answered by being told, in his own words, that the appointment to office is a mere matter of favour, and that to exclude an individual or a class from office is no injury? Surely, on consideration, he must admit that official appointments ought not to be subject to regulations purely arbitrary, to regulations for which no reason can be given but mere caprice, and that those who would exclude any class from public employment are bound to show some special reason for the exclusion.

My honourable friend has appealed to us as Christians. Let me

then ask him how he understands that great commandment which
comprises the law and the prophets. Can we be said to do unto
others as we would that they should do unto us if we wantonly
inflict on them even the smallest pain? As Christians, surely we are
bound to consider, first, whether, by excluding the Jews from all
public trust, we give them pain; and, secondly, whether it be necessary to give them that pain in order to avert some greater evil.
That by excluding them from public trust we inflict pain on them
my honourable friend will not dispute. As a Christian, therefore, he
is bound to relieve them from that pain, unless he can show, what
I am sure he has not yet shown, that it is necessary to the general
good that they should continue to suffer.

But where, he says, are you to stop, if once you admit into the
House of Commons people who deny the authority of the Gospels?
Will you let in a Mussulman? Will you let in a Parsee? Will you
let in a Hindoo, who worships a lump of stone with seven heads?
I will answer my honourable friend's question by another. Where
does he mean to stop? Is he ready to roast unbelievers at slow fires?
If not, let him tell us why: and I will engage to prove that his
reason is just as decisive against the intolerance which he thinks a
duty, as against the intolerance which he thinks a crime. Once admit
that we are bound to inflict pain on a man because he is not of our
religion; and where are you to stop? Why stop at the point fixed
by my honourable friend rather than at the point fixed by the honourable Member for Oldham*, who would make the Jews incapable
of holding land? And why stop at the point fixed by the honourable
Member for Oldham rather than at the point which would have
been fixed by a Spanish Inquisitor of the sixteenth century? When
once you enter on a course of persecution, I defy you to find any
reason for making a halt till you have reached the extreme point.
When my honourable friend tells us that he will allow the Jews to
possess property to any amount, but that he will not allow them to
possess the smallest political power, he holds contradictory language. Property is power. The honourable Member for Oldham sees
very clearly that it is impossible to deprive a man of political power
if you suffer him to be the proprietor of half a county, and therefore very consistently proposes to confiscate the landed estates of
the Jews.

* William Cobbett (1762–1835).

But even the honourable Member for Oldham does not go far enough. He has not proposed to confiscate the personal property of the Jews. Yet it is perfectly certain that any Jew who has a million may easily make himself very important in the state. By such steps we pass from official power to landed property, and from landed property to personal property, and from property to liberty, and from liberty to life. In truth, those persecutors who use the rack and the stake have much to say for themselves. They are convinced that their end is good; and it must be admitted that they employ means which are not unlikely to attain the end. Religious dissent has repeatedly been put down by sanguinary persecution. In that way the Albigenses were put down. In that way Protestantism was suppressed in Spain and Italy, so that it has never since reared its head. But I defy anybody to produce an instance in which disabilities such as we are now considering have produced any other effect than that of making the sufferers angry and obstinate. My honourable friend should either persecute to some purpose, or not persecute at all.

He dislikes the word persecution, I know. He will not admit that the Jews are persecuted. And yet I am confident that he would rather be sent to the King's Bench Prison for three months, or be fined a hundred pounds, than be subject to the disabilities under which the Jews lie. How can he then say that to impose such disabilities is not persecution and that to fine and imprison is persecution? All his reasoning consists in drawing arbitrary lines. What he does not wish to inflict he calls persecution. What he does wish to inflict he will not call persecution. What he takes from the Jews he calls political power. What he is too good-natured to take from the Jews he will not call political power. The Jew must not sit in Parliament: but he may be the proprietor of all the ten-pound houses in a borough. He may have more fifty-pound tenants than any peer in the kingdom. He may give the voters treats to please their palates, and hire bands of gipsies to break their heads, as if he were a Christian and a Marquess.

All the rest of the system is of a piece. The Jew may be a juryman, but not a judge. He may decide issues of fact, but not issues of law. He may give a hundred thousand pounds damages; but he may not in the most trivial case grant a new trial. He may rule the money-market: he may influence the exchanges: he may be summoned to congresses of Emperors and Kings. Great potentates, instead of negotiating a loan with him by tying him in a chair and pulling out his grinders, may treat with him as with a great potentate, and may postpone the declaring of war or the signing of a treaty till they have conferred with him. All this is as it should be: but he must not be a Privy Councillor. He must not be called Right Honourable, for that is political power.

And who is it that we are trying to cheat in this way? Even Omniscience. Yes, Sir; we have been gravely told that the Jews are under the divine displeasure, and that if we give them political power, God will visit us in judgment. Do we then think that God cannot distinguish between substance and form? Does not He know that, while we withhold from the Jews the semblance and name of political power, we suffer them to possess the substance? The plain truth is that my honourable friend is drawn in one direction by his opinions, and in a directly opposite direction by his excellent heart. He halts between two opinions. He tries to make a compromise between principles which admit of no compromise. He goes a certain way in intolerance. Then he stops, without being able to give a reason for stopping. But I know the reason. It is his humanity. Those who formerly dragged the Jew at a horse's tail, and singed his beard with blazing furze-bushes, were much worse men than my honourable friend; but they were more consistent than he.

It has been said that it would be monstrous to see a Jew judge try a man for blasphemy. In my opinion it is monstrous to see any judge try a man for blasphemy under the present law. But, if the law on that subject were in a sound state, I do not see why a conscientious Jew might not try a blasphemer. Every man, I think, ought to be at liberty to discuss the evidences of religion; but no man ought to be at liberty to force on the unwilling ears and eyes of others sounds and sights which must cause annoyance and irritation. The distinction is clear. I think it wrong to punish a man for selling Paine's *Age of Reason* in a backshop to those who choose to buy, or for delivering a Deistical lecture in a private room to those who choose to listen. But if a man exhibits at a window in the Strand a hideous caricature of that which is an object of awe and adoration to nine hundred and ninety-nine out of every thousand of the people who pass up and down that great thoroughfare; if a man in a place of public resort applies opprobrious epithets to names held in reverence by all Christians; such a man ought, in my

opinion, to be severely punished, not for differing from us in opion-
ion, but for committing a nuisance which gives us pain and disgust.
He is no more entitled to outrage our feelings by obtruding his
impiety on us, and to say that he is exercising his right of discussion, than to establish a yard for butchering horses close to our
houses, and to say that he is exercising his right of property, or to
run naked up and down the public streets, and to say that he is
exercising his right of locomotion. But he must use all his rights
so as not to infringe the rights of others.

These, Sir, are the principles on which I would frame the law
of blasphemy; and if the law were so framed, I am at a loss to
understand why a Jew might not enforce it as well as a Christian.
I am not a Roman Catholic; but if I were a judge at Malta, I should
have no scruple about punishing a bigoted Protestant who should
burn the Pope in effigy before the eyes of thousands of Roman
Catholics. I am not a Mussulman; but if I were a judge in India,
I should have no scruple about punishing a Christian who should
pollute a mosque. Why, then, should I doubt that a Jew, raised by
his ability, learning, and integrity to the judicial bench, would deal
properly with any person who, in a Christian country, should insult
the Christian religion?

But, says my honourable friend, it has been prophesied that the
Jews are to be wanderers on the face of the earth, and that they are
not to mix on terms of equality with the people of the countries in
which they sojourn. Now, Sir, I am confident that I can demonstrate
that this is not the sense of any prophecy which is part of Holy
Writ. For it is an undoubted fact that, in the United States of
America, Jewish citizens do possess all the privileges possessed by
Christian citizens. Therefore, if the prophecies mean that the Jews
never shall, during their wanderings, be admitted by other nations
to equal participation of political rights, the prophecies are false.
Therefore their meaning cannot be that which is attributed to them
by my honourable friend.

Another objection which has been made to the motion is that the
Jews look forward to the coming of a great deliverer, to their return
to Palestine, to the rebuilding of their Temple, to the revival of
their ancient worship, and that therefore they will always consider
England, not their country, but merely as their place of exile. But,
surely, Sir, it would be the grossest ignorance of human nature to

imagine that the anticipation of an event which is to happen at some time altogether indefinite, of an event which has been vainly expected during many centuries, of an event which even those who confidently expect that it will happen do not confidently expect that they or their children or their grandchildren will see, can ever occupy the minds of men to such a degree as to make them regardless of what is near and present and certain. Indeed Christians, as well as Jews, believe that the existing order of things will come to an end. Many Christians believe that Jesus will visibly reign on earth during a thousand years. Expositors of prophecy have gone so far as to fix the year when the Millennial period is to commence. The prevailing opinion is, I think, in favour of the year 1866; but according to some commentators, the time is close at hand. Are we to exclude all Millenarians from Parliament and office, on the ground that they are impatiently looking forward to the miraculous monarchy which is to supersede the present dynasty and the present constitution of England, and that therefore they cannot be heartily loyal to King William?

In one important point, Sir, my honourable friend, the Member for the University of Oxford, must acknowledge that the Jewish religion is of all erroneous religions the least mischievous. There is not the slightest chance that the Jewish religion will spread. The Jew does not wish to make proselytes. He may be said to reject them. He thinks it almost culpable in one who does not belong to his race to presume to belong to his religion. It is therefore not strange that a conversion from Christianity to Judaism should be a rarer occurrence than a total eclipse of the sun.

There was one distinguished convert in the last century, Lord George Gordon; and the history of his conversion deserves to be remembered. For if ever there was a proselyte of whom a proselytising sect would have been proud, it was Lord George; not only because he was a man of high birth and rank; not only because he had been a member of the legislature; but also because he had been distinguished by the intolerance, nay, the ferocity, of his zeal for his own form of Christianity. But was he allured into the synagogue? Was he even welcomed to it? No, Sir; he was coldly and reluctantly permitted to share the reproach and suffering of the chosen people; but he was sternly shut out from their privileges. He underwent the painful rite which their law enjoins. But when, on his death-bed, he begged hard to be buried among them according to their ceremonial, he was told that his request could not be granted. I understand that cry of "Hear." It reminds me that one of the arguments against this motion is that the Jews are an unsocial people, that they draw close to each other, and stand aloof from strangers. Really, Sir, it is amusing to compare the manner in which the question of Catholic emancipation was argued formerly by some gentlemen with the manner in which the question of Jew emancipation is argued by the same gentlemen now. When the question was about Catholic emancipation, the cry was, "See how restless, how versatile, how encroaching, how insinuating, is the spirit of the Church of Rome. See how her priests compass earth and sea to make one proselyte, how indefatigably they toil, how attentively they study the weak and strong parts of every character, how skillfully they employ literature, arts, sciences, as engines for the propagation of their faith. You find them in every region and under every disguise, collating manuscripts in the Bodleian, fixing telescopes in the observatory of Pekin, teaching the use of the plough and the spinning wheel to the savages of Paraguay. Will you give power to the members of a Church so busy, so aggressive, so insatiable?" Well, now the question is about people who never try to seduce any stranger to join them, and who do not wish anybody to be of their faith who is not also of their blood. And now you exclaim, "Will you give power to the members of a sect which remains sullenly apart from other sects, which does not invite, nay, which hardly even admits neophytes?"

The truth is, that bigotry will never want a pretence. Whatever the sect be which it is proposed to tolerate, the peculiarities of that sect will, for the time, be pronounced by intolerant men to be the most odious and dangerous that can be conceived. As to the Jews, that they are unsocial as respects religion is true; and so much the better: for, surely, as Christians, we cannot wish that they should bestir themselves to pervert us from our own faith. But that the Jews would be unsocial members of the civil community, if the civil community did its duty by them, has never been proved. My right honourable friend who made the motion which we are discussing has produced a great body of evidence to show that they have been grossly misrepresented; and that evidence has not been refuted by my honourable friend the Member for the University of Oxford.

But what if it were true that the Jews are unsocial? What if it were true that they do not regard England as their country? Would not the treatment which they have undergone explain and excuse their antipathy to the society in which they live? Has not similar antipathy often been felt by persecuted Christians to the society which persecuted them? While the bloody code of Elizabeth was enforced against the English Roman Catholics, what was the patriotism of Roman Catholics? Oliver Cromwell said that in his time they were Espaniolised. At a later period it might have been said that they were Gallicised. It was the same with the Calvinists. What more deadly enemies had France in the days of Louis the Fourteenth than the persecuted Huguenots? But would any rational man infer from these facts that either the Roman Catholic as such, or the Calvinist as such, is incapable of loving the land of his birth? If England were now invaded by Roman Catholics, how many English Roman Catholics would go over to the invader? If France were now attacked by a Protestant enemy, how many French Protestants would lend them help? Why not try what effect would be produced on the Jews by that tolerant policy which has made the English Roman Catholic a good Englishman and the French Calvinist a good Frenchman?

Another charge has been brought against the Jews, not by my honourable friend the Member for the University of Oxford—he has too much learning and too much good feeling to make such a charge—but by the honourable Member for Oldham, who has, I am sorry to see, quitted his place. The honourable Member for Oldham tells us that the Jews are naturally a mean race, a sordid race, a money-getting race; that they are averse to all honourable callings; that they neither sow nor reap; that they have neither flocks nor herds; that usury is the only pursuit for which they are fit; that they are destitute of all elevated and amiable sentiments.

Such, Sir, has in every age been the reasoning of bigots. They never fail to plead in justification of persecution the vices which persecution has engendered. England has been to the Jews less than half a country; and we revile them because they do not feel for England more than a half patriotism. We treat them as slaves, and wonder that they do not regard us as brethren. We drive them to mean occupations, and then reproach them for not embracing honourable professions. We long forbade them to possess land; and we complain that they chiefly occupy themselves in trade. We shut them out from all the paths of ambition; and then we despise them for taking refuge in avarice. During many ages we have, in all our dealings with them, abused our immense superiority of force; and then we are disgusted because they have recourse to that cunning which is the natural and universal defence of the weak against the violence of the strong.

But were they always a mere money-changing, money-getting money-hoarding race? Nobody knows better than my honourable friend the Member for the University of Oxford that there is nothing in their national character which unfits them for the highest duties of citizens. He knows that, in the infancy of civilisation, when our island was as savage as New Guinea, when letters and arts were still unknown to Athens, when scarcely a thatched hut stood on what was afterwards the site of Rome, this condemned people had their fenced cities and cedar palaces, their splendid Temple, their fleets of merchant ships, their schools of sacred learning, their great statesmen and soldiers, their natural philosophers, their historians and their poets. What nation ever contended more manfully against overwhelming odds for its independence and religion? What nation ever, in its last agonies, gave such signal proofs of what may be accomplished by a brave despair? And if, in the course of many centuries, the oppressed descendants of warriors and sages have degenerated from the qualities of their fathers, if, while excluded from the blessings of law, and bowed under the yoke of slavery, they have contracted some of the vices of outlaws and of slaves, shall we consider this as matter of reproach to them? Shall we not rather consider it as matter of shame and remorse to ourselves?

Let us do justice to them. Let us open to them the door of the House of Commons. Let us open to them every career in which ability and energy can be displayed. Till we have done this, let us not presume to say that there is no genius among the countrymen of Isaiah, no heroism among the descendants of the Maccabees.

Sir, in supporting the motion of my honourable friend, I am, I firmly believe, supporting the honour and the interests of the Christian religion. I should think that I insulted that religion if I said that it cannot stand unaided by intolerant laws. Without such laws it was established, and without such laws it may be maintained. It triumphed over the superstitions of the most refined and of the most savage nations, over the graceful mythology of Greece and the bloody idolatry of the Northern forests. It prevailed over the power and policy of the Roman empire. It tamed the barbarians by whom that empire was overthrown. But all these victories were gained not by the help of intolerance, but in spite of the opposition of intolerance.

The whole history of Christianity proves that she has little indeed to fear from persecution as a foe, but much to fear from persecution as an ally. May she long continue to bless our country with her benignant influence, strong in her sublime philosophy, strong in her spotless morality, strong in those internal and external evidences to which the most powerful and comprehensive of human intellects have yielded assent, the last solace of those who have outlived every earthly hope, the last restraint of those who are raised above every earthly fear! But let not us, mistaking her character and her interests, fight the battle of truth with the weapons of error, and endeavour to support by oppression that religion which first taught the human race the great lesson of universal charity.

FRIEDRICH WILHELM NIETZSCHE:

"The Christian, that ultima ratio *of lying, is the Jew all over again—he is* threefold *the Jew." (1895)*

Friedrich Wilhelm Nietzsche (1844–1900) was a German philosopher who was influenced, during his early years, by Schopenhauer and Richard Wagner. Beginning his studies as a theological student at the University of Bonn, Nietzsche quickly abandoned theology (and Christianity itself) to devote himself entirely to the writing and teaching of philosophy. In 1869 he was appointed professor at the University of Basle, but ten years

From F. W. Nietzsche, *The Antichrist* (1895), translated by H. L. Mencken (New York: Alfred A. Knopf, 1920), pp. 78–90, 124–128; Copyright 1920 by Alfred A. Knopf, Inc.

later he was forced to resign his post because of poor health. He experienced a complete mental and physical breakdown in 1888–1889, the result, in part, of the rejection of his doctrines by the majority of scholars in Germany and elsewhere.

Nietzsche's best known book, *Thus Spake Zarathustra* (1883–1885), proclaimed the gospel of the Superman and the super race. According to Nietzsche, the world had been poisoned by an effete Christianity which he regarded as essentially Jewish in origin and nature. Although the Jews had once been a vigorous and self-reliant people, they eventually became demoralized by embracing values that emphasized humility, caution, mendacity, and adaptability. Through Christianity, the morality of the "subject race" (the Jews) had become the morality of the civilized world. Thus all that was decadent in Judaism became incorporated in Christianity. What was needed, therefore, was a new race of men who were capable of rejecting Judaic-Christianity morality in favor of bolder, more virile principles. The new race, Nietzsche believed, would ultimately produce Superman, and he made it clear that he was writing for this new race of men "which does not yet exist: for the lords of the earth. . . ."

The following selection is from Nietzsche's *The Antichrist,* first published in 1895.

The Jews are the most remarkable people in the history of the world, for when they were confronted with the question, to be or not to be, they chose, with perfectly unearthly deliberation, to be *at any price:* this price involved a radical *falsification* of all nature, of all naturalness, of all reality, of the whole inner world, as well as of the outer. They put themselves *against* all those conditions under which, hitherto, a people had been able to live, or had even been *permitted* to live; out of themselves they evolved an idea which stood in direct opposition to *natural* conditions—one by one they distorted religion, civilization, morality, history and psychology until each became a *contradiction* of its *natural significance.* We meet with the same phenomenon later on, in an incalculably exaggerated form, but only as a copy: the Christian church, put beside the "people of God," shows a complete lack of any claim to originality. Precisely for this reason the Jews are the most *fateful* people in the history of the world: their influence has so falsified the reasoning of mankind in this matter that today the Christian can cherish anti-Semitism without realizing that it is no more than the *final consequence of Judaism.*

In my "Genealogy of Morals" I give the first psychological explanation of the concepts underlying those two antithetical things, a noble morality and a *ressentiment* morality, the second of which is a mere product of the denial of the former. The Judaeo-Christian moral system belongs to the second division, and in every detail. In order to be able to say Nay to everything representing an *ascending* evolution of life—that is, to well-being, to power, to beauty, to self-approval—the instincts of *ressentiment*, here become downright genius, had to invent an *other* world in which the *acceptance of life* appeared as the most evil and abominable thing imaginable. Psychologically, the Jews are a people gifted with the very strongest vitality, so much so that when they found themselves facing impossible conditions of life they chose voluntarily, and with a profound talent for self-preservation, the side of all those instincts which make for *décadence*—not as if mastered by them, but as if detecting in them a power by which "the world" could be *defied*. The Jews are the very opposite of *décadents*: they have simply been forced into *appearing* in that guise, and with a degree of skill approaching the *non plus ultra* of histrionic genius they have managed to put themselves at the head of all *décadent* movements (—for example, the Christianity of Paul—), and so make of them something stronger than any party frankly saying *Yes* to life. To the sort of men who reach out for power under Judaism and Christianity,—that is to say, to the *priestly* class—*décadence* is no more than a means to an end. Men of this sort have a vital interest in making mankind sick, and in confusing the values of "good" and "bad," "true" and "false" in a manner that is not only dangerous to life, but also slanders it.

The history of Israel is invaluable as a typical history of an attempt to *denaturize* all natural values: I point to five facts which bear this out. Originally, and above all in the time of the monarchy, Israel maintained the *right* attitude of things, which is to say, the natural attitude. Its Jahveh was an expression of its consciousness of power, its joy in itself, its hopes for itself: to him the Jews looked for victory and salvation and through him they expected nature to give them whatever was necessary to their existence—above all, rain. Jahveh is the god of Israel, and *consequently* the god of justice: this is the logic of every race that has power in its hands and a good conscience in the use of it. In the religious ceremonial of the Jews both aspects of this self-approval stand revealed. The nation is grateful for the high destiny that has enabled it to obtain dominion; it is grateful for the benign procession of the seasons, and for the good fortune attending its herds and its crops.—This view of things remained an ideal for a long while, even after it had been robbed of validity by tragic blows: anarchy within and the Assyrian without. But the people still retained, as a projection of their highest yearnings, that vision of a king who was at once a gallant warrior and an upright judge—a vision best visualized in the typical prophet (*i.e.*, critic and satirist of the moment), Isaiah.—But every hope remained unfulfilled. The old god no longer *could* do what he used to do. He ought to have been abandoned. But what actually happened? Simply this: the conception of him was *changed*—the conception of him was *denaturized;* this was the price that had to be paid for keeping him.—Jahveh, the god of "justice"—he is in accord with Israel *no more,* he no longer visualizes the national egoism; he is now a god only conditionally. . . . The public notion of this god now becomes merely a weapon in the hands of clerical agitators, who interpret all happiness as a reward and all unhappiness as a punishment for obedience or disobedience to him, for "sin": that most fraudulent of all imaginable interpretations, whereby a "moral order of the world" is set up, and the fundamental concepts, "cause" and "effect," are stood on their heads. Once natural causation has been swept out of the world by doctrines of reward and punishment some sort of *un*natural causation becomes necessary: and all other varieties of the denial of nature follow it. A god who *demands*—in place of a god who helps, who gives counsel, who is at bottom merely a name for every happy inspiration of courage and self-reliance. . . . *Morality* is no longer a reflection of the conditions which make for the sound life and development of the people; it is no longer the primary life-instinct; instead it has become abstract and in opposition to life—a fundamental perversion of the fancy, an "evil eye" on all things. *What* is Jewish, *what* is Christian morality? Chance robbed of its innocence; unhappiness polluted with the idea of "sin"; well-being represented as a danger, as a "temptation"; a physiological disorder produced by the canker worm of conscience. . . .

The concept of god falsified; the concept of morality falsified;—but even here Jewish priest-craft did not stop. The whole history of

Israel ceased to be of any value: out with it!—These priests accomplished that miracle of falsification of which a great part of the Bible is the documentary evidence; with a degree of contempt unparalleled, and in the face of all tradition and all historical reality, they translated the past of their people into *religious* terms, which is to say, they converted it into an idiotic mechanism of salvation, whereby all offences against Jahveh were punished and all devotion to him was rewarded. We would regard this act of historical falsification as something far more shameful if familiarity with the *ecclesiastical* interpretation of history for thousands of years had not blunted our inclinations for uprightness *in historicis*. And the philosophers support the church: the *lie* about a "moral order of the world" runs through the whole of philosophy, even the newest. What is the meaning of a "moral order of the world"? That there is a thing called the will of God which, once and for all time, determines what man ought to do and what he ought not to do; that the worth of a people, or of an individual thereof, is to be measured by the extent to which they or he obey this will of God; that the destinies of a people or of an individual are *controlled* by this will of God, which rewards or punishes according to the degree of obedience manifested.—In place of all that pitiable lie *reality* has this to say: the *priest*, a parasitical variety of man who can exist only at the cost of every sound view of life, takes the name of God in vain: he calls that state of human society in which he himself determines the value of all things "the kingdom of God"; he calls the means whereby that state of affairs is attained "the will of God"; with cold-blooded cynicism he estimates all peoples, all ages and all individuals by the extent of their subservience or opposition to the power of the priestly order. One observes him at work: under the hand of the Jewish priesthood the *great* age of Israel became an age of decline; the Exile, with its long series of misfortunes, was transformed into a *punishment* for that great age—during which priests had not yet come into existence. Out of the powerful and *wholly free* heroes of Israel's history they fashioned, according to their changing needs, either wretched bigots and hypocrites or men entirely "godless." They reduced every great event to the idiotic formula: "obedient *or* disobedient to God."—They went a step further: the "will of God" (in other words some means necessary for preserving the power of the priests) had to be *determined*—and to this end they had to have a "revelation." In plain English, a gigantic literary fraud had to be perpetrated, and "holy scriptures" had to be concocted—and so, with the utmost hierarchical pomp, and days of penance and much lamentation over the long days of "sin" now ended, they were duly published. The "will of God," it appears, had long stood like a rock; the trouble was that mankind had neglected the "holy scriptures." . . . But the "will of God" had already been revealed to Moses. . . . What happened? Simply this: the priest had formulated, once and for all time and with the strictest meticulousness, what tithes were to be paid to him, from the largest to the smallest (—not forgetting the most appetizing cuts of meat, for the priest is a great consumer of beefsteaks); in brief, he let it be known just *what he wanted,* what "the will of God" was. . . . From this time forward things were so arranged that the priest became *indispensable everywhere;* at all the great natural events of life, at birth, at marriage, in sickness, at death, not to say at the *"sacrifice"* (that is, at meal-times), the holy parasite put in his appearance, and proceeded to *denaturize* it—in his own phrase, to "sanctify" it. . . . For this should be noted: that every natural habit, every natural institution (the state, the administration of justice, marriage, the care of the sick and of the poor), everything demanded by the life-instinct, in short, everything that has any value *in itself,* is reduced to absolute worthlessness and even made the *reverse* of valuable by the parasitism of priests (or, if you chose, by the "moral order of the world"). The fact requires a sanction—a power to *grant values* becomes necessary, and the only way it can create such values is by denying nature. . . . The priest depreciates and desecrates nature: it is only at this price that he can exist at all.—Disobedience to God, which actually means to the priest, to "the law," now gets the name of "sin"; the means prescribed for "reconciliation with God" are, of course, precisely the means which bring one most effectively under the thumb of the priest; he alone can "save." . . . Psychologically considered, "sins" are indispensable to every society organized on an ecclesiastical basis; they are the only reliable weapons of power; the priest *lives* upon sins; it is necessary to him that there be "sinning." . . . Prime axiom: "God forgiveth him that repenteth"—in plain English, *him that submitteth to the priest.*

Christianity sprang from a soil so corrupt that on it everything natural, every natural value, every *reality* was opposed by the deepest instincts of the ruling class—it grew up as a sort of war to the death upon reality, and as such it has never been surpassed. The "holy people," who had adopted priestly values and priestly names for all things, and who, with a terrible logical consistency, had rejected everything of the earth as "unholy," "worldly," "sinful"—this people put its instinct into a final formula that was logical to the point of self-annihilation: as *Christianity* it actually denied even the last form of reality, the "holy people," the "chosen people," *Jewish* reality itself. The phenomenon is of the first order of importance: the small insurrectionary movement which took the name of Jesus of Nazareth is simply the Jewish instinct *redivivus*—in other words, it is the priestly instinct come to such a pass that it can no longer endure the priest as a fact; it is the discovery of a state of existence even more fantastic than any before it, of a vision of life even more *unreal* than that necessary to an ecclesiastical organization. Christianity actually *denies* the church. . . .

I am unable to determine what was the target of the insurrection said to have been led (whether rightly or *wrongly*) by Jesus, if it was not the Jewish church—"church" being here used in exactly the same sense that the word has today. It was an insurrection against the "good and just," against the "prophets of Israel," against the whole hierarchy of society—*not* against corruption, but against caste, privilege, order, formalism. It was *unbelief* in "superior men," a Navy flung at everything that priests and theologians stood for. But the hierarchy that was called into question, if only for an instant, by this movement was the structure of piles which, above everything, was necessary to the safety of the Jewish people in the midst of the "waters"—it represented their *last* possibility of survival; it was the final *residuum* of their independent political existence; an attack upon it was an attack upon the most profound national instinct, the most powerful national will to live, that has ever appeared on earth. This saintly anarchist, who aroused the people of the abyss, the outcasts and "sinners," the Chandala of Judaism, to rise in revolt against the established order of things—and in language which, if the Gospels are to be credited, would get him sent to Siberia today —this man was certainly a political criminal, at least in so far as it was possible to be one in so *absurdly unpolitical* a community. This is what brought him to the cross: the proof thereof is to be found in the inscription that was put upon the cross. He died for his *own* sins—there is not the slightest ground for believing, no matter how often it is asserted, that he died for the sins of others.—

—The gospels are invaluable as evidence of the corruption that was already persistent *within* the primitive community. That which Paul, with the cynical logic of a rabbi, later developed to a conclusion was at bottom merely a process of decay that had begun with the death of the Saviour.—These gospels cannot be read too carefully; difficulties lurk behind every word. I confess—I hope it will not be held against me—that it is precisely for this reason that they offer first-rate joy to a psychologist—as the *opposite* of all merely naïve corruption, as refinement *par excellence,* as an artistic triumph in psychological corruption. The gospels, in fact, stand alone. The Bible as a whole is not to be compared to them. Here we are among Jews: this is the *first* thing to be borne in mind if we are not to lose the thread of the matter. This positive genius for conjuring up a delusion of personal "holiness" unmatched anywhere else, either in books or by men; this elevation of fraud in word and attitude to the level of an *art*—all this is not an accident due to the chance talents of an individual, or to any violation of nature. The thing responsible is *race.* The whole of Judaism appears in Christianity as the art of concocting holy lies, and there, after many centuries of earnest Jewish training and hard practice of Jewish technic, the business comes to the stage of mastery. The Christian, that *ultima ratio* of lying, is the Jew all over again—he is *threefold* the Jew. . . . The underlying will to make use only of such concepts, symbols and attitudes as fit into priestly practice, the instinctive repudiation of every *other* mode of thought, and every other method of estimating values and utilities—this is not only tradition, it is *inheritance:* only as an inheritance is it able to operate with the force of nature. The whole of mankind, even the best minds of the best ages (with one exception, perhaps hardly human—), have permitted themselves to be deceived. The gospels have been read as a *book of innocence* . . . surely no small indication of the high skill with which the trick has been done.—Of course, if we could actually *see* these astounding bigots and bogus saints, even if only for an instant, the farce would come to an end,—and it is precisely because *I* cannot read a word of theirs without seeing their attitudinizing that *I have made an end of them.* . . . I simply cannot endure the way they have of rolling up their eyes.—For the majority, happily enough, books are mere *literature.*—Let us not be led astray: they say "judge not," and yet they condemn to hell whoever stands in their way. In letting God sit in judgment they judge themselves; in glorifying God they glorify themselves; in *demanding* that every one show the virtues which they themselves happen to be capable of—still more, which they *must* have in order to remain on top—they assume the grand air of men struggling for virtue, of men engaging in a war that virtue may prevail. "We live, we die, we sacrifice ourselves *for the good*" (—"the truth," "the light," "the kingdom of God"): in point of fact, they simply do what they cannot help doing. Forced, like hypocrites, to be sneaky, to hide in corners, to slink along in the shadows, they convert their necessity into a *duty:* it is on grounds of duty that they account for their lives of humility, and that humility becomes merely one more proof of their piety. . . . Ah, that humble, chaste, charitable brand of fraud! "Virtue itself shall bear witness for us." . . . One may read the gospels as books of *moral* seduction: these petty folks fasten themselves to morality—they know the uses of morality! Morality is the best of all devices for leading mankind *by the nose!*—The fact is that the conscious conceit of the chosen here disguises itself as modesty: it is in this way that *they,* the "community," the "good and just," range themselves, once and for always, on one side, the side of "the truth"—and the rest of mankind, "the world," on the other. . . . In *that* we observe the most fatal sort of megalomania that the earth has ever seen: little abortions of bigots and liars began to claim exclusive rights in the concepts of "God," "the truth," "the light," "the spirit," "love," "wisdom" and "life," as if these things were synonyms of themselves and thereby they sought to fence themselves off from the "world"; little super-Jews, ripe for some sort of madhouse, turned values upside down in order to meet *their* notions, just as if the Christian were the meaning, the salt, the standard and even the *last judgment* of all the rest. . . . The whole disaster was only made possible by the fact that there already existed in the world a similar megalomania, allied to this one in race, to wit, the *Jewish:* once a chasm began to yawn between Jews and Judaeo-Christians, the latter had no choice but to employ the self-preservative measures that the Jewish instinct had devised, even *against* the Jews themselves, whereas the Jews had employed them only against non-Jews. The Christian is simply a Jew of the "reformed" confession.—

WERNER SOMBART:

*"Liberalism we have already shown to be
a near relative of Judaism, and so we
have the kindred trio of Capitalism,
Liberalism, and Judaism." (1911)*

Werner Sombart (1863–1941) was a German political economist who specialized in the analysis of modern capitalism. A professor first at the University of Breslau and eventually at the University of Berlin, Sombart during his early years was a socialist, and at one time wrote a biography of Karl Marx. When the Nazi movement began to flourish in Germany, he joined it and became one of its foremost academic apologists. In a book, *German Socialism*, published in 1934, Sombart justified the exclusion of Jews from German life on the grounds that capitalism was essentially an expression of the "Hebraic spirit."

Sombart's earlier book, *The Jews and Modern Capitalism* (1911), anticipated the later one in arguing that Judaism and capitalism were basically synonymous. Capitalism, for Sombart, was the offspring, so to speak, of the marriage between Jewish religion and the Jewish character structure that had been created by the conditions of nomadic life. Regarding capitalism as alien to Nordic culture, Sombart believed that the "commercial spirit" of the Jews was responsible not only for the rise of capitalism, but for the survival of the Jews in hostile environments. Sombart's thesis in *The Jews and Modern Capitalism*, however exaggerated or distorted, was not overtly anti-Semitic, but it was widely used by anti-Semites, and played a prominent role in Nazi propaganda.

A portion of *The Jews and Modern Capitalism* is reprinted in the following selection.

If we think for a moment of human history we must needs construct for ourselves the hypothesis of a sort of "collective soul."

From Werner Sombart, *The Jews and Modern Capitalism* (1911), translated by M. Epstein (Glencoe, Illinois: The Free Press, 1951), pp. 253–278.

When, for example, we talk of the Jewish religion we are bound to connect it with the Jewish people whose genius gave it birth. Or, when we say the Jews had an influence on modern economic development, it follows surely that there must have been something essentially Jewish that brought it about. Otherwise we might as well assert that it would have made no difference to the economic history of Western Europe if Eskimos had taken the place of Jews, or perhaps even gorillas would have done equally well!

This *reductio ad absurdum* shows plainly enough that there must be some specifically Jewish characteristic. But let us consider the matter from a slightly different point of view. Let us glance at the objective circumstances in the Jewish aptitude for modern capitalism. There was first, as we have seen, the dispersion of the Jews over a wide area. Now without recourse to subjective forces the Diaspora can be as little explained as the effects of the Diaspora. And one thing is evident. The dispersion of a people in itself does not necessarily have either economic or cultural results; nay, very often dispersion may lead to fusion and ultimate disappearance.

It has been claimed—and with truth—that it was the dispersion of the Jews which fitted them to become intermediaries. Granted, but did it also tend to make of them negotiators and private advisers of princes, callings which have from time immemorial been the stepping-stones of the interpreter to higher posts? Were the capacities essential to these new offices not inherent in the Jews themselves?

We have admitted that the dispersion of the Jews was responsible for no little of their success in international commerce and credit. But is not the postulate to this success the fact that the Jews everywhere kept together? What would have happened if, like so many other scattered races, they had not maintained their bonds of union?

Lastly, let us not forget that the Jews came among just those peoples who happened to be mature enough to receive capitalism. But even so, if Jewish influence was strong (and it is so still) in Holland, in England, in Germany, in Austria-Hungary—stronger far than their influence on the Spaniards, Italians, Greeks or Arabs—it was in a large measure due to the contrasts between them and their hosts. For it would seem that the more slow-witted, the more thick-skulled, the more ignorant of business a people is, the more effective is Jewish influence on their economic life. And can this be satisfactorily accounted for except through special Jewish peculiarities?

No matter what was the origin of their innate dissimilarity from their hosts, the salient point is that this strangeness should have obtained lasting influence in economic life. Once more it is impossible to fathom this without the assumption of inherent Jewish characteristics. That a people or a tribe is hated and persecuted does not furnish sufficient reason for spurring them on to redoubled efforts in their activities. On the contrary, in most cases this contempt and ill-treatment but serve to destroy morals and initiative. Only where man is possessed of exceptional qualities do these become, under the stress of circumstance, the source of regenerated energy.

Again, look at their semi-citizenship. Does not the identical argument hold good here also? It is so obvious as to become almost a truism. Nowhere did the Jews enjoy the same advantages as their fellow-citizens, and yet everywhere they achieved economically much more than the rest of the population. There can be but one explanation for this—the specifically Jewish characteristics.

On the other hand, the legal position of the Jews varied in different countries and at different times. In some States they were allowed to engage in certain occupations; in others these same occupations were forbidden them; in others again, such as England, they were on a perfectly equal footing with the rest of the people in this respect. And yet they devoted themselves almost everywhere to particular callings. In England and America they began their commercial mission by becoming bullion-merchants or storekeepers. And can this be accounted for in any other way than by once more pointing to their peculiar characteristics?

As for the wealth of the Jews, that alone will hardly suffice to explain their great achievements in the sphere of economic activities. A man who possesses vast sums must have a number of intellectual qualities in addition, if his money is to be usefully employed in the capitalistic sense. That surely requires no proof.

Jewish characteristics must therefore exist. It remains only to discover what they are.

Our first thought of the Jews as a unit will naturally be associated with their religion. But before we proceed another step I should like to premise that on the one hand I shall limit the group lumped together under the Jewish religion, and on the other hand, I shall enlarge it. I shall limit it by only considering the Jews since their expulsion from Spain and Portugal, that is, from the end of the Middle Ages. I shall enlarge it by including within the circle of my observations the descendants of Jews, even if they themselves have left the faith.

Moreover, I should like to touch upon the arguments urged against the existence of Jewish peculiarities.

(1) It has been remarked that the Jews of Western Europe and America have to a large extent assimilated with the peoples among whom they dwell. This need not be denied, even if specifically Jewish characteristics were as clear as daylight. Is it not possible for social groups to intermingle? A man may be a German, have all the characteristics of a German, and yet be an individual in the group "international proletariat!" Or take another instance. Are not the German Swiss at one and the same time Swiss and German?

(2) The Jews in the Diaspora, it is maintained, are not a "nation" or a "people" in the commonly accepted meaning of the term, since they are not a political, cultural or linguistic community. The reply to this objection is that there are many other qualifications besides those mentioned (e.g., a common origin) which must be considered. But speaking generally, it is as well not to press a definition too closely.

(3) The differences between the Jews themselves have been made much of. It has been said that there is no homogeneity among Jews, that one section is bitterly opposed to the other. The Western Jews are different from the Eastern Jews, the Sephardim from the Ashkenazim, the Orthodox from the Liberals, the everyday Jew from the Sabbath Jew (to use a phrase of Marx). This also there is no need to deny. But it does not by any means preclude the possibility of common Jewish characteristics. Is it so difficult to conceive of wheels within wheels? Cannot a large group contain lesser groups side by side? Think of the many groups to which an Englishman may belong. He may be a Catholic or a Protestant, a farmer or a professor, a northerner or a southerner and Heaven only knows what else besides. But he remains an Englishman all the same. So with the Jew. He may belong to one circle within the whole, may possess certain characteristics that mark all individuals in that circle, but he retains the specifically Jewish characteristics nevertheless.

Finally, I must make it plain that I have no intention of outlining all Jewish characteristics. I propose to deal with those only that have reference to economic life. I shall not content myself with the old-fashioned expressions, such as the Jewish "commercialism," the "bartering spirit" and the like. I say nothing of the practice of some to include the desire for profit as a characteristic of a social group. The desire for profit is human—all too human. In fact, I must reject all previous analyses of the Jewish soul (in so far as they touch economic life), and for the following reasons. First, what the Jew was well-fitted for was never clearly enough designated. "For trade" is much too vague a term to be of the slightest use. I have therefore tried to show, in a special chapter, the circle of economic activities for which Jews are specifically fitted. Secondly, mere description is not explanation. If I want to prove that a man has all the capabilities necessary to make him an admirable speculator on the Stock Exchange, it will not be enough if I say that he will make a fine jobber. It is like saying indigence is due to poverty. Yet that is how Jewish economic talents have been treated. Our method will be different. We shall try to discover certain properties of the soul which are congenial to the exercise of economic functions in a capitalistic organism.

And now, having cleared the way, I shall proceed to demonstrate what the real Jewish peculiarities are.

It is surprising to find that despite the enormity of the problem there is yet a great degree of unanimity in the different views about the Jews. In literature no less than in actual life, unprejudiced observers agree on one or other point of importance. Read Jellinek or Fromer, Chamberlain or Marx, Heine or Goethe, Leroy-Beaulieu or Picciotto—read the pious or the nonconforming Jew, the anti-Semitic or the philo-Semitic non-Jew—and you get the impression that all of them are conscious of the same peculiarities. This is comforting to one who is about to describe the Jewish genius once more. At any rate, he will say nothing that other people might not have said, even though his standpoint be slightly different. In my own case I shall attempt to show the connexion between the characteristics and the natural gifts of the Jews and the capitalistic economic system. I shall first try to sketch a detailed picture of Jewish qualities and then proceed to bring them into relation with capitalism.

Unlike most other writers on the subject I will begin by noting a
Jewish quality which, though mentioned often enough, never received the recognition which its importance merited. I refer to the
extreme intellectuality of the Jew. Intellectual interests and intellectual skill are more strongly developed in him than physical
(manual) powers. Of the Jew it may certainly be said, "l'intelligence
prime le corps." Everyday experience proves it again and again,
and many a fact might be cited in its support. No other people has
valued the learned man, the scholar, so highly as the Jews. "The
wise man takes precedence of the king, and a bastard who is a
scholar of a high-priest who is an ignoramus." So the Talmud has
it. Any one who is acquainted with Jewish students knows well
enough that this over-rating of mere knowledge is not yet a thing
of the past. And if you could not become "wise," at least it was your
duty to be educated. At all times instruction was compulsory in
Israel. In truth, to learn was a religious duty; and in Eastern Europe
the synagogue is still called the Shool (Schule, School). Study and
worship went hand in hand; nay, study was worship and ignorance
was a deadly sin. A man who could not read was a boor in this
world and damned in the next. In the popular sayings of the Ghetto,
nothing had so much scorn poured upon it as foolishness. "Better
injustice than folly," and "Ein Narr ist ein Gezar" (A fool is a misfortune) are both well known.

The most valuable individual is the intellectual individual; humanity at its best is intellectuality at its highest. Listen to what a
sensible Jew has to say when he pictures the ideal man, the superman if you like, of the future. He takes it all as a matter of course;
those who are differently constituted must surely tremble at the
prospect. "In the place of the blind instincts . . . civilized man will
possess intellect conscious of purpose. It should be every one's
unswerving ideal to crush the instincts and replace them by will-
power, and to substitute reflection for mere impulse. The individual
only becomes a man in the fullest sense of the word when his
natural predisposition is under the control of his reasoning powers.
And when the process of emancipation from the instincts is complete we have the perfect genius with his absolute inner freedom
from the domination of natural laws. Civilization should have but
one aim—to liberate man from all that is mystic, from the vague
impulsiveness of all instinctive action, and to cultivate the purely

rational side of his being." Only think. Genius, the very essence of instinctive expression, conceived as the highest form of the rational and the intellectual!

One consequence of this high evaluation of the intellect was the esteem in which callings were held according as they demanded more "headwork" or more "handwork." The former were almost in all ages placed higher than the latter. It is true that there may have been, and still may be, Jewish communities in which hard bodily labour is done every day, but this hardly applies to the Jews of Western Europe. Even in Talmud times Jews preferred those callings which necessitated a lesser expenditure of physical energy. As Rabbi said, "The world needs both the seller of spices and the tanner, but happy he who is a seller of spices." Or again, R. Meir used to say, "A man should have his son taught a clean and easy handicraft."

The Jews were quite alive to their predominant quality and always recognized that there was a great gulf between their intellectuality and the brute force of their neighbours. One or two sayings popular among Polish Jews express the contrast with no little humour. "God help a man against Gentile hands and Jewish heads." "Heaven protect us against Jewish *moach* (brains) and Gentile *koach* (physical force)." *Moach v. Koach*—that is the Jewish problem in a nutshell. It ought to be the motto of this book.

The predominance of intellectual interests could not but lead in a people so gifted as the Jews to intellectual skill. "Say what you like about a Jew, you cannot say he is a fool." "A gallant Greek, a stupid Jew, an honest Gipsy—all are unthinkable" is a popular saying among Roumanians. And a Spanish proverb has it, "A hare that is slow and a Jew who is a fool: both are equally probable." Who that has had dealings with Jews but will not confirm that on an average they possess a greater degree of understanding, that they are more intelligent than other people? I might even call it astuteness or sagacity, as was remarked by one of the keenest observers of Jews a century or more ago, who characterized them as "intellectual and endowed with great genius for things of the present age," though, he added, "to a less degree than in the past."

"The Jewish mind is an instrument of precision; it has the exactness of a pair of scales": most people will agree with this judgment of Leroy-Beaulieu. And when H. S. Chamberlain speaks of the under-development of Jewish "understanding" he must surely be using the term in a special sense. He cannot possibly mean by it quick thought, precise analysis, exact dissection, speedy combination, the power of seeing the point at once, of suggesting analogies, distinguishing between synonymous things, of drawing final conclusions. The Jew is able to do all this, and Jellinek, who rightly lays stress on this side of the Jewish character, points out that Hebrew is particularly rich in expressions for activities demanding qualities of the mind. It has no fewer than eleven words for seeking or researching, thirty-four for distinguishing or separating, and fifteen for combining.

There is no doubt that these mental gifts make the Jews prominent as chess-players, as mathematicians and in all calculating work. These activities postulate a strong capacity for abstract thought and also a special kind of imagination, which Wundt has so happily christened the combinatory. Their skill as physicians (ability at diagnosis) may also be traced to their calculating, dissecting and combining minds, which "like lightning, illuminate dark places in a flash."

It is not unknown that often enough Jewish mental ability degenerates into hair-splitting. (When the mill has no corn to grind it grinds itself.) But this does not matter so much as another fact. The intellectuality of the Jew is so strong that it tends to develop at the expense of other mental qualities, and the mind is apt to become one-sided. Let us take a few instances. The Jew lacks the quality of instinctive understanding; he responds less to feeling than to intellect. We can scarcely think of a Jewish mystic like Jacob Böhme, and the contrast becomes still more striking when we remember the sort of mysticism found in the Kabbala. In the same way all romance is alien to this particular view of life; the Jew cannot well sympathize with losing oneself in the world, in mankind or in nature. It is the difference between frenzied enthusiasm and sober, matter-of-fact thought.

Akin to this characteristic is that of a certain lack of impressionability, a certain lack of receptive and creative genius. When I was in Breslau a Jewish student from the far East of Siberia came to me one day "to study Karl Marx." It took him nearly three weeks to reach Breslau, and on the very day after his arrival he called on me and borrowed one of Marx's works. A few days later he came again, discussed with me what he had read, brought back the book and borrowed another. This continued for a few months. Then he returned to his native village. The young man had received absolutely no impressions from his new surroundings; he had made no acquaintances, never taken a walk, hardly knew in fact where it was that he was staying. The life of Breslau passed him by completely. No doubt it was the same before he came to Breslau, and will be the same throughout the future. He will walk through the world without seeing it. But he had made himself acquainted with Marx. Is this a typical case? I think so. You may meet with it every day. Are we not continually struck by the Jew's love for the inconcrete, his tendency away from the sensuous, his constant abiding in a world of abstractions? And is it only accidental that there are far fewer Jewish painters than literary men or professors? Even in the case of Jewish artists is there not something intellectual about their work? Never was word more truly spoken than when Friedrich Naumann compared Max Liebermann with Spinoza, saying, "He paints with his brain."

The Jew certainly sees remarkably clearly, but he does not see much. He does not think of his environment as something alive, and that is why he has lost the true conception of life, of its oneness, of its being an organism, a natural growth. In short, he has lost the true conception of the personal side of life. General experience must surely support this view; but if other proofs are demanded they will be found in the peculiarities of Jewish law, which, as we have already seen, abolished personal relationships and replaced them by impersonal, abstract connexions or activities or aims.

As a matter of fact, one may find among Jews an extraordinary knowledge of men. They are able with their keen intellects to probe, as it were, into every pore, and to see the inside of a man as only Röntgen rays would show him. They muster all his qualities and abilities, they note his excellences and his weaknesses; they detect at once for what he is best fitted. But seldom do they see the whole man, and thus they often make the mistake of ascribing actions to him which are an abomination to his inmost soul. Moreover, they seldom appraise a man according to his personality, but rather according to some perceptible characteristic and achievement.

Hence their lack of sympathy for every status where the nexus is a personal one. The Jews' whole being is opposed to all that is usually understood by chivalry, to all sentimentality, knight-errantry, feudalism, patriarchalism. Nor does he comprehend a social order based on relationships such as these. "Estates of the realm" and craft organizations are a loathing to him. Politically he is an individualist. A constitutional State in which all human intercourse is regulated by clearly defined legal principles suits him well. He is the born representative of a "liberal" view of life in which there are no living men and women of flesh and blood with distinct personalities, but only citizens with rights and duties. And these do not differ in different nations, but form part of mankind, which is but the sum-total of an immense number of amorphous units. Just as so many Jews do not see themselves—do they not deny their obvious characteristics and assert that there is no difference between them and Englishmen or Germans or Frenchmen?—so they do not see other people as living beings but only as subjects, citizens, or some other such abstract conception. It comes to this, that they behold the world not with their "soul" but with their intellect. The result is that they are easily led to believe that whatever can be neatly set down on paper and ordered aright by the aid of the intellect must of necessity be capable of proper settlement in actual life. How many Jews still hold that the Jewish Question is only a political one, and are convinced that a liberal regime is all that is required to remove the differences between the Jew and his neighbour. It is nothing short of astounding to read the opinion of so soundly learned a man as the author of one of the newest books on the Jewish Question that the whole of the anti-Semitic movement during the last thirty years was the result of the works of Marx and Dühring. "The thousand victims of the pogroms and the million sturdy workers who emigrated from their homes are but a striking illustration of the power of—Eugen Dühring" (!). Is not this opposing ink and blood, understanding and instinct, an abstraction and a reality?

The conception of the universe in the mind of such an intellectual people must perforce have been that of a structure well-ordered in accordance with reason. By the aid of reason, therefore, they sought to understand the world; they were rationalists, both in theory and in practice.

Now as soon as a strong consciousness of the ego attaches itself to the predominating intellectuality in the thinking being, he will tend to group the world round that ego. In other words, he will look at the world from the point of view of end, or goal, or purpose. His outlook will be teleological, or that of practical rationalism. No peculiarity is so fully developed in the Jew as this, and there is complete unanimity of opinion on the subject. Most other observers start out with the teleology of the Jew; I for my part regard it as the result of his extreme intellectuality, in which I believe all the other Jewish peculiarities are rooted. In saying this, however, I do not in the least wish to minimize the very great importance of this Jewish characteristic.

Take any expression of the Jewish genius and you will be certain to find in it this teleological tendency, which has sometimes been called extreme subjectivity. Whether or no the Indo-Germanic races are objective and the Semitic subjective, certain it is that the Jews are the most subjective of peoples. The Jew never loses himself in the outer world, never sinks in the depth of the cosmos, never soars in the endless realms of thought, but, as Jellinek well puts it, dives below the surface to seek for pearls. He brings everything into relation with his ego. He is for ever asking why, what for, what will it bring? *Cui bono?* His greatest interest is always in the result of a thing, not in the thing itself. It is un-Jewish to regard any activity, be it what you will, as an end in itself; un-Jewish to live your life without having any purpose, to leave all to chance; un-Jewish to get harmless pleasure out of Nature. The Jew has taken all that is in Nature and made of it "the loose pages of a text-book of ethics which shall advance the higher moral life." The Jewish religion, as we have already seen, is teleological in its aim; in each of its regulations it has the ethical norm in view. The entire universe, in the Jew's eyes, is something that was made in accordance with a plan. This is one of the differences between Judaism and heathenism, as Heine saw long ago. "They [the heathens] all have an endless, eternal 'past,' which is in the world and develops with it by the laws of necessity; but the God of the Jews was outside the world, which He created as an act of free-will."

No term is more familiar to the ear of the Jew than *Tachlis*, which means purpose, aim, end or goal. If you are to do anything it must have a *tachlis*; life itself, whether as a whole or in its single activities, must have some *tachlis*, and so must the universe. Those who assert that the meaning of Life, of the World, is not *tachlis* but tragedy, the Jew will reckon as foolish visionaries.

How deeply the teleological view of things is embedded in the
nature of the Jew may be seen in the case of those of them who,
like the Chassidim, pay no attention to the needs of practical life
because "there is no purpose in them." There is no purpose in making a living, and so they let their wives and children starve, and
devote themselves to the study of their sacred books. But we may
see it also in all those Jews who, with a soul-weariness within them
and a faint smile on their countenances, understanding and forgiving everything, stand and gaze at life from their own heights, far
above this world. I have in mind such choice spirits among the
literary men of our day as George Hirschfeld, Arthur Schnitzler and
George Hermann. The great charm of their work lies in this world-
aloofness with which they look down on our hustle and bustle, in
the quiet melancholy pervading all their poetry, in their sentiment.
Their very lack of will-power is only strength of will in a kind of
negative form. Through all their ballads sounds the same soft plaint
of grief: how purposeless and therefore how sad is the world! Nature
herself is tinged with this sorrow; autumn always lurks in ambush
though wood and meadow be bright with gay spring blossoms; the
wind plays among the fallen leaves and the sun's golden glory, be
it never so beautiful, must go down at last. Subjectivity and the
conception that all things must have an aim (and the two are the
same) rob the poetry of Jewish writers of naïveté, freshness and
directness, because Jewish poets are unable simply to enjoy the
phenomena of this world, whether it be human fate or Nature's
vagaries; they must needs cogitate upon it and turn it about and
about. Nowhere is the air scented with the primrose and the violet,
nowhere gleams the spray of the rivulet in the wood. But to make
up for lack of these they possess the wonderful aroma of old wine
and the magic charm of a pair of beautiful eyes gazing sadly into
the distance.

When this attitude of mind that seeks for a purpose in all things
is united with a strong will, with a large fund of energy (as is generally the case with the Jew), it ceases to be merely a point of view;
it becomes a policy. The man sets himself a goal and makes for it,
allowing nothing whatever to turn him aside from his course; he is
determined, if you like, stiff-necked. Heine in characterizing his
people called it stubbornness, and Goethe said that the essence of
the Jewish character was energy and the pursuit of direct ends.

My next point is mobility, but I am not quite sure whether this can be ascribed to all Jews or only to the Ashkenazi (German) Jews. Writers who have sung the praises of the Sephardim (Spanish Jews) always lay stress on a certain dignified air which they have, a certain superciliousness of bearing. Their German brethren, on the other hand, have always been described as lively, active and somewhat excitable. Even to-day you may meet with many Spanish Jews, especially in the Orient, who strike you as being dignified, thoughtful and self-restrained, who do not in the least appear to have that mobility, moral or physical, which is so often noticeable in European Jews. But mobility of mind—quick perception and mental versatility—all Jews possess.

These four elements, intellectuality, teleology, energy and mobility, are the corner-stones of Jewish character, so complicated in its nature. I believe that all the qualities of the Jew may be easily traced to one or more of these elements. Take two which are of special import in economic life—extreme activity and adaptability.

The Jew is active, or if you will, industrious. In the words of Goethe, "No Jew, not even the most insignificant, but is busy towards the achievement of some worldly, temporary or momentary aim." This activity often enough degenerates into restlessness. He must for ever be up and doing, for ever managing something and carrying it to fruition. He is always on the move, and does not care much if he makes himself a nuisance to those who would rest if they could. All musical and social "affairs" in our large towns are run by Jews. The Jew is the born trumpeter of progress and of its manifold blessings. And why? Because of his practical-mindedness and his mobility combined with his intellectuality. The last more especially, because it never strikes deep root. All intellectuality is in the long run shallowness; never does it allow of probing to the very roots of a matter, never of reaching down to the depths of the soul, or of the universe. Hence intellectuality makes it easy to go from one extreme to the other. That is why you find among Jews fanatical orthodoxy and unenlightened doubt side by side; they both spring from one source.

But to this shallow intellectuality the Jew owes perhaps the most valuable of his characteristics—his adaptability—which is unique in history. The Jews were always a stiff-necked people, and their adaptability no less than their capacity to maintain their national traits are both due to the one cause. Their adaptability enabled them to submit for the time being, if circumstances so demanded, to the laws of necessity, only to hark back to their wonted ways when better days came. From of old the Jewish character was at one and the same time resistant and submissive, and though these traits may appear contradictory they only seem so. As Leroy-Beaulieu well said, "The Jew is at once the most stubborn and the most pliant of men, the most self-willed and the most malleable."

The leaders and the "wise" men of the Jewish people were in all ages fully alive to the importance, nay the necessity, of this flexibility and elasticity, if Israel was to continue, and they were therefore never tired of insisting upon it. Jewish literature abounds in instances. "Be as pliant as the reed which the wind blows in this direction and in that, for the Torah can be observed only by him that is of a contrite spirit. Why is the Torah likened unto water? To tell you that just as water never flows up to the heights but rather runs down to the depths, so too the Torah does not abide with the haughty but only with the lowly." Or again, "When the fox is in authority bow down before him." Once more, "Bend before the wave and it passes over you; oppose it, and it will sweep you away." Finally, a supplication from the Prayer Book runs as follows: "May my soul be as the dust to every one."

It was in this spirit that the Rabbis counselled their flocks to pretend to accept the dominant faiths in those countries where their existence depended on the renunciation of their own. The advice was followed to a large extent, and in the words of Fromer, "The Jewish race, by simulating death from time to time, was able to live on and on."

There are very few, if any, make-believe Christians or Moslems to-day. Nevertheless, the remarkable power of the Jew to adapt himself to his environment has more scope than ever. The Jew of Western Europe and America to-day no longer wishes to maintain his religion and his national character intact; on the contrary, he wishes, in so far as the nationalist spirit has not yet awakened in him, to lose his characteristics and to assimilate with the people in whose midst his lot happens to be cast. And lo, this too he can successfully achieve.

Perhaps the clearest illustration of the way in which Jewish traits manifest themselves is the fact that the Jew in England becomes like an Englishman, in France like a Frenchman, and so forth. And if he does not really become like an Englishman or a Frenchman, he appears to be like one. That a Felix Mendelssohn should write German music, that a Jacques Offenbach French and a Souza Yankee-doodle; that Lord Beaconsfield should set up as an Englishman, Gambetta as a Frenchman, Lassalle as a German; in short, that Jewish talent should so often have nothing Jewish about it, but be in accord with its environment, has curiously enough again and again been urged as evidence that there are no specifically Jewish characteristics, whereas in truth it proves the very opposite in a striking fashion. It proves that the Jews have the gift of adaptability in an eminently high degree. The Jew might go from one planet to another, but his strangeness amid the new surroundings would not continue for long. He quickly feels his way and adapts himself with ease. He is German where he wants to be German, and Italian if that suits him better. He does everything and dabbles in everything, and with success. He can be a pure Magyar in Hungary, he can belong to the Irredenta in Italy, and be an anti-Semite in France (Drumont!). He is an adept in seizing upon anything which is still germinating, and bringing it with all speed to its full bloom. All this his adaptability enables him to do.

I have already said that this peculiar capacity for adaptation is rooted in the four elements of the Jewish character. But perhaps the rationalism of the Jew is responsible for it to a greater degree than the other three. Because of his rationalism he is able to look at everything from without. If the Jew is anything, it is not because he must but because he determines to be so. Any convictions he may have do not spring from his inmost soul; they are formulated by his intellect. His standpoint is not on solid earth but an imaginary castle in the air. He is not organically original but mechanically rational. He lacks depth of feeling and strength of instinct. That is why he is what he is, but he can also be different. That Lord Beaconsfield was a Conservative was due to some accident or other, or some political conjuncture; but Stein and Bismarck and Carlyle were Conservatives because they could not help it; it was in their blood. Had Marx or Lassalle been born in another age, or in another environment, they might quite easily have become Conservatives instead of Radicals. As a matter of fact, Lassalle was already coquetting with the idea of becoming a reactionary, and no doubt he would have played the part of a Prussian Junker as brilliantly as that of socialist agitator.

The driving power in Jewish adaptability is of course the idea of a purpose, or a goal, as the end of all things. Once the Jew has made up his mind what line he will follow, the rest is comparatively easy, and his mobility only makes his success more sure.

How mobile the Jew can be is positively astounding. He is able to give himself the personal appearance he most desires. As in days of old through simulating death he was able to defend himself, so now by colour adaptation or other forms of mimicry. The best illustrations may be drawn from the United States, where the Jew of the second or third generation is with difficulty distinguished from the non-Jew. You can tell the German after no matter how many generations; so with the Irish, the Swede, the Slav. But the Jew, in so far as his racial physical features allow of it, has been successful in imitating the Yankee type, especially in regard to outward marks such as clothing, bearing and the peculiar method of hairdressing.

Easier still, on account of his mental and moral mobility, is it for the Jew to make the intellectual atmosphere of his environment his own. His mental mobility enables him quickly to seize upon the "tone" of any circle, quickly to notice what it is that matters, quickly to feel his way into things. And his moral mobility? That helps him to remove troublesome hindrances, either ethical or aesthetical, from his path. And he can do this with all the more facility because he has only to a small degree what may be termed personal dignity. It means little to him to be untrue to himself, if it is a question of attaining the wished-for goal.

Is this picture faithful to life? The obvious adaptability of the Jew to the changing conditions of the struggle for existence is surely proof enough. But there is further proof in some of the special gifts which Jews possess. I refer to their undoubted talent for journalism, for the Bar, for the stage, and all of it is traceable to their adaptability.

Adolf Jellinek, in the book we have referred to more than once, has drawn a clever little sketch showing the connexion between the two. "The journalist," he say, "must be quick, mobile, lively, enthusiastic, able to analyze quickly and as quickly to put two and two together; must be able to enter *in medias res*, to have the gist of any question of the day or the central fact of a debate in his mind's eye; must be able to deal with his subject in clear and well-marked outlines, to describe it epigrammatically, antithetically, sententiously, in short arresting sentences, to breathe life into it by means of a certain amount of pathos, to give it colour by means of esprit, to make it spicy by means of seasoning." Are not all these Jewish traits?

The actor's calling, no less than the barrister's, depends for success on his ability to place himself quickly in a strange world of ideas, to take a right view of men and conditions without much difficulty, to form a correct estimate of them and to use them for his own end. The Jew's gift of subjectivity stands him here in good stead, for by its aid he can easily put himself in the position of another, take thought for him and defend him. To be sure, jurisprudence is the bulk of the contents of Jewish literature!

Now comes the question, how and in what way did the Jewish characteristics enable Jews to become financiers and speculators, indeed, to engage as successfully in economic activities within the framework of the capitalistic system as to be mathematicians, statisticians, physicians, journalists, actors and advocates? To what extent, that is, does a special talent for capitalistic enterprise spring from the elements in the Jewish character?

Speaking generally, we may say in this connexion what we have already remarked about capitalism and the Jewish religion, that the fundamental ideas of capitalism and those of the Jewish character show a singular similarity. Hence we have the triple parallelism between Jewish character, the Jewish religion and capitalism. What was it we found as the all-controlling trait of the Jewish people? Was it not extreme intellectuality? And is not intellectuality the quality which differentiates the capitalistic system from all others? Organizing ability springs from intellectuality, and in the capitalistic system we find the separation between head and hands, between the work of directing and that of manufacturing. "For the greatest work to be completely done, you need of hands a thousand, of minds but only one." That sums up the capitalistic state of things.

The purest form of capitalism is that wherein abstract ideas are most clearly expressed. That they are part and parcel of the Jewish character we have already seen; there is no occasion to labour the close kinship in this respect between capitalism and the Jew. Again, the quality of abstraction in capitalism manifests itself in the substitution of all qualitative differences by merely quantitative ones (value in exchange). Before capitalism came, exchange was a many-sided, multi-coloured and technical process; now it is just one specialized act—that of the dealer: before there were many relationships between buyer and seller; there is only one now—the commercial. The tendency of capitalism has been to do away with different manners, customs, pretty local and national contrasts, and to set up in their stead the dead level of the cosmopolitan town. In short, there has been a tendency towards uniformity, and in this capitalism and Liberalism have much in common. Liberalism we have already shown to be a near relative of Judaism, and so we have the kindred trio of Capitalism, Liberalism, and Judaism.

How is the inner resemblance between the first and the last best manifested? Is it not through the agency of money, by means of which capitalism succeeds so well in its policy of bringing about a drab uniformity? Money is the common denominator, in terms of which all values are expressed; at the same time it is the be-all and end-all of economic activity in a capitalistic system. Hence one of the conspicuous things in such a system is success. Is it otherwise with the Jew? Does he not also make the increase of capital his chief aim? And not only because the abstractness of capital is congenial to the soul of the Jew, but also because the great regard in which (in the capitalistic system) money is held strikes another sympathetic note in the Jewish character—its teleology. Gold becomes the great means, and its value arises from the fact that you can utilize it for many ends. It needs but little skill to show that a nature intent on working towards some goal should feel itself drawn to something which has value only because it is a means to an end. Moreover, the teleology of the Jew brings it about that he prizes success. (Another point of similarity, therefore, with capitalism.) Because he rates success so highly he sacrifices to-day for to-morrow, and his mobility only helps him to do it all the better. Here again we may observe a likeness to capitalism. Capitalism is constantly on the look-out for something new, for some way of expanding, for abstaining to-day for the sake of to-morrow. Think of our whole system of credit. Does not this characteristic show itself there clearly enough? Now remember also that the Jews were very much at home in the organization of credit—in which values or services which may, or can, become effective some time in the future are made available to-day. Human thought can plainly picture future experiences and future needs, and credit offers the opportunity through present economic activities of producing future values. That credit is extensively found in modern life scarcely requires pointing out. The reason too is obvious: it offers golden chances. True, we must give up the joys that spring from "completely throwing ourselves into the present." But what of that? The Jewish character and capitalism have one more point in common—practical rationalism, by which I mean the shaping of all activities in accordance with reason.

To make the whole parallelism even more plain, let me illustrate it by concrete instances. The Jew is well fitted for the part of undertaker because of his strength of will and his habit of making for some goal or other. His intellectual mobility is accountable for his readiness to discover new methods of production and new possibilities of marketing. He is an adept at forming new organizations, and in these his peculiar capacity for finding out what a man is best fitted for stands him in good stead. And since in the world of capitalism there is nothing organic or natural but only what is mechanical or artificial, the Jew's lack of understanding of the former is of no consequence. Even undertaking on a large scale is itself artificial and mechanical; you may extend a concern or contract it; you may change it according to circumstances. That is why Jews are so successful as organizers of large capitalistic undertakings. Again, the Jew can easily grasp impersonal relationships. We have already noted that he has the feeling of personal dependence only in a slight measure. Hence, he does not care for your hoary "patriarchalism," and pays little attention to the dash of sentimentality which is still sometimes found in labour contracts. In all relations between sellers and buyers, and between employers and employed, he reduces everything to the legal and purely business basis. In the struggle of the workers to obtain collective agreements between themselves and the masters, which shall regulate the conditions of their labour, the Jew is almost invariably on the side of the first.

But if the Jew is well fitted to be an undertaker, still more is he cut out for the part of the trader. His qualities in this respect are almost innumerable.

The trader lives in figures, and in figures the Jew has always been in his element. His love of the abstract has made calculation easy for him; it is his strong point. Now a calculating talent combined with a capacity for working always with some aim in view has already won half the battle for the trader. He is enabled to weigh aright the chances, the possibilities and the advantages of any given situation, to eliminate everything that is useless, and to appraise the whole in terms of figures. Give this sober calculator a strong dose of imagination and you have the perfect speculator before you. To take stock of any given state of things with lightning speed, to see a thousand eventualities, to seize upon the most valuable and to act in accordance with that—such, as we have already pointed out, is the aim of the dealer. For all this the Jew has the necessary gifts of mind. I should like expressly to emphasize the close kinship between the activities of the clever speculator and those of the clever physician who can successfully diagnose a disease. The Jew, because of his qualities, is eminently fitted for both.

A good dealer must be a good negotiator. What cleverer negotiators are there than the Jews, whose ability in this direction has long been recognized and utilized? To adapt yourself to the needs of a market, to meet any specified form of demand, is the one prime essential for the dealer. That the Jew with his adaptability can do this as well as any other is obvious. The second is the power of suggestion, and in this also the Jew is well qualified by his ability to think himself into the situation of another.

Wherever we look the conclusion forces itself upon us that the combination of no other set of qualities is so well fitted, as are those of the Jew, for realizing the best capitalistic results. There is no need for me to take the parallelism further; the intelligent reader can easily do so for himself. I would only direct his attention to one point more before leaving the subject—the parallel between the feverish restlessness of Stock Exchange business, always intent on upsetting the tendency towards an equilibrium, and the restless nature of the Jew.

In another place I have sought to characterize the ideal undertaker in three words—he must be wide-awake, clever and resourceful. Wide-awake: that is to say, quick of comprehension, sure in judgment, must think twice before speaking once, and be able to seize upon the right moment.

Clever: that is to say, he must possess a knowledge of the world, must be certain of himself in his judgment and in his treatment of men, certain in his judgment on a given conjuncture; and above all, acquainted with the weaknesses and mistakes of those around him.

Resourceful: that is to say, full of ideas.

The capitalistic undertaker must have three additional qualities: he must be active, sober and thorough. By sober, I mean free from passion, from sentiment, from unpractical idealism. By thorough, I mean reliable, conscientious, orderly, neat and frugal.

I believe this rough sketch will, in broad outline, stand for the capitalistic undertaker no less than for the Jew.

ADOLF HITLER:

"Was there any form of filth or profligacy, particularly in cultural life, without at least one Jew involved in it?" (1925)

Adolf Hitler (1889–1945), Nazi ruler of Germany 1933–1945, left as his memorial not only World War II and the destruction of the German Third Reich, but the graves of more than six million Jews. The most fanatical enemy of the Jews in all of history, Hitler became an anti-Semite in the aftermath of the First World War. Like other German anti-Semites, Hitler became convinced that the Jews were responsible for Germany's defeat. In a speech of 1922, he declared that the Jews of Germany had secretly conspired to promote an Allied victory, and that the result of the war was a Jewish victory which had as its ultimate purpose the destruction of Aryan civilization. Regarding the Weimar Republic as "The Paradise of Jews," Hitler in 1923 charged that democracy and Marxism were Jewish inventions, both designed to subvert the world in the interest of Jewish domination.

Although Hitler made no secret of his virulent anti-Semitism in his book, *Mein Kampf* (1925), his overt intentions regarding the Jews were not immediately clear when he came to power in January, 1933. As a result, many German Jews, especially those wholly or partly assimilated, believed that Nazi regulations would not affect Jews whose families had lived in Germany for several centuries, or whose German patriotism was a matter of record. Shortly after taking office, however, the Nazis promoted a boycott of Jewish businesses. In 1935 Jewish children were

From Adolf Hitler, *Mein Kampf*, tr. Ralph Manheim (London: Hurst & Blackett Ltd., 1940; Boston: Houghton Mifflin Company, 1943), pp. 51–65.

excluded from public schools. The notorious Nuremberg Laws of that year denied Jews citzenship, and prohibited marriages between Jews and "Aryans." The assassination in Paris of a German Embassy official by a Jew, Herschel Grynspan, in November, 1938, gave the Nazis a pretext for destroying more than four hundred synagogues and a large number of Jewish-owned stores and commercial enterprises. The German Jews were also fined a billion marks, and thousands of Jews were sent to concentration camps. Had World War II ended in a Nazi victory, there can be no question that Adolf Hitler would have proceeded to exterminate the whole of European, and perhaps world, Jewry.

The account here reprinted, which deals with Hitler's early conversion to anti-Semitism and with his attitude toward the Jewish "question," is from *Mein Kampf.*

Today it is difficult, if not impossible, for me to say when the word 'Jew' first gave me ground for special thoughts. At home I do not remember having heard the word during my father's lifetime. I believe that the old gentleman would have regarded any special emphasis on this term as cultural backwardness. In the course of his life he had arrived at more or less cosmopolitan views which, despite his pronounced national sentiments, not only remained intact, but also affected me to some extent.

Likewise at school I found no occasion which could have led me to change this inherited picture.

At the *Realschule,* to be sure, I did meet one Jewish boy who was treated by all of us with caution, but only because various experiences had led us to doubt his discretion and we did not particularly trust him; but neither I nor the others had any thoughts on the matter.

Not until my fourteenth or fifteenth year did I begin to come across the word 'Jew,' with any frequency, partly in connection with political discussions. This filled me with a mild distaste, and I could not rid myself of an unpleasant feeling that always came over me whenever religious quarrels occurred in my presence.

At that time I did not think anything else of the question.

There were few Jews in Linz. In the course of the centuries their outward appearance had become Europeanized and had taken on a human look; in fact, I even took them for Germans. The absurdity of this idea did not dawn on me because I saw no distinguishing feature but the strange religion. The fact that they had, as I believed, been persecuted on this account sometimes almost turned my distaste at unfavorable remarks about them into horror.

Thus far I did not so much as suspect the existence of an organized opposition to the Jews.

Then I came to Vienna.

Preoccupied by the abundance of my impressions in the architectural field, oppressed by the hardship of my own lot, I gained at first no insight into the inner stratification of the people in this gigantic city. Notwithstanding that Vienna in those days counted nearly two hundred thousand Jews among its two million inhabitants, I did not see them. In the first few weeks my eyes and my senses were not equal to the flood of values and ideas. Not until calm gradually returned and the agitated picture began to clear did I look around me more carefully in my new world, and then among other things I encountered the Jewish question.

I cannot maintain that the way in which I became acquainted with them struck me as particularly pleasant. For the Jew was still characterized for me by nothing but his religion, and therefore, on grounds of human tolerance, I maintained my rejection of religious attacks in this case as in others. Consequently, the tone, particularly that of the Viennese anti-Semitic press, seemed to me unworthy of the cultural tradition of a great nation. I was oppressed by the memory of certain occurrences in the Middle Ages, which I should not have liked to see repeated. Since the newspapers in question did not enjoy an outstanding reputation (the reason for this, at that time, I myself did not precisely know), I regarded them more as the products of anger and envy than the results of a principled, though perhaps mistaken, point of view.

I was reinforced in this opinion by what seemed to me the far more dignified form in which the really big papers answered all these attacks, or, what seemed to me even more praiseworthy, failed to mention them; in other words, simply killed them with silence.

I zealously read the so-called world press (*Neue Freie Presse, Wiener Tageblatt,* etc.) and was amazed at the scope of what they offered their readers and the objectivity of individual articles. I respected the exalted tone, though the flamboyance of the style sometimes caused me inner dissatisfaction, or even struck me unpleasantly. Yet this may have been due to the rhythm of life in the whole metropolis.

Since in those days I saw Vienna in that light, I thought myself justified in accepting this explanation of mine as a valid excuse.

But what sometimes repelled me was the undignified fashion in which this press curried favor with the Court. There was scarcely an event in the Hofburg which was not imparted to the readers either with raptures of enthusiasm or plaintive emotion, and all this to-do, particularly when it dealt with the 'wisest monarch' of all time, almost reminded me of the mating cry of a mountain cock.

To me the whole thing seemed artificial.

In my eyes it was a blemish upon liberal democracy.

To curry favor with this Court and in such indecent forms was to sacrifice the dignity of the nation.

This was the first shadow to darken my intellectual relationship with the 'big' Viennese press.

As I had always done before, I continued in Vienna to follow events in Germany with ardent zeal, quite regardless whether they were political or cultural. With pride and admiration, I compared the rise of the Reich with the wasting away of the Austrian state. If events in the field of foreign politics filled me, by and large, with undivided joy, the less gratifying aspects of internal life often aroused anxiety and gloom. The struggle which at that time was being carried on against William II did not meet with my approval. I regarded him not only as the German Emperor, but first and foremost as the creator of a German fleet. The restrictions of speech imposed on the Kaiser by the Reichstag angered me greatly because they emanated from a source which in my opinion really hadn't a leg to stand on, since in a single session these parliamentarian imbeciles gabbled more nonsense than a whole dynasty of emperors, including its very weakest numbers, could ever have done in centuries.

I was outraged that in a state where every idiot not only claimed the right to criticize, but was given a seat in the Reichstag and let loose upon the nation as a 'lawgiver,' the man who bore the imperial crown had to take 'reprimands' from the greatest babblers' club of all time.

But I was even more indignant that the same Viennese press which made the most obsequious bows to every rickety horse in the Court, and flew into convulsions of joy if he accidentally swished his tail, should, with supposed concern, yet, as it seemed to me, ill-concealed malice, express its criticisms of the German Kaiser. Of course it had no intention of interfering with conditions within the German Reich—oh, no, God forbid—but by placing its finger on these wounds in the friendliest way, it was fulfilling the duty imposed by the spirit of the mutual alliance, and, conversely, fulfilling the requirements of journalistic truth, etc. And now it was poking this finger around in the wound to its heart's content.

In such cases the blood rose to my head.

It was this which caused me little by little to view the big papers with greater caution.

And on one such occasion I was forced to recognize that one of the anti-Semitic papers, the *Deutsches Voksblatt,* behaved more decently.

Another thing that got on my nerves was the loathsome cult for France which the big press, even then, carried on. A man couldn't help feeling ashamed to be a German when he saw these saccharine hymns of praise to the 'great cultural nation.' This wretched licking of France's boots more than once made me throw down one of these 'world newspapers.' And on such occasions I sometimes picked up the *Volksblatt,* which, to be sure, seemed to me much smaller, but in these matters somewhat more appetizing. I was not in agreement with the sharp anti-Semitic tone, but from time to time I read arguments which gave me some food for thought.

At all events, these occasions slowly made me acquainted with the man and the movement, which in those days guided Vienna's destinies: Dr. Karl Lueger[1] and the Christian Social Party.

When I arrived in Vienna, I was hostile to both of them.

The man and the movement seemed 'reactionary' in my eyes.

My common sense of justice, however, forced me to change this judgment in proportion as I had occasion to become acquainted

[1]Karl Lueger (1844–1910). In 1897, as a member of the anti-Semitic Christian Social Party, he became mayor of Vienna and kept the post until his death. At first opposed by the Court for his radical nationalism and anti-Semitism, toward the end of his career he became more moderate and was reconciled with the Emperor.

with the man and his work; and slowly my fair judgment turned
to unconcealed admiration. Today, more than ever, I regard this
man as the greatest German mayor of all times.

How many of my basic principles were upset by this change in
my attitude toward the Christian Social movement!

My views with regard to anti-Semitism thus succumbed to the
passage of time, and this was my greatest transformation of all.

It cost me the greatest inner soul struggles, and only after months
of battle between my reason and my sentiments did my reason
begin to emerge victorious. Two years later, my sentiment had
followed my reason, and from then on became its most loyal
guardian and sentinel.

At the time of this bitter struggle between spiritual education
and cold reason, the visual instruction of the Vienna streets had
performed invaluable services. There came a time when I no longer,
as in the first days, wandered blindly through the mighty city; now
with open eyes I saw not only the buildings but also the people.

Once, as I was strolling through the Inner City, I suddenly encountered an apparition in a black caftan and black hair locks. Is
this a Jew? was my first thought.

For, to be sure, they had not looked like that in Linz. I observed
the man furtively and cautiously, but the longer I stared at this
foreign face, scrutinizing feature for feature, the more my first
question assumed a new form:

Is this a German?

As always in such cases, I now began to try to relieve my doubts
by books. For a few hellers I bought the first anti-Semitic pamphlets of my life. Unfortunately, they all proceeded from the supposition that in principle the reader knew or even understood the
Jewish question to a certain degree. Besides, the tone for the most
part was such that doubts again arose in me, due in part to the dull
and amazingly unscientific arguments favoring the thesis.

I relapsed for weeks at a time, once even for months.

The whole thing seemed to me so monstrous, the accusations so
boundless, that, tormented by the fear of doing injustice, I again
became anxious and uncertain.

Yet I could no longer very well doubt that the objects of my
study were not Germans of a special religion, but a people in themselves; for since I had begun to concern myself with this question

and to take cognizance of the Jews, Vienna appeared to me in a different light than before. Wherever I went, I began to see Jews, and the more I saw, the more sharply they became distinguished in my eyes from the rest of humanity. Particularly the Inner City and the districts north of the Danube Canal swarmed with a people which even outwardly had lost all resemblance to Germans.

And whatever doubts I may still have nourished were finally dispelled by the attitude of a portion of the Jews themselves.

Among them there was a great movement, quite extensive in Vienna, which came out sharply in confirmation of the national character of the Jews: this was the *Zionists.*

It looked, to be sure, as though only a part of the Jews approved this viewpoint, while the great majority condemned and inwardly rejected such a formulation. But when examined more closely, this appearance dissolved itself into an unsavory vapor of pretexts advanced for mere reasons of expedience, not to say lies. For the so-called liberal Jews did not reject the Zionists as non-Jews, but only as Jews with an impractical, perhaps even dangerous, way of publicly avowing their Jewishness.

Intrinsically they remained unalterably of one piece.

In a short time this apparent struggle between Zionistic and liberal Jews disgusted me; for it was false through and through, founded on lies and scarcely in keeping with the moral elevation and purity always claimed by this people.

The cleanliness of this people, moral and otherwise, I must say, is a point in itself. By their very exterior you could tell that these were no lovers of water, and, to your distress, you often knew it with your eyes closed. Later I often grew sick to my stomach from the smell of these caftan-wearers. Added to this, there was their unclean dress and their generally unheroic appearance.

All this could scarcely be called very attractive; but it became positively repulsive when, in addition to their physical uncleanliness, you discovered the moral stains on this 'chosen people.'

In a short time I was made more thoughtful than ever by my slowly rising insight into the type of activity carried on by the Jews in certain fields.

Was there any form of filth or profligacy, particularly in cultural life, without at least one Jew involved in it?

If you cut even cautiously into such an abscess, you found, like

a maggot in a rotting body, often dazzled by the sudden light—
a kike!

What had to be reckoned heavily against the Jews in my eyes
was when I became acquainted with their activity in the press, art,
literature, and the theater. All the unctuous reassurances helped
little or nothing. It sufficed to look at a billboard, to study the names
of the men behind the horrible trash they advertised, to make you
hard for a long time to come. This was pestilence, spiritual pestilence, worse than the Black Death of olden times, and the people
were being infected with it! It goes without saying that the lower
the intellectual level of one of these art manufacturers, the more
unlimited his fertility will be, and the scoundrel ends up like a
garbage separator, splashing his filth in the face of humanity. And
bear in mind that there is no limit to their number; bear in mind
that for one Goethe Nature easily can foist on the world ten thousand of these scribblers who poison men's souls like germ-carriers
of the worse sort, on their fellow men.

It was terrible, but not to be overlooked, that precisely the Jew,
in tremendous numbers, seemed chosen by Nature for this shameful
calling.

Is this why the Jews are called the 'chosen people'?

I now began to examine carefully the names of all the creators
of unclean products in public artistic life. The result was less and
less favorable for my previous attitude toward the Jews. Regardless
how my sentiment might resist, my reason was forced to draw its
conclusions.

The fact that nine tenths of all literary filth, artistic trash, and
theatrical idiocy can be set to the account of a people, constituting
hardly one hundredth of all the country's inhabitants, could simply
not be talked away; it was the plain truth.

And I now began to examine my beloved 'world press' from this
point of view.

And the deeper I probed, the more the object of my former admiration shriveled. The style became more and more unbearable;
I could not help rejecting the content as inwardly shallow and banal;
the objectivity of exposition now seemed to me more akin to lies
than honest truth; and the writers were—Jews.

A thousand things which I had hardly seen before now struck

my notice, and others, which had previously given me food for thought, I now learned to grasp and understand.

I now saw the liberal attitude of this press in a different light; the lofty tone in which it answered attacks and its method of killing them with silence now revealed itself to me as a trick as clever as it was treacherous; the transfigured raptures of their theatrical critics were always directed at Jewish writers, and their disapproval never struck anyone but Germans. The gentle pinpricks against William II revealed its methods by their persistency, and so did its commendation of French culture and civilization. The trashy content of the short story now appeared to me as outright indecency, and in the language I detected the accents of a foreign people; the sense of the whole thing was so obviously hostile to Germanism that this could only have been intentional.

But who had an interest in this?

Was all this a mere accident?

Gradually I became uncertain.

The development was accelerated by insights which I gained into a number of other matters. I am referring to the general view of ethics and morals which was quite openly exhibited by a large part of the Jews, and the practical application of which could be seen.

Here again the streets provided an object lesson of a sort which was sometimes positively evil.

The relation of the Jews to prostitution and, even more, to the white-slave traffic, could be studied in Vienna as perhaps in no other city of Western Europe, with the possible exception of the southern French ports. If you walked at night through the streets and alleys of Leopoldstadt, at every step you witnessed proceedings which remained concealed from the majority of the German people until the War gave the soldiers on the eastern front occasion to see similar things, or, better expressed, forced them to see them.

When thus for the first time I recognized the Jew as the cold-hearted, shameless, and calculating director of this revolting vice traffic in the scum of the big city, a cold shudder ran down my back.

But then a flame flared up within me. I no longer avoided discussion of the Jewish question; no, now I sought it. And when I learned to look for the Jew in all branches of cultural and artistic life and its various manifestations, I suddenly encountered him in a place where I would least have expected to find him.

When I recognized the Jew as the leader of the Social Democracy, the scales dropped from my eyes. A long soul struggle had reached its conclusion.

Even in my daily relations with my fellow workers, I observed the amazing adaptability with which they adopted different positions on the same question, sometimes within an interval of a few days, sometimes in only a few hours. It was hard for me to understand how people who, when spoken to alone, possessed some sensible opinions, suddenly lost them as soon as they came under the influence of the masses. It was often enough to make one despair. When, after hours of argument, I was convinced that now at last I had broken the ice or cleared up some absurdity, and was beginning to rejoice at my success, on the next day to my disgust I had to begin all over again; it had all been in vain. Like an eternal pendulum their opinions seemed to swing back again and again to the old madness.

All this I could understand: that they were dissatisfied with their lot and cursed the Fate which often struck them so harshly; that they hated the employers who seemed to them the heartless bailiffs of Fate; that they cursed the authorities who in their eyes were without feeling for their situation; that they demonstrated against food prices and carried their demands into the streets: this much could be understood without recourse to reason. But what inevitably remained incomprehensible was the boundless hatred they heaped upon their own nationality, despising its greatness, besmirching its history, and dragging its great men into the gutter.

This struggle against their own species, their own clan, their own homeland, was as senseless as it was incomprehensible. It was unnatural.

It was possible to cure them temporarily of this vice, but only for days or at most weeks. If later you met the man you thought you had converted, he was just the same as before.

His old unnatural state had regained full possession of him.

I gradually became aware that the Social Democratic press was directed predominantly by Jews; yet I did not attribute any special significance to this circumstance, since conditions were exactly the same in the other papers. Yet one fact seemed conspicuous: there was not one paper with Jews working on it which could have been regarded as truly national, according to my education and way of thinking.

I swallowed my disgust and tried to read this type of Marxist press production, but my revulsion became so unlimited in so doing that I endeavored to become more closely acquainted with the men who manufactured these compendiums of knavery.

From the publisher down, they were all Jews.

I took all the Social Democratic pamphlets I could lay hands on and sought the names of their authors: Jews. I noted the names of the leaders; by far the greatest part were likewise members of the 'chosen people,' whether they were representatives in the Reichsrat or trade-union secretaries, the heads of organizations or street agitators. It was always the same gruesome picture. The names of the Austerlitzes, Davids, Adlers, Ellenbogens, etc., will remain forever graven in my memory. One thing had grown clear to me: the party with whose petty representatives I had been carrying on the most violent struggle for months was, as to leadership, almost exclusively in the hands of a foreign people; for, to my deep and joyful satisfaction, I had at last come to the conclusion that the Jew was no German.

Only now did I become thoroughly acquainted with the seducer of our people.

A single year of my sojourn in Vienna had sufficed to imbue me with the conviction that no worker could be so stubborn that he would not in the end succumb to better knowledge and better explanations. Slowly I had become an expert in their own doctrine and used it as a weapon in the struggle for my own profound conviction.

Success almost always favored my side.

The great masses could be saved, if only with the gravest sacrifice in time and patience.

But a Jew could never be parted from his opinions.

At that time I was still childish enough to try to make the madness of their doctrine clear to them; in my little circle I talked my tongue sore and my throat hoarse, thinking I would inevitably succeed in convincing them how ruinous their Marxist madness was; but what I accomplished was often the opposite. It seemed as though their increased understanding of the destructive effects of

Social Democratic theories and their results only reinforced their determination.

The more I argued with them, the better I came to know their dialectic. First they counted on the stupidity of their adversary, and then, when there was no other way out, they themselves simply played stupid. If all this didn't help, they pretended not to understand, or, if challenged, they changed the subject in a hurry, quoted platitudes which, if you accepted them, they immediately related to entirely different matters, and then, if again attacked, gave ground and pretended not to know exactly what you were talking about. Whenever you tried to attack one of these apostles, your hand closed on a jelly-like slime which divided up and poured through your fingers, but in the next moment collected again. But if you really struck one of these fellows so telling a blow that, observed by the audience, he couldn't help but agree, and if you believed that this had taken you at least one step forward, your amazement was great the next day. The Jew had not the slightest recollection of the day before, he rattled off his same old nonsense as though nothing at all had happened, and, if indignantly challenged, affected amazement; he couldn't remember a thing, except that he had proved the correctness of his assertions the previous day.

Sometimes I stood there thunderstruck.

I didn't know what to be more amazed at: the agility of their tongues or their virtuosity at lying.

Gradually I began to hate them.

All this had but one good side: that in proportion as the real leaders or at least the disseminators of Social Democracy came within my vision, my love for my people inevitably grew. For who, in view of the diabolical craftiness of these seducers, could damn the luckless victims? How hard it was, even for me, to get the better of this race of dialectical liars! And how futile was such success in dealing with people who twist the truth in your mouth, who without so much as a blush disavow the word they have just spoken, and in the next next minute take credit for it after all.

No. The better acquainted I became with the Jew, the more forgiving I inevitably became toward the worker.

In my eyes the gravest fault was no longer with him, but with all those who did not regard it as worth the trouble to have mercy on him, with iron righteousness giving the son of the people his just deserts, and standing the seducer and corrupter up against the wall.

Inspired by the experience of daily life, I now began to track down the sources of the Marxist doctrine. Its effects had become clear to me in individual cases; each day its success was apparent to my attentive eyes, and, with some exercise of my imagination, I was able to picture the consequences. The only remaining question was whether the result of their action in its ultimate form had existed in the mind's eye of the creators, or whether they themselves were the victims of an error.

I felt that both were possible.

In the one case it was the duty of every thinking man to force himself to the forefront of the ill-starred movement, thus perhaps averting catastrophe; in the other, however, the original founders of this plague of the nations must have been veritable devils; for only in the brain of a monster—not that of a man—could the plan of an organization assume form and meaning, whose activity must ultimately result in the collapse of human civilization and the consequent devastation of the world.

In this case the only remaining hope was struggle, struggle with all the weapons which the human spirit, reason, and will can devise, regardless on which side of the scale Fate should lay its blessing.

Thus I began to make myself familiar with the founders of this doctrine, in order to study the foundations of the movement. If I reached my goal more quickly than at first I had perhaps ventured to believe, it was thanks to my newly acquired, though at that time not very profound, knowledge of the Jewish question. This alone enabled me to draw a practical comparison between the reality and the theoretical flim-flam of the founding fathers of Social Democracy, since it taught me to understand the language of the Jewish people, who speak in order to conceal or at least to veil their thoughts; their real aim is not therefore to be found in the lines themselves, but slumbers well concealed between them.

For me this was the time of the greatest spiritual upheaval I have ever had to go through.

I had ceased to be a weak-kneed cosmopolitan and become an anti-Semite.

Just once more—and this was the last time—fearful, oppressive thoughts came to me in profound anguish.

When over long periods of human history I scrutinized the activity of the Jewish people, suddenly there rose up in me the fearful question whether inscrutable Destiny, perhaps for reasons unknown to us poor mortals, did not with eternal and immutable resolve, desire the final victory of this little nation.

Was it possible that the earth had been promised as a reward to this people which lives only for this earth?

Have we an objective right to struggle for our self-preservation, or is this justified only subjectively within ourselves?

As I delved more deeply into the teachings of Marxism and thus in tranquil clarity submitted the deeds of the Jewish people to contemplation, Fate itself gave me its answer.

The Jewish doctrine of Marxism rejects the aristocratic principle of Nature and replaces the eternal privilege of power and strength by the mass of numbers and their dead weight. Thus it denies the value of personality in man, contests the significance of nationality and race, and thereby withdraws from humanity the premise of its existence and its culture. As a foundation of the universe, this doctrine would bring about the end of any order intellectually conceivable to man. And as, in this greatest of all recognizable organisms, the result of an application of such a law could only be chaos, on earth it could only be destruction for the inhabitants of this planet.

If, with the help of his Marxist creed, the Jew is victorious over the other peoples of the world, his crown will be the funeral wreath of humanity and this planet will, as it did thousands of years ago, move through the ether devoid of men.

Eternal Nature inexorably avenges the infringement of her commands.

Hence today I believe that I am acting in accordance with the will of the Almighty Creator: *by defending myself against the Jew, I am fighting for the work of the Lord.*

NIKITA KHRUSHCHEV:

*"The Jews have always preferred artisan
trades; they are tailors, glass workers,
jewelers, traders, druggists, and carpenters.
But, if you take the building trades, or
metallurgy, you would not encounter
a single Jew to my knowledge." (1958)*

The treatment of Jews in the countries of Eastern Europe has, for centuries, furnished material for some of the bloodiest chapters in Jewish history. At the mercy of tsars, Cossacks, and peasants, Russian and Polish Jews were massacred by the thousands and even the hundreds of thousands during the Middle Ages. As late as the nineteenth and early twentieth centuries, the *pogrom* (which itself is a Russian word) spelled torture and death for whole communities of Jews.

When the Communists seized power in Russia in 1917, there was some expectation, in world Gentile and Jewish circles alike, that the end of tsarism and feudalism would also mark the end, at least in the Soviet Union, of organized anti-Semitism. For one thing, Karl Marx was himself of Jewish origin, and a number of Jews played leading roles in the revolution, notably Leon Trotsky (born Lev Davidovich Bronstein). But more important, Marxist principles appeared to be antagonistic to doctrines of racism and ethnic chauvinism. On the contrary, it was often argued by Communist sympathizers, the Bolsheviks would prove to be stanch friends of persecuted minorities everywhere, including the Jewish minority. Indeed, well into the nineteen forties Communist parties in the West were insisting that there was no official, and very little unofficial, anti-Semitism in the USSR.

Despite recurrent rumors of organized and unorganized Soviet anti-Semitism—rumors hotly denied by Communists and sympathizers with Communism—there was a considerable shock throughout the world in November, 1952, when eleven men—eight of whom were publicly identified as "of Jewish origin"—were indicted and convicted in Prague, Czechoslovakia, of having served as the conspiratorial agents of world Jewry, and the Zionist movement. International reaction was hardly less subdued when certain Jewish doctors in Moscow were accused of endeavoring to poison leading Soviet officials. Both the Prague trials, an

From Peter Meyer, "Stalin Follows in Hitler's Footsteps," originally published in *Commentary*, reprinted in Elliot E. Cohen, editor, *The New Red Anti-Semitism: a Symposium* (Boston: The Beacon Press, 1953), pp. 2–4, 6–8. Copyright 1953 by American Jewish Committee.

official account of which is here reprinted, and the so-called "Doctors' Plot" served to confirm the impression that one of the cruder varieties of anti-Semitism was firmly entrenched in the highest official circles of the Soviet Union.

With the death of Joseph Stalin in early 1953, and the subsequent disavowal by Khrushchev of the "Doctors' Plot," there were hopes, again, that the Jews of Eastern Europe would no longer be singled out for special treatment and discrimination. And thus far there have been no repeat performances of the Prague trials or the "Doctors' Plot." On the other hand, Jewish religious and cultural activities are carefully regulated, or suppressed altogether, in most Iron Curtain countries. Moreover, the *Figaro* interview of 1958 with the present Chairman of the Council of Ministers of the USSR, a portion of which follows, suggests that Nikita Khrushchev's effort to stereotype Jews has something in common with the earlier efforts of his tsarist and Communist predecessors.

From the Prague Trials of 1952

Defendant Rudolf Slansky

Former Secretary General of the Communist Party of Czechoslovakia

PRESIDING JUDGE: "Accused Slansky, step before the microphone. Are you guilty of the four described criminal acts?"

SLANSKY: "Yes."

PRESIDING JUDGE: "The first crime is espionage."

SLANSKY: "Yes."

PRESIDING JUDGE: "Sabotage."

SLANSKY: "Yes."

PRESIDING JUDGE: "High treason."

SLANSKY: "Yes."

PRESIDING JUDGE: "Military treason."

SLANSKY: "Yes."

PRESIDING JUDGE: "Will you please tell us in what respect you admit your guilt?"

SLANSKY: "First of all I wish to confess my guilt that, as the enemy of the Communist party and the People's Democratic regime, I formed the anti-state conspiratorial center at the head of which I stood for several years. . . ."

PRESIDING JUDGE: "How is it that you, who have been a member of the Czechoslovak Communist party for thirty years, could become a servant of the imperialists and the organizer and leader of a conspiracy against the Czechoslovak People's Democratic Republic?"

In reply to this question Slansky gave an outline of his origins and political past. He said he came from a bourgeois family of a rich village merchant and this had influenced his "personal traits and character." In 1921 he joined the Communist party still burdened with "petty bourgeois opinions, which I never abandoned. This prevented me from becoming a real Communist. Therefore I did not act as a Communist, and I did not fulfill honorably the duties arising from my membership in the Communist party. . . ."

The Prosecutor . . . asked Slansky to explain how his center of conspiracy "was linked with the Western imperialist powers or imperialist circles and in what manner these circles directed the activities of the center." Slansky said one link had been the various people who at different times had become agents of the imperialist intelligence service of Great Britain, the United States, France, and Yugoslavia. Another link had been diverse organizations such as the Zionists and Freemasons—all interconnected and ruled by the Anglo-U.S. imperialists. . . .

The Prosecutor then asked Slansky to elaborate his admission that he had placed Zionists in important posts. Slansky explained that he did so "because the Zionists were conducting hostile activity aimed at the liquidation of the popular democratic regime in Czechoslovakia. I collaborated with them and I placed various Zionist elements into important posts in the administrative, economic, and party apparatus. . . ."

The significance of this, he said, lay in the fact that Zionist organizations in Czechoslovakia were in turn connected with similar Zionist organizations in the capitalist countries. "The whole worldwide Zionist movement was, in fact, led and ruled by the imperialists—in particular the U.S. imperialists through the American Zionists. For American Zionists, who as in other countries are the financially most powerful and politically most influential Zionists, form part of the ruling imperialist circles of America."

The Zionist organization, moreover, was a channel through which the imperialists carried out extensive espionage and subversive work in Czechoslovakia. The "Joint" organization [American Jewish Joint Distribution Committee] in Prague was "a branch of the American Zionists" and played an important part in various hostile machinations. One of these was "the abuse of the emigration scheme under which Jewish citizens left for the capitalist countries, thereby removing from Czechoslovakia unjustifiably large property values and causing grave economic damage."

Slansky admitted that he [tolerated] the legal existence in Czechoslovakia, both before and after February 1948, of these nationalist bourgeois Zionist organizations. Though his attention was drawn to the hostile work conducted by them he protected them: "I deliberately shielded them by perverting the campaign against so-called anti-Semitism. By proposing that a big campaign be waged against anti-Semitism, by magnifying the danger of anti-Semitism, and by proposing various measures against anti-Semitism—such as the writing of articles, the publication of pamphlets, the holding of lectures, and so forth—I criminally prevented the waging of a campaign against Zionism and the revelation of the hostile character of Zionist ideology, and the unmasking of the hostile activity of Zionists and Zionist organizations."

Slansky said he had discussed these matters with Geminder, Svermova, Frank, and others. In addition to the campaign against anti-Semitism there had also been a press publicity drive for the State of Israel without its being pointed out that Israel was a bourgeois state and in fact represented the most advanced outpost of the American imperialists in the Near East. "I deliberately shielded Zionism by publicly speaking out against the people who pointed to the hostile activities of Zionists and by describing these people as anti-Semites—just as did my collaborators—so that these people were in the end prosecuted and persecuted and sometimes even excluded from the party, as happened to certain members of the Central Secretariat. I thus created an atmosphere in which people were afraid—even prominent officials in the state apparatus—to oppose Zionism and Zionist organizations."

With regard to the emigration scheme—in which Geminder as [well as] Fischl played important parts—he had condoned the exportation from Czechoslovakia of excessive quantities of valuable property. In this he and his group collaborated with members of the Israeli delegation, such as the Israeli Minister Ueberall, "who is in fact an agent of the U.S. imperialists."

Another field in which his conspiratorial group worked through the Zionists was foreign trade. Here Loebl and Margolius played important parts. Czechoslovak foreign trade was misused to the advantage of Zionist organizations at home and abroad, thereby supporting the bourgeois State of Israel. Czechoslovakia suffered economic damage as a result of her goods being sold at unfavorable prices, lower than in the capitalist market, while manufactures from capitalist countries were imported at high prices. Huge profits went to Zionist organizations and benefited Israel. . . .

PROSECUTOR: "In your subversive activities have you also made use of other organizations?"

SLANSKY: "Yes."

PROSECUTOR: "Which were they?"

SLANSKY: "Freemasons. The anti-state conspiratorial center made use in their activities of Zionist organizations as well as Freemasons and their lodges. I myself had connections with Freemasons, for example with Ing. Machon and Dr. Vancura, who were outstanding officials of Freemason lodges. . . ."

In the field of foreign trade Slansky and his associates also had done their utmost to organize sabotage and cause damage. . . . Owing to their Zionist convictions, these associates cooperated with various American agents and endeavored to link the Czechoslovak economy to the capitalist West; machinery and equipment was bought in the capitalist West although it could have been supplied at more favorable prices by the USSR. . . .

In reply to the Prosecutor's questions about his anti-state activities other than those mentioned in his evidence today, Slansky said: "In my hostile activities I relied on the support of various hostile organizations such as the Zionists and Freemasons and on hostile elements among partisans, false trade unionists, and so forth. . . ."

PROSECUTOR: "Further, it is clear from the evidence you have given that you formed an anti-state conspiratorial center which was preparing the overthrow of the People's Democratic regime and the restoration of capitalism, and that you carried on these activities in the service of the Western imperialists and primarily in the service of the U.S. aspirants to world domination—"

SLANSKY: "I admit this."

PROSECUTOR: "—in order to become a Czechoslovak Tito. Is this so?"

SLANSKY: "Yes."

Defendant André Simone

Former Editor of Rude Pravo

The commentator said that Simone was a former editor of the Communist daily *Rude Pravo,* and described him as a cunning globetrotter, a spy without backbone, who as a son of a wealthy manufacturer obstinately hated the working class. . . .

PRESIDING JUDGE: "What led you to actively fight the People's Democratic regime in Czechoslovakia?"

SIMONE: "I shall tell the truth. I am the son of a manufacturer and educated in the spirit of the bourgeois ideology. The working class was alien to me. This was why my surroundings were formed of people spiritually akin to me, from the ranks of traitors against the working people, Trotskyites, right-wing socialists, and bourgeois elements. For thirty years I defended the bourgeois ideology, disrupted the unity of the working class and the workers' movement in various capitalist countries, and I carried on similar activities in Czechoslovakia as a participant in Slansky's conspiracy. . . ."

STATE PROSECUTOR: "When and how did you become associated with the French espionage service?"

SIMONE: "In September 1939, I pledged myself to the French Minister Mandel in Paris."

Continuing, Simone said that Mandel had maintained his own espionage service with the help of Jewish and some French capitalist magnates. In 1939 Mandel had discussed with the accused the Daladier plan and had told him about his belief that a second world war would break out. Mandel had expected Germany's defeat and had stressed the point that after the war matters would have to be settled with the Soviet Union.

The accused had agreed with Mandel's view and had told him that he, Mandel, could always rely on his cooperation. . . .

STATE PROSECUTOR: "In 1939 you pledged your cooperation to the British Intelligence Service. Tell us about it."

SIMONE: "I pledged my collaboration with the British Intelligence Service in Paris in 1939 in the office of the agent Paul Willert. . . ."

In February 1946, before his departure for Czechoslovakia, he had been asked by the British Vice Consul to report in London to

Willert, which he did. He met Willert twice in London in April.
Simone told the court that he informed Willert on the first occasion
that in New York he, Simone, had agreed with the Jewish nationalist
and U.S. intelligence agent Schoenbrunn to cooperate on behalf of
the U.S. Intelligence Service. . . .

They met at a restaurant and Schoenbrunn informed him that he
was instructed by the U.S. Secret Service to negotiate with him.
Schoenbrunn emphasized that the United States was conducting the
same policy as Mandel, who, if he were still alive, would whole-
heartedly back Washington. Mandel had rendered splendid service
to capitalist Jewry.

Schoenbrunn said: "It is the duty of every Jew to support the
Americans even if he does not agree with every detail of their policy." Simone's best way of showing his support was by providing
"information" which the prosecutor interpreted as "espionage information."

Simone then explained what he knew of the background of
Schoenbrunn. He was the son of a Jewish capitalist who migrated
to the United States before the First World War. In 1946-47 Schoenbrunn was in the service of the U.S. Overseas News Agency, "which
is an organ of the U.S. Jewish capitalists," financed among others
by Bernard Baruch. This agency "is one of the important links among
the U.S. Zionists and Jewish nationalists in the United States and
cooperates closely with the State Department." Through this agency
the U.S. Psychological Warfare Board was spreading "outrageous
lies and slander against the Peace Camp." Simone knew all this when
he agreed to work for Schoenbrunn.

He was then asked to say something more about the U.S. Psychological Warfare Board. He said that the members were officials of
the State Department, War Department, the Catholic and Protestant
churches, and Jewish organizations.

The Board "organizes murder, sabotage, and diversionary activities in China, and so forth. It had at its disposal hundreds of millions
of dollars of the Mutual Security Act with which to achieve the
same purposes in the USSR and the People's Democracies, as well
as for the recruitment of exile emigrés for the U.S. Forces. The
correct name for the Board ought to be the 'U.S. Board for a Shooting War and for the Liquidation of Progressive People, for Murder-
ous Atomic Aggression on the USSR and the People's Democracies,

and for the Elimination of Anything in the Way of the U.S. Imperialists. . . .' "

Simone . . . had given Slansky a full report about his close connections with Jewish nationalists and Zionist circles in Mexico and as editor of the paper [one word missing] *Israelite.*

Slansky had accepted this news as a matter of course. Slansky had shown particular interest in the activities of Browder, former Secretary General of the U.S. Communists, "unmasked in 1944 as an enemy of the working people. His interest in details of Browder's technique as a liquidator" became understandable to Simone only later when he realized that Slansky wanted to "emulate Browder and Tito in usurping power and liquidating the Marx-Lenin Communist party of Czechoslovakia," whereby he would have tried to destroy the popular democratic regime. . . .

In 1946 Slansky told him [Simone] of the need to "popularize Tito and Yugoslavia's specific roads to Socialism." At that time he had not known that Slansky had talked with Tito. Slansky had also shown great interest in cooperation with the Zionists and [Jewish] nationalists in Mexico.

The Presiding Judge asked Simone why he thought Slansky had confided to him his "hostile intentions."

Simone replied: "He wanted to ensnare me in his conspiratorial center in Czechoslovakia." Due to Simone's background, Slansky had found it easy to win him over. . . .

Simone had renewed his contacts with the intelligence service agent Willert, in August 1946 at the Paris Peace Conference, when he supplied him with a detailed report of his activities in Czechoslovakia and when "I told him that Slansky had his own notions and plans for future development in Czechoslovakia." Willert had asked many questions about Slansky. . . .

PROSECUTOR: "Who contacted you and gave you the password agreed upon with Willert after your return from the Peace Conference?"

SIMONE: "In 1947 the British spy Alexander Werth called me up and asked me to meet him. We met in the National Club where Werth immediately identified himself with Willer's password. From 1947 on I had espionage contacts with the British spy Alexander Werth on the occasion of his trips to Czechoslovakia right up to the autumn of 1949. I met him four times, always after telephone conversations.

"I used to meet Werth either in the Hotel Alcron, in the National Club, or in the Restaurant Lippert. With every important report which I gave to Werth, I quoted its source. Werth always asked me about my work and my position and always showed interest in the development of my relations with Slansky and Clementis. . . ."

Simone stated that information for his espionage reports had been given to him by Slansky, Geminder, Loebl, Frejka, Clementis, and Hajdu.

"When I was unable to supply these Western agents with the information they required, I put them in touch with other members of the espionage center, above all, Slansky. In March 1948 I arranged a meeting between Slansky and two hostile Labor Members of Parliament, Crossman and Wigg. I arranged this meeting by telephone and it was to be held in the Communist party secretariat. Slansky wanted me to act as interpreter at this meeting, but as I could not do this he used Vilem Novy as an interpreter. After his return to Britain, Crossman wrote a number of hostile articles against People's Democratic Czechoslovakia.

"During the Paris Peace Conference I put Clementis in touch with the U.S. Agents Schoenbrunn, Howard Smith, and Edgar Allan Mowrer. Later I arranged meetings of Schoenbrunn and Hindus with Clementis. . . .

"As a conspirator I am responsible for every action and crime of each Jewish member of the conspiratorial center.

"Which are the countries where fierce anti-Semitism is on the increase? The United States and Great Britain. I have joined the spies of those states. Which country has a law against racialism and anti-Semitism? The USSR. I have joined U.S., British, and French anti-Semites against the Soviet Union. Therein lies my crime.

"I am a writer, supposedly an architect of the soul. What sort of architect have I been—I who have poisoned people's souls? Such an architect of the soul belongs to the gallows. The only service I can still render is to warn all who by origin or character are in danger of following the same path to hell. The sterner the punishment . . . [unintelligible]."

[The commentator wound up by saying that the evidence of this "cynical enemy of the working people," like that of all the other defendants, had once again revealed the depths to which that "scum of society," that "gang of adventurers and lickspittles in the service of U.S. armament kings," had sunk. The people "will mete out rigorous and just punishment."]

An Interview with Nikita Khrushchev, 1958*

The political policies followed by the Soviet towards other nationalities are as just as they are generous. The U.S.S.R. was the first nation in the world to decide to help the Jews, not individually but as a people. For this purpose we chose a sparsely populated region in Siberia, north of Manchuria—Birobidjan. We put it at the disposal of the Jews, and accorded it a special statute. This was a remarkable gift. Actually the lands of Birobidjan are the most fertile in existence. Over there the climate is temperate; the cultivation of the soil is a pleasure. There is water and sun. There are immense forests, fertile lands, an abundance of minerals, and rivers teeming with fish. What happened? The Jews left in masses for Birobidjan. They were enthusiastic and in high spirits. From all corners of the Soviet Union they came, and I should add from all the European countries from which they were able to come, fleeing from persecution. And now? Very few remain there. Currently the comings and goings continue, but one must admit that there are more returning than going.

How many Jews remain in that beautiful region? Here is something I cannot tell you exactly, as there are no records of any kind available on this. There must certainly be quite a number remaining. In 1955, I myself crossed through Birobidjan, and . . . I perceived numerous Yiddish inscriptions in the stations and on the streets around the stations.

If one draws a balance sheet, it must be admitted that Jewish colonization in Birobidjan has been a failure. They arrive there all fired with enthusiasm and then one after the other they leave.

How can you explain this unfortunate state of affairs? In my opinion it is due to historical conditions. The Jews have always preferred artisan trades; they are tailors, glass workers, jewelers, traders,

* From an interview with Nikita Khrushchev, reported in *Le Figaro* (Paris), April 9, 1958. Translated by Jacques Duroux.

druggists, and carpenters. But, if you take the buildings trades, or metallurgy, you would not encounter a single Jew to my knowledge. They do not like collective work, or group discipline. They are individualists.

Let us set aside the new State of Israel. For tens of centuries the Jews have never been able to resolve to live together among themselves and to draw their livelihood and equilibrium from themselves alone, apart from other communities. A second characteristic is that the Jews are in essence intellectuals. They never consider themselves sufficiently educated. As soon as they can possibly manage it they want to go to the university, despite the necessary sacrifices to achieve that aim. You ask me why there are no Hebrew schools in Birobidjan or elsewhere? Because it is impossible to compel the Jews to attend Jewish schools. Also, their interests are too divergent and often too much at odds to make it possible to satisfy them in any region where they would find themselves all together, face to face. This does not depend on the non-Jews. A true Jewish cultural community is no more possible of attainment than a political community: the Jews are interested in everything, want to get to the bottom of everything, discuss on all topics and finish up by having very diverse and deep cultural concepts.

In the U.S.S.R. there are nationalities which are less numerous than the Jews, or who are less gifted. But these non-Jews are better at organizing a common existence. That is why it is possible for them to build durable national institutions. I could quote you innumerable examples. One cannot fight against the wish to create nor against negative ideas. That is why I am skeptical as to what is required for the permanency of Jewish collectivism.

On the subject of the Jews, I believe that the Israel experience is a success.

We Communists sympathize greatly with the Jews who have immigrated to Israel. The letters which we receive from them are moving in their numbers and their sorrow. Over there it is the housing which is lacking, and it is the lack of being accustomed to agricultural labor. Then there is the difficulty of assimilation between exiles coming from so many different places. For what did all those Jews go there? They realized they were returning to the land of their ancestors. These are not sufficient grounds to enable them to live close to one another and cement a true nation.

Israel has not adopted happy positions for the Jewish people. The U.S.S.R. had voted for Israel at the United Nations. She had supported that state at its birth, in a very useful manner. Israel showed herself ungrateful and unfortunate in her choices. That nation plays the game of imperialists and enemies of socialist countries. We buy only a few oranges from Israel. We could do without.

In conclusion, it is Israelite imperialists who relate the horrors about Birobidjan. At the same time the capitalists try to incite nasty accounts of the rights of nationalities in the Soviet Union, where all people can exist happily in socialist liberty. All that is anti-Soviet propaganda. Discussion on this subject is useless.

ERNEST JONES:

". . . the greater part of this bulky Jewish question is related to a central characteristic of Jews that may very reasonably be derived from their peculiar belief of being God's chosen people: . . ." (1959)

Ernest Jones, M.D. (1879–1958), was, for many years, the leading figure in the British psychoanalytical movement. Of Welsh background, Jones was a practicing neurologist during his early years in London. In 1907 he paid his first visit to Sigmund Freud in Vienna, and shortly afterward began to specialize in psychiatry and psychoanalysis. Long after many of Freud's early co-workers had taken issue with Freud's theories, notably Carl Jung and Alfred Adler, Jones remained loyal to the founder of psychoanalysis, and ultimately became one of his foremost disciples. Widely credited with introducing psychoanalysis in Britain and the United States, Jones founded the *International Journal of Psychoanalysis*, and was one of the founders, in 1911, of the American Psychoanalytical Society. Author of a large number of books and monographs, Jones is best known for his three-volume biography, *The Life and Work of Sigmund Freud* (1953–1957).

The selection here reprinted is from Jones's posthumously published autobiography, *Free Associations: Memories of a Psycho-Analyst*, which appeared in the United States in 1959.

From Ernest Jones, *Free Associations: Memories of a Psycho-analyst* (New York: Basic Books, Inc., 1959), pp. 208–212.

The situation was still further complicated to some extent by the curious circumstance that, with the exception of the small Swiss group—who nearly all parted company after four or five years—and myself, all the early workers in psycho-analysis were Jews. I imagine the reasons for this were mainly local ones in Austria and Germany, since, except to some slight extent in the United States, it is a feature that has not been repeated in any other country; in England, for example, only two analysts have been Jews (apart from refugee immigrants). In Vienna it was obviously easier for Jewish doctors to share Freud's ostracism, which was only an exacerbation of the life they were accustomed to, and the same was true of Berlin and Budapest, where anti-Semitism was almost equally pronounced. The aptness of Jews for psychological intuition, and their ability to withstand public obloquy, may also have contributed to this state of affairs. It was one that had some influence on the form taken, especially at first, by the psycho-analytical "movement." It also had personal results for myself, since I found, to my surprise, that henceforth my life was to be lived mainly in Jewish company and that my best friends would for the greater part be Jews. This could not but be a matter of interest to me, and it makes it inevitable that I should say something about my attitude to this vexed and delicate topic.

Until this time I had had no friends among Jews, and had met very few of them. In childhood I remember my grandmother telling me that Jews were people who kept pawnshops, a fact with hardly any meaning to me, and that they were obstinate people who kept apart from the rest, even going to the length of having non-Christian synagogues of their own. So I suppose I started life with the usual vague prejudice against them. There were none in any school I went to, and only one or two in college or hospital; there was nothing, therefore, to arouse my interest in them. I doubt if I connected them much with the ancient Jews of the Old Testament, about whom I was of course fully informed. These lived far away and long ago, and had presumably disappeared, for the remarkable and incredible stories one read of their doings were hard to connect with any real everyday world.

The Jews I was now to get to know were of course all foreigners, from whom one must expect standards of all sorts and attitudes of mind different from English ones, so it was some time before I came to discriminate between them and other foreigners and to remark on their own distinguishing characteristics. As time went on, however, my position as the only Gentile sharing deeply their main preoccupation with, I think I may say, my own unusual capacity for adaptation and sympathetic understanding, led to my being admitted to their intimacy on practically equal terms. They would almost forget my Gentile extraction, and would freely share with me their characteristic jokes, anecdotes, points of view, and outlook on life. After a quarter of a century's such experience I came to feel that I knew their characteristics with an intimacy that must have fallen to the lot of few Gentiles, and I have reflected much on them and the social problems that surround their lives. I am going to prove this to any Jewish readers of this book by an anecdote which I shall not attempt to translate to others. When the Nazis took possession of Vienna one of the urgent problems that arose was how to help the patients of the Psycho-Analytical Clinic there. The Nazis said we might for the moment continue to treat them, but that the Directorship of the Clinic must be in "Aryan" hands. On inquiring about Dr. Sterba, one of our colleagues who happened to be a Gentile, I was told he had left for Switzerland, whereupon, to the general amusement, I exclaimed: *"O weh, unser einziger Shabbes-Goy ist fort."*

In one important respect, however, my knowledge on this topic is singularly deficient. It has never been my fortune to know a Jew possessing any religious belief, let alone an orthodox one. It may well be said that this quite disqualifies me from holding any opinion worth anything on any Jewish question, for to empty it of its religious kernel is surely to make it into a *Hamlet* without the Danish Prince. I should not myself agree, however. I fully admit that the greater part of what is called the Jewish problem emanates from their remarkable religious history, but I am sufficiently familiar with that history both from my first-hand experience in childhood and from extensive subsequent reading.

Well, after this preamble, all I am going to say here on a topic that might well fill an interesting book amounts to two personal expressions of opinion. The first is that the greater part of this bulky Jewish problem is related to a central characteristic of Jews that may very reasonably be derived from their peculiar belief of being

God's Chosen People: namely, their intense, and practically universal, determination not merely to regard themselves as different from other people but also fundamentally to remain so despite any superficial compromise they may appear to make. Although every distinct community possesses something of this quality, no other seems to possess it in anything like the same degree, and no other maintains it when living as a minority amidst other communities.

My second observation is that, whatever other qualities Jews may possess, likable or the reverse, no one who knows them well can deny that they are personally interesting. By that I mean, specially alive, alert, quick at comprehending people or events and at making pungent or witty comments on them. My Celtic mind, a little impatient of Anglo-Saxon placidity, complacency, and slowness of imagination, responded gratefully to these qualities, and it was perhaps the chief reason why I enjoyed Jewish society. One might at times find the rather hothouse family atmosphere, with its intensities and frictions, somewhat trying, but one could be sure of never being bored. These are the qualities, together with the resulting swift facility in apprehension of knowledge, that go to support the Jewish belief, which they often impose on other people too, concerning the superiority of their intellectual powers. I have never been convinced of that myself, for one should not take one kind of intelligence for the whole of what the brain can do, and I greatly doubt if the first-class names in science, art, or literature are more often Jewish than their numbers or opportunities would lead one to expect.

These last considerations have a considerable bearing on the reactions of the psycho-analytical group when faced with their difficult internal and external situation. The opposition to psycho-analysis, inevitable in any event, was doubtless heightened by anti-Semitic prejudice, which, curiously enough, has often had a sexual accompaniment, just as the anti-"colour" prejudices of English and Americans have. A Jew was, so to speak, the wrong person to announce that the sexual instinct was a far more subtle and significant factor in mental life than had ever been supposed; and the fact that—in Central Europe at least, where anti-Semitism was so strong—only Jews could be found to support the new views confirmed the suspicions of outsiders. The Jews themselves, with their proneness, so often justified, to interpret any criticism or opposition as actuated by anti-Semitism, also tended to confuse the issue in the same way; and their natural eagerness to make converts conflicted with their innate tendency to retire behind ghetto walls with an outlook of suspicion and resentment.

V

THE JEW IN AMERICA
1654–1958

HISTORICAL NOTE

The American Jewish community, numerically the world's largest with a population of more than five million, began with the arrival at New Amsterdam in 1654 of twenty-three Jewish refugees from Recife in Brazil. These early immigrants, known as Sephardic Jews (the word *Sephardim* is derived from the Hebrew term for Spain) were descendants of the Jews who had been expelled from Spain in 1492. The original *Sephardim* had moved from Spain to various parts of Europe, and a small group had chosen to settle in the New World. When Recife passed from Dutch to Portugese hands, the Jews again became refugees, and set out for North America. They were later joined by other Sephardic Jews, but the *Sephardim* never constituted a numerous following in the United States.

New Amsterdam, under Peter Stuyvesant, initially accorded the Jews a hostile reception. Stuyvesant made no secret of his personal animosity toward Jews, and he first endeavored to exclude them from the Dutch colony. Although the effort failed, the Jews for a time were subjected to a number of restrictions. For example, they were prohibited from serving in the forces that stood guard against Indian attacks; instead, they were required to pay a special tax to support such forces. But gradually, after successive appeals to Stuyvesant's employers, the West India Company in Holland, the New Amsterdam Jews achieved equal citizenship.

In 1658 a group of New Amsterdam Jews emigrated to Newport, Rhode Island, attracted by Roger Williams's offer of full religious toleration. During the following century, additional Jewish settlers arrived from England, Holland, the West Indies, and elsewhere. Most of them engaged in mercantile occupations, and established homes and businesses on the Atlantic seaboard and along the main arteries of commerce. By 1776 Jewish communities existed in New York, Newport, Philadelphia, Charleston, and Savannah. From 1790 to 1830, the number of Jews in the United States increased from 2,500 to approximately 10,000.

The large-scale emigration of German Jews to the United States occurred between 1830 and 1880. Although the majority arrived impoverished from German ghettos, their social and economic status rapidly improved. By the time of the Civil War, a number of German Jews had become successful merchants and manufacturers, and a few were engaged in banking. As a result of the emancipation of German Jewry in 1871, the movement of German Jews to the United States was sharply reduced.

The wave of German Jewish emigration was followed by a vast influx of Jews from Eastern Europe. In the late nineteenth century, pogroms in Russia, the Ukraine, Poland, and Rumania forced millions of Jews to flee from their homes, and by 1924, when the Johnson-Lodge bill halting their immigration was passed into law, some 2,500,000 Eastern European Jews had arrived in the United States. The bulk of these immigrants settled in New York, and large numbers of them became workers in the garment industry.

In our own time, Jewish immigrants in the United States have largely consisted of refugees from Nazi Europe and, more recently, Communist countries. The majority of the 150,000 refugees who arrived between 1936 and the end of World War II were of middle-class origin, and they had little difficulty adjusting themselves to American conditions. Since World War II, more than 100,000 refugees, many of them destitute survivors of the concentration camps, have entered the United States.

American Jews, for the most part, have fared better than the Jews of any other country. Although there have been vigorous outbreaks of anti-Semitism—during and after the Civil War, and, again, in the nineteen twenties and nineteen thirties—anti-Semitism has never been a matter of official government policy. The United States Constitution states explicitly that no religious test shall ever be required for public office, and no American President has ever been a declared anti-Semite. Moreover, while no Jew has ever been nominated for the presidency, Jews have served with distinction as Supreme Court Justices, Governors, Senators, and Congressmen.

The discriminations affecting Jews have largely been social and occupational. Thus Jews are often not permitted to join country clubs, and at many universities Jews are enrolled under a so-called "quota" system. In the earlier period, especially, Jews had difficulty making careers for themselves in heavy industry, banking, transportation, mining, insurance, and public utilities. It was also true, in the late nineteenth and early twentieth centuries, that discrimination in employment forced many Jews into sweatshops where, as foreigners, they were ruthlessly exploited. Restricted covenants in housing, if not requiring the establishment of a ghetto, have nevertheless limited residential choice (but Jews, it need hardly be added, have never been as severely restricted as Negroes).

Nevertheless, when this history is fairly reviewed, it becomes apparent that the experience of American Jewry has been quite different from that of European Jewry. If there has been occasional indulgence, by a minority, in vicious Jew-baiting and anti-Semitism, there have never been massacres of Jews, or pogroms, or inquisitions, or concentration camps. The influenza epidemic after World War I was not blamed on the Jews, and the South did not attribute its defeat in the Civil War to a Jewish conspiracy. Moreover, while social discrimination remains, today one notes fewer hotel and resort advertisements that include the phrase "Christians Only." Universities each year appear to make less use of "quota" systems, and every year also sees an increase in the number of mixed fraternities and sororities on campuses. Although "hate" sheets still circulate, it is doubtful that the American Nazi party will become a mass movement in the foreseeable future.

Indeed the history of American Jewry lends testimony to the strength of the "melting pot" tradition. "Only in America," as Harry Golden might say, could integration of Jews have proceeded so far as to produce, by the mid-twentieth century, the "Farfel Frolics" and "Herring Hops" that are as much a part of Jewish temple as their counterparts are of Protestant church life. As Will Herberg has remarked, the temples and churches have in common "the same corporate structure, the same proliferation of men's clubs, sisterhoods, junior congregations, youth groups, 'young marrieds,' Sunday school classes, discussion circles, adult education projects, breakfasts, 'brunches,' dinners, and suppers." And one could add: Scout Troops, Cub Packs, picnics, baseball teams, and bowling leagues. Small wonder, then, that for many American Jews the United States, not Israel, has become the Promised Land, and the city in which they dwell, the new Jerusalem.

Yet the destiny of American Jewry, as of Jewry everywhere, is not indicated clearly by either past or present. Although Jews have a firm footing in the United States, they contribute millions of dollars annually to Zionist organizations in America and abroad. Israeli bonds have a ready market in Jewish circles, and each summer thousands of American Jews visit Tel Aviv, Haifa, and the *Kibbutzim*. In recent years there has been some revival of Orthodox Judaism, and many young adults, who formerly took their religion lightly or not at all, are now raising their children in the Orthodox fashion. Do these developments betoken security and confidence in the future, or insecurity and a lack of confidence? Is it possible that the American Jew, for all of his belief that he has found the Promised Land, occasionally catches a gleam of history in the eye of his Gentile neighbor—a gleam of the nightmare from which Stephen Dedalus was attempting to awaken?

These are questions which each Jew and Gentile must answer for himself.

PETER STUYVESANT:

*"The Jews who have arrived would nearly
all like to remain here . . . [but we] have
deemed it useful to require them in a
friendly way to depart." (1654)*

Peter Stuyvesant (1592–1672) was Dutch Colonial governor of New Amsterdam. Somewhat arbitrary and despotic in manner, Stuyvesant's governorship was characterized by disputes with leading Dutch merchants over questions of representation and trade policy. Stuyvesant also aroused opposition through his efforts to increase taxes, and to prohibit the sale of liquor and firearms to the Indians. Generally unpopular, he returned to Holland in 1665 where he was blamed for the political and financial difficulties in North America of the parent West India Company. Returning to New Amsterdam in 1667, Stuyvesant spent the remaining five years of his life on his farm, the "Bouwerie," in that section of New York City now known as the "Bowery."

In addition to opposing Jewish settlement in New Amsterdam, Stuyvesant also persecuted Lutherans and Quakers. As the following selections demonstrate, Stuyvesant was unsuccessful in his efforts to exclude Jews, but for some years Jewish residents of New Amsterdam were not permitted to open retail shops or to engage in certain professions. Moreover, the West India Company specified that the Jews, in buying real estate, should live "close together," although the Company did not indicate in what neighborhood or locality. In adopting a more tolerant attitude toward Jews than that displayed by Stuyvesant, the Directors in Holland were guided by the fact that a number of Jews were important stockholders in the Company, and that, further, Jewish trade and commerce were an asset to the economic well-being of the new colony.

From Jacob R. Marcus, editor, *The Jew in the Medieval World* (Cincinnati, Ohio: The Union of American Hebrew Congregations, 1938), pp. 69–72; Copyright 1938 by Union of American Hebrew Congregations; reprinted 1960 by the Jewish Publication Society of America, Philadelphia, Pa.

Letter of Peter Stuyvesant to the West India Company,
September 22, 1654

The Jews who have arrived would nearly all like to remain here, but learning that they (with their customary usury and deceitful trading with the Christians) were very repugnant to the inferior magistrates, as also to the people having the most affection for you; the Deaconry also fearing that owing to their present indigence they might become a charge in the coming winter, we have, for the benefit of this weak and newly developing place and the land in general, deemed it useful to require them in a friendly way to depart; praying also most seriously in this connection, for ourselves as also for the general community of your worships, that the deceitful race—such hateful enemies and blasphemers of the name of Christ—be not allowed further to infect and trouble this new colony, to the detraction of your worships and the dissatisfaction of your worships' most affectionate subjects.

Petition of the Amsterdam Jews to the West India Company,
January, 1655

To the Honorable Lords, Directors of the Chartered West India Company, Chamber of the City of Amsterdam

The merchants of the Portuguese nation residing in this City respectfully remonstrate to your Honors that it has come to their knowledge that your Honors raise obstacles to the giving of permits or passports to the Portuguese Jews to travel and to go to reside in New Netherland, which if persisted in will result

Granted [February 15, 1655] that they may reside and traffic, provided they shall not become a charge upon the Deaconry or the Company.

to the great disadvantage of the Jewish nation. It can also be of no advantage to the general Company but rather damaging.

There are many of the nation who have lost their possessions at Pernambuco and have arrived from there in great poverty, and part of them have been dispersed here and there. So that your petitioners had to expend large sums of money for their necessaries of life, and through lack of opportunity all cannot remain here to live. And as they cannot go to Spain or Portugal because of the Inquisition, a great part of the aforesaid people must in time be obliged to depart for other territories of their High Mightinesses the States-General and their Companies, in order there, through their labor and efforts, to be able to exist under the protection of the administrators of your Honorable Directors, observing and obeying your Honors' orders and commands.

It is well known to your Honors that the Jewish nation in Brazil have at all times been faithful and have striven to guard and maintain that place, risking for that purpose their possessions and their blood.

Yonder land is extensive and spacious. The more loyal people that go to live there, the better it is in regard to the population of the country as in regard to the payment of various excises and taxes which may be imposed there, and in regard to the increase of trade, and also to the importation of all the necessaries that may be sent there.

Your Honors should also consider that the Honorable Lords, the Burgomasters of the City and the Honorable High Illustrious Mighty Lords, the States-General, have in political matters always protected and considered the Jewish nation as upon the same footing as all the inhabitants and burghers. Also it is conditioned in the treaty of perpetual peace with the King of Spain that the Jewish nation shall also enjoy the same liberty as all other inhabitants of these lands.

Your Honors should also please consider that many of the Jewish nation are principal shareholders in the Company. They having always striven their best for the Company, and many of their nation have lost immense and great capital in its shares and obligations.

The Company has by a general resolution consented that those who wish to populate the Colony shall enjoy certain districts of land gratis. Why should now certain subjects of this State not be allowed to travel thither and live there? The French consent that the Portuguese Jews may traffic and live in Martinique, Christopher, and others of their territories, whither also some have gone from here, as your Honors know. The English also consent at the present time that the Portuguese and Jewish nation may go from London and settle at Barbados, whither also some have gone.

As foreign nations consent that the Jewish nation may go to live and trade in their territories, how can your Honors forbid the same and refuse transportation to this Portuguese nation who reside here and have been settled here well on to about sixty years, many also being born here and confirmed burghers, and this to a land that needs people for its increase?

Therefore the petitioners request, for the reasons given above (as also others which they omit to avoid prolixity), that your Honors be pleased not to exclude but to grant the Jewish nation passage to and residence in that country; otherwise this would result in a great prejudice to their reputation. Also that by an Apostille and Act the Jewish nation be permitted, together with other inhabitants, to travel, live, and traffic there, and with them enjoy liberty on condition of contributing like others, etc.

*"Letters from the Directors of the West India Company, Department of Amsterdam, Holland, to Peter Stuyvesant and Council in New Netherland, 1655–56."**

26th of April 1655

Honorable, Prudent, Pious, Dear, Faithful.
. . . We would have liked to agree to your wishes and request, that the new territories should not be further invaded by people of the Jewish race, for we foresee from such immigration the same difficulties, which you fear, but after having further weighed and considered this matter, we observe, that it would be unreasonable and unfair, especially because of the considerable loss, sustained by the Jews in the taking of *Brasil* and also because of the large amount of capital which they have invested in shares of this company. After many consultations we have decided and resolved upon a certain petition made by said *Portuguese* Jews, that they shall have permission to sail to and trade in *New Netherland* and to live and remain there, provided the poor among them shall not become a burden to the Company or the community, but be supported by their own nation. You will govern yourself accordingly. . . .

13th of March 1656

Honorable, Prudent, Pious, Dear, Faithful.
. . . The permission given to the *Jews*, to go to *New-Netherland* and enjoy there the same privileges, as they have here, has been granted only as far as civil and political rights are concerned, with-

* From *Documents Relating to the History of the Early Colonial Settlements* (Albany, N.Y.: Weed, Parsons and Company, 1883).

out giving the said *Jews* a claim to the privilege of exercising their religion in a synagogue or at a gathering; as long therefore, as you receive no request for granting them this liberty of religious exercise, your considerations and anxiety about this matter, are premature and when later something shall be said about it, you can do no better, than to refer them to us and await the necessary order. . . .

14th of June 1656

Honorable, Vigorous, Pious, Dear, Faithful.

. . . We have seen and heard with displeasure, that against our orders of the 15th of February 1655, issued at the request of the *Jewish* or *Portuguese* nation, you have forbidden them to trade to *Fort Orange* and the South river, also the purchase of real estate, which is granted to them without difficulty here in this country, and we wish it had not been done and that you had obeyed our orders, which you must always execute punctually and with more respect: *Jews* or *Portuguese* people however shall not be employed in any public service, (to which they are neither admitted in this city), nor allowed to have open retail shops, but they may quietly and peacefully carry on their business as before said and exercise in all quietness their religion within their houses, for which end they must without doubt endeavor to build their houses close together in a convenient place on one or the other side of *New Amsterdam,*—at their own choice—as they have done here. . . .

COTTON MATHER:

". . . I lifted up my cries: For the conversion of the Jewish Nation, and for my own having the happiness, at some time or other, to baptize a Jew. . . ." (1696)

Cotton Mather (1663–1728), distinguished Congregational minister and author, was born in Boston. The foremost spokesman of early American Puritanism, Mather combined an interest in science—for example, he was

From the *Diaries* of Cotton Mather, quoted in Lee M. Friedman, "Cotton Mather and the Jews," *Publications of the American Jewish Historical Society,* No. 26 (Baltimore: The Lord Baltimore Press, 1918), 201–210.

a proponent of inoculation for smallpox—with a belief in witchcraft and a literal interpretation of Scriptures. A conservative by instinct and preference, Mather nevertheless was a leader of opposition in Massachusetts to the policies pursued by the Royal Governor, and in 1718 his religious orthodoxy had mellowed sufficiently to permit him to assist at the ordination of a Baptist minister. On the other hand, Mather was an outspoken critic of Roger Williams, and upon hearing that Williams was willing to accept Jews in the new colony of Rhode Island, Mather denounced Newport as "the common receptacle of the convicts of Jerusalem and the outcasts of the land."

Mather regarded the conversion of the Jews to Christianity as a part of his own personal mission. The following excerpts from his *Diaries* suggest that his labors in that direction extended over a period of many years.

July 18, 1696

This day, from the dust, where I lay prostrate, before the Lord, I lifted up my cries: For the conversion of the Jewish Nation, and for my own having the happiness, at some time or other, to baptize a Jew, that should by my ministry, bee brought home unto the Lord.

April 9, 1699

This week, I attempted a further service to the name of the my Lord Jesus Christ. I considered, that when the Evangelical Elias, was to prepare the Jewish Nation, and the coming of the Messiah, he was to do it, by bringing down the Heart of the Fathers before the children. And I considered, that would not only confirm us Christians in our Faith exceedingly to see every article of it, asserted in the express words of the Old Testament, but that it would mightily convince and confound the Jewish Nation. Ye, who Knowes, what use the Lord may make of such an Essay? Wherefore, with much contrivance, I draw up a Catechism of the whole Christian Religion, and contrived the Questions to fitt the answers, whereof I brought every one out of the Old Testament. I prefased the Catechism, with an address unto the Jewish Nation, telling them in some lively terms, that if they would but return to the faith of the Old Testament, and believe with their own Ancient and blessed Patriarchs, this was all that wee desired of them or for them. I gave this book to the Printer, and it was immediately published. Its Title is, *The Faith of the Fathers*.

[From the Dedication of *The Faith of the Fathers*]

To the Jewish Nation:
One thing that satisfies us Christians, in the Truth of Christianity, is your obstinate aversion to that Holy Religion, our Blessed Jesus, the Author of our Faith, foretold your continuance under the circumstances now come upon you until the Ties of the Gentiles in the four monarchies, just now expiring, are expired. . . . Here is now put into your Hands an irresistible and inefragable demonstration that tho' you say, you are Jews you are not so. . . . Be amazed, O ye Rebellious and rejected People of our Great Lord Messiah. . . . Return O backsliding Israel!

April 28, 1699

And whereas, I have now for divers years, employ'd much prayer for, and some discourse with, an infidel Jew in this Town; thro' a Desire to glorify my Lord Jesus Christ in the Conversion of that Infidel, if Hee please to accept mee in that Service. I this day renew'd my Request unto Heaven for it. And writing a short letter to the Jew, wherein I enclosed my, Faith of the Fathers, and, La Fedel Christiano, I sent it unto him.

May 21, 1699

I had advice from Heaven—Yea, more than this; That I shall shortly see some Harvest of my Prayers and Pains, and the Jewish Nation also.

September 2, 1699

This Day, I understand by letters from Carolina, a thing that exceedingly refreshes me, a Jew there embracing the Christian faith, and my little book, *The Faith of the Fathers,* therein a special instrument of good unto him.

October 28, 1700

American Tears upon the Ruines of the Greek Churches. Moreover, a very charming relation of Conversion made by a Jew, one Shalom Ben Shalomoh, at his joining lately to a Congregational Church in London falling into our Hands, I foresaw many advantages to glorify the Lord Jesus Christ by Reprinting it. Wherefore, composing a preface to make the Transition agreeable, I procured this to be added as an appendix to the book of the Greek Churches.

February 12, 1710–11

Song of Jubilation. And that the Lord may be glorified in the Conversion of that poor Jew, and where I was concerned now 16 or 17 years ago; and towards whom the Dispensations of Heaven have been singular and wonderful.

April 11–12, 1711

Vigil—prayer. I cried unto the Lord, that I might yet see one (opportunity) and a very Rich one, in the conversion of that poor Jew, for whose conversion and salvation we have been for 6 or 7 years more than waiting on him.

July 4–5, 1713

Vigil—prayer. For the conversion of the poor Jew, who is this Day returned once more unto New England, and who has now for 19 years together been the Subject of our Cares and Hopes, and Prayers.

August 29, 1713

Prayer. For the conversion of the Jew for whom I have been so long and so much concerned!

[From a letter to John Winthrop Mather]

August 15, 1716

. . . a strange and miraculous motion from God upon the minds of the Jewish children in the City of Berlin. The little Jews, from eight to twelve years of age, fled to the Protestant ministers, that they might be initiated into Christianity. They embraced it with such rapture that when they saw the name of Jesus, in a book, they kissed it a hundred times, and shed floods of tears upon it. No methods used by their parents to reduce them are effectual; but they say to their parents, "We shall not return to you; it is time for you to come over to us!" This German divine saw happy auspices in this rare occurrence.

October 15, 1716, A.D.

A late and strange Impression of Grace, on the Jewish Children, in the City of Berlin: May I not improve it, and an Excitation of Piety in my flock, and sway the young people of it.

August 10, 1717

G.D. I hear of a Jew in this place. I would seek conversation with him.

January 17, 1717/8

G.D. I am this week entertained, with surprising advice, concerning the Jew, with whom and for whom we were so much concerned three and twenty years ago.

PETER KALM:

*"The Rabbi stood in the middle of the
synagogue, and read with his face turned
toward the east; he spoke, however, so
fast, as to make it almost impossible for
anyone to understand what he said." (1748)*

Peter Kalm, of Sweden, traveled in America in 1748. Like many other European visitors in the eighteenth century, Kalm came from a country where there were few Jews, and as a result Jewish religion and customs held some fascination for him.

The following account is based on a visit of Kalm's to a Jewish synagogue in New York City in November, 1748.

November the 2d. [1748] Besides the different sects of Christians, there are many Jews settled in New York, who possess great priv-

"Impressions of Peter Kalm, a Swedish Traveler, regarding the Jews of New York," reprinted in Jacob R. Marcus, editor, *The Jew in the Medieval World* (Cincinnati, Ohio: The Union of American Hebrew Congregations, 1938), pp. 72–73; Copyright of 1938 by Union of American Hebrew Congregations; reprinted 1960 by the Jewish Publication Society of America, Philadelphia, Pa.

ileges. They have a synagogue and houses, and great country-seats of their own property, and are allowed to keep shops in town. They have likewise several ships, which they freight and send out with their own goods. In fine, they enjoy all the privileges common to the other inhabitants of this town and province.

During my residence at New York, this time, and in the next two years, I was frequently in company with Jews. I was informed, among other things, that these people never boiled any meat for themselves on Saturday, but that they always did it the day before; and that in winter they kept a fire [going continuously] during the whole Saturday [for kindling fire anew on the Sabbath is prohibited by Jewish law]. They commonly eat no pork; yet I have been told by several men of credit, that many of them (especially among the young Jews) when traveling, did not make the least difficulty about eating this, or any other meat that was put before them; even though they were in company with Christians.

I was in their synagogue last evening for the first time, and this day at noon I visited it again, and each time I was put into a particular seat, which was set apart for strangers or Christians. A young rabbi read the divine service, which was partly in Hebrew, and partly in the rabbinical dialect. Both men and women were dressed entirely in the English fashion; the former had all of them their hats on, and did not once take them off during service. The galleries, I observed, were appropriated to the ladies, while the men sat below. During prayers, the men spread a white cloth over their heads, which perhaps is to represent sackcloth. But I observed that the wealthier sort of people had a much richer sort of cloth than the poorer ones. Many of the men had Hebrew books, in which they sang and read alternately. The Rabbi stood in the middle of the synagogue, and read with his face turned towards the east; he spoke, however, so fast, as to make it almost impossible for any one to understand what he said.

EZRA STILES:

". . . Providence seems to make everything to work for Mortification to the Jews." (1762)

Ezra Stiles (1727–1795) was something of a prince among Renaissance men of the eighteenth century in America. As learned as Jefferson and as wise as Franklin, Stiles's multiple interests embraced theology, law, science, philosophy, comparative religion, and the study of languages. A graduate of Yale and an ordained minister, Stiles's restless pursuit of knowledge may have been related to his difficulties in accepting certain formal tenets of Christianity. Although in 1755 he was appointed minister of the Second Congregational Church in Newport, Rhode Island, he attended services, from time to time, in Quaker, Epsiscopal, Reformed Dutch, and Catholic Churches, and in Jewish Synagogues. He also found time to study Arabic, French, and Hebrew, perform experiments in chemistry, and raise his own silkworms in an effort to promote the manufacture of silk in America. Chosen President of Yale in 1778, he discovered that the Newport Church refused to release him as minister, and in true Yale fashion he continued to serve God and man, Newport, and New Haven, until 1786.

Stiles's interest in the Jews and in Jewish religion developed shortly after he arrived in Newport. The future Yale President was endlessly fond of discussing the finer points of Biblical interpretation with visiting Rabbis and Talmudic scholars, especially with reference to the Second Coming of the Messiah. Like other Christian clergymen of his day, he was an advocate of the conversion of the Jews, but unlike others he did not devote himself to the conversion of Jewish friends and acquaintances.

Stiles's *Diaries,* from which the following selections are taken, provide us with much insight into the relations between New England Jews and Gentiles in the latter half of the eighteenth century.

March 18, 1762

Josephus says, "had all the Happiness that ever Jerusalem enjoyed been equal to the Miseries it suffered in this Siege, it had doubtless been the envy of all the world."—War of the Jews Abrig^d, 163.

From "References to the Jews in the Diary of Ezra Stiles" by Prof. Morris Jastrow, Jr., *Publications of the American Jewish Historical Society,* 1902, No. 10, 5–36.

There are about 15 fam⁵ of Jews in Newport. Some of the principal of them last year made Application to the Supreme Court (610-S. C. Rh. Jsl. Newport ss. March term 1762) to be naturalized. The Court declined or deferred acting. The Jews then applied to the General Assembly, which referred it to to Sup. Court again as their business to determine, which Sup. Court at Newport March Term 1762 gave their judgment and determination upon the Petition of Aron Lopez & Isaac Elizur, copied two Leaves back. It was remarkable that before this Term there had been three Trials for Felony, of which two were capital, all guilty by Jury. And on the eleventh day of March, 1762, Sentence was pronounced upon the Criminals purposely bro't to the Bar; first upon Jn°-Sherman, a noted Thief & Burglar for Burglary, sentenced to be hanged; secondly upon Fortune an abandoned Negro who set Fire to the Warehouses at End Long Wharf 19th Feb⁷ which did Damage 5,000 ster. & endangered the Conflagration of the Town, sentenced to be hanged: Thirdly upon V. Lawton for perjury in swaring to an account which he had falsely forged against another, sentenced to the Pillory. . . . And then the Jews were called up to hear their almost equally mortifying Sentence and Judg' which dismissed their Petition for Naturalization. Whether this was designedly or accidental in proceding upon the Business of the Court I do not learn. But this I remark that Providence seems to make everything to work for Mortification to the Jews & to prevent their incorporating into any Nation; that thus they may continue a distinct people. Tho' the Naturalization Act passed the Parliament a few years ago, yet it produced such a national Disgust towards the Hebrews, that the Jews themselves joyned in Petition to Parliament to repeal that Act, & it was therefore repealed for Britain. And tho' it was continued by way of Permission in the Plantation, upon seven years Residence, yet the Tumult at New York in procuring the Taking place of their Natural—there; and the opposition it has met with in Rhode Island forbodes that the Jews will never become incorporated with the pple. of America, any more than in Europe, Asia and Africa.

December 2, 1763

In the Afternoon was the dedication of the New Synagogue in this Town. It began by a handsome procession in which were carried the Books of the Law, to be deposited in the Ark. Several Portions of Scripture, & of their Service with a Prayer for the Royal Family, were read and finely sung by the priests & People. There were present many Gentlemen & Ladies. The Order and Decorum, the Harmony & Solemnity of the Musick, together with a handsome Assembly of People, in a Edifice the most perfect of the Temple kind perhaps in America, & splendidly illuminated, could not but raise in the Mind a faint Idea of the Majesty & Grandeur of the Ancient Jewish Worship mentioned in Scripture.

Dr. Isaac de Abraham Touro performed the Service. The Synagogue is about perhaps fourty foot long & 30 wide, of Brick on a Foundation of free Stone: it was begun about two years ago, & is now finished except the Porch & the Capitals of the Pillars. The Front representation of the holy of holies or its Partition Veil, consists only of wainscotted Breast Work on the East End, in the lower part of which four long Doors cover an upright Square Closet the depth of which is about a foot or the thickness of the Wall, & in this Apartment (vulgarly called the Ark) were deposited three Copies & Rolls of the Pentateuch, written on Vellum or rather tanned Calf Skin; one of these Rolls I was told by Dr. Touro was presented from Amsterdam & is Two Hundred year old; the Letters have the Rabbinical Flourishes.

A Gallery for the Women runs round the whole Inside, except the East End supported by Columns of Ionic order, over which are placed correspondent Columns of the Corinthian order supporting the Cieling of the Roof. The Depth of the Corinthian Pedestal is the height of the Balustrade which runs round the Gallery. The Pulpit for Reading the Law, is a raised Pew with an extended front table; this placed about the center of the Synagogue or nearer the West End, being a Square embalustraded Comporting with the Length of the indented Chancel before & at the Foot of the Ark.

On the middle of the North Side & affixed to the Wall is a raised Seat for the Parnas or Ruler, & for the Elders; the Breast and Back interlaid with Chinese Mosaic Work. A Wainscotted Seat runs round the Sides of the Synagogue below, & another in the Gallery. There are no other Seats or pews. There may be Eighty Souls of Jews or 15 families now in Town. The Synagogue has already cost Fifteen Hundred Pounds Sterling. There are to be five Lamps pendant from a lofty Cieling.

November 23, 1772

This Afternoon visited by Rabbi Moses and Mr. Touro. The Whimsical Visionary though I hope honest Mr. Pipels being present, I told Rabbi Moses that this Man had seen visions of Angels, . . . R. Moses smiled, and Mr. Pipels began to relate his Extraordinaries with warmth. R. Moses asked him the Color of the Angel, said he was mistaken as to his vision, for that he was the Angel that appeared to him, but was sure he told him no such Thing. This humor & sarcasm toutched and a little confounded Mr. Pipels who after some Talk took Leave and departed to cross the ferries and return to Pennsylvania. R. Moses spent the rest of the Afternoon in my study, explaining the Zohar to me. . . . This day I paid for my Zohar 22/6 sterling. This Forenoon I spent read^g Dionysius Areopag whom I find to have the same sublime Mysteries as the Zohar.

November 23, 1773

The Rabbi (Tobiah Bar Jehudah) visited me again or came to my house but I was not at home. In the Evening I visited him at Mr. Tauro's—and supped with them, the only Time I ever happened at Meal with a Jew. Just before they sat down to supper, Water was bro't by the Maid in a white earthen Bottle which stood in a Vase or Bason: they two washed their hands, taking up the bottle and pouring the Water on the hand. I asked if this was טבל (because the Baptists say this word denotes total, not partial, Immersions) they said yes—& quoted a passage of the Talmud that none can eat till they had thus washed themselves in which I recollect the word טבל was twice repeated. I did not wash, but sat down and eat with them. After sitting, each in a whispering voice said Grace for himself. The Rabbi said, that in the days of Messiah, it would be allowed to the Jews to eat Swines Flesh—. I said that Abraham, Isaac and Jacob when they come with Messiah, would not eat Food as formerly; he said they would.—I said Circumcision must cease—he said not—I added Childbearing must cease when the World was full as it would be in Messiahs day, and then there would be no more to circumcise and so it must cease.—I asked him the value of a couple of Pearls I had & of the dimensions I described; he said if good 500 Ducats, which is about £100 sterling. . . .

He is a great *Cabbalist* and Philosopher; which two Branches of knowledge are far more to his Tast than the Talmud. He has a son of about 13 years age—when aet. 12 he had read thro' the Talmud. This Rabbi was educated and spent 26 years in Amsterdam, whither he was sent aet. 8. He told me he was of the Family and ninth Descendant of R. *Selomoh Ishaaci* the celebrated Commentator who died A.D. 1180.

March 30, 1773

This afternoon the Rabbi [Isaac Karigal] came to visit me in Company with Mr. Lopez. The Rabbi is aet. 39, a large Man, neat and well dressed in Turkish Habit. We conversed largely on the Gemara, the 2 Talmuds (of which he preferred the Babylonish) the Changes of the Hebrew Language in different Ages &c &c. He was born in Hebron where he says are only 107 Families of Jews. From aet. 7, has followed his Studies. He says, one may breakfast at Hebron and dine at Jerusalem, which are but six hour apart. He has been at Samaria, Tiberias, and thro' the Holy Land, at Constantinople &c. &c. He spake of Aly Bey, and shewed me a passage in the *Zohar* which he said predicted that the *Russians should conquer the Turks.* I observed that in the Original it was that *Edom* should conquer the *Ismaelites*—he replied that Edom there denoted a Northern Power and the Ismaelites those of their Religion. He said he did not understand *Arabic* to read it, upon my showing an Arabic Extract from Eutychius. Yet he said it was the common Tongue now in the holy Land, only the Jews were not allowed to learn the Writings. I shewed him the first Psalm in Arabic but in Hebrew Letters—he read it off freely—and I suppose I then for the first Time heard the true pronunciation of Arabic. He did not perfectly understand it. He said the vernacular Arabic now was different from the antient. We talked upon the difference of the Dialects of the Chaldee, Syriac, and rabbinical Hebrew, on the Tagums &c. Evening coming on he took Leave in a polite & friendly manner.

June 14, 1773

. . . In the Forenoon I went to visit the Rabbi—discoursed on Ventriloquism & the Witch of Endor & the Reality of bringing up Samuel. He had not heard of Ventriloquism before & still doubted

it. He shewed me a Hebrew Letter from Isaac Pinto a Jew in N.
York, in which Mr. Pinto who is now reading Aben Ezra desires
R. Carigal's Tho'ts upon some Arabic in Aben Ezra. But the Rabbi
says he supposes Aben Ezra wrote in the Coran Arabic which he
doth not understand. The Rabbi . . . is extremely fond of persuad^g
himself that there has been no change in the Pentateuch since
Moses left it; and shewed me a passage of St. *Austin* de Civitate
Dei in a Hebrew Book of *David Nieto;* it was rendered into Hebrew
to this Effect, that there was an Impossibility that the Jews shd.
have corrupted their holy Books, since in all Dispersions they were
found the same. He was much pleased that he was able to shew
me something out of our Fathers for my Extracts out of his Rabbins.
I turned him to the strong Expression in his Letter "your Love has
made such an indelible impression upon the inmost Tho'ts. & Affections of my Heart that Volumes of Book are not sufficient to write
the thousandth part of the eternal Love wherewith I love thee"—
and asked him how he could use so strong an Expression of Friendship? He in reply said he wished well to others besides his own
nation, he loved all Mankind, & turned me to Levit. xix, 18,—*thou
shalt love thy Neighbour as thyself.*

April 8, 1773

This day is Passover with the Jews. I went to the Synagogue.
The Chocam Rabbi was there; he was one called up to the Reading
of the Law—but I observed that he *did not read his own portion* of
the Law—which I wondered at; however he audibly pronounced
the short prayer instead of the Huzzan before reading his part, and
after the Huzzan had read the portion, the Rabbi alone and without the Chuzan lift up his voice and pronounced the Blessing. This
is repeated by the Chuzan usually for every one of the 7 persons—
but this part the Rabbi did for himself; and he performed no other
part of the Service as distinct from the Congregation.

The Rabbi's Dress of Aparrel: Common English Shoes, black
Leather, Silver flowered Buckles, White Stockings. His general
Habit was Turkish. A *green Silk Vest* or long under Garment reach-
ing down more than half way the Legs or within 3 Inches of the
Ankles; the ends of the Sleeves of this Vest appeared on the Wrists
in a foliage Turn-up of 3 inches, & the Opening little larger than

that the hand might pass freely. A Girdle or Sash of different Colors red and green girt the Vest around his Body. It appeared not to be open at bottom but to come down like a petticoat; and no Breeches could be discovered. This Vest however had an opening above the Girdle—and here he put in his *Handkerchief,* and *Snuff-box,* and *Watch.* Under this was an inner Vest of Calico besides other Jewish Talismans. Upon the vest first mentioned was a *scarlet outer Garment* of Cloth, one side of it was Blue, the *outside scarlet;* it reached down about an Inch lower than the Vest, or near the Ankles: It was open before, no range of Buttons &c along the Edge, but like a Scholars Gown in the Body but plain and without many gatherings at the Neck, the sleeves strait or narrow and slit open 4 or 5 Inches at the End, and turned up with a *blue silk Quarter Cuff,* higher up than the End of the sleeve of the Vest. When he came into the Synagogue he put over all, the usual *Alb* or white *Surplice,* which was like that of other Jews, except that its Edge was striped with *Blue straiks,* and had *more Fringe.* He had a White Cravat round his Neck. He had a long black beard, the upper Lip partly shaven— his Head shaved all over. On his head a high Fur (Sable) Cap, exactly like a Womans Muff, and about 9 or 10 inches high, the Aperture atop was closed with green cloth. He behaved modestly and reverently. Some part of the Singing in the Synagogue this day was exceeding fine & melodious.

April 23, 1773

I visited the Rabbi. He shewed me the form of the Candlesticks of Moses and Zechariah. We discoursed on many Things.

. . . I asked him whether Moses wrote all the Pentateuch, particularly the account of his own death? & also Gen. 36, 31?—he answered yes: that he wrote of Things future as present, so Isaiah wrote of Cyrus. I asked him whether by the usual Intercalation, the *Hebrew Chronology* was perfect—the Jewish year exactly solar? —yes. How long their Chronology had been reduced to perfection, & whether antiently there were no Errors or Deviations from Solar Time? He said, *it was perfect from the Beginning,* the principles of it were laid down in the six Days Creation, & had been delivered down in the earliest Antiquity. I wanted more closely to attend to this Matter, as he spake with the deliberate Confidence of Demonstration—and he is a man of great Modesty & Candor, & most remote from a disposition to obtrude his own Assertions without being ready to open the Reasons. But we had not Time.

July 15, 1773

Spent the Afternoon with the Rabbi, partly at the Redwood Library and partly at my House. I asked him whether the Rabbins of this Age thought themselves to have any particular Reasons for expecting the Messiah immediately? He said not; but he thought it was high Time for him to come; He added, that if all Nations were in War and universal Tumult and Confusion, then he should expect him immediately, but this not being more the Case now than in every current Age, &c. . . . The Rabbi has the Zohar in 3 vol. 4ᵗᵒ printed to Constantinople.

July 16, 1773

Comparing my Zohar with the Rabbi's. In company with the Rabbi. He told me he rode over the River Jordan on Horse-back against *Jericho* which was near the River: he said it was a very shallow River and almost dry in Summer. He had been at all the twelve or 13 Synagogues in the holy Land, and gave me the following account which I wrote from his Mouth.

One Thousand Families Jews in all Judea or Holy Land A.D. 1773	5 Synagogues at Jerusalem, large 2 at Saphat large 1 at Tiberias small 1 at Hebron large 107 Families 1 at Gaza large 1 at Shechem small 1 at Acco—large ⎯⎯⎯ 12 and 1 at Jaffa only a Chamber for Worship occasionally, but not every Sabbath	2 at Damascus 1 at Sidon 1 at Alleppo large Only 12 *Synagogues* in the Holy Land.

He said there were more Synagogues in Syria than Palestine.

June 28, 1773

This afternoon the Rabbi visited me. We spent the Afternoon very agreeably. He told me that there was one Rabbi at the Syna-

gogue in *Jamaica,* another at Surinam, and a third at *Eustatia* or
Curacoa. Thus there are now *three Rabbies* settled in America.
There are none on the Continent of No. America. The Rabbi has
a prospect of settling in the Synagogue in Antigua, and this will
make a fourth in America.

June 8, 1782

On 28th of May died that amiable, benevolent, most hospitable
& very respectable Gentleman, Mr. *Aaron Lopez* Merchant, who
retir from Newp Rhd. Isld in these Times resided from 1775 to his
Death at Leicester in Massachusetts. He was a Jew by Nation, came
from Spain or Portugal about 1754 & settled at Rh. Isld. He was
a Merchant of the first Eminence; for Honor and Extent of Commerce probably surpassed by no Merch^t in America. He did Business with the greatest Ease & Clearness—always carried about with
him a Sweetness of Behav. a calm Urbanity an agreeable & unaffected Politeness of manners. Without a single Enemy & the most
Universally beloved by an extensive Acquaintance of any man I
ever knew. His Beneficence to his Fam^y connexions, to his Nation
& to all the World is almost without a Parallel. He was my intimate
Friend & Acquaintance! Oh! how often have I wished that sincere
pious & candid mind could have perceived the Evidences of X^ty,
perceived the Truth as it is in Jesus Christ, known that *Jesus* was
the *Messiah* predicted by Moses & the Prophets. The amiable &
excellent Characters of a *Lopez,* of a *Manasseh Ben Israel,* of a
Socrates & a *Gangenelli,* would almost persuade us to hope that their
Excellency was infused by Heaven, and that the virtuous & good of
all Nations & Religions, notwithstand^g their Delusions, may be bro't
together in Paradise on the Xtian System, finding Grace with all
benevolent & adorable Emmanuel who with his expiring breath &
in his deepest agonies, prayed for those who knew not what they
did.

Mr. Lopez was journey^g with his Wife & some of his Fam^y on
a visit to Newport, and within five Miles of Providence at Scotts
pond as he was water^g his Horse, the Horse plunged beyond his
Depth with the Sulky, when M^rLopez leaped into the Water; and
tho his serv^t attempted to save him he was lost. His Corps was carried to Newport & there interred in the Jew Burying Ground there
—the Demonstration of universal Sorrow attended the Funeral.

THOMAS JEFFERSON, JAMES
MADISON, AND JOHN ADAMS:

*"Your sect [Judaism] by its sufferings has
furnished a remarkable proof of the
universal spirit of religious intolerance
inherent in every sect, disclaimed by all
while feeble, and practiced by all
when in power." (Thomas Jefferson, 1818)*

The following selections present letters of John Adams, Thomas Jefferson, and James Madison, written on the occasion of the consecration of the Mill Street (New York) Synagogue in 1818.

John Adams (1735–1826), second President of the United States, was interested in the history of religions, and he had a considerable knowledge of Judaism. His studies had convinced him, he once wrote Jefferson, that ". . . in spite of Bolingbroke and Voltaire I will insist that the Hebrews have done more to civilize men than any other nation. If I were an atheist, and believed in blind eternal fate, I should still believe that fate had ordained the Jews to be the most essential instrument for civilizing nations."

Thomas Jefferson (1743–1826), who succeeded Adams in the White House, was a lifelong advocate of toleration and religious freedom. Although less acquainted than Adams with Jewish history and traditions, Jefferson had many Jewish friends, among them Commodore Uriah P. Levy (1792–1862). When Jefferson died in 1826, the Levy family became the owners of Jefferson's estate at Monticello, and preserved it as a memorial to the author of the Declaration of Independence.

James Madison (1751–1836) was the fourth President of the United States. Madison was personally acquainted with Haym Solomon, a Jewish banker who helped finance the Revolutionary War, and on certain occasions before he became President, when he himself was in financial straits, Madison borrowed money from Solomon. Solomon, apparently, refused to accept interest on such loans. In a letter to Edmund Randolph of 1782, Madison wrote:

Letters from Thomas Jefferson, James Madison, and John Adams to Mordecai M. Noah, on the occasion of the consecration of the Mill Street (New York) Synagogue in 1818, reprinted in Lewis Abraham, "Correspondence Between Washington and Jewish Citizens." Papers presented at the Third Annual Meeting of the American Jewish Historical Society, December 26–27, 1894, *Publications of the American Jewish Historical Society*, No. 3, 1895, 94–96.

The kindness of our little friend (Solomon) in Front Street, near the coffee-house, is a fund that will preserve me from extremities, but I never resort to it [without] great mortification, as he obstinately rejects all recompense. The price of money is so usurious that he thinks it ought to be extorted from none but those who aim at profitable speculations. To a necessitous delegate, he gratuitously spares a supply out of his private stock.

When Madison was President (1813–1821) he appointed a number of Jews to office, and found posts for several in the diplomatic service.

Monticello, *May* 28, 1818.

Sir:—I thank you for the discourse on the consecration of the Synagogue in your city, with which you have been pleased to favor me. I have read it with pleasure and instruction, having learnt from it some valuable facts in Jewish history which I did not know before. Your sect by its sufferings has furnished a remarkable proof of the universal spirit of religious intolerance inherent in every sect, disclaimed by all while feeble, and practiced by all when in power. Our laws have applied the only antidote to this vice, protecting our religious, as they do our civil rights, by putting all on an equal footing. But more remains to be done, for although we are free by the law, we are not so in practice; public opinion erects itself into an Inquisition, and exercises its office with as much fanaticism as fans the flames of an *Auto-de-fe*.

The prejudice still scowling on your section of our religion, although the elder one, cannot be unfelt by yourselves; it is to be hoped that individual dispositions will at length mould themselves to the model of the law, and consider the moral basis, on which all our religions rest, as the rallying point which unites them in a common interest; while the peculiar dogmas branching from it are the exclusive concern of the respective sects embracing them, and no rightful subject of notice to any other; public opinion needs reformation on that point, which would have the further happy effect of doing away the hypocritical maxim of '*intus et lubet, foris ut moris.*' Nothing, I think, would be so likely to effect this, as to your sect particularly, as the more careful attention to education, which you recommend, and which, placing its members on the equal and commanding benches of science, will exhibit them as equal objects of respect and favor. I salute you with great respect and esteem.

(Signed)   Thomas Jefferson.

M. M. Noah, Esq.

Montpelier, *May* 15, 1818.

Sir:—I have received your letter of the 6th, with the eloquent discourse delivered at the consecration of the Synagogue. Having ever regarded the freedom of religious opinions and worship as equally belonging to every sect, and the secure enjoyment of it as the best human provision for bringing all, either into the same way of thinking, or into that mutual charity which is the only proper substitute, I observe with pleasure the view you give of the spirit in which your sect partake of the common blessings afforded by our Government and laws.

As your foreign mission took place whilst I was in the administration, it cannot but be agreeable to me to learn that your accounts have been closed in a manner so favorable to you.

(Signed)   James Madison.

Quincy, *July* 31, 1818.

Sir:—Accept my best thanks for your polite and obliging favour of the 24th, and especially for the discourse inclosed. I know not when I have read a more liberal or more elegant composition.

You have not extended your ideas of the right of private judgment and the liberty of conscience, both in religion and philosophy, farther than I do. Mine are limited only by morals and propriety.

I have had occasion to be acquainted with several gentlemen of your nation, and to transact business with some of them, whom I found to be men of as liberal minds, as much honor, probity, generosity and good breeding, as any I have known in any sect of religion or philosophy.

I wish your nation may be admitted to all privileges of citizens in every country of the world. This country has done much. I wish it may do more; and annul every narrow idea in religion, government, and commerce. Let the wits joke; the philosophers sneer! What then? It has pleased the Providence of the 'first cause,' the universal cause, that Abraham should give religion, not only to Hebrews, but to Christians and Mahometans, the greatest part of the modern civilized world.

(Signed) John Adams.

LYDIA MARIA CHILD:

"The effect produced on my mind, by witnessing the ceremonies of the Jewish Synagogue, were strange and bewildering." (1841)

Lydia Maria Child, schoolteacher, novelist, militant abolitionist, and Bostonian, was born in 1802. Among her other distinctions was the publication in 1833 of the first book-length antislavery work printed in the United States, *Appeal for That Class of Americans Called Africans*. A friend of John Brown, Whittier, Charles Sumner, and other luminaries of the day, Mrs. Child was celebrated in a poem of James Russell Lowell's, "Fable for Critics," a portion of which reads:

> There come Philothea, her face all aglow,
> She has just been dividing some poor creature's woe,
> And can't tell which pleases her most, to relieve
> His want, or his story to hear and believe; . . .

Like other Americans of puritan stock,[1] Mrs. Child had some interest in Jews, based on a reverence for the Old Testament and a tendency to think of the early Puritans as heirs of the prophetic tradition. But it does not appear that she knew many, if any, Jews in Boston. At any rate, her visit to the Crosby Street Synagogue in New York City, reported in the following selection, was her first venture into a Jewish place of worship.

Mrs. Child's account first appeared as one of a series of letters published in the *Boston Courier*. The letters were later reprinted in two volumes, issued in 1843, and 1845, titled *Letters from New York*.

From Lydia Maria Child, *Letters From New York* (New York and Boston, 1843), reprinted in Lee M. Friedman, "Mrs. Child's Visit to a New York Synagogue in 1841," *Publications of the American Jewish Historical Society*, No. XXXVIII, Part 3, March, 1949, 176–184.

[1] See below, Edmund Wilson, "The Jews," pp. 354–371.

September 23, 1841

I lately visited the Jewish Synagogue in Crosby-street, to witness the Festival of the New Year, which was observed for two days, by religious exercises and a general suspension of worldly business. The Jewish year, you are aware, begins in September; and they commemorate it in obedience to the following text of Scripture: "In the first day of the seventh month ye shall have a Sabbath, a memorial of blowing of trumpets, a holy convocation. Ye shall do no servile work therein."

It was the first time I ever entered any place of worship where Christ was not professedly believed in. Strange vicissitudes of circumstances, over which I had no control, have brought me into intimate relation with almost every form of Christian faith, and thereby given me the power of looking candidly at religious opinions from almost any point of view. But beyond the pale of the great sect of Christianity I had never gone; though far back in my early years, I remember an intense desire to be enough acquainted with some intelligent and sincere Mohammedan, to enable me to look at the Koran through *his* spectacles.

The women were seated separately, in the upper part of the house. One of the masters of Israel came, and somewhat gruffly ordered me, and the young lady who accompanied me, to retire from the front seats of the synagogue. It was uncourteous; for we were very respectful and still, and not in the least disposed to intrude upon the daughters of Jacob. However, my sense of justice was rather gratified at being treated contemptuously as a Gentile and "a Nazarene;" for I remembered the contumely with which *they* had been treated throughout Christendom, and I imagined how they must feel, on entering a place of Christian worship, to hear us sing,

> With hearts as hard as stubborn Jews,
> That unbelieving race.

The effect produced on my mind, by witnessing the ceremonies of the Jewish Synagogue, was strange and bewildering; spectral and flitting; with a sort of vanishing resemblance to reality; the magic lantern of the Past.

Veneration and Ideality, you know, would have made me wholly a poet, had not the inconvenient size of Conscientiousness forced me into reforms; between the two, I look upon the Future with active hope, and upon the Past with loving reverence. My mind was, therefore, not only unfettered by narrow prejudice, but solemnly impressed with recollections of those ancient times when the Divine Voice was heard amid the thunders of Sinai, and the Holy Presence shook the mercy-seat between the cherubim. I had, moreover, ever cherished a tenderness for

> Israel's wandering race, that go
> Unblest through every land;
> Whose blood hath stained the polar snow
> And quenched the desert sand:
> Judea's homeless hearts, that turn
> From all earth's shrines to thee,
> With their lone faith for ages borne
> In sleepless memory.

Thus prepared, the scene would have strongly excited my imagination and my feelings, had there not been a heterogeneous jumbling of the Present with the Past. There was the Ark containing the Sacred Law, written on scrolls of vellum, and rolled, as in the time of Moses; but between the Ark and the congregation, instead of the "brazen laver," wherein those who entered into the tabernacle were commanded to wash, was a common bowl and ewer of English delf, ugly enough for the chamber of a country tavern. All the male members of the congregation, even the little boys, while they were within the synagogue, wore fringed silk mantles, bordered with blue stripes; for Moses was commanded to "Speak unto the children of Israel, and bid them that they make them fringes in the borders of their garments, throughout their generations, and that they put upon the fringe of their borders a ribbon of blue;"—but then these mantles were worn over modern broadcloth coats, and fashionable pantaloons with straps. The Priest indeed approached more nearly to the gracefulness of oriental costume; for he wore a full black silk robe, like those worn by the Episcopal clergy; but the large white silk shawl which shaded his forehead, and fell over his shoulders, was drawn over a common black hat! Ever and anon, probably in parts of the ceremony deemed peculiarly sacred, he drew the shawl entirely over his face, as he stooped forward and laid his forehead on the book before him. I suppose this was done because Moses, till he had done speaking with the congregation, put a veil upon his face. But through the whole, priest and people kept on their hats. My spirit was vexed with this incongruity. I had turned away from the turmoil of the Present, to gaze quietly for a while on the grandeur of the Past; and the representatives of the Past walked before me, not in the graceful oriental turban, but the useful European hat! It broke the illusion completely.

The ceremonies altogether impressed me with less solemnity than those of the Catholic Church; and gave me the idea of far less faith and earnestness in those engaged therein. However, some allowance must be made for this; first, because the common bond of faith in Christ was wanting between us; and secondly, because all the services were performed in Hebrew, of which I understood not one syllable. To see mouths opened to chant forth a series of unintelligible sounds, has the same kind of fantastic unreality about it, that there is in witnessing a multitude dancing, when you hear no music. But after making all these allowances, I could not escape the conclusion that the ceremonies were shuffled through in a cold, mechanical style. The priest often took up his watch, which lay before him; and assuredly this chanting of prayers "by Shrewsbury clock" is not favourable to solemnity.

The chanting was unmusical, consisting of monotonous ups and downs of the voice, which, when the whole congregation joined in it, sounded like the continuous roar of the sea.

The trumpet, which was blown by a Rabbi, with a shawl drawn over his hat and face, was of the ancient shape, somewhat resembling a cow's horn. It did not send forth a spirit-stirring peal; but the sound groaned and struggled through it—not at all reminding one of the days when

> There rose the choral hymn of praise,
>   And trumph and timbrel answered keen,
> And Zion's daughters poured their lays,
>   With priest and warrior's voice between.

I observed, in the English translation on one side of an open prayer book, these words: "When the trumpet shall blow on the holy mountain, let all the earth hear! Let them which are scattered in Assyria, and perishing in Egypt, gather themselves together in the Holy City." I looked around upon the congregation, and I felt that Judea no longer awoke at the sound of the trumpet!

The ark, on a raised platform, was merely a kind of semi-circular closet, with revolving doors. It was surmounted by a tablet, bearing a Hebrew inscription in gilded letters. The doors were closed and opened at different times, with much ceremony; sometimes, a man stood silently before them, with a shawl drawn over his hat and face. When opened, they revealed festoons of white silk damask, suspended over the sacred rolls of the Pentateuch; each roll enveloped in figured satin, and surmounted by ornaments with silver bells. According to the words of Moses, "Thou shalt put into the ark the testimony which I shall give thee." Two of these rolls were brought out, opened by the priest, turned round toward all the congregation, and after portions of them had been chanted for nearly two hours, were again wrapped in satin, and carried slowly back to the ark, in procession, the people chanting the Psalms of David, and the little bells tinkling as they moved.

While they were chanting an earnest prayer for the coming of the Promised One, who was to restore the scattered tribes, I turned over the leaves, and by a singular coincidence my eye rested on these words: "Abraham said, see ye not the splendid light now shining on Mount Moriah? And they answered, *nothing but caverns do we see.*" I thought of Jesus, and the whole pageant became more spectral than ever; so strangely vague and shadowy, that I felt as if under the influence of magic.

The significant sentence reminded me of a German friend, who shared his sleeping apartment with another gentleman, and both were in the habit of walking very early in the morning. One night, his companion rose much earlier than he intended; and perceiving his mistake, placed a lighted lamp in the chimney corner, that its glare might not disturb the sleeper, leaned his back against the fire-place, and began to read. Sometime after, the German rose, left him reading, and walked forth into the morning twilight. When he returned, the sun was shining high up in the heavens; but his companion, unconscious of the change, was still reading by lamplight in the chimney corner. And this the Jews are now doing, as well as a very large proportion of Christians.

Ten days from the Feast of Trumpets, comes the Feast of the

Atonement. Five days after, the Feast of Tabernacles is observed for seven days. Booths of evergreen are erected in the synagogue, according to the injunction, "Ye shall dwell in booths seven days; all that are Israelites born shall dwell in booths. And ye shall take the boughs of goodly trees, branches of palm trees, and the boughs of thick trees, and willows of the brook; and ye shall rejoice before the Lord your God seven days."

Last week, a new synagogue was consecrated in Attorney-street; making, I believe, five Jewish Synagogues in this city, comprising in all about ten thousand of this ancient people. The congregation of the new synagogue are German emigrants, driven from Bavaria, the Duchy of Baden, etc. by oppressive laws. One of these laws forbade Jews to marry; and among the emigrants were many betrothed couples, who married as soon as they landed on our shores; trusting their future support to the God of Jacob. If not as "rich as Jews," they are now most of them doing well in the world; and one of the first proofs they gave of prosperity, was the erection of a place of worship.

The oldest congregation of Jews in New York, were called *Shewith [sic] Israel*. The Dutch governors would not allow them to build a place of worship; but after the English conquered the colony, they erected a small wooden synagogue, in Mill-street, near which a creek ran up from the East River, where the Jewish women performed their ablutions. In the course of improvement this was sold; and they erected the handsome stone building in Crosby-street, which I visited. It is not particularly striking or magnificent, either in its exterior or interior; nor would it be in good keeping, for a people gone into captivity to have garments like those of Aaron, "for glory and for beauty," or an "ark overlaid with pure gold, within and without, and a crown of gold to it round about."

There is something deeply impressive in this remnant of scattered people, coming down to us in continuous links through the long vista of recorded time; preserving themselves carefully unmixed by intermarriage with people of other nations and other faith, and keeping up the ceremonial forms of Abraham, Isaac, and Jacob, through all the manifold changes of revolving generations. Moreover, our religions are connected, though separated; they are shadow and substance, type and fulfilment. To the Jews only, with all their blindness and waywardness, was given the idea of one God, spiritual and invisible; and, therefore, among them only could such a one as Jesus have appeared. To us they have been the medium of glorious truths; and if the murky shadow of their Old dispensation rests too heavily on the mild beauty of the New, it is because the Present can never quite unmoor itself from the Past; and well for the world's safety that it is so.

Quakers were mixed with the congregation of Jews; thus oddly brought together, were the representatives of the extreme of conservatism, and the extreme of innovation!

I was disappointed to see so large a proportion of this peculiar people fair-skinned and blue-eyed. As no one who marries a Gentile is allowed to remain in their synagogues, one would naturally expect to see a decided predominance of the dark eyes, jetty locks, and olive complexions of Palestine. But the Jews furnish incontrovertible evidence that colour is the effect of climate. In the mountains of Bavaria they are light-haired and fair-skinned: in Italy and Spain they are dark: in Hindostan swarthy. The *Black* Jews of Hindostan are said to have been originally African and Hindoo slaves, who received their freedom as soon as they became converted to Judaism, and had fulfilled the rites prescribed by the ceremonial law; for the Jews, unlike Christians, deem it unlawful to hold any one of their own religious faith in slavery. In another respect they put us to shame; for they held a Jubilee of Freedom once in fifty years, and on that occasion emancipated all, even of their heathen slaves.

Whether the Black Jews, now a pretty large class in Hindostan, intermarry with other Jews we are not informed. Moses, their great lawgiver married an Ethiopian. Miriam and Aaron were shocked at it, as they would have been at any intermarriage with the heathen tribes, of whatever colour. Whether the Ethiopian woman had adopted the faith of Israel is not mentioned; but we are told that the anger of the Lord was kindled against Aaron and his sister for their conduct on this occasion.

The anniversary meetings of the New York Hebrew Benevolent Society presents a singular combination. There meet together pilgrims from the Holy Land, merchants from the Pacific Ocean and the East Indies, exiles from the banks of the Vistula, the Danube, and the Dnieper, bankers from Vienna and Paris, and dwellers on the shores of the Hudson and the Susquehannah. Suspended in their dining hall, between the American and English flags, may be seen the Banner of Judah, with Hebrew inscriptions in golden letters. How this stirs the sea of memory! That national banner has not been unfurled for eighteen hundred years. The last time it floated to the breeze was over the walls of Jerusalem, besieged by Titus Vespasianus. Then *our* stars and stripes were not foreseen, even in dim shadow, by the vision of a prophet; and here they are intertwined together over this congress of nations!

In New York, as elsewhere, the vending of "old-clo'" is a prominent occupation among the Jews; a fact in which those who look for spiritual correspondences can perceive significance; although singularly enough Sartor Resartus makes no allusion to it, in his "Philosophy of Clothes." When I hear Christian ministers apologizing for slavery by the example of Abraham, defending war, because the Lord commanded Samuel to hew Agag in pieces, and sustaining capital punishment by the retaliatory code of Moses, it seems to me it would be most appropriate to have Jewish criers at the doors of our theological schools, proclaiming at the top of their lungs, "Old Clothes! Old Clothes! Old Clothes all the way from Judea!"

The proverbial worldliness of the Jews, their unpoetic avocations, their modern costume, and mechanical mode of perpetuating ancient forms, cannot divest them of a sacred and even romantic interest. The religious idea transmitted by this remarkable people, has given them a more abiding and extended influence on the world's history, than Greece attained by her classic beauty, or Rome by her triumphant arms. Mohammedanism and Christianity, the two forms of theology which include nearly all the civilized world, both grew from the stock planted by Abraham's children. On them lingers the long-reflected light of prophecy; and we, as well as they, are watching for its fulfilment. And verily, all things seem tending toward it. Through all their wanderings, they have followed the direction of Moses, to be *lenders* and not *borrowers*. The sovereigns of Europe and Asia, and the republics of America, are their debtors, to an immense amount. The Rothschilds are Jews; and they have wealth enough to purchase all Palestine if they choose; a large part of Jerusalem is in fact mortgaged to them. The oppressions of the Turkish government, and the incursions of hostile tribes, have hitherto rendered Syria an unsafe residence; but the Sultan has erected it into an independent power, and issued orders throughout his empire, that the Jews shall be as perfectly protected in their religious and civil rights, as any other class of his subjects; moreover, the present controversy between European nations and the East seems likely to result in placing Syria under the protection of Christian nations. It is reported that Prince Metternich, Premier of Austria, has determined, if possible, to constitute a Christian kingdom out of Palestine, of which Jerusalem is to be the seat of government. The Russian Jews, who number about 2,000,000, have been reduced to the most abject condition by contempt and tyranny; but there, too, government is now commencing a movement in their favour, without requiring them to renounce their faith. As long ago as 1817 important privileges were conferred by law on those Jews who consented to embrace Christianity. Land was gratuitously bestowed upon them, where they settled, under the name of The Society of Israelitish Christians.

These signs of the times cannot, of course, escape the observation, or elude the active zeal, of Christians of the present day. England has established many missions for the conversion of the Jews. The Presbyterian Church of Scotland have lately addressed a letter of sympathy and expostulation to the scattered children of Israel, which has been printed in a great variety of Oriental and Occidental languages.

In Upper Canada, a Society of Jews converted to Christianity, have been organized to facilitate the return of the wandering tribes to the Holy Land.

The Rev. Solomon Michael Alexander, a learned Rabbi, of the tribe of Judah, has been proselyted to Christianity, and sent to Palestine by the Church of England; being consecrated the first Bishop of Jerusalem.

Moreover the spirit of schism appears among them. A numerous and influential body in England have seceded, under the name of Reformed Jews. They denounce the Talmud as a mass of absurdities, and adhere exclusively to the authority of Moses; whereas, orthodox Jews consider the rabbinical writings of equal authority with the Pentateuch. They have sent a Hebrew circular to the Jews of this country, warning them against the seceders. A General Convention is likewise proposed, to enable them to draw closer the bonds of union.

What a busy, restless age is this in which we are cast! What a difficult task for Israel to walk through its midst, with mantles untouched by the Gentiles.

> And hath she wandered thus in vain,
>   A pilgrim of the past?
> No! long deferred her hope hath been.
>   But it shall come at last;
> For in her wastes a voice I hear,
>   As from some prophet's urn,
> It bids the nations build not there,
>   For Jacob shall return.

HENRY WADSWORTH LONGFELLOW:

"Closed are the portals of their Synagogue.
No Psalms of David now the silence break,
No Rabbi reads the ancient Decalogue
In the grand dialect the Prophets spake."
(1852)

Henry Wadsworth Longfellow (1807–1882) was born in Portland, Maine. His early years were spent in private schools, and in 1824, at the age of seventeen, he was graduated from Bowdoin College (in a class which included Nathaniel Hawthorne). After some years in Europe, he returned to Bowdoin as professor and college librarian. In 1834 he accepted a position at Harvard, and for eighteen years directed Harvard's modern language program. Hawthorne's major interest, however, was literature, especially poetry. The publication in 1839 of *Voices of the Night,* a collection of his poetry, brought him some success, and it was followed by a number of poems which brought him fame: "The Wreck of the Hesperus" (1841), *Song of Hiawatha* (1855), *The Courtship of Miles Standish* (1858), and others.

Longfellow's interest in early New England history was joined to a sympathetic and somewhat romanticized regard for Indians, slaves, and Jews. His "Sandalphon" (1858) was based on an old Talmudic legend

Henry Wadsworth Longfellow, "The Jewish Cemetery at Newport" (1852), in Cecil Shepard, *Henry Wadsworth Longfellow* (New York: American Book Company, 1934).

concerning an angel who was capable of transforming prayers into flowers; and his five-act tragedy *Judas Maccabeus* (1872) dealt with the relations between Judaism and Hellenism.

The poem here reprinted was written following a visit to the oldest Jewish cemetery in the United States, located at Newport, Rhode Island.

THE JEWISH CEMETERY AT NEWPORT

How strange it seems! These Hebrews in their graves,
    Close by the street of this fair seaport town,
Silent beside the never-silent waves,
    At rest in all this moving up and down!

The trees are white with dust, that o'er their sleep
    Wave their broad curtains in the south-wind's breath,
While underneath these leafy tents they keep
    The long, mysterious Exodus of Death.

And these sepulchral stones, so old and brown,
    That pave with level flags their burial-place,
Seem like the tablets of the Law, thrown down
    And broken by Moses at the mountain's base.

The very names recorded here are strange,
    Of foreign accent, and of different climes;
Alvares and Rivera interchange
    With Abraham and Jacob of old times.

"Blessed be God, for he created Death!"
    The mourners said, "and Death is rest and peace";
Then added, in the certainty of faith,
    "And giveth Life that never more shall cease."

Closed are the portals of their Synagogue,
    No Psalms of David now the silence break,
No Rabbi reads the ancient Decalogue
    In the grand dialect the Prophets spake.

Gone are the living, but the dead remain,
  And not neglected; for a hand unseen,
Scattering its bounty, like a summer rain,
  Still keeps their graves and their remembrance green.

How came they here? What burst of Christian hate,
  What persecution, merciless and blind,
Drove o'er the sea—that desert desolate—
  These Ishmaels and Hagars of mankind?

They lived in narrow streets and lanes obscure,
  Ghetto and Judenstrass, in mirk and mire;
Taught in the school of patience to endure
  The life of anguish and the death of fire.

All their lives long, with the unleavened bread
  And bitter herbs of exile and its fears,
The wasting famine of the heart they fed,
  And slaked its thirst with marah of their tears.

Anathema maranatha! was the cry
  That rang from town to town, from street to street;
At every gate the accursed Mordecai
  Was mocked and jeered, and spurned by Christian feet.

Pride and humiliation hand in hand
  Walked with them through the world where'er they went;
Trampled and beaten were they as the sand,
  And yet unshaken as the continent.

For in the background figures vague and vast
  Of patriarchs and of prophets rose sublime,
And all the great traditions of the Past
  They saw reflected in the coming time.

And thus forever with reverted look
  The mystic volume of the world they read,
Spelling it backward, like a Hebrew book,
  Till life became a Legend of the Dead.

But ah! what once has been shall be no more!
 The groaning earth in travail and in pain
Brings forth its races, but does not restore,
And the dead nations never rise again.

ULYSSES S. GRANT:

*"The Jews, as a class . . .
are hereby expelled from the
department." (1862)*

Ulysses Simpson Grant (1822–1885), eighteenth President, spent the first forty years of his life in relative obscurity. Graduating in the middle of his class at West Point, he spent the next ten years at various Army posts in the Western United States. In 1854, while stationed at an obscure post in California, Grant was reprimanded by his Commanding Officer for heavy drinking. In a fit of anger he resigned his Army commission, his resignation being accepted, ironically, by the then Secretary of the Army, Jefferson Davis. Grant was unable to obtain a commission from Washington during the first weeks of the Civil War, but he was finally appointed Colonel of the 21st Illinois Volunteers by the Governor of Illinois. By August, 1861, he was serving as Brigadier General in the Western Department of the Union Army, with headquarters at Cairo, Illinois.

Grant's promotion to Major General of Volunteers in early 1862 was almost immediately followed by two major defeats of his troops. On April 6 and 7 his troops were badly mauled at Shiloh, and November saw another failure in the first advance against Vicksburg. It was at that time that a number of military orders, aimed at Jews, were issued over his signature, culminating in the release on December 17, 1862, of the notorious General Order No. 11.

Although Grant subsequently insisted that he had "no prejudice against sect or race," he never specifically denied authorship of No. 11. It is also doubtful that the Order would have been revoked had it not been brought to the attention of Congress and President Lincoln. But it should be mentioned in Grant's favor that as President he offered the Cabinet post of Secretary of the Treasury to New York banker Joseph Seligman, and in 1870 he appointed Benjamin F. Peixotto United States Consul in Bucharest. The Peixotto appointment was especially novel in that Peixotto, a

From "General Ulysses S. Grant and the Jews" by Joseph Lebowich, *Publications of the American Jewish Historical Society*, 1909, No. 17, 71–99.

258   THE JEW IN AMERICA

past grand master of B'nai B'rith, was financed by B'nai B'rith money,
since no funds had been allocated for an American Consulate in Bucharest.
Peixotto's special mission was to alleviate the perscution of Jews in Eastern
Europe. Moreover Grant is probably the only President who ever con-
tributed to the dowry of a Jewish bride in Jerusalem. Informed that a
Jewish resident of Jerusalem, wishing to honor Grant, had invited him to
contribute to his daughter's dowry, Grant asked, "Is this man serious?"
Told that he was, Grant sent the man a check for twenty-five dollars!

LaGrange, Tenn.,
November 9, 1862.

Major-General Hurlbut,
Jackson, Tenn.:

Refuse all permits to come south of Jackson for the present. The
Israelites especially should be kept out.

What troops have you now, exclusive of Stevenson's brigade?

U. S. Grant,
Major-General

LaGrange, Tenn.,
November 10, 1862.

General Webster,
Jackson, Tenn.:

Give orders to all the conductors on the road that no Jews are to
be permitted to travel on the railroad southward from any point.
They may go north and be encouraged in it; but they are such an
intolerable nuisance that the department must be purged of them.

U. S. Grant,
Major-General

Holly Springs, Miss.,
December 8, 1862.

General Order

On account of the scarcity of provisions all cotton speculators,
Jews, and other vagrants having no honest means of support, except
trading upon the misery of the country, and in general all persons
from the North not connected with the army whatever, and having
no permission from the Commanding-General to remain in town,

will leave in twenty-four (24) hours or will be put to duty in the
intrenchments.

By order of Col. Jno. V. Du Bois, U.S. Army.

> Hdqrs. Thirteenth A.C.,
> Dept. of the Tenn.,
> Oxford, Miss.,
> December 17, 1862.

Hon. C. P. Wolcott,
Assistant Secretary of War,
Washington, D.C.:

I have long since believed that in spite of all vigilance that can
be infused into post commanders, the specie regulations of the
Treasury Department have been violated, and that mostly by Jews
and other unprincipled traders. So well satisfied have I been of this
that I instructed the commanding officer at Columbus to refuse all
permits to Jews to come South, and I have frequently had them
expelled from the department, but they come in with their carpet-
sacks in spite of all that can be done to prevent it. The Jews seem
to be a privileged class that can travel everywhere. They will land
at any wood-yard on the river and make their way through the
country. If not permitted to buy cotton themselves they will act as
agents for someone else, who will be at a military post with a Treasury permit to receive cotton and pay for it in Treasury notes which
the Jew will buy up at an agreed rate, paying gold.

There is but one way that I know of to reach this case; that is,
for the Government to buy all the cotton at a fixed rate and send
it to Cairo, Saint Louis, or some other point to be sold. Then all
traders (they are a curse to the army) might be expelled.

> U. S. Grant,
> Major-General.

General Orders,)
   No. 11.   )

> Hdqrs. Thirteenth A.C.,
> Dept. of the Tenn.,
> Holly Springs,
> December 17, 1862.

The Jews, as a class violating every regulation of trade established
by the Treasury Department and also department orders, are hereby

expelled from the department within twenty-four hours from the receipt of this order.

Post commanders will see that all of this class of people be furnished passes and required to leave, and any one returning after such notification will be arrested and held in confinement until an opportunity occurs of sending them out as prisoners, unless furnished with permit from headquarters.

No passes will be given these people to visit headquarters for the purpose of making personal applications for trade permits.

By order of Maj.-Gen. U. S. Grant.

Jno. A. Rawlins,
Assistant Adjutant-General

Paducah, Ky.,
Dec. 29, 1862.

Hon. Abraham Lincoln,
President of the United States.

General Order No. 11 issued by General Grant at Oxford, Miss., December the 17th, commands all post commanders to expel all Jews without distinction within twenty-four hours from his entire Department. The undersigned good and loyal citizens of the United States and residents of this town, for many years engaged in legitimate business as merchants, feel greatly insulted and outraged by this inhuman order; the carrying out of which would be the grossest violation of the Constitution and our rights as good citizens under it, and would place us, besides a large number of other Jewish families of this town, as outlaws before the world. We respectfully ask your immediate attention to this enormous outrage on all law and humanity and pray for your effectual and immediate interposition. We would especially refer you to the post commander and post adjutant as to our loyalty, and to all respectable citizens of this community as to our standing as citizens and merchants. We respectfully ask for immediate instructions to be sent to the Commander of this Post.

D. Wolff & Bros.
C. F. Kaskel
J. W. Kaskel

War Department,
Washington,
January 4, 1863.

Major-General Grant,
Holly Springs, Miss.

A paper purporting to be General Orders, No. 11, issued by you December 17, has been presented here. By its terms it expels all Jews from your department.

If such an order has been issued, it will be immediately revoked.

H. W. Halleck,
General-in-Chief.

Circular

Hdqrs. Thirteenth A.C.,
Dept. of the Tenn.,
Holly Springs, Miss.,
January 7, 1863.

By direction of General-in-Chief of the Army, at Washington, the general order from these headquarters expelling Jews from the department is hereby revoked.

By order of Maj.-Gen. U. S. Grant.

Jno. A. Rawlins,
Assistant Adjutant-General.

Five years later, during the Presidential campaign of 1868, General Order No. 11 was the basis for charges that Grant was anti-Semitic. Simon Wolf, Jewish leader and friend of Grant's, was convinced that the Order had been issued by a subordinate on Grant's staff, without his permission, under pressure from General Sherman. Wolf later declared that Grant's rather evasive reply to his request for clarification was occasioned by the fact that the General "did not wish anyone, as he stated, to suppose that he was seeking public applause; he would rather suffer in silence." General Badeau was one of Grant's close associates.

My Dear Mr. Wolf:

I have brought your request to the attention of Gen. Grant, and while he would like very much indeed to comply therewith, yet he fears that any statement made by him now would be misconstrued by the general public. He, therefore, prefers not to make any explanation other than what you have already received. He desires me to express his hearty and sincere appreciation for the interest you have taken, knowing that your motives are actuated by friendship and a desire to do justice, not only to himself, but to the people whom you so worthily represent.

Very truly yours,

March, 1868.   Adam Badeau.

The issue of Grant's alleged anti-Semitism was not yet settled, however. On August 25, 1868, Mr. Adolph Moses of Chicago published a letter in the Chicago *Times* claiming that "General Grant in insulting the Jews, has violated a principle guaranteed by the charter of our liberties . . . we can oppose him, and not for insulting the Jews or anybody else." Congressman I. N. Morris of Illinois, a supporter of Grant's, brought the letter to Grant's attention.

Grant's reply to Morris contains his last written reference to General Order No. 11. He does not refer to it in his Memoirs.

[From a Letter to Congressman I. N. Morris, September 14, 1868]

At the time of its (General Order No. 11) publication, I was incensed by a reprimand received from Washington for permitting acts which Jews within my lines were engaged in. There were many other persons within my lines equally bad with the worst of them, but the difference was that the Jews could pass with impunity from one army to the other, and gold, in violation of orders, was being smuggled through the lines, at least so it was reported. The order was issued and sent without any reflection and without thinking of the Jews as a sect or race to themselves, but simply as persons who had successfully (I say successfully instead of persistently, because there were plenty of others within my lines who envied their success) violated an order, which greatly inured to the help of the rebels.

Give Mr. Moses assurance that I have no prejudice against sect or race, but want each individual to be judged by his own merit. Order No. 11 does not sustain this statement, I admit, but then I do not sustain that order. It never would have been issued if it had not been telegraphed the moment it was penned, and without reflection.

Yours truly,
U. S. Grant.

MARK TWAIN:

"The Jew is not a disturber of the peace of any country. Even his enemies will concede that. He is not a loafer, he is not a sot, he is not noisy, he is not a brawler nor a rioter, he is not quarrelsome." (1899)

Mark Twain, born Samuel Langhorne Clemens (1835–1910), grew up in a poverty-stricken home in Missouri. As a boy, Twain learned to set type for the Hannibal (Missouri) *Journal,* and eventually became a journeyman printer. After a few years in New York and Philadelphia, Twain returned to Missouri and became a pilot on Mississippi River boats (the pseudonym "Mark Twain" was derived from a call used by river pilots in taking depth soundings). With the decline of river trade during the Civil War Twain first tried gold mining in Nevada, and, with the failure of that venture, journalism. The publication of *The Celebrated Jumping Frog of Calaveras County* brought him immediate fame, and with the writing of *Tom Sawyer* and its sequel, *Huckleberry Finn,* he became a world literary figure. Honored with degrees from Oxford, Yale, and the University of Missouri, Twain in 1906 built a house at Redding, Connecticut, where he resided until his death.

His essay, "Concerning the Jews," here reprinted, was first published in *Harper's Magazine* in September, 1899.

Some months ago I published a magazine article descriptive of a remarkable scene in the Imperial Parliament in Vienna. Since then I have received from Jews in America several letters of inquiry.

From Mark Twain, "Concerning the Jews," first published in *Harper's Magazine,* September, 1899; reissued in pamphlet form (New York: Harper and Brothers, 1934), reprinted by permission of Harper and Brothers.

They were difficult letters to answer, for they were not very definite. But at last I received a definite one. It is from a lawyer, and he really asks the questions which the other writers probably believed they were asking. By help of this text I will do the best I can to publicly answer this correspondent, and also the others—at the same time apologizing for having failed to reply privately. The lawyer's letter reads as follows:

I have read "Stirring Times in Austria." One point in particular is of vital import to not a few thousand people, including myself, being a point about which I have often wanted to address a question to some disinterested person. The show of military force in the Austrian Parliament, which precipitated the riots, was not introduced by any Jew. No Jew was a member of that body. No Jewish question was involved in the *Ausgleich* or in the language proposition. No Jew was insulting anybody. In short, no Jew was doing any mischief toward anybody whatsoever. In fact, the Jews were the only ones of the nineteen different races in Austria which did not have a party—they are absolutely non-participants. Yet in your article you say that in the rioting which followed all classes of people were unanimous only on one thing—*viz.*, in being against the Jews. Now will you kindly tell me why, in your judgment, the Jews have thus ever been, and are even now, in these days of supposed intelligence, the butt of baseless, vicious animosities? I dare say that for centuries there has been no more quiet, undisturbing, and well-behaving citizen, as a class, than that same Jew. It seems to me that ignorance and fanaticism cannot alone account for these horrible and unjust persecutions.

Tell me, therefore, from your vantage-point of cold view, what in your mind is the cause. Can American Jews do anything to correct it either in America or abroad? Will it ever come to an end? Will a Jew be permitted to live honestly, decently, and peaceably like the rest of mankind? What has become of the golden rule?

I will begin by saying that if I thought myself prejudiced against the Jew, I should hold it fairest to leave this subject to a person not crippled in that way. But I think I have no such prejudice. A few years ago a Jew observed to me that there was no uncourteous reference to his people in my books, and asked how it happened. It happened because the disposition was lacking. I am quite sure that (bar one) I have no race prejudices, and I think I have no color prejudices nor caste prejudices nor creed prejudices. Indeed, I know it. I can stand any society. All that I care to know is that a man is a human being—that is enough for me; he can't be any worse. I have no special regard for Satan; but I can at least claim that I have no prejudice against him. It may even be that I lean a little his way, on account of his not having a fair show. All religions issue bibles against him, and say the most injurious things about him, but we never hear *his* side. We have none but the evidence for the prosecution, and yet we have rendered the verdict. To my mind, this is irregular. It is un-English; it is un-American; it is French. Without this precedent Dreyfus could not have been condemned. Of course Satan has some kind of a case, it goes without saying. It may be a poor one, but that is nothing; that can be said about any of us. As soon as I can get at the facts I will undertake his rehabilitation myself, if I can find an unpolitic publisher. It is a thing which we ought to be willing to do for any one who is under a cloud. We may not pay him reverence, for that would be indiscreet, but we can at least respect his talents. A person who has for untold centuries maintained the imposing position of spiritual head of four-fifths of the human race, and political head of the whole of it, must be granted the possession of executive abilities of the loftiest order. In his large presence the other popes and politicians shrink to midges for the microscope. I would like to see him. I would rather see him and shake him by the tail than any other member of the European Concert. In the present paper I shall allow myself to use the word Jew as if it stood for both religion and race. It is handy; and, besides, that is what the term means to the general world.

In the above letter one notes these points:

1. The Jew is a well-behaved citizen.
2. Can ignorance and fanaticism *alone* account for his unjust treatment?
3. Can Jews do anything to improve the situation?
4. The Jews have no party; they are non-participants.
5. Will the persecution ever come to an end?
6. What has become of the golden rule?

Point No. 1.—We must grant proposition No. 1, for several sufficient reasons. The Jew is not a disturber of the peace of any country. Even his enemies will concede that. He is not a loafer, he is not a sot, he is not noisy, he is not a brawler nor a rioter, he is not quarrelsome. In the statistics of crime his presence is conspicuously rare —in all countries. With murder and other crimes of violence he has but little to do: he is a stranger to the hangman. In the police court's daily long roll of "assaults" and "drunk and disorderlies" his name seldom appears. That the Jewish home is a home in the truest sense is a fact which no one will dispute. The family is knitted together by the strongest affections; its members show each other every due respect; and reverence for the elders is an inviolate law of the house. The Jew is not a burden on the charities of the state nor of the city; these could cease from their functions without affecting him. When he is well enough, he works; when he is incapacitated, his own people take care of him. And not in a poor and stingy way, but with a fine and large benevolence. His race is entitled to be called the most benevolent of all the races of men. A Jewish beggar is not impossible, perhaps; such a thing may exist, but there are few men that can say they have seen that spectacle. The Jew has been staged in many uncomplimentary forms, but, so far as I know, no dramatist has done him the injustice to stage him as a beggar. Whenever a Jew has real need to beg, his people save him from the necessity of doing it. The charitable institutions of the Jews are supported by Jewish money, and amply. The Jews make no noise about it; it is done quietly; they do not nag and pester and harass us for contributions; they give us peace, and set us an example—an example which we have not found ourselves able to follow; for by nature we are not free givers, and have to be patiently and persistently hunted down in the interest of the unfortunate.

These facts are all on the credit side of the proposition that the Jew is a good and orderly citizen. Summed up, they certify that he is quiet, peaceable, industrious, unaddicted to high crimes and brutal dispositions; that his family life is commendable; that he is not a burden upon public charities; that he is not a beggar; that in benevolence he is above the reach of competition. These are the very quintessentials of good citizenship. If you can add that he is as honest as the average of his neighbors— But I think that question is affirmatively answered by the fact that he is a successful business man. The basis of successful business is honesty; a business cannot thrive where the parties to it cannot trust each other. In the matter of numbers the Jew counts for little in the overwhelming population of New York; but that his honesty counts for much is guaranteed by the fact that the immense wholesale business of Broadway, from the Battery to Union Square, is substantially in his hands.

I suppose that the most picturesque example in history of a

trader's trust in his fellow-trader was one where it was not Christian trusting Christian, but Christian trusting Jew. That Hessian Duke who used to sell his subjects to George III to fight George Washington with got rich at it; and by and by, when the wars engendered by the French Revolution made his throne too warm for him, he was obliged to fly the country. He was in a hurry, and had to leave his earnings behind—nine million dollars. He had to risk the money with some one without security. He did not select a Christian, but a Jew— a Jew of only modest means, but of high character; a character so high that it left him lonesome—Rothschild of Frankfort. Thirty years later, when Europe had become quiet and safe again, the Duke came back from overseas, and the Jew returned the loan, with interest added.

The Jew has his other side. He has some discreditable ways, though he has not a monopoly of them, because he cannot get entirely rid of vexatious Christian competition. We have seen that he seldom transgresses the laws against crimes of violence. Indeed, his dealings with courts are almost restricted to matters connected with commerce. He has a reputation for various small forms of cheating, and for practising oppressive usury, and for burning himself out to get the insurance, and arranging for cunning contracts which leave him an exit but lock the other man in, and for smart evasions which find him safe and comfortable just within the strict letter of the law, when court and jury know very well that he has violated the spirit of it. He is a frequent and faithful and capable officer in the civil service, but he is charged with an unpatriotic disinclination to stand by the flag as a soldier—like the Christian Quaker.

Now if you offset these discreditable features by the creditable ones summarized in a preceding paragraph beginning with the words, "These facts are all on the credit side," and strike a balance, what must the verdict be? This, I think: that, the merits and demerits being fairly weighed and measured on both sides, the Christian can claim no superiority over the Jew in the matter of good citizenship.

Yet, in all countries, from the dawn of history, the Jew has been persistently and implacably hated, and with frequency persecuted.

Point No. 2.—"Can fanaticism alone account for this?"

Years ago I used to think that it was responsible for nearly all of it, but latterly I have come to think that this was an error. Indeed, it is now my conviction that it is responsible for hardly any of it. In this connection I call to mind Genesis, chapter xlvii.

We have all thoughtfully—or unthoughtfully—read the pathetic story of the years of plenty and the years of famine in Egypt, and how Joseph, with that opportunity, made a corner in broken hearts, and the crusts of the poor, and human liberty—a corner whereby he took a nation's money all away, to the last penny; took a nation's land away, to the last acre; then took the nation itself, buying it for bread, man by man, woman by woman, child by child, till all were slaves; a corner which took everything, left nothing; a corner so stupendous that, by comparison with it, the most gigantic corners in subsequent history are but baby things, for it dealt in hundreds of millions of bushels, and its profits were reckonable by hundreds of millions of dollars, and it was a disaster so crushing that its effects have not wholly disappeared from Egypt today, more than three thousand years after the event.

Is it presumable that the eye of Egypt was upon Joseph, the foreign Jew, all this time? I think it likely. Was it friendly? We must doubt it. Was Joseph establishing a character for his race which would survive long in Egypt? And in time would his name come to be familiarly used to express that character—like Shylock's? It is hardly to be doubted. Let us remember that this was *centuries before the crucifixion.*

I wish to come down eighteen hundred years later and refer to a remark made by one of the Latin historians. I read it in a translation many years ago, and it comes back to me now with force. It was alluding to a time when people were still living who could have seen the Saviour in the flesh. Christianity was so new that the people of Rome had hardly heard of it, and had but confused notions of what it was. The substance of the remark was this: Some Christians were persecuted in Rome through error, they being *"mistaken for Jews."*

The meaning seems plain. These pagans had nothing against Christians, but they were quite ready to persecute Jews. For some reason or other they hated a Jew before they even knew what a Christian was. May I not assume, then, that the persecution of Jews is a thing which *antedates* Christianity and was not born of Christianity? I think so. What was the origin of the feeling?

When I was a boy, in the back settlements of the Mississippi Val-

ley, where a gracious and beautiful Sunday-school simplicity and
unpracticality prevailed, the "Yankee" (citizen of the New England
states) was hated with a splendid energy. But religion had nothing
to do with it. In a trade, the Yankee was held to be about five times
the match of the Westerner. His shrewdness, his insight, his judgment, his knowledge, his enterprise, and his formidable cleverness
in applying these forces were frankly confessed, and most compe-
tently cursed.

In the cotton states, after the war, the simple and ignorant negroes
made the crops for the white planter on shares. The Jew came down
in force, set up shop on the plantation, supplied all the negro's wants
on credit, and at the end of the season was proprietor of the negro's
share of the present crop and of part of his share of the next one.
Before long the whites detested the Jew, and it is doubtful if the
negro loved him.

The Jew is being legislated out of Russia. The reason is not concealed. The movement was instituted because the Christian peasant
and villager stood no chance against his commercial abilities. He
was always ready to lend money on a crop, and sell vodka and other
necessaries of life on credit while the crop was growing. When settlement day came he owned the crop; and next year or year after
he owned the farm, like Joseph.

In the dull and ignorant England of John's time everybody got
into debt to the Jew. He gathered all lucrative enterprises into his
hands; he was the king of commerce; he was ready to be helpful in
all profitable ways; he even financed crusades for the rescue of the
Sepulcher. To wipe out his account with the nation and restore business to its natural and incompetent channels he had to be banished
the realm.

For the like reasons Spain had to banish him four hundred years
ago, and Austria about a couple of centuries later.

In all the ages Christian Europe had been obliged to curtail his
activities. If he entered upon a mechanical trade, the Christian had
to retire from it. If he set up as a doctor, he was the best one, and
he took the business. If he exploited agriculture, the other farmers
had to get at something else. Since there was no way to successfully
compete with him in any vocation, the law had to step in and save
the Christian from the poorhouse. Trade after trade was taken away
from the Jew by statute till practically none was left. He was for-

bidden to engage in agriculture; he was forbidden to practise law; he was forbidden to practise medicine, except among Jews; he was forbidden the handicrafts. Even the seats of learning and the schools of science had to be closed against this tremendous antagonist. Still, almost bereft of employments, he found ways to make money, even ways to get rich. Also ways to invest his takings well, for usury was not denied him. In the hard conditions suggested, the Jew without brains could not survive, and the Jew with brains had to keep them in good training and well sharpened up, or starve. Ages of restriction to the one tool which the law was not able to take from him—his brain—have made that tool singularly competent; ages of compulsory disuse of his hands have atrophied them, and he never uses them now. This history has a very, very commercial look, a most sordid and practical commercial look, the business aspect of a Chinese cheap-labor crusade. Religious prejudices may account for one part of it, but not for the other nine.

Protestants have persecuted Catholics, but they did not take their livelihoods away from them. The Catholics have persecuted the Protestants with bloody and awful bitterness, but they never closed agriculture and the handicrafts against them. Why was that? That has the candid look of genuine religious persecution, not a trade-union boycott in a religious disguise.

The Jews are harried and obstructed in Austria and Germany, and lately in France; but England and America give them an open field and yet survive. Scotland offers them an unembarrassed field too, but there are not many takers. There are a few Jews in Glasgow, and one in Aberdeen; but that is because they can't earn enough to get away. The Scotch pay themselves that compliment, but it is authentic.

I feel convinced that the Crucifixion has not much to do with the world's attitude toward the Jew; that the reasons for it are older than that event, as suggested by Egypt's experience and by Rome's regret for having persecuted an unknown quantity called a Christian, under the mistaken impression that she was merely persecuting a Jew. *Merely* a Jew—a skinned eel who was used to it, presumably. I am persuaded that in Russia, Austria, and Germany nine-tenths of the hostility to the Jew comes from the average Christian's inability to compete successfully with the average Jew in business—in either straight business or the questionable sort.

In Berlin, a few years ago, I read a speech which frankly urged the expulsion of the Jews from Germany; and the agitator's *reason* was as frank as his proposition. It was this: *that eighty-five per cent.* of the successful lawyers of Berlin were Jews, and that about the same percentage of the great and lucrative businesses of all sorts in Germany were in the hands of the Jewish race! Isn't it an amazing confession? It was but another way of saying that in a population of 48,000,000 of whom only 500,000 were registered as Jews, eighty-five per cent. of the brains and honesty of the whole was lodged in the Jews. I must insist upon the honesty—it is an essential of successful business, taken by and large. Of course it does not rule out rascals entirely, even among Christians, but it is a good working rule, nevertheless. The speaker's figures may have been inexact, but *the motive of persecution* stands out as clear as day.

The man claimed that in Berlin the banks, the newspapers, the theaters, the great mercantile, shipping, mining, and manufacturing interests, the big army and city contracts, the tramways, and pretty much all other properties of high value, and *also* the small businesses —were in the hands of the Jews. He said the Jew was pushing the Christian to the wall all along the line; that it was all a Christian could do to scrape together a living; and that the Jew *must* be banished, and soon—there was no other way of saving the Christian. Here in Vienna, last autumn, an agitator said that all these disastrous details were true of Austria-Hungary also; and in fierce language he demanded the expulsion of the Jews. When the politicians come out without a blush and read the baby act in this frank way, *unrebuked,* it is a very good indication that they have a market back of them, and know where to fish for votes.

You note the crucial point of the mentioned agitation; the argument is that the Christian cannot *compete* with the Jew, and that hence his very bread is in peril. To human beings this is a much more hate-inspiring thing than is any detail connected with religion. With most people, of a necessity, bread and meat take first rank, religion second. I am convinced that the persecution of the Jew is not due in any large degree to religious prejudice.

No, the Jew is a money-getter; and in getting his money he is a very serious obstruction to less capable neighbors who are on the same quest. I think that that is the trouble. In estimating world values the Jew is not shallow, but deep. With precocious wisdom he found out in the morning of time that some men worship rank, some worship heroes, some worship power, some worship God, and that over these ideals they dispute and cannot unite—but that they all worship money; so he made it the end and aim of his life to get it. He was at it in Egypt thirty-six centuries ago; he was at it in Rome when that Christian got persecuted by mistake for him; he has been at it ever since. The cost to him has been heavy; his success has made the whole human race his enemy—but it has paid, for it has brought him envy, and that is the only thing which men will sell both soul and body to get. He long ago observed that a millionaire commands respect, a two-millionaire homage, a multi-millionaire the deepest deeps of adoration. We all know that feeling; we have seen it express itself. We have noticed that when the average man mentions the name of a multi-millionaire he does it with that mixture in his voice of awe and reverence and lust which burns in a Frenchman's eye when it falls on another man's centime.

Point No. 4.—"The Jews have no party; they are non-participants."

Perhaps you have let the secret out and given yourself away. It seems hardly a credit to the race that it is able to say that; or to you, sir, that you can say it without remorse; more, that you should offer it as a plea against maltreatment, injustice, and oppression. Who gives the Jew the right, who gives any race the right, to sit still, in a free country, and let somebody else look after its safety? The oppressed Jew was entitled to all pity in the former times under brutal autocracies, for he was weak and friendless, and had no way to help his case. But he has ways now, and he has had them for a century, but I do not see that he has tried to make serious use of them. When the Revolution set him free in France it was an act of grace—the grace of other people; he does not appear in it as a helper. I do not know that he helped when England set him free. Among the Twelve Sane Men of France who have stepped forward with great Zola at their head to fight (and win, I hope and believe) the battle for the most infamously misused Jew of modern times, do you find a great or rich or illustrious Jew helping? In the United States he was created free in the beginning—he did not need to help, of course. In Austria, and Germany, and France he has a vote, but of what considerable use is it to him? He doesn't seem to know how to apply it to the best effect. With all his splendid capacities and

all his fat wealth he is to-day not politically important in any country. In America, as early as 1854, the ignorant Irish hodcarrier, who
had a spirit of his own and a way of exposing it to the weather,
made it apparent to all that he must be politically reckoned with;
yet fifteen years before that we hardly knew what an Irishman
looked like. As an intelligent force, and numerically, he has always
been away down, but he has governed the country just the same.
It was because he was *organized*. It made his vote valuable—in fact,
essential.

You will say the Jew is everywhere numerically feeble. That is
nothing to the point—with the Irishman's history for an object-lesson.
But I am coming to your numerical feebleness presently. In all parliamentary countries you could no doubt elect Jews to the legisla-
tures—and even *one* member in such a body is sometimes a force
which counts. How deeply have you concerned yourselves about this
in Austria, France, and Germany? Or even in America for that matter? You remark that the Jews were not to blame for the riots in
this Reichsrath here, and you add with satisfaction that there wasn't
one in that body. That is not strictly correct; if it were, would it not
be in order for you to explain it and apologize for it, not try to make
a merit of it? But I think that the Jew was by no means in as large
force there as he ought to have been, with his chances. Austria opens
the suffrage to him on fairly liberal terms, and it must surely be his
own fault that he is so much in the background politically.

As to your numerical weakness. I mentioned some figures awhile
ago—500,000—as the Jewish population of Germany. I will add some
more 6,000,000 in Russia, 5,000,000 in Austria, 250,000 in the United
States. I take them from memory! I read them in the *Encyclopaedia
Britannica* about ten years ago. Still, I am entirely sure of them. If
those statistics are correct, my argument is not as strong as it ought
to be as concerns America, but it still has strength. It is plenty strong
enough as concerns Austria, for ten years ago 5,000,000 was nine
per cent. of the empire's population. The Irish would govern the
Kingdom of Heaven if they had a strength there like that.

I have some suspicions; I got them at second hand, but they have
remained with me these ten or twelve years. When I read in the
E. B. that the Jewish population of the United States was 250,000,
I wrote the editor, and explained to him that I was personally acquainted with more Jews than that in my country, and that his

figures were without doubt a misprint for 25,000,000. I also added that I was personally acquainted with *that* many there; but that was only to raise his confidence in me, for it was not true. His answer miscarried, and I never got it; but I went around talking about the matter, and people told me they had reason to suspect that for business reasons many Jews whose dealings were mainly with the Christians did not report themselves as Jews in the census. It looked plausible; it looks plausible yet. Look at the city of New York; and look at Boston, and Philadelphia, and New Orleans, and Chicago, and Cincinnati, and San Francisco—how your race swarms in those places!—and everywhere else in America, down to the least little village. Read the signs on the marts of commerce and on the shops: Goldstein (gold stone), Edelstein (precious stone), Blumenthal (flower-vale), Rosenthal (rose-vale), Veilchenduft (violet odor), Singvogel (song-bird), Rosenzweig (rose branch), and all the amazing list of beautiful and enviable names which Prussia and Austria glorified you with so long ago. It is another instance of Europe's coarse and cruel persecution of your race; not that it was coarse and cruel to outfit it with pretty and poetical names like those, but that it was coarse and cruel to make it *pay* for them or else take such hideous and often indecent names that to-day their owners never use them; or, if they do, only on official papers. And it was the many, not the few, who got the odious names, they being too poor to bribe the officials to grant them better ones.

Now why was the race renamed? I have been told that in Prussia it was given to using fictitious names, and often changing them, so as to beat the tax-gatherer, escape military service, and so on; and that finally the idea was hit upon of furnishing all the inmates of a house with *one and the same surname,* and then holding the house responsible right along for those inmates, and accountable for any disappearances that might occur; it made the Jews keep track of *each other,* for self-interest's sake, and saved the government the trouble.

If that explanation of how the Jews of Prussia came to be renamed is correct, if it is true that they fictitiously registered themselves to gain certain advantages, it may possibly be true that in America they refrain from registering themselves as Jews to fend off the damaging prejudices of the Christian customer. I have no way of knowing whether this notion is well founded or not. There may be other and better ways of explaining why only that poor little 250,000 of our Jews got into the *Encyclopaedia*. I may, of course, be mistaken, but I am strongly of the opinion that we have an immense Jewish population in America.

Point No. 3.—"Can Jews do anything to improve the situation?"

I think so. If I may make a suggestion without seeming to be trying to teach my grandmother how to suck eggs, I will offer it. In our days we have learned the value of combination. We apply it everywhere—in railway systems, in trusts, in trade-unions, in Salvation Armies, in minor politics, in major politics, in European Concerts. Whatever our strength may be, big or little, we *organize* it. We have found out that that is the only way to get the most out of it that is in it. We know the weakness of individual sticks, and the strength of the concentrated fagot. Suppose you try a scheme like this, for instance. In England and America put every Jew on the census-book *as* a Jew (in case you have not been doing that). Get up volunteer regiments composed of Jews solely, and, when the drum beats, fall in and go to the front, so as to remove the reproach that you have few Massenas among you, and that you feed on a country but don't like to fight for it. Next, in politics, organise your strength, band together, and deliver the casting vote where you can, and, where you can't, compel as good terms as possible. You huddle to yourselves already in all countries, but you huddle to no sufficient purpose, politically speaking. You do not seem to be organized, except for your charities. There you are omnipotent; there you compel your due of recognition—you do not have to beg for it. It shows what you can do when you band together for a definite purpose.

And then from America and England you can encourage your race in Austria, France, and Germany, and materially help it. It was a pathetic tale that was told by a poor Jew in Galicia a fortnight ago during the riots, after he had been raided by the Christian peasantry and despoiled of everything he had. He said his vote was of no value to him, and he wished he could be excused from casting it, for indeed casting it was a sure *damage* to him, since no matter which party he voted for, the other party would come straight and take its revenge out of him. Nine per cent. of the population of the empire, these Jews, and apparently they cannot put a plank into any candidate's platform! If you will send our Irish lads over here I think they will organize your race and change the aspect of the Reichsrath.

You seem to think that the Jews take no hand in politics here, that they are "absolutely non-participants." I am assured by men competent to speak that this is a very large error, that the Jews are exceedingly active in politics all over the empire, but that they scatter their work and their votes among the numerous parties, and thus lose the advantages to be had by concentration. I think that in America they scatter too, but you know more about that than I do.

Speaking of concentration, Dr. Herzl has a clear insight into the value of that. Have you heard of his plan? He wishes to gather the Jews of the world together in Palestine, with a government of their own—under the suzerainty of the Sultan, I suppose. At the convention of Berne, last year, there were delegates from everywhere, and the proposal was received with decided favor. I am not the Sultan, and I am not objecting; but if that concentration of the cunningest brains in the world was going to be made in a free country (bar Scotland), I think it would be politic to stop it. It will not be well to let that race find out its strength. If the horses knew theirs, we should not ride any more.

Point No. 5.—"Will the persecution of the Jews ever come to an end?"

On the score of religion, I think it has already come to an end. On the score of race prejudice and trade, I have the idea that it will continue. That is, here and there in spots about the world, where a barbarous ignorance and a sort of mere animal civilization prevail; but I do not think that elsewhere the Jew need now stand in any fear of being robbed and raided. Among the high civilizations he seems to be very comfortably situated indeed, and to have more than his proportionate share of the prosperities going. It has that look in Vienna. I suppose the race prejudice cannot be removed; but he can stand that; it is no particular matter. By his make and ways he is substantially a foreigner wherever he may be, and even the angels dislike a foreigner. I am using this word foreigner in the German sense—*stranger*. Nearly all of us have an antipathy to a stranger, even of our own nationality. We pile grip-sacks in a vacant seat to keep him from getting it; and a dog goes further, and does as a savage would—challenges him on the spot. The German dictionary seems to make no distinction between a stranger and a foreigner; in its view a stranger *is* a foreigner—a sound position, I think. You will always be by ways and habits and predilections substantially strangers—foreigners—wherever you are, and that will probably keep the race prejudice against you alive.

But you were the favorites of Heaven originally, and your manifold and unfair prosperities convince me that you have crowded back into that snug place again. Here is an incident that is significant. Last week in Vienna a hailstorm struck the prodigious Central Cemetery and made wasteful destruction there. In the Christian part of it, according to the official figures, 621 window-panes were broken; more than 900 singing-birds were killed; five great trees and many small ones were torn to shreds and the shreds scattered far and wide by the wind; the ornamental plants and other decorations of the graves were ruined, and more than a hundred tomb-lanterns shattered; and it took the cemetery's whole force of 300 laborers more than three days to clear away the storm's wreckage. In the report occurs this remark—and in its italics you can hear it grit its Christian teeth: ". . . lediglich die *israelitische* Abtheilung des Friedhofes vom Hagelwetter *ganzlich verschont* worden war." Not a hailstone hit the Jewish reservation! Such nepotism makes me tired.

Point No. 6.—"What has become of the golden rule?"

It exists, it continues to sparkle, and is well taken care of. It is Exhibit A in the Church's assets, and we pull it out every Sunday and give it an airing. But you are not permitted to try to smuggle it into this discussion, where it is irrelevant and would not feel at home. It is strictly religious furniture, like an acolyte, or a contribution-plate, or any of those things. It has never been intruded into business; and Jewish persecution is not a religious passion, it is a business passion.

To conclude.—If the statistics are right, the Jews constitute but *one per cent.* of the human race. It suggests a nebulous dim puff of star dust lost in the blaze of the Milky Way. Properly the Jew ought hardly to be heard of; but he is heard of, has always been heard of. He is as prominent on the planet as any other people, and his commercial importance is extravagantly out of proportion to the smallness of his bulk. His contributions to the world's list of great names in literature, science, art, music, finance, medicine, and abstruse learning are also away out of proportion to the weakness of his numbers. He has made a marvelous fight in this world, in all the ages; and has done it with his hands tied behind him. He could be vain of himself, and be excused for it. The Egyptian, the Babylonian, and the Persian rose, filled the planet with sound and splendor, then faded to dreamstuff and passed away; the Greek and the Roman followed, and made a vast noise, and they are gone; other peoples have sprung up and held their torch high for a time, but it burned out, and they sit in twilight now, or have vanished. The Jew saw them all, beat them all, and is now what he always was, exhibiting no decadence, no infirmities of age, no weakening of his parts, no slowing of his energies, no dulling of his alert and aggressive mind. All things are mortal but the Jew: all other forces pass, but he remains. What is the secret of his immortality?

GROVER CLEVELAND:

"Nor can we overlook, if we are decently just, the valuable aid cheerfully contributed by our Jewish fellow-countrymen in every national emergency that has since overtaken us." (1905)

Grover Cleveland (1837–1908), President of the United States 1885–1889, and 1893–1897, was born in New Jersey, the son of a Presbyterian minister. Educated in the law, Cleveland's early career combined law and politics in Erie County, New York. As Mayor of Buffalo in 1881 and Governor of New York in 1882, Cleveland achieved national prominence, and as a result received the Democratic party's nomination for the Presidency in 1884.

The following selection is taken from an address delivered by Cleveland in Carnegie Hall, New York City, on November 30, 1905. The occasion commemorated was the two hundred and fiftieth anniversary of Jewish settlement in the United States.

Address by Former President Grover Cleveland delivered on the occasion of the Two Hundred and Fiftieth Anniversary of the Settlement of the Jews in the United States, Carnegie Hall, New York, November 30 (Thanksgiving Day), 1905, Publications of the American Jewish Historical Society, No. 14, 1906.

Mr. Chairman and Ladies and Gentlemen: Among the large enterprises and undertakings which have become familiar to the people of the United States, there may be mentioned the extravagant celebration, especially in these latter days, of all sorts of anniversaries and events. Many of these undoubtedly tend to the improvement and stimulation of patriotic sentiment. But there is good reason to believe that others have no better justification than the indulgence of local pride or the furtherance of narrow and selfish interests.

We join to-day in "the celebration of the two hundred and fiftieth anniversary of the settlement of the Jews in the United States." This event created such an important epoch in our country's development, and its relationship to our nation's evolution is so clearly seen in the light of present conditions, that every thoughtful American citizen must recognize the fitness and usefulness of its commemoration. To those of the Jewish faith it recalls a foothold gained, that meant for them a home and peaceful security, after centuries of homelessness and ruthless persecution. To those of us professing a different religious faith, it brings to mind the landing upon our soil of an element of population whose wonderful increase and marked traits of character have added a powerful factor to our national progress and achievement. All nationalities have contributed to the composite population of the United States—many of them in greater number than the Jews. And yet I believe that it can be safely claimed that few, if any, of those contributing nationalities have directly and indirectly been more influential in giving shape and direction to the Americanism of to-day. What our Jewish fellow-citizens have done to increase the material advancement of the United States is apparent on every hand and must stand confessed. But the best and highest Americanism is something more than materialistic. Its spirit, which should make it imperishable and immortal, exists in its patriotic aspirations and exalting traditions. On this higher plain of our nationality, and in the atmosphere of ennobling sentiment, we also feel the touch of Jewish relationship. If the discovery of America prophesied the coming of our nation and fixed the place of its birth, let us not forget that Columbus, on his voyage in search of a new world, was aided in a most important way by Jewish support and comradeship. If the people of the United States glory in their free institutions as the crown of man's aspiration for self-government, let them not be unmindful of the fact that

280 THE JEW IN AMERICA

the Jews among us have in their care and keeping the history and traditions of an ancient Jewish commonwealth astonishingly like our own Republic in its democracy and underlying intention. This ancient commonwealth was ordained of God for the government of His chosen people; and we should not close our minds to a conception of the coincidence in divine purpose discoverable in the bestowal, by the Ruler of the universe, of a similar plan of rule, after thousands of years, upon the people of the United States, who also had their beginning in willing submission to God's sovereignty, and the assertion of freedom in His worship. When with true American enthusiasm and pride we recall the story of the war for our independence, and rejoice in the indomitable courage and fortitude of our Revolutionary heroes, we should not fail to remember how well the Jews of America performed their part in the struggle and how in every way they usefully and patriotically supported the interests of their newly found home. Nor can we overlook, if we are decently just, the valuable aid cheerfully contributed by our Jewish fellow-countrymen in every national emergency that has since overtaken us. They gave convincing evidence of their assimilation of the best sentiment of American patriotism by heartily joining in the popular acclaim that met the selection of Washington as the first President of our new Republic. In support of this statement it certainly cannot be amiss to quote the following passages from a letter addressed to General Washington after his election to the presidency, by the Hebrew congregation in Newport, Rhode Island:

"Deprived as we hitherto have been of the inalienable rights of free citizens, we now, with a deep sense of gratitude to the almighty Disposer of all events, behold a government erected by the majesty of the people, a government which to bigotry gives no sanction, to persecution no assistance, but generously affording to all liberty of conscience and immunities of citizenship, deeming every one, of whatever nation, tongue, and language, equal parts of the great government machine.

"This so ample and extensive Federal Union, whose base is philanthropy, mutual confidence, and public virtue, we cannot but acknowledge to be the work of the great God who rules in the armies of the heavens and among the inhabitants of the earth, doing whatever seemeth to Him good."

These expressions, besides bearing on the hearty participation of our Jewish fellow-citizens in the patriotic sentiments of the time, illustrate how thoroughly they appreciated the new opportunities and the new security offered to them by a free, just, and popular government.

And thus it happened that the Jewish immigrants who were driven to our colonies by religious persecution, and their descendants, have, under the kindly influence of toleration and equality, coöperated in nation-building with those of different religious faiths, whose ancestors, or they themselves, had also sought, amid hard and inhospitable surroundings, freedom to worship God. Jewish patriotism, which had been for centuries submerged and smothered in homeless wanderings and nationless existence, in the more cheerful light and warmth of a safe abiding place, sprang up and flourished. It has been said: "If you persecute, you make slaves; only by declaring equal rights for all will you make good citizens." The rule that equality in right is essential to good citizenship has never been better supported than by the result of according equal rights to the Jews who found a home on the soil of the United States.

I do not overlook the fact that the full enjoyment by the Jews of religious and industrial freedom was not without restraint or limitation at the time of their first arrival. Nor am I in the least inclined to claim that Jewish characteristics or the Jewish religion is, or ever had been, absolutely preventive of bad men and bad citizens. It cannot be denied, however, that with even the limited equality of rights at first accorded to the Jews by the American colonies, their loyalty and effective patriotism when needed were not wanting.

We have to-day only to look about us to discover that, in every phase of present American enterprise and effort, the Jews of the United States, with unrestricted toleration and equality, are making their impress more and more deep and permanent upon our citizenship. They accumulate wealth without exhibiting or encouraging harmful extravagance and business recklessness. They especially care for their poor, but they do it sensibly, and in a way that avoids pauper-making. On every side are seen monuments of their charitable work, and evidences of their determination to furnish their children and youth equipment for usefulness and self-support. It is not among them that dangerous discontent and violent demonstrations against peace and order are hatched and fostered. There may be something of separateness in their social life among us, but this should be naturally expected among those who are not altogether free from the disposition born of persecution and the loss of nationality, to seek in a common devotion to their peculiar religious creed the strongest bond of their social fellowships. And yet, with it all, they are by no means laggards in the civic duty and the work in behalf of the general welfare of the state, which are the badges of good citizenship.

It is time for the unreserved acknowledgment that the toleration and equal opportunity accorded to the Jews of the United States have been abundantly repaid to us. And in making up the accounts, let us not omit to put to their credit the occasion presented to us through our concession to them of toleration and equality, for strengthening, by wholesome exercise, the spirit of broad-minded justice and consideration, which, as long as we are true to ourselves, we must inflexibly preserve as the distinguishing and saving traits of our nationality.

I know that human prejudice—especially that growing out of race or religion—is cruelly inveterate and lasting. But wherever in the world prejudice against the Jews still exists, there can be no place for it among the people of the United States, unless they are heedless of good faith, recreant to the underlying principles of their free government, and insensible to every pledge involved in our boasted equality of citizenship.

Roger Williams, the pioneer of religious liberty in America, expressed the fear, long before the United States became a nation, that England and the other nations had a score to pay to the Jews, and he added these words: "I desire not the liberty to myself which I would not freely and impartially weigh out to all the consciences of the world beside." Our nation will have no score to pay to the Jews. As a people we shall never suffer the humiliation of appealing to them for favors with the shamefacedness of intolerance unforgotten and unforgiven. The Jews of the United States have become our fellow-citizens, and, like us, have at heart the prosperity and safety of our common country—forasmuch as we have desired not that liberty to ourselves which we would not freely and impartially weigh out to all the consciences of the world beside.

After all it comes to this: We celebrate an event in the history of our country fraught with important results, and deeply concerning us all as citizens of the United States. In the spirit of true Americanism let us all rejoice in the good which the settlement we commemorate has brought to the nation in which we all find safety and protection; and, uninterrupted by differences in religious faith, let us, under the guidance of the genius of Toleration and Equality, here consecrate ourselves more fully than ever to united and devoted labor in the field of our common nation's advancement and exaltation.

JOHN JAY CHAPMAN:

"I'm glad I'm a Jew." (1897)

"I'm glad I don't have more Jewish blood in me than I have." (1919)

John Jay Chapman (1862–1933) was not a Jew, of course, nor was he descended from Jews. Born in New York City, Chapman could trace his ancestry to Huguenot and Dutch forebears in early Colonial America. His immediate family was violently opposed to slavery, and even after the Civil War the slavery issue was the dominant topic in family conversations. As a youth at St. Paul's School in Concord, New Hampshire, Chapman was devoutly, if not fanatically, religious. He appears to have been ill a good part of the time, and throughout his life there were dark periods of physical and mental collapse. It is possible to suppose that Chapman's rigid Puritan conscience played a major role in his illnesses, and occasionally precipitated extreme forms of behavior. In 1887, while still a student at the Harvard Law School, Chapman was involved in a fist-fight caused by courtship rivalry. His opponent was severely beaten, and in expiation Chapman burned his left hand so badly that it had to be amputated.

In the years that followed, Chapman devoted himself to a variety of interests. A poet, playwright, and translator of Greek classics, he also wrote a number of polemics directed against Big Business, Wall Street, and the Catholic Church. Although Chapman's critical style was that of an honest man who did not believe in Diogenes, a number of his writings, notably his famous Coatesville Address of August 19, 1911, are acute and discerning analyses of the problems they deal with.

Chapman's metamorphosis with regard to the Jews is not easily squared with the spirit of his memorable Coatesville protest of a Negro lynching. But it may be worth noting that the twenty-year period which saw his attitude change encompassed severe illness, disillusionment, and the deaths of his first wife and a son. (Chapman's son, Victor, was the first American pilot lost in World War I.) The shift in Chapman's views may well have been simply an individual expression of the historic relationship between social or personal conditions and the treatment accorded Jews.

The following selections are taken from Chapman's *Notes on Religion* (1915), *Learning and Other Essays* (1910), and M. A. DeWolfe Howe, editor, *John Jay Chapman and His Letters* (1937).

From a Letter to Elizabeth Chanler, September 14, 1897

There is a depth of human feeling in the Jew that no other race ever possessed. We do no more than imitate it—and follow it. David, for instance, and his conduct about Uriah's wife and the child that died—and Absalom—and Jonathan. Compare the Greek—the Chinese, the Roman. These Jews are more human than any other men. It is the cause of the spread of their religion—for we are all adopted into Judah. The heart of the world is Jewish. There is the same spirit in the Old Testament as in the New. What monstrous perversion—that we should worship their God and despise themselves! We admire the Pyramids and the Egyptians, but the history of the Jews is the most remarkable, the most notable thing, on the globe. Their sacred books and chronicles and traditions and history make the annals of every other nation mere rubbish—and I feel this same power in the Jews I know. They are the most humane and the strongest people morally, mentally and physically. They persist. I'm glad I'm a Jew. I believe that's the reason why this paper-faced civilization impresses me so little. . . .[1]

From "The Comic," 1910

We have been speaking of Greek thought and Greek life; yet between that life and ourselves there have intervened some centuries of Christianity, including the Middle Ages, during which Jewish influence pervaded and absorbed other thought. The Hebrew ruled and subdued in philosophy, poetry, and religion. The Hebrew influence is the most powerful influence ever let loose upon the world.

[1] M. A. DeWolfe Howe, ed., *John Jay Chapman and His Letters* (Boston: Houghton Mifflin Company, 1937) pp. 170–71.

Every book written since this Hebrew domination is saturated with Hebrew. It has thus become impossible to see the classics as they were. Between them and us is an atmosphere of mordant, powerful, Hebraic thought, which transmutes and fantastically recolors them. How the classics would have laughed over our conception of them! Virgil was a witch during the Middle Ages and now he is an acolyte, a person over whom the modern sentimental school maunders in tears. The classics would feel toward our notions of them somewhat as a Parisian feels toward a French vaudeville after it has been prepared for the American stage. Christianity is to blame.

I have perhaps spoken as if Christianity has blown over with the Middle Ages; but it has not. The Middle Ages have blown over; but Christianity seems, in some ways, never to have been understood before the nineteenth century. It is upon us, sevenfold strong. Its mysteries supersede the other mysteries; its rod threatens to eat up the rods of the other magicians. These tigers of Christian criticism within us attack the classics. The half-formed objections to Plato which I have mentioned are seriously reinforced by the Hebrew dispensation, which somehow reduces the philosophic speculations of Greece to the status of favors at a cotillion. It is senseless to contrast Christ with Socrates; it is unfair and even absurd to review Greek life and thought by the light of Hebrew life and thought. But to do so is inevitable. We are three parts Hebrew in our nature and we see the Mediterranean culture with Hebrew eyes. The attempts of such persons as Swinburne and Pater to writhe themselves free from the Hebrew domination always betray that profound seriousness which comes from the Jew. These men make a break for freedom—they will be joyous, antique, and irresponsible. Alas, they are sadder than the Puritans and shallower than Columbine.

It has become forever and perpetually impossible for any one to treat Greek thought on a Greek basis: the basis is gone. As I wrote the words a page or two back about "Comedy having been placed by Plato in the heaven of man's highest endeavor," I thought to myself, "Perhaps I ought to say highest *artistic* endeavor." There spoke the Jew monitor which dogs our classical studies, sniffing at them and hinting that they are trivial. In the eye of that monitor there is no room for the comic in the whole universe: there is no such thing as the comic. The comic is something outside of the

Jewish dispensation, a kind of irreducible unreason, a skeptical or satanic element.

One would conclude from their records that the Jews were people who never laughed except ironically. To be sure, Michal laughed at David's dancing, and Sara laughed at the idea of having a child, and various people in the New Testament laughed others "to scorn." But nobody seems to have laughed heartily and innocently. One gets the impression of a race devoid of humor. This is partly because it is not the province of religious writings to record humor; but it is mainly because Jewish thought condemns humor. Wherever humor arises in a Christian civilization—as in the popular Gothic humor—it is a local race-element, an unsubdued bit of something foreign to Judah. Where the Bible triumphs utterly, as in Dante and Calvin, there is no humor.[1]

From "The Effect of Hebraic Thought on Western Europe," 1915

It was the Jew who discovered God; and Christ, who re-delivered God to us, was a Jew. A Jew, yet much more than a Jew. The ancient Hebrew race knew religion, and laid the foundations for morality, as the Greeks did for the fine arts. No one has added a line to the Bible, whether to the Old or to the New Testament. Whence comes this natural ascendancy in spiritual matters, this insight, which the ancient Jew possessed? Perhaps it comes from racial, ancestral, age-long preoccupation. The Semitic wise men had been handling these themes for thousands of years. Certainly the book of Job exhibits a school of practical ethics that runs straight up into celestial speculation—showing a gamut of thought and a vigor of expression that have never since been reached—except by the Jew.

The God of the Jews was at first a racial God; but the mind of the Jew was stronger than his patriotism, and by degrees the racial idea of piety was supplanted by a universal idea. All through the Old Testament we find the thought of Jehovah cracking the old Mosaic Dispensation. You can see the seams in it here and there, from Genesis onward. A Universe has been discerned through the

[1] John Jay Chapman, *Learning and Other Essays* (New York: Moffat, Yard and Company, 1910), pp. 166–169.

rifts, and wine has broken the cask. Also, in the New Testament, Christ's power shatters the whole structure of the Mosaic Dispensation till you can hardly find the frame work; and yet the adumbration of a Christ has been at the back of that Jewish Theology. The New Testament, without the Old, can be but half-comprehended. The very figures of speech are the same in each, and half of Christ's thought is to be found in Moses.

Let us now turn, almost at random, to the sayings of the Jews, and examine a few of the metaphors of this old Wisdom, in order to illustrate the intellectual heights at which these Semitic thinkers habitually walked. "The battle is not to the strong, neither is the race to the swift. The stone which the builders rejected has become the head of the corner. . . . As thou knowest not what is the way of the spirit, nor how the bones do grow in the womb of her that is with child: even so thou knowest not the works of God who maketh all."

With all this profundity, with all this human feeling, there is never a note of falsetto in Jewish sentiment. The poetry of the Psalms and of the Prophets touches many kinds of religious feeling—joyous, sad, mystic, impassioned, elegiac; yet it is always robust. The straining after religious emotion which characterizes Christianity in Western Europe was not seen in Isaiah. If you contrast any page of mediaeval piety with a page of the Psalms, or contrast any legend or anecdote out of the Middle Ages with one from the New Testament, you will find that the desire to *experience religion* is what characterizes European Christianity. This straining after emotion began in the earliest Christian era. You might say that this note of hysteric feeling is one of the immediate effects which Jewish thought produced upon the Gentile nature. Jewish thought was like a strong brew that upset the stomach of less hardy men. How could the Roman colonist Augustine, living under the African sun, digest the fiery doctrine of Israel and yet retain the phlegm of Israel? The metaphysics of the Hebrew put Europe to its purgation; and, down to quite recent times—yes, down almost to yesterday—the Western brain has been turned by this Eastern drug: the drug drives us mad.[1]

[1] John Jay Chapman, *Notes on Religion* (New York: Laurence J. Gomme, 1915), pp. 49–52.

From a Letter to Chanler Chapman, December 29, 1919. The letter was written in Atlantic City.

Judea—Israel—the Lost Tribes—lost no more! found—very much found, increased—multiplied—as the sands of the sea—upon the sands of the sea—in city of the sea—Atlantic City—with cliff dwellings of 10,000 souls each—and regurgitating with Hebrews—only Hebrews. Families of tens and dozens—grave old plodders, gay young friskers—angel Jews, siren Jewesses—puppy Jews—mastiff Jews—bulging matrons—spectacled backfish—golden-haired Jewish Dianas—sable-eyed Jewish Pucks, Jewish Mirandas—Romeos and Juliets, Jew Caesars—only no Shylock. It is a heathen menagerie of Israel. Only one Christian—a big Scottish Y.M.C.A. looking man who is starter of the facade of elevators—and is out of his real job just now, for I am sure that his real job is to watch the bathers in summer and save the drowners—when the nation is in the water. For they would never trust a Jew.

Dear Mo and I lie in bed, or on the beds and read Virgil aloud— also Le Notre and the journals. She has her meals sent up—so far— but I descend into the amphibious theatre and prowl amid the animals. The young I like. They submit to caresses and their parents are pleased. The young have aplomb as well as the old in Judea.

Food, cigars, clothing, bien-être—this people understands enjoyment. They are uncritical: life is a simple matter to them:—a bank account and the larder. No, they will never rule the world. They are too easily deflected—absorbed and satisfied. It is foolish to rule the world, and the Jew knows it. They are crumbling material for the hands of their leaders and ropes of sand. They have too much sense—and will go for the glittering garments and not murder Progress. They strike me as an inferior race in spite of their great advantages. Did it ever occur to you how much Napoleon must have despised the French? He had not a drop of French blood in his veins, and was born just before or just after Corsica was ceded to France. What sort of a nation must that be that can be ruled by such a shyster? At the time of his Brumaire coup d'état—three or four men could have done for him. But Frenchmen cannot act together. He ruled them by terror and espionage, by flummery and gloire, by their vanity and their basenesses. He made monkeys of them,—and today they are proud of him! But I ought not to foment your critical dislike of the French—and their ways and vanities. You are young, and easily influenced; and something I said might stick in your mind and cause a gangrene. But to return to the Jews, my long acquaintance with Klein and his club makes me at home with them—but I'm glad I haven't *more* Jewish blood in me than I have. I don't want any more. They are losing their quality by the loss of their education. These people don't know anything. They have no religion, no customs except eating and drinking.

Imagine the job of an American Jewish rabbi. They have good hearts and charities I know, but no thrills, and O my, they *look* so grotesque that I could never preach to them.[1]

LINCOLN STEFFENS:

". . . the weeping and gnashing of teeth of the old Jews who were doomed and knew it." (Circa 1890–1900)

Lincoln Steffens (1866–1936), crusading journalist and muckraker, spent his early years in the West. Following graduation from the University of California in 1884, he traveled extensively in Europe and America before launching a journalistic career in New York City. As a reporter for the New York *Evening Post* and, later, a variety of magazines, he acquired an intimate knowledge of Wall Street, business and political corruption, and social conditions. His writings established him as one of the foremost "angry young men" of his generation, and his anger touched reformers as well as stand-patters. At first friendly to reform and some of its leaders, notably Robert M. LaFollette, his experiences convinced him that nothing less than radical reconstruction of institutions would solve the problem of corruption. Disillusioned with the possibilities in America, he became extremely sympathetic to revolutionary movements abroad. He supported the Mexican Revolution, and after visiting Lenin in Russia in 1919, he wrote in one of his letters: "I have seen the future, and it works." He seems also to have been impressed, in the early twenties, by Mussolini.

[1] M. A. DeWolfe Howe, ed., *John Jay Chapman and His Letters* (Boston: Houghton Mifflin Company, 1937) pp. 367–368.

From *The Autobiography of Lincoln Steffens* (copyright 1931 by Harcourt, Brace and Company, Inc.; renewed by Peter Steffens) pp. 243–245. Used by permission of the publishers.

Steffens had numerous Jewish friends throughout his life. As City Editor of the *Commercial Advertiser* in 1897 he was instrumental in hiring Abraham Kahan, well known Jewish intellectual, and through Kahan he acquired a considerable knowledge of Jewish affairs. He was also employed for a time by Edward A. Filene, noted Jewish businessman and philanthropist, to investigate conditions in Boston.

Steffens' two principal books are *The Shame of the Cities* (1904) which deals with municipal corruption, and his *Autobiography* (1931). The following selection is taken from the *Autobiography*, and relates to the period when he was working for the New York *Evening Post*.

I soon found out that by going with the reporters to a fire or the scene of an accident was a way to see the town and the life of the town.

A synagogue that burned down during a service introduced me to the service; I attended another synagogue, asked questions, and realized that it was a bit of the Old Testament repeated after thousands of years, unchanged. And so I described that service and other services. They fascinated me, those old practices, and the picturesque customs and laws of the old orthodox Jews from Russia and Poland. Max, an East Side Jew himself, told me about them; I read up and talked to funny old, fine rabbis about them, and about their conflicts with their Americanized children. The *Post* observed all the holy days of the Ghetto. There were advance notices of their coming, with descriptions of the preparations and explanations of their sacred, ancient, biblical meaning, and then an account of them as I saw these days and nights observed in the homes and the churches of the poor. A queer mixture of comedy, tragedy, orthodoxy, and revelation, they interested our Christian readers. The uptown Jews complained now and then. Mr. Godkin himself required me once to call personally upon a socially prominent Jewish lady who had written to the editor asking why so much space was given to the ridiculous performances of the ignorant, foreign East Side Jews and none to the uptown Hebrews. I told her. I had the satisfaction of telling her about the comparative beauty, significance, and character of the uptown and downtown Jews. I must have talked well, for she threatened and tried to have me fired, as she put it. Fortunately, the editorial writers were under pressure also from prominent Jews to back up their side of a public controversy over the blackballing of a rich Jew by an uptown social club. "We" were fair to the Jews, editorially, but personally irritated. I was not "fired"; I was sent out to interview the proprietor of a hotel which excluded Jews, and he put his case in a very few words.

"I won't have one," he said. "I have had my experience and so learned that if you let one in because he is exceptional and fine, he will bring in others who are not exceptional, etc. By and by they will occupy the whole house, when the Christians leave. And then, when the Christians don't come any more, the Jews quit you to go where the Christians have gone, and there you are with an empty or a second-class house."

It would have been absurd to discharge me since I at that time was almost a Jew. I had become as infatuated with the Ghetto as eastern boys were with the wild west, and nailed a mazuza on my office door; I went to the synagogue on all the great Jewish holy days; on Yom Kippur I spent the whole twenty-four hours fasting and going from one synagogue to another. The music moved me most, but I knew and could follow with the awful feelings of a Jew the beautiful old ceremonies of the ancient orthodox services. My friends laughed at me; especially the Jews among them scoffed. "You are more Jewish than us Jews," they said, and since I have traveled I realize the absurdity of the American who is more French than the French, more German than the Kaiser. But there were some respecters of my respect. When Israel Zangwill, the author of *Tales of the Ghetto*, came from London to visit New York, he heard about me from Jews and asked me to be his guide for a survey of the East Side; and he saw and he went home and wrote *The Melting Pot*.

The tales of the New York Ghetto were heart-breaking comedies of the tragic conflict between the old and the new, the very old and the very new; in many matters, all at once: religion, class, clothes, manners, customs, language, culture. We all know the difference between youth and age, but our experience is between two generations. Among the Russian and other eastern Jewish families in New York it was an abyss of many generations; it was between parents out of the Middle Ages, sometimes out of the Old Testament days hundreds of years B.C., and the children of the streets of New York today. We saw it everywhere all the time. Responding to a reported suicide, we would pass a synagogue where a score or more of boys were sitting hatless in their old clothes, smoking cigarettes on the

steps outside, and their fathers, all dressed in black, with their high
hats, uncut beards, and temple curls, were going into the synagogues,
tearing their hair and rending their garments. The reporters stopped
to laugh; and it was comic; the old men, in their thrift, tore the
lapels of their coats very carefully, a very little, but they wept tears,
real tears. It was a revolution. Their sons were rebels against the
law of Moses; they were lost souls, lost to God, the family, and to
Israel of old. The police did not understand or sympathize. If there
was a fight—and sometimes the fathers did lay hands on their sons,
and the tough boys did biff their fathers in the eye; which brought
out all the horrified elders of the whole neighborhood and all the
sullen youth—when there was a "riot call," the police would rush in
and club now the boys, now the parents, and now, in their Irish
exasperation, both sides, bloodily and in vain. I used to feel that
blood did not hurt, but the tears did, the weeping and gnashing of
teeth of the old Jews who were doomed and knew it. Two, three,
thousand years of continuous devotion, courage, and suffering for a
cause lost in a generation.

HENRY ADAMS:

*"The atmosphere [in Washington] really
has become a Jew atmosphere. It is curious
and evidently good for some people, but
it isolates me." (1914)*

Henry Adams (1838–1918), great-grandson of the second President of
the United States, was a distinguished historian and one-time novelist.
After graduation from Harvard in 1858 Adams studied abroad, and for
a time served as private secretary to his father, Charles Francis Adams,
when the latter was a congressman and minister to Britain. As a political
writer in Washington, he was revolted by the mediocrity and corruption
of post-Civil War national politics, and in 1870 he joined the Harvard
faculty as an assistant professor of history. While at Harvard he became
editor of the *North American Review*, one of the most influential maga-

From Worthington Chauncey Ford, editor, *Letters of Henry Adams (1892–
1918)* (Boston and New York: Houghton Mifflin Company, 1938), pp. 338,
620.

zines of its time. The years after 1877, when he left Harvard, were devoted to travel, historical research, and ultimately the writing of the famous autobiography, *The Education of Henry Adams*. Adams' other books include a nine-volume history of the United States during the Jefferson and Madison administrations, biographies of Albert Galatin and John Randolph, and the well known *Mont Saint-Michel and Chartres*.

The following excerpts from two of Adams' letters were written in 1901 and 1914. Adams, if not quite a full-blown anti-Semite, found Jews rather distasteful, and he was capable at times, especially in his old age, of believing that Jews were becoming the supreme influence in the political, economic, and cultural life of the nation.

From a Letter to Elizabeth Cameron

Wednesday, Warsaw. [August 14, 1901] We arrived here yesterday afternoon, after a tiresome night and day in what they call an express, through a country flatter than Florida, and less varied. But we had the pleasure of seeing at last the Polish Jew, and he was a startling revelation even to me, who have seen *pas mal de Jew*. The country is not bad; on the contrary, it is a good deal like our plains, more or less sandy, but well watered. It is the people that make one tired. You would gratify all your worst instincts if you see a dozen women reaping the grain, and one big, clumsy man standing over them, superintending and doing nothing. With what pleasure should I have called your attention to it, knowing your ferocious and evil nature in regard to my sex! While Sister Anne is really so indifferent to masculine crime, wrapped up as she is in the passion for her two hulking boys! I can get very little fun out of her on that account, and she seems to grow worse always. She bore the journey well,— better than I expected, for I found it fatiguing; but we've a worse one tomorrow to Moscow, and I shall be glad to see her well over it. Warsaw is a big, bustling city, like all other cities, only mostly Jew, in which it is peculiar to Poland. I see little to remark in the streets; nothing in the shops. The people are uglier than on Pennsylvania Avenue which is otherwise my lowest standard. Like all other cities and places, it is evidently flattened out, and has lost most of its characteristics. The Jews and I are the only curious antiquities in it. My only merit as a curio is antiquity, but the Jew is also a curiosity. He makes me creep.

From a Letter to Charles Milnes Gaskell

Washington, 19 February, 1914.

The winter is nearly over, I am seventy-six years old, and nearly over too. As I go, my thoughts turn towards you and I want to know how you are. Of myself, I have almost nothing to tell. It is quite astonishing how the circle narrows. I think that in reality as many people pass by, and I hear as much as I ever did, but it is no longer a part of me. I am inclined to think it not wholly my fault. The atmosphere really has become a Jew atmosphere. It is curious and evidently good for some people, but it isolates me. I do not know the language, and my friends are as ignorant as I. We are still in power, after a fashion. Our sway over what we call society is undisputed. We keep Jews far away, and the anti-Jew feeling is quite rabid. We are anti-everything and we are wild up-lifters; yet we somehow seem to be more Jewish every day. This is not my own diagnosis. I make none. I care not a straw what happens provided the fabric lasts a few months more; but will it do so? I am uneasy about you. I judge you to be worse than we. At least you are making almost as much howl about it.

THORSTEIN VEBLEN:

"It is a fact which must strike any dispassionate observer that the Jewish people have contributed much more than an even share to the intellectual life of modern Europe." (1919)

Thorstein Veblen (1857–1929), distinguished American political economist, grew up in Minnesota. His Norwegian parents, although they had enjoyed little formal education, were cultured people, and at an early age Veblen learned Greek, Latin, and German, in addition to Norwegian and

From *Essays in Our Changing Order* in *The Portable Veblen*, Max Lerner, ed., pp. 467–479, copyright 1934 by The Viking Press. First published in the *Political Science Quarterly*, March, 1919, reprinted by permission of The Academy of Political Science and The Viking Press.

English. Following graduation from Carleton College in 1880, Veblen did graduate work at Johns Hopkins and Yale. An iconoclast, agnostic, and increasingly acidulous critic of American economic and social institutions, Veblen had great difficulty in locating himself in the academic world. He taught at Cornell, Chicago, Stanford, Missouri, and the New School for Social Research; at each university his professional views, combined with a rather unorthodox personal life, brought him into conflict with trustees, administrators, and colleagues [all of whom are the targets of his bitter book on academic life, *The Higher Learning in America* (1918)]. As a consequence, and despite a considerable publishing record, he was almost fifty years old before he reached the rank, at Stanford, of associate professor.

Unlike the books of most of his contemporaries, Veblen's works—*The Theory of the Leisure Class* (1899), *The Theory of Business Enterprise* (1904), *The Instinct of Workmanship* (1914), *Imperial Germany and the Industrial Revolution* (1915), and others—are still read, and at many universities are required reading in social science courses. Indeed Veblen's merciless analyses of the business world, with special reference to its manners, morals, practices, and influence, have been neither equaled nor surpassed by any critic since his time.

The selection that follows, "The Intellectual Pre-eminence of Jews in Modern Europe" (1919), has a contemporary ring in the sense that it deals with the problem, much discussed today by Jews and Gentiles alike, of Jewish alienation. Whether or not one agrees with Veblen that the intellectual contributions of the Jews are in large measure dependent upon their "immunity from the inhibitions of intellectual quietism," it is fair to comment that his attitude toward assimilation is shared by large numbers of Jews and non-Jews everywhere.

Among all the clamorous projects of national self-determination which surround the return of peace, the proposal of the Zionists is notable for sobriety, good will, and a poise of self-assurance. More confidently and perspicuously than all the others, the Zionists propose a rehabilitation of their national integrity under a regime of live and let live, "with charity for all, with malice toward none." Yet it is always a project for withdrawal upon themselves, a scheme of national demarcation between Jew and gentile; indeed, it is a scheme of territorial demarcation and national frontiers of the conventional sort, within which Jews and Jewish traits, traditions, and aspirations are to find scope and breathing space for a home-bred culture and a free unfolding of all that is best and most characteristic of the endowment of the race. There runs through it all a dominant bias of isolation and inbreeding, and a confident persuasion that this isolation and inbreeding will bring great and good results for all concerned. The Zionists aspire to bring to full fruition all that massive endowment of spiritual and intellectual capacities of which their people have given evidence throughout their troubled history, and not least during these concluding centuries of their exile.

The whole project has an idyllic and engaging air. And any disinterested bystander will be greatly moved to wish them godspeed. Yet there comes in a regret that this experiment in isolation and inbreeding could not have been put to the test at an earlier date, before the new order of large-scale industry and universal intercourse had made any conclusive degree of such national isolation impracticable, before this same new order had so shaped the run of things that any nation or community drawn on this small scale would necessarily be dependent on and subsidiary to the run of things at large. It is now, unhappily, true that any "nation" of the size and geographical emplacement of the projected Zion will, for the present and the calculable future, necessarily be something of a national make-believe. The current state of the industrial arts will necessarily deny it a rounded and self-balanced national integrity in any substantial sense. The days of Solomon are long past.

Yet much can doubtless be done by taking thought and making the most of that spirit of stubborn clannishness which has never been the least among the traits of this people. But again, to any disinterested bystander there will come the question: What is the use of it all? It is not so much a question of what is aimed at, as of the chances of its working-out. The logic of the Zionist project plainly runs to the effect that, whereas this people have achieved great things while living under conditions of great adversity, scattered piecemeal among the gentiles of Europe, they are due to achieve much greater things and to reach an unexampled prosperity so soon as they shall have a chance to follow their own devices untroubled within the shelter of their own frontiers. But the doubt presents itself that the conditioning circumstances are not the same or of the same kind in the occidental twentieth century A.D. as in the oriental twelfth century B.C.; nor need it follow that those things which scattered Jews have achieved during their dispersion among the gentiles of Europe are a safe index of what things may be expected of a nation of Jews turned in upon themselves within the insulating frontiers of the Holy Land. It is on this latter point that a question is raised here as to the nature and causes of Jewish achievement in gentile Europe; and the contrast of the conditions offered by the projected Zion will present itself without argument.

It is a fact which must strike any dispassionate observer that the Jewish people have contributed much more than an even share to the intellectual life of modern Europe. So also it is plain that the civilization of Christendom continues today to draw heavily on the Jews for men devoted to science and scholarly pursuits. It is not only that men of Jewish extraction continue to supply more than a proportionate quota to the rank and file engaged in scientific and scholarly work, but a disproportionate number of the men to whom modern science and scholarship look for guidance and leadership are of the same derivation. Particularly is this true of the modern sciences, and it applies perhaps especially in the field of scientific theory, even beyond the extent of its application in the domain of workday detail. So much is notorious.

This notable and indeed highly creditable showing has, of course, not escaped the attention of those men of Jewish race who interest themselves in the fortunes of their own people. Not unusually it is set down as a national trait, as evidence of a peculiarly fortunate intellectual endowment, native and hereditary, in the Jewish people. There is much to be said for such a view, but it should not follow that any inquiry into the place and value of the Jewish people in western civilization should come to rest with this broad assertion of pre-eminence in point of native endowment.

It is true that the history of the Chosen People, late and early, throws them into a position of distinction among the nations with which they have been associated; and it will commonly be accepted without much argument that they have, both late and early, shown distinctive traits of temperament and aptitude, such as to mark them off more or less sharply from all the gentiles among whom it has been their lot to be thrown. So general is the recognition of special Jewish traits, of character and of capacity, that any refusal to recognise something which may be called a Jewish type of hereditary endowment would come to nothing much better than a borrowing of trouble.

That there should be such a tenacious spiritual and intellectual heritage transmissible within the Jewish community and marking that people off in any perceptible degree from their gentile neighbors is all the more notable in view of the known life-history of the children of Israel. No unbiased ethnologist will question the fact that the Jewish people are a nation of hybrids; that gentile blood of many kinds has been infused into the people in large proportions in the course of time. Indeed, none of the peoples of Christendom has been more unremittingly exposed to hybridisation, in spite of all the stiff conventional precautions that have been taken to keep the breed pure. It is not a question of a surreptitious hybrid strain, such as would show itself in sporadic reversions to an alien type; but rather it is a question whether the Jewish strain itself, racially speaking, can at all reasonably be held to account for one half of the pedigree of the Jewish nation as it stands.

The hybrid antecedents of the Children of Israel are not a mere matter of bookish record. Evidence of their hybrid descent is written all over them, wherever they are to be met with, so that in this respect the Jews of Europe are in the same case as the other Europeans, who are also universally cross-bred. It would perplex any anthropologist to identify a single individual among them all who could safely be set down as embodying the Jewish racial type without abatement. The variations in all the measurable traits that go to identify any individual in the schedules of the anthropologists are wide and ubiquitous as regards both their physical and their spiritual traits, in respect to anthropometric measurements as well as in temperament and capacities. And yet, when all is said in abatement of it, the Jewish type, it must be admitted, asserts itself with amazing persistence through all the disguises with which it has been overlaid in the course of age-long hybridisation. Whatever may be found true elsewhere, in their contact with other racial types than those of Europe, it still appears that within this European racial environment the outcome given by any infusion of Jewish blood in these cross-bred individuals is something which can be identified as Jewish. Cross-breeding commonly results in a gain to the Jewish community rather than conversely; and the hybrid offspring is a child of Israel rather than of the gentiles.

In effect, therefore, it is the contribution of this Jewish-hybrid people to the culture of modern Europe that is in question. The men of this Jewish extraction count for more than their proportionate share in the intellectual life of western civilisation; and they count particularly among the vanguard, the pioneers, the uneasy guild of pathfinders and iconoclasts, in science, scholarship, and institutional change and growth. On its face it appears as if an infusion of Jewish blood, even in some degree of hybrid attenuation, were the one decisive factor in the case; and something of that sort may well be allowed, to avoid argument if for no more substantial reason. But even a casual survey of the available evidence will leave so broad a claim in doubt.

Of course, there is the fact to be allowed for at the outset, so far as need be, that these intellectuals of Jewish extraction are, after all, of hybrid extraction as well; but this feature of the case need be given no undue weight. It is of consequence in its bearing on the case of the Jews only in the same manner and degree as it is of consequence for any other hybrid people. Cross-breeding gives a wider range of variation and a greater diversity of individual endowment than can be had in any passably pure-bred population; from which results a greater effectual flexibility of aptitudes and capacities in such a people when exposed to conditions that make for change. In this respect the Jews are neither more nor less fortunate than their gentile compatriots.

It may be more to the purpose to note that this intellectual pre-eminence of the Jews has come into bearing within the gentile community of peoples, not from the outside; that the men who have been its bearers have been men immersed in this gentile culture in which they have played their part of guidance and incitement, not bearers of a compelling message from afar or proselyters of enlightenment conjuring with a ready formula worked out in the ghetto and carried over into the gentile community for its mental regeneration. In point of fact, neither these nor other Jews have done effectual missionary work, in any ordinary sense of that term, in this or any other connection; nor have they entertained a design to do so. Indeed, the Chosen People have quite characteristically never been addicted to missionary enterprise; nor does the Jewish scheme of right and honest living comprise anything of the kind. This, too, is notorious fact; so much so that this allusion to it may well strike any Jew as foolish insistence on a commonplace matter of course. In their character of a Chosen People, it is not for them to take thought of their unblest neighbors and seek to dispel the darkness that overlies the soul of the gentiles.

The cultural heritage of the Jewish people is large and rich, and it is of ancient and honorable lineage. And from time immemorial this people has shown aptitude for such work as will tax the powers of thought and imagination. Their home-bred achievements of the ancient time, before the Diaspora, are among the secure cultural monuments of mankind; but these achievements of the Jewish ancients neither touch the frontiers of modern science nor do they fall in the lines of modern scholarship. So also the later achievements of the Jewish scholars and savants, in so far as their intellectual enterprise has gone forward on what may be called distinctively Jewish lines, within the confines of their own community and by the leading of their own home-bred interest, untouched by that peculiar drift of inquiry that characterises the speculations of the modern gentile world—this learning of the later generations of home-bred Jewish scholars is also reputed to have run into lucubrations that have no significance for contemporary science or scholarship at large.

It appears to be only when the gifted Jew escapes from the cultural environment created and fed by the particular genius of his own people, only when he falls into the alien lines of gentile inquiry and becomes a naturalised, though hyphenate, citizen in the gentile republic of learning, that he comes into his own as a creative leader in the world's intellectual enterprise. It is by loss of allegiance, or at the best by force of a divided allegiance to the people of his origin, that he finds himself in the vanguard of modern inquiry.

It will not do to say that none but renegade Jews count effectually in the modern sciences. Such a statement would be too broad; but, for all its excessive breadth, it exceeds the fact only by a margin. The margin may seem wide, so wide as to vitiate the general statement, perhaps, or at least wide enough materially to reduce its cogency. But it would be wider of the mark to claim that the renegades are to be counted only as sporadic exceptions among a body of unmitigated Jews who make up the virtual total of that muster of creative men of science which the Jewish people have thrown into the intellectual advance of Christendom.

The first requisite for constructive work in modern science, and indeed for any work of inquiry that shall bring enduring results, is a skeptical frame of mind. The enterprising skeptic alone can be counted on to further the increase of knowledge in any substantial fashion. This will be found true both in the modern sciences and in the field of scholarship at large. Much good and serviceable workmanship of a workday character goes into the grand total of modern scientific achievement; but that pioneering and engineering work of guidance, design, and theoretical correlation, without which the most painstaking collection and canvass of information is irrelevant, incompetent, and impertinent—this intellectual enterprise that goes forward presupposes a degree of exemption from hard-and-fast preconceptions, a skeptical animus, Unbefangenheit, release from the dead hand of conventional finality.

The intellectually gifted Jew is in a peculiarly fortunate position in respect of this requisite immunity from the inhibitions of intellectual quietism. But he can come in for such immunity only at the cost of losing his secure place in the scheme of conventions into which he has been born, and at the cost, also, of finding no similarly secure place in that scheme of gentile conventions into which he is thrown. For him as for other men in the like case, the skepticism that goes to make him an effectual factor in the increase and diffusion of knowledge among men involves a loss of that peace of mind that is the birthright of the safe and sane quietist. He becomes a disturber of the intellectual peace, but only at the cost of becoming an intellectual wayfaring man, a wanderer in the intellectual no-man's-land, seeking another place to rest, farther along the road, somewhere over the horizon. They are neither a complaisant nor a contented lot, these aliens of the uneasy feet; but that is, after all, not the point in question.

The young Jew who is at all gifted with a taste for knowledge will unavoidably go afield into that domain of learning where the gentile interests dominate and the gentile orientation gives the outcome. There is nowhere else to go on this quest. He comes forthwith to realise that the scheme of traditions and conventional verities handed down within the pale of his own people are matters of habit handed down by tradition, that they have only such force as belongs to matters of habit and convention, and that they lose their binding force so soon as the habitually accepted outlook is given up or seriously deranged. These nationally binding convictions of what is true, good, and beautiful in the world of the human spirit are forthwith seen to be only contingently good and true; to be binding only so far as the habitual will to believe in them and to seek the truth along their lines remains intact. That is to say, only so long as no scheme of habituation alien to the man's traditional outlook has broken in on him, and has forced him to see that those convictions and verities which hold their place as fundamentally and eternally good and right within the balanced scheme of received traditions prove to be, after all, only an ephemeral web of habits of thought; so soon as his current habits of life no longer continue to fall in those traditional lines that keep these habits of thought in countenance.

Now it happens that the home-bred Jewish scheme of things, human and divine, and the ways and means of knowledge that go with such a scheme, are of an archaic fashion, good and true, perhaps, beyond all praise, for the time and conditions that gave rise to it all, that wove that web of habituation and bound its close-knit tissue of traditional verities and conventions. But it all bears the date-mark, "B.C." It is of a divine complexion, monotheistic even, and perhaps intrinsically thearchic; it is ritualistic, with an exceedingly and beautifully magical efficacy of ritual necessity. It is imperiously self-balanced and self-sufficient, to the point of sanctity; and as is always true of such schemes of sanctity and magical sufficiency, it runs on a logic of personal and spiritual traits, qualities and relations, a class of imponderables which are no longer of the substance of those things that are inquired into by men to whom the ever increasingly mechanistic orientation of the modern time becomes habitual.

When the gifted young Jew, still flexible in respect of his mental habits, is set loose among the iron pots of this mechanistic orientation, the clay vessel of Jewish archaism suffers that fortune which is due and coming to clay vessels among the iron pots. His beautifully rounded heirloom, trade-marked "B.C.", goes to pieces between his hands, and they are left empty. He is divested of those archaic conventional preconceptions which will not comport with the intellectual environment in which he finds himself. But he is not thereby invested with the gentile's peculiar heritage of conventional preconceptions which have stood over, by inertia of habit, out of the gentile past, which go, on the one hand, to make the safe and sane gentile, conservative and complacent, and which conduce also, on the other hand, to blur the safe and sane gentile's intellectual vision, and to leave him intellectually sessile.

The young Jew finds his own heritage of usage and outlook untenable; but this does not mean that he therefore will take over and inwardly assimilate the traditions of usage and outlook which the gentile world has to offer; or at the most he does not uncritically take over all the intellectual prepossessions that are always standing over among the substantial citizens of the republic of learning. The idols of his own tribe have crumbled in decay and no longer cumber the ground, but that release does not induce him to set up a new line of idols borrowed from an alien tribe to do the same disservice. By consequence he is in a peculiar degree exposed to the unmediated facts of the current situation; and in a peculiar degree, therefore, he takes his orientation from the run of the facts as he finds them, rather than from the traditional interpretation of analogous facts in the past. In short, he is a skeptic by force of circumstances over which he has no control. Which comes to saying that he is in line to become a guide and leader of men in that intellectual enterprise out of which comes the increase and diffusion of knowledge among men, provided always that he is by native gift endowed with that net modicum of intelligence which takes effect in the play of the idle curiosity.

Intellectually he is likely to become an alien; spiritually he is more than likely to remain a Jew; for the heartstrings of affection and consuetude are tied early, and they are not readily retied in after life. Nor does the animus with which the community of safe and sane gentiles is wont to meet him conduce at all to his personal incorporation in that community, whatever may befall the intellectual assets which he brings. Their people need not become his people nor their gods his gods, and indeed the provocation is forever and irritably present all over the place to turn back from following after them. The most amiable share in the gentile Community's life that is likely to fall to his lot is that of being interned. One who goes away from home will come to see many unfamiliar things, and to take note of them; but it does not follow that he will swear by all the strange gods whom he meets along the road.

As bearing on the Zionist's enterprise in isolation and nationality, this fable appears to teach a two-fold moral: If the adventure is carried to that consummate outcome which seems to be aimed at, it should apparently be due to be crowned with a large national complacency and, possibly, a profound and self-sufficient content on the part of the Chosen People domiciled once more in the Chosen Land; and when and in so far as the Jewish people in this way turn inward on themselves, their prospective contribution to the world's intellectual output should, in the light of the historical evidence, fairly be expected to take on the complexion of Talmudic lore, rather than that character of free-swung skeptical initiative which their renegades have habitually infused into the pursuit of the modern sciences abroad among the nations. Doubtless, even so the supply of Jewish renegades would not altogether cease, though it should presumably fall off to a relatively inconsiderable residue. And not all renegades are fit guides and leaders of men on the quest of knowledge, nor is their dominant incentive always or ordinarily the quest of the idle curiosity.

There should be some loss to Christendom at large, and there might be some gain to the repatriated Children of Israel. It is a sufficiently difficult choice between a life of complacent futility at home and a thankless quest of unprofitable knowledge abroad. It is, after all, a matter of the drift of circumstances: and behind that lies a question of taste, about which there is no disputing.

THE DEARBORN INDEPENDENT:

"Every influence that leads to lightness and
looseness in Gentile youth today heads up
in a Jewish source. . . . Who direct all
the cheap jewelry houses, the bridge-head
show parks, the 'coney islands,' the
centers of nervous thrills and looseness?"
(1920)

The Dearborn Independent, a weekly newspaper in Dearborn, Michigan, became the property of Henry Ford, the automobile manufacturer, on January 11, 1919. Ford dealers and automobile buyers were encouraged to purchase it, and in time it achieved a readership of some 700,000 persons. While Ford took a personal interest in the newspaper, the effective editor was William J. Cameron, formerly of the *Detroit News,* and admirer in his youth of Robert Ingersoll and William Jennings Bryan.

From *The Dearborn Independent,* August 7, 1920, reprinted in *The International Jew: the World's Foremost Problem* (Dearborn, Michigan: The Dearborn Publishing Company, 1920), pp. 129–140.

In the first decade of its existence under Ford's ownership, *The Dearborn Independent* published a large number of virulent anti-Semitic articles, one of which is reprinted in the following selection. The first article appeared on May 20, 1920, and was titled "The International Jew: The World's Problem." Thereafter, for ninety-one consecutive issues, world and American Jewry were charged with a variety of sins, failings, and, above all, with a conspiracy to dominate the world. According to the Dearborn newspaper, the Jews symbolized capitalism at its worst, dominated Wall Street, and were engaged in an effort to subvert Christianity, in accordance with the "master plan" developed in the *Protocols of Zion.*

Ultimately, following a libel suit which was settled out of court, Ford disavowed his alleged anti-Semitism, and through an intermediary, submitted a full retraction of *The Dearborn Independent* articles to representatives of the American Jewish Committee. In December, 1927, the Ford Motor Company placed $156,000 worth of advertising in Jewish and Yiddish newspapers. Nevertheless, during its anti-Semitic phase, *The Dearborn Independent* was circulated widely in anti-Jewish circles in Europe and America. Under the title of *The International Jew,* the articles were reprinted in Germany in 1927, and as early as 1922, a *New York Times* correspondent who interviewed Adolf Hitler noticed a large picture of Henry Ford hanging on the wall beside the desk in Hitler's Munich office. While the effect, if any, of *The International Jew* on anti-Semitism here and abroad is difficult to gauge, there can be no disputing the fact that in the early twenties *The Dearborn Independent* gave aid and comfort to anti-Semites in the United States, Germany, and elsewhere.

As a mere literary curiosity, these documents which are called "The Protocols of the Learned Elders of Zion," would exercise a fascination by reason of the terrible completeness of the World Plan which they disclose. But they discourage at every turn the view that they are literature; they purport to be statesmanship, and they provide within their own lines the clue by which their status may be determined. Besides the things they look forward to doing, they announce the things they have done and are doing. If, in looking about the world, it is possible to see both the established conditions and the strong tendencies to which these Protocols allude, it will not be strange if interest in a mere literary curiosity gives way to something like alertness, and it may be alarm.

A few general quotations will serve to illustrate the element of present achievement in the assertions of these documents, and in order that the point may be made clear to the reader the key words will be emphasized.

Take this from Protocol Nine:

> In reality there are no obstacles before us. Our super-government *has* such an extra-legal status that it may be called by the energetic and strong word—dictatorship. I can conscientiously say that, at the present time, *we are* the lawmakers. *We create* courts and jurisprudence. *We rule* with a strong will because *we hold* in our hands the remains of a once strong party, now subjugated by us.

And this from the Eighth Protocol:

> We will surround our government with a whole world of economists. It is for this reason that *the science of economics is the chief subject of instruction taught by the Jews.* We shall be surrounded by a whole galaxy of bankers, industrialists, capitalists, and especially by millionaires because, actually, everything will be decided by an appeal to figures.

These are strong claims, but not too strong for the facts that can be marshaled to illustrate them. They are, however, but an introduction to further claims that are made and equally paralleled by the facts. All through the Protocols, as in this quotation from the Eighth, the preeminence of the Jews in the teaching of political economy is insisted upon, and the facts bear that out. They are the chief authors of those vagaries which lead the mob after economic impossibilities, and they are also the chief teachers of political economy in our universities, the chief authors of those popular textbooks in the subject, which hold the conservative classes to the fiction that economic *theories* are economic *laws.* The *idea,* the *theory,* as instruments of social disintegration are common to both the university Jew and the Bolshevik Jew. When all this is shown in detail, public opinion upon the importance of academic and radical economics may undergo a change.

And, as claimed in the quotation just given from the Ninth Protocol, the Jewish world power does today constitute a super-government. It is the Protocol's own word, and none is more fitting. No nation can get all that it wants, but the Jewish World Power can get all that it wants, even though its demands exceed Gentile equality. "*We are* the lawmakers," say the Protocols, and Jewish influences have been lawmakers in a greater degree than any but the specialists realize. In the past ten years Jewish international rule, or the power of the group of International Jews has quite dominated the world. More than that, it has been powerful enough to prevent the passage of salutary laws, and where one law may have slipped through to a place on the statute books, it has been powerful enough to get it interpreted in a sense that rendered it useless for its purpose. This, too, can be illustrated by a large collection of facts.

Moreover, the method by which this is done was outlined long ago in the program of which the Protocols purport to be an outline. "*We create* courts," continues the quotation, and it is followed in other Protocols by numerous references to "our judges." There is a Jewish court sitting in a public building in the city of New York every week, and other courts, for the sole advantage and use of this people whose spokesmen deny that they are a "separate people," are in formation everywhere. The Zionist plan has already been used in some of the smaller European countries to confer an extra-citizenship upon Jews who already enjoy citizenship in the lands of their residence, and in addition to that a degree of self-rule under the very governments which they demand to protect them. Wherever Jewish tendencies are permitted to work unhindered, the result is not "Americanization," nor "Anglicization" nor any other distinctive nationalism, but a strong and ruling reversion back to essential "Judaization."

The "agents" referred to in the first quotation will receive attention in another article. To resume the claims of the Protocols: This from the Seventeenth Protocol:

We have taken good care long ago to discredit the Gentile clergy and thereby to destroy their mission, which at present might hamper us considerably. Their influence over the people diminishes daily.

Freedom of conscience *has been* proclaimed everywhere. Consequently it is only a question of time when the complete crash of the Christian religion will occur. It will be easier still to handle the other religions, but it is too early to discuss this phase of the subject.

This will be of considerable interest, perhaps, to those clergymen who are laboring with Jewish rabbis to bring about some kind of religious union. Such a union would of necessity dispose of Christ as a well-meaning but wholly mistaken Jewish prophet, and thus distinctive Christianity would cease to exist insofar as the "union" was effective. The principal religious aversion of the Protocols, however, so far as it is expressed, is against the Catholic church in general and the pontifical office in particular.

A curious paragraph in this Protocol claims for the Jewish race a particular skill in the art of insult:

Our contemporary press will expose governmental and religious affairs and the incapacity of the Gentiles, always using expressions so derogatory as to approach insult, the faculty of employing which is so well known to our race.

This from the Fifth Protocol:

Under our influence the execution of the laws of the Gentiles *is* reduced to a minimum. Respect for the law *is* undermined by the liberal interpretation we have introduced in this sphere. The courts *decide* as we dictate, even in the most important cases in which are involved fundamental principles or political issues, *viewing* them in the light in which *we present* them to the Gentile administration through agents with whom we have apparently nothing in common, through newspaper opinion and other avenues.

In Gentile society where *we have* planted discord and protestantism****

The word "protestantism" is evidently not used in the religious or sectarian sense, but to denote a temper of querulous fault-finding destructive or harmonious collective opinion.

This from the Fourteenth Protocol:

In countries called advanced, *we have created* a senseless, filthy and disgusting literature. For a short time after our entrance into power we shall encourage its existence so that it may show in greater relief the contrast between it and the written and spoken announcements which will emanate from us.

Discussing in the Twelfth Protocol the control of the Press—a subject which must be treated more extensively in that article—the claim is made:

We have attained this at the present time to the extent that all news is received through several agencies in which it is centralized from all parts of the world. These agencies will then be to all intents and purposes our own institutions and will publish only that which we permit.

This from the Seventh Protocol bears on the same subject:

We must force the Gentile governments to adopt measures which will promote our broadly conceived plan, already approaching its triumphant goal, by bringing to bear the pressure of stimulated public opinion, *which has been organized by us* with the help of the so-called "great power" of the press. With a few exceptions not worth considering, *it is already* in our hands.

To resume the Twelfth Protocol:

If *we have already managed* to dominate the mind of Gentile society to such a point that almost all see world affairs through the colored lenses of the spectacles which *we place* before their eyes, and *if now there is not one government with barriers erected against our access* to that which by Gentile stupidity is called *state secrets,* what then will it be when we are the recognized masters of the world in the person of our universal ruler?

The Jewish nation is the only nation that possesses the secrets of all the rest. No nation long protects a secret which directly concerns another nation, but even so, no nation has all the secrets of all the other nations. Yet it is not too much to say that the International Jews have this knowledge. Much of it, of course, amounts to nothing and their possession of it does not materially add to their power, but the fact that they have the *access,* that they can get whatever they want when they want it is the important point— as many a secret paper could testify if it could talk, and many a custodian of secret papers could tell if he would. The real secret diplomacy of the world is that which hands over the world's so-called secrets to a few men who are members of one race. The surface of diplomacy, those activities which get written down in the memoirs of comfortably aging statesmen, those coups and treaties which are given high-sounding fame as if they really were important—that is incomparable with the diplomacy of Judah, and its matchless enginery for worming out the hidden knowledge of every ruling group. The United States is included in all these statements. Perhaps there is no government in the world so completely at their service as is our own at present, their control having been gained during the past five or six years.

The Protocols do not regard the dispersal of the Jews abroad upon the face of the earth as a calamity, but as a providential arrangement by which the World Plan can be the more certainly executed, as see these words of the Eleventh Protocol:

God gave to us, His Chosen People, as a blessing, the dispersal, and *this which has appeared to all to be our weakness* has been our *whole strength. It has now brought us* to the threshold of universal rule.

The claims to accomplishment which are put forth in the Ninth Protocol would be too massive for words were they too massive for concrete realization, but there is a point where the word and the actuality meet and tally.

In order not to destroy prematurely the Gentile institutions, *we have* laid our efficient hands on them, and rasped the strings of their mechanism. They were formerly in strict and just order, but *we have* replaced them with a liberal disorganized and arbitrary administration. *We have* tampered with jurisprudence, the franchise, the press, freedom of the person, and, most important of all, education and culture, the corner stone of free existence.

We have misled, stupefied and demoralized the youth of the Gentiles by means of education in principles and theories patently false to us, but which *we have* inspired.

Above existing laws, without actual change but by distorting them through contradictory interpretations, *we have* created something stupendous in the way of results.

Everyone knows that, in spite of the fact that the air was never so full of theories of liberty and wild declarations of "rights," there has been a steady curtailment of "personal freedom." Instead of being socialized, the people, under a cover of socialistic phrases, are being brought under an unaccustomed bondage to the state. The Public Health is one plea. Various forms of Public Safety are other pleas. Children are hardly free to play nowadays except under playmasters appointed by the State, among whom, curiously enough, an astonishing proportion of Jews manage to find a place. The streets are no longer as free as they were; laws of every kind are hedging upon the harmless liberties of the people. A steady tendency toward systematization, every phase of the tendency based upon some very learnedly stated "principle," has set in, and curiously enough, when the investigator pursues his way to the authoritative center of these movements for the regulation of the people's life, he finds Jews in power. Children are being lured away from the "social center" of the home for other "centers"; they are being led away (and we are speaking of Gentile children—no Gentiles are ever allowed to regulate the lives of Jewish children) from their natural leaders in home, church and school, to institutionalized "centers" and scientific "play spots," under "trained leaders" whose whole effect, consciously or unconsciously, is to lead the modern child to look to the State, instead of its natural environment, for leadership. All this focuses up to the World Plan for the subjugation of the Gentiles, and if it is not the Jewish World Plan it would be interesting to know why the material for it is so largely Gentile children and the leaders of it so often of the Jewish race.

Jewish liberties are the best safeguarded in the United States. Gentiles take their chance with public matters, but every Jewish community is surrounded by special protectors who gain special recognition by various devices—political and business threats not the least of them. No public spirited Gentiles are welcomed to the task of regulating the lives of Jewish children. The Jewish community in every city is all-sufficient in itself as far as such activities go. The most secret of all parochial schools are the Jewish schools, whose very locations are not all known to the officials of large cities. The Jew is almost anxious in his efforts to mold the Gentile mind; he insists on being permitted to tell the Gentile what to think, especially about the Jew; he is not averse to influencing general Gentile thought in a manner which, though it come about by wide circles, works ultimately into the Jewish scheme of things. The anxiety and the insistence, so well known to all who have observed them, are only reflections of the Jew's conviction that his is the superior race and is capable of directing the inferior race—of which there is but one, including the whole non-Jewish world.

Every influence that leads to lightness and looseness in Gentile youth today heads up in a Jewish source. Did the young people of the world devise the "sport clothes" which have had so deleterious an effect on the youth of the times that every publicist has thought it worthy of mention? Those styles come out of Jewish clothing concerns, where certainly art is not the rule nor moral influence the main consideration. The moving picture is an interesting development of photography allied with the show business, but whose is the responsibility for its development along such lines as make it a menace to the minds of millions—so serious a menace that it has not escaped observation and condemnation everywhere? Who are the masters of musical jazz in the world? Who direct all the cheap jewelry houses, the bridge-head show parks, the "coney islands," the centers of nervous thrills and looseness? It is possible to take the showy young man and woman of trivial outlook and loose sense of responsibility, and tag them outwardly and inwardly, from their clothing and ornaments to their hectic ideas and hopes, with the same tag, "Made, introduced and exploited by a Jew."

There is, therefore, something most sinister in the light which events cast upon that paragraph:

We have misled, stupefied, and demoralized the youth of the Gentiles by means of education in principles and theories, patently false to us, but which we have inspired.

"Principles and theories" do not necessarily imply lofty or even modest intellectual qualities. The youngster who spends his noon hours and evenings at the movies is getting his "principles and theories" just as the more intellectual youngster from a higher grade of society who listens to a Jewish "liberal" expound "sex liberty" and the "control of population" is getting his. The looseness which inheres in these "principles and theories" does not emanate from the Gentile home, or the Gentile church, or from any line of money-making which is filled principally with Gentiles, but from theories, movements and lines of money-making mostly fancied by Jews. This line of accusation could be run much deeper, but it is preferred to restrict it to what is observable by decent eyes everywhere.

And that "the youth of the Gentiles" are the principal victims, and not the youth of the Jews, is also observable. While a certain percentage of Jewish youth itself is overcome by this social poison, the percentage is almost nothing compared with the results among the youth of the Gentiles. It is a significant fact that Jews who link this process of enervation of Gentiles with large profits are not themselves, nor are their sons and daughters, the victims of this enervation. Jewish youth comes through more proudly and more cleanly than the mass of Gentile youth.

Many a father and mother, many a sound-minded uncorrupted young person, and thousands of teachers and publicists have cried out against *luxury*. Many a financier, observing the manner in which the people earned and flung away their money, has warned against *luxury*. Many an economist, knowing that the nonessential industries were consuming men and materials that were necessary to the stabilizing of essential industries; knowing that men are making knick-knacks who should be making steel; knowing that men are engaged in making gew-gaws who should be working on the farm; that materials are going into articles that are made only to *sell* and never to *use*, and that materials are thus diverted from the industries that support the people's life—every observer knowing this crazy insistence on luxurious nonessentials has lifted up a strong voice against it.

But, according to these Protocols, we have been starting at the wrong end. The people, it is true, buy these senseless *nonessentials* which are called *luxuries*. But the people do not devise them. And the people grow tired of them one by one. But the stream of varieties continues—always something else being thrust at the people, dangled before their eyes, set bobbing down the avenue on enough manikins to give the impression that it is "style"; newspaper print and newspaper pictures; movie pictures; stage costumes enough to force the new thing into "fashion" with a kind of force and compulsion which no really worthy essential thing can command.

Where does it come from? What power exists whose long experience and deliberate intent enable it to frivolize the people's minds and tastes and compel them to pay most of their money for it too? Why this spasm of luxury and extravagance through which we have just passed? How did it occur that before luxury and extravagance were apparent, all the material to provoke and inflame them had been prepared beforehand and shipped beforehand, ready for the stampede which also had been prepared?

If the people of the United States would stop to consider, when the useless and expensive thing is offered them—if they would trace its origin, trace the course of the enormous profits made out of it, trace the whole movement to flood the market with uselessness and extravagance and thus demoralize the Gentile public financially, intellectually and socially—if, in short, it could be made clear to them that Jewish financial interests are not only pandering to the loosest elements in human nature, but actually engaged in a calculated effort to render them loose in the first place and keep them loose—it would do more than anything else to stop this sixfold waste—the waste of material, the waste of labor, the waste of Gentile money, the waste of Gentile mind, the waste of Jewish talent, and the worse than waste of Israel's real usefulness to the world.

We say the *Gentile public* is the victim of this stimulated trade in useless luxuries. Did you ever see Jewish people so victimized? They might wear very noticeable clothing, but its price and its quality agree. They might wear rather large diamonds, but they are diamonds. The Jew is not the victim of the Jew, the craze for luxuries is just like the "coney island" crowd to him; he knows what attracts them and the worthlessness of it.

And it is not so much the financial loss that is to be mourned, nor yet the atrocities committed upon good taste, but the fact that the silly Gentile crowds walk into the net willingly, even gaily, supposing the change of the fashion to be as inevitable as the coming of spring, supposing the new demand on their earnings to be as necessary and as natural as taxes. The crowds think that some-how they have part in it, when their only part is to pay, and then pay again for the new extravagance when the present one palls. There are men in this country who know two years ahead what the frivolities and extravagances of the people will be, because they decree what they shall be. These things are all strictly business, demoralizing to the Gentile majority, enriching to the Jewish minority.

Look at the Sixth Protocol for a sidelight on all this:

This is an excerpt from a longer passage dealing with the plans by which the people's interest could be swung from political to industrial questions, how industry could be made insecure and unfair by the introduction of speculation into its management, and finally how against this condition the people could be rendered restless and helpless. Luxury was to be the instrument:

To destroy Gentile industry, we shall, as an incentive to this speculation, *encourage among the Gentiles a strong demand for luxuries—all enticing luxuries.*

And in the First Protocol:

Surely we cannot allow our own people to come to this. The people of the Gentiles are stupefied with spirituous liquors * * *

—incidentally, the profits of spirituous liquors flow in large amounts to Jewish pockets. The history of the whiskey ring in this country will show this. Historically, *the whole prohibition movement may be described as a contest between Gentile and Jewish capital,* and in this instance, thanks to the Gentile majority, the Gentiles won.

The amusement, gambling, jazz song, scarlet fiction, side show, cheap-dear fashions, flashy jewelry, and every other activity that lived by reason of an invisible pressure upon the people, and that exchanged the most useless of commodities for the prices that would just exhaust the people's money surplus and no more—every such activity has been under the mastery of Jews.

They may not be conscious of their participation in any wholesale demoralization of the people. They may only be conscious of "easy money." They may sometimes yield to surprise as they contrast the silly Gentiles with their own money-wise and fabric-wise and metal-wise Jews. But however this may be, there is the conception of a program by which a people may be deliberately devastated materially and spiritually, and yet kept pleasant all the time—and there also is the same program translated into terms of daily transactions and for the most part, perhaps altogether under control of the members of one race.

H. L. MENCKEN:

*"The case against the Jews
is long and damning;
it would justify ten
thousand times as many
pogroms as now go on in
the world." (1920)*

Henry L. Mencken (1880–1956), journalist, author, and critic, was widely known during his lifetime as the "Sage of Baltimore." After attending the Baltimore Polytechnic Institute, Mencken in 1899 became a reporter for the Baltimore *Morning Herald.* A few years later he joined the staff of the Baltimore *Sun,* in which a number of his better known journalistic pieces subsequently appeared, notably his reportorial accounts

From H. L. Mencken, "Introduction" to F. W. Nietzsche, *The Antichrist,* translated by H. L. Mencken (New York: Alfred A. Knopf, 1920), pp. 29–31, Copyright 1920 bv Alfred A. Knopf, Inc.

of the Scopes trial in Tennessee in 1924, the nomination in Chicago of
Franklin D. Roosevelt for President in 1932, and Henry A. Wallace's
Progressive Party Convention in 1948. But reporting the news was only
one of Mencken's interests. In 1908 he became literary critic of *The
Smart Set,* a magazine somewhat similar to *The New Yorker,* and in
1914 joint editor (with George Jean Nathan). He was one of the founders
of *The American Mercury* in 1924, and served as its editor until 1933.
Of a variety of books, including one on the plays of George Bernard
Shaw, Mencken's most serious work was *The American Language* (1919,
with supplements published in 1945 and 1948), an analysis of usage and
expression, including slang, which marked American "English" as a
unique language form.

Although Mencken was essentially a satirist and a cynic—he had no
use for religion, democracy, or the conventions of ordinary life—he read
widely in history and philosophy. An admirer of Nietzsche, he was
inclined, like the German philosopher, to regard Christianity as a Jewish
invention that had done the world more harm than good.

The selection here reprinted was first published in 1920. It forms part
of Mencken's introduction to an American edition of Nietzsche's *The
Antichrist* (New York, 1920).

On the Continent, the day is saved by the fact that the plutocracy tends to become more and more Jewish. Here the intellectual
cynicism of the Jew almost counterbalances his social unpleasant-
ness. If he is destined to lead the plutocracy of the world out of
Little Bethel he will fail, of course, to turn it into an aristocracy—
i.e., a caste of gentlemen—, but he will at least make it clever, and
hence worthy of consideration. The case against the Jews is long
and damning; it would justify ten thousand times as many pogroms
as now go on in the world. But whenever you find a Davidsbündler-
schaft making practise against the Philistines, there you will find a
Jew laying on. Maybe it was this fact that caused Nietzsche to
speak up for the children of Israel quite as often as he spoke against
them. He was not blind to their faults, but when he set them beside
Christians he could not deny their general superiority. Perhaps in
America and England, as on the Continent, the increasing Jewishness of the plutocracy, while cutting it off from all chance of ever
developing into an aristocracy, will yet lift it to such a dignity that
it will at least deserve a certain grudging respect.

But even so, it will remain in a sort of half-world, midway between the gutter and the stars. Above it will still stand the small

group of men that constitutes the permanent aristocracy of the race—the men of imagination and high purpose, the makers of genuine progress, the brave and ardent spirits, above all petty fears and discontents and above all petty hopes and ideals no less. There were heroes before Agamemnon; there will be Bachs after Johann Sebastian. And beneath the Judaized plutocracy, the sublimate *bourgeoisie*, there the immemorial proletariat, I venture to guess, will roar on, endlessly tortured by its vain hatreds and envies, stampeded and made to tremble by its ancient superstitions, prodded and made miserable by its sordid and degrading hopes. It seems to me very likely that, in this proletariat, Christianity will continue to survive. It is nonsense, true enough, but it is sweet. Nietzsche, denouncing its dangers as a poison, almost falls into the error of denying it its undoubtedly sugary smack. Of all the religions ever devised by the great practical jokers of the race, this is the one that offers most for the least money, so to speak, to the inferior man. It starts out by denying his inferiority in plain terms: *all* men are equal in the sight of God. It ends by erecting that inferiority into a sort of actual superiority: it is a merit to be stupid, and miserable, and sorely put upon—of such are the celestial elect. Not all the eloquence of a million Nietzsches, nor all the painful marshalling of evidence of a million Darwins and Harnacks, will ever empty that great consolation of its allure.

LOUIS THOMAS McFADDEN:

"Mr. Speaker, there is no real persecution of Jews in Germany. Hitler and the Warburgs, the Mendelssohns and the Rothschilds, appear to be on the best of terms." (1933)

Louis T. McFadden (1876–1936), banker and Congressman, was born in Troy, Pennsylvania. As a boy, McFadden worked on a farm, but his rise in the banking and commercial world was rapid. At the age of

Congressman Louis T. McFadden, from a speech entitled "Financial Interests Should Not Dictate Foreign Policy of United States Government," *Congressional Record*, House of Representatives, June 15, 1933. (Seventy-Third Congress, First Session, Vol. 77, part 6, 6225–6226.)

sixteen he was employed by the First National Bank of Canton, Pennsylvania, and in 1916 he became its president. He also served as treasurer of the Pennsylvania Bankers Association in 1906, and as president of the Association in 1914.

Entering politics in 1915, McFadden served in Congress from 1915 to 1934. A maverick Republican, McFadden introduced on December 13, 1932, a 4,500-word resolution which moved the impeachment of President Herbert Hoover for "high crimes and misdemeanors." The resolution charged that Hoover had failed to uphold a Congressional mandate against the cancellation of war debts, and Hoover was also accused of indulging in "recent conversations" with "international bankers." The resolution was defeated, and, in addition to costing McFadden valuable patronage, probably contributed to his defeat by a Democrat in the 1934 Congressional election. While in Congress McFadden achieved prominence as a critic of the Federal Reserve System, and as an avowed foe of "international bankers" and their alleged connection with Judaism and Zionism.

The selection here reprinted is taken from a speech of McFadden's delivered in the House of Representatives on June 15, 1933.

Mr. Speaker, I doubt if the history of the relations between this country and Russia is known to every American citizen. It may not be considered amiss, therefore, if I dwell for a few moments on our past relations with that strange and interesting country. To do so it will be necessary for me to go back to the late eighties and the early nineties of the last century, when the United States was turning the corner and becoming rich and powerful. At that time a man named Jacob Schiff came to this country as the agent of certain foreign money lenders. His mission was to get control of American railroads. This man was a Jew. He was the son of a rabbi. He was born in one of the Rothschilds' houses in Frankfort, Germany. He was a small fellow with a pleasant face and, if I remember correctly, his eyes were blue. At an early age he set out from Frankfort to seek his fortune and went to Hamburg, Germany. At Hamburg he entered the Warburg banking establishment. The Warburgs of Hamburg are bankers of long standing, with branches in Amsterdam and Sweden. After Schiff had served his time with them, he went to London and worked with their London correspondents. He was also connected with the firm of Samuel Montagu & Co., the London gold merchants. When he came to this country, he was well equipped to do business as an international money changer. He knew how to be polite, he could write a smooth letter, and he always pretended to be a man of holiness and a philantropist.

Sometime before Schiff's arrival there was a firm of Jewish peddlers or merchants in Lafayette, Ind., by the name of Kuhn & Loeb. I think they were there about 1850. Probably they made money out of the new settlers who passed through Indiana on their way to the Northwest. This firm of Jews had finally moved to New York and had set themselves up as private bankers and had grown rich. Jacob Schiff married Teresa Loeb and became the head of Kuhn, Loeb & Co. Schiff made a great deal of money here for himself and for the Jewish money lenders of London. He began to give orders to Presidents almost as a matter of course. He appears to have been a man who would stop at nothing to gain his own ends. I do not blame him for being a Jew. I blame him for being a trouble maker.

Russia had a powerful enemy in this man, Jacob Schiff. The people of the United States were taught to believe that this enmity of his was caused by wrongs done to Russian Jews. I look elsewhere for the motives which animated him.

In the 1890's Schiff was the agent in this country of Ernest Cassell and other London money lenders. These money lenders were looking forward to a war between England and Russia and were making preparations for propaganda designed to support England in the United States. This country was then a debtor nation, paying a high yearly tribute to Schiff and his principals. Schiff accordingly took it upon himself to create a prejudice in the United States against Russia. He did this by presenting the supposed wrongs of the Russian Jews to the American public. Unpleasant tales began to appear in print. School children in this country were told that Jewish children were crippled for life by Russian soldiers wielding the knout. By unfair means a wedge was driven between Russia and the United States.

One of Schiff's schemes was a sort of wholesale importation of Russian Jews into the United States. He drew up divers and sundry regulations for the temporary transplantation of these Jewish emigrants. He would not, he said, have them enter this country through the port of New York, because they might like New York too well to leave it for the outposts he had selected for them. He said it would be best to have them come in at New Orleans and to have them stay there 2 weeks, "so that they could pick up a few words of English and get a little money" before setting off for what he called the "American hinterland." How they were to get the money he did not say.

Aided by Schiff and his associates, many Russian Jews came to this country about that time and were naturalized here. A number of these naturalized Jews then returned to Russia. Upon their return to that country, they immediately claimed exemption there from the regulations of domicile imposed on Jews; that is, they claimed the right to live on purely Russian soil because they were American citizens, or "Yankee" Jews. Disorders occurred and were exploited in the American press. Riots and bombings and assassinations, for which somebody furnished money, took place. The perpetrators of these outrages appear to have been shielded by powerful financial interests. While this was going on in Russia, a shameless campaign of lying was conducted here, and large sums of money were spent to make the general American public believe that the Jews in Russia were a simple and guileless folk ground down by the Russians and needing the protection of the great benefactor of all the world— Uncle Sam. In other words, we were deceived. We were so deceived that we allowed them to come in here and to take the bread out of the mouths of our own American citizens. . . .

Mr. Speaker, the restrictions upon Jews in Russia at that time may or may not have been onerous. But onerous or not, before the Russians had time to change them, Schiff had the 80-year-old treaty of friendship and good will between Russia and the United States denounced. Speaking of this matter, Count Witte says in his autobiography: "The Russians lost the friendship of the American people."

Mr. Speaker, I cannot believe that those people—the real Russians—ever lost the true friendship of the American people. They were done away with to suit the ambitions of those who intend to be the financial masters of the world, and some of us were deceived into thinking that in some mysterious way they, themselves, were to blame. The chasm that suddenly opened between ourselves and our old friends and well-wishers in Russia was a chasm created by Schiff the vindictive in his inhuman greed, and he created it in the name of the Jewish religion.

Mr. Speaker, it was a mistake for the United States to permit the integrity of its foreign policy to be jeopardized or affected adversely by such religious, racial, and financial meddling as that practiced upon us by Schiff and his London associates. The United States should manage its foreign affairs with more distinction than that which is implied in the picture of Jacob Schiff shaking his fist at the White House and muttering threats against William Howard Taft, then President of the United States, a man who was excessively distinguished in his chosen field and who represented the integrity and the patriotic Americanism of every generation of New Englanders from the first of Massachusetts Bay Colony to his own, and represented them well.

Mr. Speaker, the people of the United States should not permit financial interests or any other special interests to dictate the foreign policy of the United States Government. But in this connection history is now repeating itself. You have heard, no doubt, of the so-called persecution of Jews in Germany.

Mr. Speaker, there is no real persecution of Jews in Germany. Hitler and the Warburgs, the Mendelssohns and the Rothschilds, appear to be on the best of terms. There is no real persecution of the Jews in Germany, but there has been a pretended persecution of them because there are 200,000 unwanted Communistic Jews in Germany, largely Galician Jews who entered Germany after the World War, and Germany is very anxious to get rid of those particular Communistic Jews. The Germans wish to preserve the purity of their own blond racial stock. They are willing to keep rich Jews like Max Warburg and Franz Mendelssohn, whose families have lived in Germany so long that they have acquired some German national characteristics. But the Germans are not willing to keep the Galician Jews, the upstarts. So a great show is put on, largely by German Jews themselves, in the hope that Uncle Sam will prove himself to be as foolish as he was before and that we will allow those Galician and Communistic Jews to come in here. That is why Miss Perkins has been placed in charge of the Department of Labor. She is there to lower the immigration bars. It is thought that, being a woman, she may disarm criticism. She is an old hand with the international Jewish bankers. If she were not, she would not be here in a Jewish-controlled administration.

When the so-called "anti-Semitic campaign" designed for American consumption was launched in Germany, France was alarmed because she feared the Galician Jews might be dumped on French soil. French newspapers published articles concerning the menace, but now that France has been shown that the purpose of the anti-Semitic campaign is to dump the 200,000 Communistic Jews on the United States she is worried no longer. "Ah", she says, "l'Oncle Sam, he is to be the goat. Very good."

Mr. Speaker, I regard it as a pity that there are Americans who love to fawn upon the money Jews and to flatter them. Some of these unfortunates are under obligations to Jewish money changers and dare not cross them. On June 6, 1933, there was a meeting in the city of Washington at which the following resolution was adopted:

America has been greatly enriched through generations past by men and women of high quality who have come to our shores as a result of persecution in their own lands. Our country is known throughout the world as the haven of those who suffer from wrong and injustices, and who seek an opportunity for freedom not afforded in their own land. The present is another critical time, and there are many victims of religious and racial persecution in Germany who, because of superior attainments and qualities of fine citizenship, would make valuable additions to our Commonwealth. We, therefore, ask the Government temporarily to relax the immigration barriers in favor of such persons and urge the passage of such measures as will effect this result.

Mr. Speaker, the time for such tactics has gone by. We would be very foolish to allow Germany to dump her unwanted Jewish population on the United States. If the money Jews are as noble as they advertise themselves to be, let them advocate the payment of the veterans' adjusted-compensation certificates. Let them ease the burdens of the consumptive Jewish boys who are hauling heavy carts of fur and other material around the garment center of New York. Let them see that the long-suffering Jewish school teachers receive the salaries which are due to them but which are now in arrears. That would be better than to bring 200,000 Jewish Communists in here for political purposes. . . .

KARL MENNINGER:

*"It is a very old observation that quarreling
Irish may throw bricks at one another,
and Italians knives, but Jews throw sharp
words. . . . To convert this talent for
verbalization into scientific purposes is
in no branch of science more useful than
in psychiatry." (1937)*

Karl Menninger, M.D., was born in Topeka, Kansas, in 1893. He attended Washburn University in Topeka and the University of Wisconsin, and in 1917 received his medical degree from Harvard University. After brief service at the Boston Psychopathic Hospital, he completed his internship at the Kansas City General Hospital. Upon returning to Topeka, he entered private practice with his father, Dr. Charles Frederick Menninger, and some years later, with his father and brother, William Menninger, founded the Menninger Clinic for the private practice of psychiatry and psychoanalysis. During World War II he served as a consultant in psychiatry to the Surgeon General of the United States Army. His books include *The Human Mind* (1930), *Man Against Himself* (1938), and *A Psychiatrist's World* (1959), a collection of his papers.

The following selection, "The Genius of the Jew in Psychiatry," reprinted in *A Psychiatrist's World,* was first published in 1937.

If we had no further illustration than the character of Sigmund Freud, we should have a basis for suspecting some connection between the Jew and psychological genius. It would carry us too far to list all the outstanding Jewish psychologists and psychiatrists, nor would it, in my own mind, be fitting to associate lesser names with that of such a master as he. It is one thing to show that proportionately many Jews have an interest in psychiatry and another to show that they have some special abilities in that direction. The fact is well known that Jewish physicians are distinguished for

From Karl Menninger, *A Psychiatrist's World* (New York: The Viking Press, 1959), pp. 415–424, Copyright © 1959 by Karl Menninger, reprinted by permission of The Viking Press, Inc.

their scientific accomplishments in all fields of medicine, and, in writing such an article as this, one is dangerously close to the dilemma that if one holds that Jews are brilliant in all fields of science, it is the more difficult to show that they have some outstanding genius in psychiatry. Furthermore, as a Gentile, I am apt—like all Gentiles—to overestimate the superiorities and attainments of the Jews (a psychological fact which no doubt contributes in part to anti-Semitic reactions).

Nevertheless, I shall proceed on the basis of my empirical impressions, an unscientific but not necessarily invalid method. Some physicians accuse psychiatry of being more of an art than a science and say that psychiatrists are, therefore, born rather than made (not in the sense of inheriting something, but of coming by their special gifts by very early childhood influences, rather than from later training). This perhaps substantiates me in my belief that some Jews seem to have a special gift which makes them more likely than the average person in those requirements that make for skill, if not genius, in psychiatry, gifts which are peculiarly related to their Jewish origin. Since the recognition of the psychological elements of disease and behavior are so rapidly increasing in scientific circles as well as among laymen, and since the demands for psychiatrists so far exceed the supply, the recognition of such gifts might therefore be of considerable practical value, and it behooves us to inquire into the reasons for it and the possibilities of its being cultivated.

We could not logically begin a consideration of such a problem in a more appropriate way than to consider that extraordinary genius, Sigmund Freud. It is neither necessary nor appropriate that I devote many lines here to show that he is one of the great minds in history. In all those sciences which deal with human beings in the course of his own generation probably no other individual has so largely altered the content and direction of human thought. What appeals to us, who are scientists, is the fact that he was able to reduce to a scientific discipline what had been known for thousands of years by those whose intuition gave them glimpses beneath the surface of things. That it led to extraordinary and unexpected findings which he then had the courage to examine, to correlate, and to present to a reluctant and even antagonistic world of science is to his inestimable credit. In working with difficult patients, with the possibilities of homicide or suicide or psychosis imminent, I have often reflected what immeasurable courage it must have taken for Freud to pursue his earliest researches in the face of the threat of scientific excommunication, legal action, social stigmatization, and above all that feeling of having brought about a disaster through blunder which all doctors dread. Freud faithfully and courageously worked through an uncharted wilderness, blazing a trail for the rest of us to follow and to explore more leisurely and more safely.

I should not have sought to establish a connection between his talent and the fact that he was a Jew, had not Freud himself repeatedly called attention to the relationship between his work and his Jewishness. Some of his own remarks on the subject were:

. . . Only to my Jewish nature did I owe the two qualities which have become indispensable to me on my hard road. Because I was a Jew I found myself free from many prejudices which limited others in the use of their intellects; and being a Jew I was prepared to enter opposition to renounce the agreement with the compact majority.

It would indeed seem presumptuous to take issue with Freud on any subject involving psychology, except that Freud himself taught us we must distrust our own motives and our own explanations. I shall, therefore, in the interest of the present theme, and encouraged by Freud's own attitude, attempt the formidable task of examining Freud's comments on this subject more carefully.

If we look very objectively at Freud's quotation above, we see that he did not explain it very fully. For example, he says, *"Only to my Jewish nature* did I owe the two qualities." This, it seems to me, is begging the question. Others than Jews have these qualities and it may well be that Freud might have had them had he not been a Jew. Let us examine what the qualities were.

First, he says he found himself free from many prejudices which limited others in the use of their intellects. Now what prejudices could Freud have meant? Is it true that Jews are freer from prejudices than Gentiles?

That, being a Jew, Freud could have the courage to identify himself with another minority group seems to have obvious validity. It should not be forgotten, however, that the original Jews were, so far as they knew or believed, the majority, and the Gentiles the inconsequential minority. I think it is fair to say that the Jewish people never became adjusted to the consequences of their dispersion over the globe, and such articles as one often reads extolling the great achievements of the Jews, the great men who have been Jews, are no doubt often motivated by a wish to show that qualitatively at least the Jews are in the majority—a spiritual majority. The wish to feel secure which is back of the wish to align oneself with the majority is certainly not lacking in any human beings, Jewish or non-Jewish; the fact that the Jews have been accustomed to the necessity of being affiliated with one minority may give them a greater endurance of such a state, but, as everyone knows, it also acts in a contrary direction and impels many people to identify themselves with whatever majorities they can, and to do so vigorously and enthusiastically.

I venture to say, then, that Freud's own explanations of the relation between his genius and his Jewishness explain nothing. On the other hand, if he were to have had recourse to his own theories, he would have considered far more important the actual experiences of his childhood. What is there in the experience of the Jewish child which is different from that of the Gentile child which might be related to later psychological perspicacity? This, I think, is our question.

Theoretically, the gift of intuitive perception as well as the interest in those who suffer spiritually rather than merely physically must come from previous experiences which rendered him forever sensitive and forever responsive to similar experiences in others. In other words, I think only certain types of suffering in childhood can make one sufficiently concerned with or understanding of suffering of others to enable one to be of help to them. Perhaps this is a clumsy attempt at scientific expression of the religious ideas connecting suffering with spiritual vision. I have no objection to these scientific ideas being allied to religious ideas, but I think we can be more precise and objective about them than in religious treatises. I think we can see in the sharp and intuitive vision and the scientific concern with the unhappy, which go to make a psychiatrist, a sublimation and social exploitation of the unhappiness which must come to many a child. And since many children suffer and will continue to suffer, no matter what happens, this is one way of exploiting suffering other than becoming masochistic oneself, as is the general tendency of many Jews (and, of course, of many others).

Clearly the psychiatrist or psychologist is one for whom emotional experiences are something very real, no less real than physical substances; and presumably in the suffering of other people there is awakened in him some recollections of his own suffering as a child, a suffering which was perhaps never completely assuaged; in this case, his wish to help the other person, his wish to see into the other person's problems and to set him aright, is in part an acting out of a wish that he himself might be saved or have been saved this pain, and in part a sublimation of the sadistic feelings of resentment that his own experiences aroused in him. The child who suffers more has more of such aggressions to release. Psychiatrists, like surgeons, have to hurt people, though when they do so in the interests of helping the patient, the unconscious aggressiveness is thereby sublimated.

Of course, this theory is not mine but an essential part of the whole psychoanalytic discipline; the point is now to apply it to the Jewish child. Does the Jewish child suffer more than the Gentile child, and, if so, does he suffer in a way which is likely to increase this propensity for interest in the sufferings of other people?

My impression is that perhaps, if we may generalize, the Jewish child does suffer somewhat more or somewhat more frequently than the Gentile child. However, I do not think that this is due to the immediate effects of Gentile prejudice. My impression is that it is due to the child's reaction to the parents' reaction to the entire social situation in which the Jews live. This includes, of course, their religious and historical traditions.

I believe that some ethnologists hold that from the physical standpoint there is little to support the theory of racial distinctness or character in Jews. Certainly from the psychological standpoint, about which I am better informed, it is now considered entirely invalid to ascribe specific qualities of human nature, or, for example, of "Jewish nature," to human beings independent of their social situation. Those things which are considered (by anyone) to be typically Jewish must be regarded as the consequences of long-continued custom, ideology, and social attitudes. In other words, from this standpoint (represented by the Gestalt psychologists, the psychoanalysts, and, indeed, most of the psychiatrists, as well as

many others) the Jew is not a biological entity, and his distinguishing characteristics are psychological and social rather than biological, hence, changeable and changing.

For the present, our social heritage is such that the average Jew
thinks of himself as a biological entity and is so regarded by the
average Gentile. The majority of Jewish children are brought up
under psychological circumstances distinctly different from those of
the average Gentile child, at least insofar as his membership character in the Jewish group is concerned. This results in certain reactions with reference to nonmembers of the group, attitudes of
hostility, fear, distrust, and repudiation mixed with wistful and uncertain longings to be liked and to be assimilated by other groups,
and reaction formations against these wishes. The corresponding
Gentile attitudes of fear, distrust, and dislike, mixed with mystical
notions of Jewish magic and divinity, are well known.

The product of this, insofar as the Jewish child is concerned, is
an emphasis upon his membership in the Jewish group, the dangers
to which he is exposed on account of it, the protection he is afforded
by it, and the loyalty he owes it. Granted that there are individual
differences in every family, one very frequently observed tendency
among Jews is their overemphasis of the family bond and their
overprotection and overdemonstrativeness toward the children. How
this arises from the parents' own sense of insecurity, bred of social
situations, I have just outlined.

The overprotective, separatistic treatment of any child, especially
if it is endorsed and supported both by custom and by sentimental
rationalizations, produces in the child a high degree of narcissism
resulting from the fact that he is encouraged to regard himself as
superlative, a misconception about himself which, however much
it may be displaced in the course of time to his relatives (e.g., to
great Jews who have shown the world what Jews can really do),
nevertheless acts as a barrier toward comfortable social relationships with his fellow men. To be sure, it may also inspire a terrific
aspiration and a compulsive striving toward superiority which may
partially account for the high scholastic ranking which Jews so
frequently achieve. But along with this there is a mounting sense
of disappointment and disillusionment as the growing child discovers that his parents, being human, were not entirely sincere in
their adulation and demonstrativeness. He discovers, too, with a

bitterness even greater than that of the less favored child, that nowhere outside of his own home is he treated with the extreme tenderness and solicitude he once enjoyed.

Psychiatrists know that such a wound, received in early childhood—a wound inflicted upon one's self-esteem and implicit faith in humanity—never heals without a scar. The thwarting and rebuffs which an overprotected and petted child receives in his first contact with an unfeeling world produce a reaction of protest in him and often lead to his setting up defenses against people. These defenses (or perhaps the inner insecurity which they breed) lead to the essential individualism of so many Jews.

Separatism and prejudice go hand in hand, and the Jewish child has separatism and the alleged need for it impressed upon him before he has had any actual experience with the prejudice. Thus he sets out to meet prejudice, so to speak. The external dangers in a Gentile society are magnified, perhaps partly because of the parents' own sorrows from this source but also because this is an essential corollary to the preservation of internal unity; the same thing is to be observed, of course, in college fraternities, political parties, and international politics. The effect on the child, however, is to instill fear into him. I have been told by Jewish psychiatrists that they regard this as the greatest sin, or shall we say error, of their parents. The child is thus impelled either to forestall this danger by befriending the Gentile in an obsequious manner, which is often transparent, or to defy the danger by being aggressive and provocative, which is also apt to be transparent (i.e., shows the motive of fear behind it), and when this attitude is responded to in kind it gives him an apparent justification for his fears and his hostility. Perhaps on this account every Jewish child must have some time in his life felt hostile toward his parents for their role in having sustained the separatism and inspired the fear which so affects his sense of security. The confusing thing is that there are actually some dangers from some Gentiles, as we have all been painfully reminded by affairs in Germany, and this would seem an inappropriate time to raise the question as to just how this prejudice arises and why it persists.

The result of this separatism, however one explains its origin, is that many Jewish children grow up with an extraordinary interest in and curiosity about people, reinforced no doubt by the background of religion and philosophy which is their heritage. Their own detachment when successfully achieved enables them to be more objective, more analytical and at the same time more discerning in their judgment of others, partly because they understand, and partly because they have been able to rise above suffering and even feel able to relieve it in others.

There is another point to be made in tracing childhood experiences to the adult vocation of psychiatry. Everyone learns sooner or later that one must expect disappointments in love—that his loved ones hurt him oftentimes as grievously as his enemies—but it has seemed to me that the individual Jew learns this at an earlier and more vulnerable age than do others. He learns it first because of his initial disappointment in his parents; their overtenderness and overestimation of him leads to inevitable disappointment because the least indifference on their part or perhaps the enthusiastic reception of another infant is interpreted by the child as a tragic rejection. Thus the individual Jew learns again what the Jews as a group (from their social experiences) long ago learned, namely, that no one can be implicitly and completely trusted. This saves them the painful disillusionment which the Gentile is continually experiencing because of his more gullible naïveté. The Jew knows from bitter experience that those who appear to love one another most, have a hostile component in their interpersonal bond which may under certain circumstances show itself directly or indirectly, overtly or covertly. They know that in one sense there is no such thing as disinterested friendship.

Theoretically—on the basis of their social experience—this attitude might be thought to apply only to Gentiles and not to fellow Jews. Practically, however, the early disillusionment extends to all relationships. Because of his experience within a closely allied group, the Jewish child has an opportunity to learn what every idealistic person who joins a social group or cause in search of understanding and inspiration discovers—that close association breeds hostilities and jealousies as well as love and sympathy.

This knowledge that even one's brothers, those whom one has been taught to turn to for comfort, are not exempt from envy, jealousy, craftiness, and hate, and, above all, actions of self-interest to the hurt of the others, leaves the Jew peculiarly exposed to *feelings of insecurity.* He has too keen an insight into human nature for his own comfort. He is so aware of the possibility of an attack or a desertion or a "double-cross" from his friends that he often anticipates it, even provokes it. But if he learns to understand and control this sensitiveness, he can turn to account his perception of unseen motives with telling effect, as he often does in psychiatry.

Still another reason that those raised in the Jewish tradition may have some special gift for psychiatry is that of the high value placed by them throughout history on verbal expression of feelings as exemplified by the incomparable poetry of the Psalms and the extraordinary quality of their religious literature, and also upon studious scholarly organization of their thinking. The Irish are gifted verbally but do not have the scientific essential of orderliness; the Swedes are orderly but not so gifted verbally. Now, in psychiatry the reduction of relatively intangible things such as feelings and attitudes to verbal expression is highly important. It is necessary to the scientific evaluation of mental processes and it has been shown by the work of Freud to have a therapeutic value for the patient. It is a very old observation that quarreling Irish may throw bricks at one another, and Italians knives, but Jews throw sharp words. This is a destructive use of the same gift. To convert this talent for verbalization into scientific purposes is in no branch of science more useful than in psychiatry.

Closely allied with this is the fact that traditionally and historically, spiritual values, that is to say, the importance of certain feelings and abstractions, have always appealed to Jews. It has always been my suspicion that the practical business talents exemplified by some Jews were a reaction against this traditional emphasis on intangibles. Be that as it may, the idea that something nonexistent may nevertheless be a psychological reality as powerful in its effect as some material substance is not hard for the Jew to grasp. It is much more difficult on the other hand for the average Anglo-Saxon, and puts him at a disadvantage in psychiatry.

When so many children must suffer in the ways I have outlined and so very few men become psychiatrists or psychologists, the question as to whether the Jewish tradition favors the development of skill in this vocation is left poorly answered, indeed. I do not believe it can be answered definitely. The psychological fact remains that some possess the saving grace of turning suffering and resentment and fear into constructive and helpful efforts based on a kind of spiritual discernment with a quantum of scientific detachment, and that this seems to occur relatively more often among Jews than among Gentiles. Would that it occurred oftener among both!

ALLEN A. ZOLL, GEORGE E. SULLIVAN, AND JOHN BOWE:

". . . I oppose Professor Frankfurter [for appointment as Associate Justice of the Supreme Court] on racial grounds. The reason is that there is today in America an anti-Jewish sentiment that is growing by leaps and bounds." (Allen A. Zoll, 1939)

Late in 1938 President Franklin D. Roosevelt sent to the Senate the name of Felix Frankfurter, Professor of Law at the Harvard Law School, for appointment as an Associate Justice of the Supreme Court. At that time, two Americans of Jewish extraction, Louis D. Brandeis and Benjamin Cardozo, had served on the Court; indeed Frankfurter's nomination was designed to fill the vacancy created by the death of Cardozo. Nevertheless, the Frankfurter appointment was opposed by a number of individuals speaking for themselves or in behalf of organizations. The charges against Frankfurter included his religion or "race," his alleged radical and/or pro-Communist views, his connections with international Jewry, and his lack of a war record. There was also some opposition to Frankfurter from Jewish circles, as there had been earlier when President Woodrow Wilson nominated Brandeis for membership on the Court. It was feared by some Jews that Frankfurter's appointment would be used by anti-Semites as additional evidence of Jewish "influence" in the New Deal and in America generally.

The following selection is taken from the hearings on Frankfurter's nomination in January, 1939.

From *Hearings Before a Subcommittee of the Committee on the Judiciary, United States Senate, Seventy-Sixth Congress, First Session, on the Nomination of Felix Frankfurter to Be an Associate Justice of the Supreme Court,* January 11 and 12, 1939, pp. 20–21, 74–77, 89–92.

Statement of George E. Sullivan

Frankfurter's appointment is being heralded in press propaganda as constituting "a new protest against racial intolerance," when, in truth and in fact, it would very greatly promote racial intolerance by making our other loyal citizens believe that Frankfurter typifies Jewish Americans generally.

Something must be done to protect, against misrepresentation, our loyal Jewish-Americans, who are devoted to the principles of the American Republic, and are always ready to sacrifice their lives—as many of them have frequently done—in defense of our Republic. They are not merely Jews in America, but loyal Americans. Jewish internationalism seeking either special benefits or world domination, has no appeal to them. They do not claim to be homeless. They recognize their homes to be, and also their undivided loyalties, in the American Republic.

SENATOR NEELY: Your time has expired. If you have anything further to say you may insert it in the record.

SENATOR McCARRAN: Mr. Chairman, the witness was interrupted a number of times by members of the committee. I suggest that the time be extended to include those interruptions.

SENATOR NEELY: Without objection it is so ordered. Mr. Sullivan, you may proceed.

MR. SULLIVAN: A large group of alien-minded Jews however, constantly seeks to make the public believe that all Jews belong to a distinct nationality extending throughout the world, and constitutes "a world community." Louis D. Brandeis has proclaimed in his book *The Jewish Problem—How to Solve It:*

Let us all recognize that we Jews are a distinct nationality of which every Jew, whatever his country, his station or shade of belief is necessarily a member (p. 25).

Organize, organize, organize—until every Jew in America must stand up and be counted—counted with us—or prove himself, wittingly or unwittingly, of the few who are against their own people (p. 26).

It is difficult to understand how such views and attitudes can be reconciled with the impartial duties of a member of the Supreme

Court! Moreover, in a leaflet, recently issued by the Anti-Defamation League of the Jewish organization B'nai B'rith, and known as Fireside Discussion Group Leaflet No. VII, it is asserted—

Approximately a race, definitely a type, and consciously a unity, we are an historic people—a world community (p. 3).

But that is not the view of the Jewish-American. Rabbi Lazeron came out against such an idea as the building up of that unity in America. He was immediately rebuffed by Rabbi Wise of the Jewish organization in March 1938, but Lazeron really represented the viewpoint and feeling of Jewish-Americans. That we do not recognize either in office holding or in respect to individual rights.

SENATOR NEELY: Would it be correct to conclude that your objections to Dr. Frankfurter are based upon the ground that he is a Jew?

MR. SULLIVAN: Absolutely not. One of my objections to him is that he has not the American mind that other Jewish Americans have, but has that international mind.

The same group of alien-minded, or international, Jews was, obviously, responsible for a so-called world-wide poll of Jewish communities during 1937, with the announced result carried in Associated Press dispatch of September 24, 1937 (published in *New York Times* of September 25, 1937), that Max Litvinoff, U.S.S.R. Commissar of Foreign Affairs, and Prof. Felix Frankfurter, had been elected to the "Jewish Hall of Fame" among the "120 greatest living Jews" held up as "living ideals" to Jewish youth. Obviously, no American-minded group of Jews or non-Jews could ever have been induced to hold "Red" Litvinoff up as a "living ideal" to any youth. Moreover, the action of a group which so holds up Litvinoff, and also Frankfurter at the same time, should make everyone possessing a grain of intelligence demand to know why Frankfurter did not register some protest, at least in the interest of Jewish youth, if not on his own account. If Litvinoff and Frankfurter belong in the same group, surely neither of them belongs on our Supreme Court.

Surely, no Senator can justify a failure to actively oppose the confirmation of Frankfurter's nomination, which should be indignantly and unanimously rejected.

Statement of Allen A. Zoll

MR. ZOLL: There are two reasons why I oppose the appointment of Prof. Felix Frankfurter to the Supreme Court of the United States. One is because I believe his record proves him unfitted for the position, irrespective of his race, and the other is because of his race.

SENATOR NEELY: You are opposed to him because he is a Jew?

MR. ZOLL: I think that I can give you reasons for that, not because I am anti-Semitic, but quite the contrary.

SENATOR NEELY: Your statement would indicate that you are opposed to him because he is a Jew.

SENATOR MCCARRAN: Perhaps the chairman did not get the full import of your statement. Will you make it again?

MR. ZOLL: There are two reasons why I oppose the appointment of Prof. Felix Frankfurter to the Supreme Court of the United States. One is because I believe his record proves him unfitted for the position, irrespective of his race, and the other is because of his race.

SENATOR NEELY: You oppose his appointment because he is a Jew, but still you are not anti-Semitic.

MR. ZOLL: That is quite right, sir. I think that my statement will clearly show the reasons for that.

Let me deal with this racial question first. I recognize that an able Jew is as able as anyone else and that a fine Jew is as fine as anyone else, and I also recognize the fact that there have been and are many brilliant Jews.

SENATOR BORAH: Are we to understand that you oppose him because he is a Jew?

MR. ZOLL: Partly, sir.

SENATOR BORAH: So far as I am concerned, I do not propose to listen to an argument against a man because of his religion.

MR. ZOLL: If you will let me finish my statement—

SENATOR BORAH (interposing): You are raising the same question that is drenching Europe in blood.

MR. ZOLL: No. I am trying to prevent that in this country.

SENATOR BORAH: In this country we do not deny any man privileges because of his religion or race.

MR. ZOLL: Quite right, sir.

SENATOR BORAH: If you deny a man the right to hold office, it is just the same as if you denied him the right to hold property. It is exactly the same question. I do not think we want to hear the race question debated in any public hearing in this country.

MR. ZOLL: Am I to understand that you forbid me to make my statement?

SENATOR BORAH: So far as I am concerned, I want it understood that I am strongly opposed to anyone raising the race question.

MR. ZOLL: Mr. Senator, may I say that I am not at all anti-Semitic. My statement will indicate that I want to prevent something that will cause anti-Semitism in this country.

SENATOR BORAH: You want this committee to reject Frankfurter because of his race.

MR. ZOLL: Partly, because it would be bad public policy.

SENATOR BORAH: That has nothing to do with the question of public policy.

MR. ZOLL: In my opinion, sir, it has everything to do with it.

SENATOR BORAH: One of our principles of our Government is that a member of any race has the same rights as a member of any other race. Why do you say you oppose him because he is a Jew?

MR. ZOLL: Because it would be bad public policy and would stir up more anti-Semitism in this country. I have a very brief statement on that subject. If you ask me not to make it, I will comply with your request.

SENATOR KING: May I say that I agree with Senator Borah that it is outrageous to oppose a man because of his race when he is entitled to hold the position. I have letters from friends who are Jews, and they take the position, though I do not agree with them, that to confirm Mr. Frankfurter might tend to develop an anti-Semitic spirit here, which they greatly deplore.

MR. ZOLL: That is exactly my argument, sir.

SENATOR BORAH: That is the same argument that has been made abroad on the question.

MR. ZOLL: Some of the leading Jews feel the same way.

SENATOR BORAH: That is the same argument being made elsewhere. You want the committee to reject him because he is a Jew.

MR. ZOLL: If that were the only ground it might not be sufficient.

SENATOR BORAH: You are making it one of the items for rejection.

MR. ZOLL: That is right, sir.

SENATOR BORAH: So far as I am concerned, I do not want to listen to argument against a man because of his race or religion.

MR. ZOLL: Without meaning to be argumentative, if it would cause an uprising in this country do you think it would be good public policy?

SENATOR BORAH: There can be no such uprising in this country.

MR. ZOLL: I believe there would be an uprising, and I believe anyone familiar with the attitude of anti-Semitism which now exists in this country will realize it. Does the Senator suggest I not include that part of my statement?

SENATOR BORAH: I only say that I do not care to hear it.

SENATOR MCCARRAN: I think that any member of this committee has a right to object to a statement. I think, however, that whatever is presented that is not offensive might be received.

SENATOR BORAH: It is offensive.

MR. ZOLL: My views are not intended to be offensive.

SENATOR NEELY: As many of you as are in favor of this gentleman's being permitted to continue his statement will say "aye."

SENATOR CONNALLY: He has already started it, and I am in favor of his going on. It might be explanatory.

SENATOR NEELY: The Chair wants the committee to decide the question. As many as are in favor of his being permitted to proceed with his statement will say "aye"; contrary, "no." The ayes appear to have it, the ayes have it, and it is so ordered.

SENATOR HUGHES: I quite agree with Senator Borah, but I think the gentleman should be permitted to say what he has to say.

MR. ZOLL: Shall I go ahead?

SENATOR NEELY: Yes; you may proceed.

MR. ZOLL: It is on account of these I oppose Professor Frankfurter on racial grounds. The reason is that there is today in America an anti-Jewish sentiment that is growing by leaps and bounds. This is recognized universally and has proved a source of grave concern to Jewish leaders. There is no time here to go into the reasons for this increasing anti-Jewish feeling nor would it be pertinent to this case except insofar as a slight résumé may show you that this actually exists.

In many quarters the Jew has been fostering movements that are subversive to our Government and whether rightfully or not, this belief has steadily increased since the advent of the New Deal. In the larger cities it has grown to an alarming degree. To place, at this time, upon the highest court another one of that race is not only a political mistake but a social one.

Even though he were the ablest lawyer in the land—even though he might believe in our constitutional form of government as much as Thomas Jefferson himself—even so, I would oppose him on the grounds mentioned, for the sake of his own people and ours. This appointment, in my opinion, would do more than any occurrence for years to intensify this spreading anti-Jewish feeling, which, if allowed to grow, will prove disastrous to Christian and Jew alike, in fact to all America.

I feel very sincerely that there is strong opposition to this man, not because he is not a brilliant man, because he is probably the most brilliant lawyer in the country, but because he is a Jew and because of the anti-Semitic feeling that is increasing day by day. I contend that this opposition is growing, and that his appointment will greatly increase that feeling and have a bad effect upon the New Deal, to those of you who are New Dealers. I think it would be the worst thing that could be done to make that appointment.

Statement of John Bowe

Now, I would like to give you Frankfurter's military record. He arrived in this country in 1894. He left Harvard University in 1906. He was Assistant United States Attorney in the southern district of New York from 1906 to 1910. He was employed in the War Department of the United States Government from 1911 to 1914. He has been a professor in Harvard Law School since September 1914.

What I am getting at is this: that Frankfurter has specialized in turning out international lawyers as compared with our national lawyers. There is a difference there. These international lawyers are the fixers in the meddling with the tariff and all such matters as that. I want to show you the difference between the different kinds of Jews, because these international people are mostly Jews. They are not the Ghetto Jews. That has come up through the years from the time of Christ.

SENATOR NEELY: Comrade, are you opposed to this confirmation on the ground that Dr. Frankfurther is a Jew?

MR. BOWE: Absolutely not on the ground—well, yes. I am not

opposed to him as a Jew, if he has proved himself. On his race, I am not; but before he should go into a responsible position he should prove he is entitled to it and understands the principles of our country. He is one that was brought up on a Communist basis rather than our constitutional basis, and should not be entrusted with a responsible position dealing with foreign countries where he could possibly do harm to our constitutional Government.

The reason I am here is by choice. I am not native born and here by accident of birth. I am here because I want to be here. You gentlemen may think what I want to say to you is a reflection on my intelligence, but I am not willing to admit that.

SENATOR NEELY: You and Dr. Frankfurter are both foreign born, and both chose to come to this country.

MR. BOWE: He was born on a Communist basis, and I was born on a Christian basis, and our Government is based on Christianity. We have our automatic checks and balances that regulate our country the same as through the threefold plan. You go through the threefold constitution into the threefold trinity, all based on the constitutional law of the land, the divine law of life and the natural law of God. We have got to be careful to preserve our Government, with Trotsky just across the border in Mexico; we have got to look out for that.

What I am going to bring up is this: During the war, when the Spanish War veterans were in the fight, Frankfurter was an assistant to the Secretary of War in the War Department and he issued the orders. Some of these gentlemen from these Jewish societies wanted to change the orderly system of American procedure in regard to majorities. Our Government is built on majorities.

SENATOR NEELY: Did Dr. Frankfurter have anything to do with that?

MR. BOWE: It was an order from the Secretary of War and he was his assistant.

SENATOR NEELY: Did Dr. Frankfurter himself have anything to do with it?

MR. BOWE: That is something I hope you gentlemen will look up, because it brings up another question. They got that order through that appointed Jewish chaplains in the Army, and before there were Christian chaplains and Roman Catholics. They never had that before.

SENATOR NEELY: The order of the Secretary of War of which you complain authorized the appointment of Jewish chaplains, and, in effect, placed Jewish rabbis, in this particular, on an equality with Catholics and Protestants? Is that correct?

MR. BOWE: Yes.

SENATOR NEELY: And you think that Dr. Frankfurter was partly responsible for the issuance of that order.

MR. BOWE: I think you gentlemen could find that.

SENATOR NORRIS: If we investigated and found out that he did not have anything to do with that terrible order, you would withdraw what you are now saying, would you not?

MR. BOWE: I am not hidebound on this. I am trying to get the facts. I want the facts about these Jewish chaplains and the Jewish welfare agency. It reaches into every section of this country.

SENATOR NEELY: Mr. Bowe, suppose that Dr. Frankfurter did prevail upon the Secretary of War to issue the order which resulted in the appointment of Jewish rabbis as chaplains in the Spanish-American War, or in the World War, or any other war. Do you think that that fact would justify this committee in rejecting his nomination?

MR. BOWE: No. What I am getting at now is that in New York City the Jewish religion is organized through these welfare associations and here is a list of possibly more than 400 organizations in New York City. Every one of them was born in a foreign country, and they are working as a unit. Here is the list. You can see what it is. I think it would be well to leave the list right here.

SENATOR NEELY: Very well.

MR. BOWE: Many of these names I can't even spell. They belong to organizations of Jews, from half a dozen different countries, but they are all welded in together.

SENATOR NEELY: That being your belief, you are of the opinion that no Jew should be made a member of the Supreme Court of the United States?

MR. BOWE: There is something back of that.

SENATOR NEELY: Is that your opinion?

MR. BOWE: I have seen fine Jews. I would not want to make it against his race. What I object to is the Communist sympathizers in their organizations.

SENATOR NEELY: Have you any specific objection to Dr. Frankfurter, excepting the one you mentioned? I mean the one based upon your supposition that he was in some manner, responsible for the order to which you have referred? Have you any other specific objection to his confirmation?

MR. BOWE: Yes, sir.

SENATOR NEELY: What is it?

MR. BOWE: He ought to have been a different kind of military man than he was. If he had been the right kind of an alien-born citizen he would have gone out and done his best to help in the war, instead of staying here in the War Department and trying to manage it, when it was something he didn't know anything about.

SENATOR NEELY: Comrade, would you outlaw all who failed to volunteer for service in the Spanish-American War?

MR. BOWE: I am not trying to outlaw anybody.

SENATOR CONNALLY: He is talking about the World War?

SENATOR NEELY: Are you talking about the World War?

MR. BOWE: The World War, and his staying home and keeping his friends at home. Rabbi Wise, that great man of the Jews, he went into the shipyards for $8 a week, and he is leading us all into another war.

SENATOR NEELY: Did not a great many native-born Protestants and Catholics and non-members of churches do likewise?

MR. BOWE: Yes, sir.

SENATOR NEELY: They worked on the railroads and in the factories and on the farms, and in the mines?

MR. BOWE: Yes, sir.

SENATOR NEELY: That was necessary. They were producing the necessaries of war and life?

MR. BOWE: Yes, sir; but that could have been done by the older men and the younger men who were not of military age. Just a minute, now. Frankfurter was assistant to the Secretary of War, and he was counsel for the Mediation Committee, assistant to the Secretary of Labor, and chairman of the Labor Policies Board. Frankfurter practically dominated the Labor Department. He had control over who went into the shipbuilding yards and who went overseas. He was in a position to get exemptions for his friends.

When the war was over, mind you, there were a number of professors who came back and practically dominated the Labor Department. Not long after 1932, these professors, in connection with the

Council of Foreign Relations, to which Frankfurter also belonged, persuaded the House to pass the legislation that put us into this international labor office in Switzerland. This appointment is going to facilitate and put over this international scheme and put us in whether we want it or not. This gentleman would be in a position to do that.

Now, I would like to say a word about these immigrants coming to this country that will facilitate and promote opening up this question of immigration and naturalization, and also through the financial agencies operating in this country.

SENATOR NEELY: Did Dr. Frankfurter have anything to do with it?

MR. BOWE: He is a part of that committee. Mr. Acheson will tell you more about that. When the treaty of peace came to be signed President Wilson went over there, and there were 119 Jews went over with the President and 38 Christians. These Jews were the men who wrote that treaty of peace. They were on the inside with the other international Jews, and today it is those same men who want to put us into this war; and that is what is going to happen if something is not done about it.

RUTH BENEDICT:

"Jews have learned the hard way, but they have learned, better than any other group, that outrages on Jews in Germany or on Yorkville tenement dwellers are ultimately threats to all Jews." (Circa 1942)

Ruth Benedict (1887–1948), distinguished anthropologist, was thirty-two years old before she became seriously interested in cultural anthropology and ethnology. Graduated from Vassar in 1909, she was first known as a poet, writing under the name of "Anne Singleton." In 1919 she enrolled at Columbia in courses taught by Franz Boas, which she initially regarded

Ruth Benedict, "The Bond of Fellowship" (circa 1942) in Margaret Mead, *An Anthropologist at Work: Writings of Ruth Benedict* (Boston: Houghton Mifflin Company, 1959), pp. 356–357.

as "busy work." Boas' influence was such, however, that she took her Ph.D. degree in 1923, and eventually ranked second only to Boas in the Department of Anthropology at Columbia. One of the first anthropologists to make use of psychoanalytical insights in the comparative study of religions and cultures, her best known books are *Patterns of Culture* (1934), *Race: Science and Politics* (1940), and *The Chrysanthemum and the Sword: Patterns of Japanese Culture* (1946).

The first of the following selections, "The Bond of Fellowship," is from an undated manuscript of Benedict's written circa 1942. The second selection, which deals with certain aspects of the care of Jewish babies in Eastern Europe, is taken from an article first published in the *American Journal of Orthopsychiatry* in 1949. Both selections reflect the author's human as well as anthropological interest in Jewish culture and identity.

From "The Bond of Fellowship"

When I was growing up in the hinterland of America I did not know any Jews. In the public schools I went to, there were no Jews, and, later, it would not have occurred to me to see anything in common among the few Jews I came to know. There was the daughter of the rich clothing merchant, the threadbare student who kept me on my toes discussing European philosophy, and the itinerant peddler who kept the farmers supplied with store goods and who stayed on to swap words of wisdom with my grandfather. They all fell, in my mind and in their own, into the usual American pigeonholes which have to do first and foremost with money income. The clothing merchant's family in Buffalo consorted with the other rich merchants of the city; they made no common cause with itinerant peddler or with schoolboy living on crusts. There was no issue that drew these Jews together.

Anti-Semitism was no issue in my childhood and we thought it had been outmoded. It has been a cruel teacher, but it has laid the basis in the last decades for a Jewish fellowship which overspans all class and national schisms. Jews have learned the hard way, but they have learned, better than any other group, that outrages on Jews in Germany or on Yorkville tenement-dwellers are ultimately threats to all Jews. They have learned too that discriminations against any minority group, whether it is Irish or Negro, Italian or Japanese, are potentially threats to the Jewish minority. They have had to recognize from their own experience that they themselves can live decently only insofar as all human beings have opportunity to live without being the butt of outrages and discriminations.

It is an eternal truth for all men, but human beings have to learn it over and over again from their own experience. Democracy has taken this truth as its foundation stone, but the democracies have been halfhearted. It has to be brought home afresh. And in our great need for drastic reaffirmation of this truth in this war and in the peace to follow, Jews can speak clearly and work courageously. More than any other minority group—and all such groups have learned this lesson also in their own persons—Jews are represented among the rich and the poor, business, the professions, and the trades. They therefore span the usual schisms in American life. More than any other group they are international. They therefore span the great modern schisms among the nations. Jews are therefore in a doubly strategic position. It would be tragedy indeed if any timidities, any wisdom of this world, made them turn their eyes away when affronts are perpetrated. Let them not keep silent. There are many Gentiles who have not yet learned the truth Jews know, and that truth must be made clear to them. No other issue in the world today is of greater importance. America desperately needs those who have learned from their own experience that altruism and self-interest coincide in every effort to secure for all human beings the right and the obligation of full and decent participation in our common life. Such efforts are the bond of fellowship which unite in one great crusade, not only Jews of every nation and of every income; it unites also the Jew and the intelligent Gentile.

From "Child Rearing in Certain European Countries"*

The swaddling of the Jewish baby, whether in Poland or the Ukraine, has characteristics of its own. The baby is swaddled on a soft pillow and in most areas the bindings are wrapped relatively loosely around the baby and his little featherbed. The mother sings to the baby as she swaddles it. The specific stress is upon warmth and comfort, and the incidental confinement of the baby's limbs is

* From "Child Rearing in Certain European Countries," first published in *American Journal of Orthopsychiatry*, XIX, No. 2 (1949), reprinted in *An Anthropologist at Work: Writings of Ruth Benedict*, pp. 449–458.

regarded with pity and commiseration. People say in describing swaddling, "Poor baby, he looks just like a little mummy," or "He lies there nice and warm, but, poor baby, he can't move." Swaddling is also good, especially for boys, because it insures straight legs. There is no suggestion that it is the beginning of a process of "hardening" or that it is necessary because the baby is inherently violent. Rather, it is the baby's first experience of the warmth of life in his own home—a warmth which at three or four he will contrast with the lack of comfort, the hard benches, the long hours of immobility and the beatings at the *cheder*, the elementary Jewish school where he is taught Hebrew. In strongest contrast to the experience of the Gentile child, swaddling is part of the child's induction into the closest kind of physical intimacy; within the family the mother will expect to know every physical detail of her children's lives and treats any attempts at privacy as a lack of love and gratitude. The pillowed warmth of his swaddling period apparently becomes a prototype of what home represents, an image which he will have plenty of opportunity to contrast with the world outside, the world of the *goy*.

It is profitable also to relate Jewish swaddling to another pattern of Eastern European Jewish life: its particular version of complementary interpersonal relations. I am using "complementary" in a technical sense as a designation of those interpersonal relations where the response of a person or group to its vis-à-vis is in terms of an opposite or different behavior from that of the original actors. Such paired actions as dominance-submission, nurturing-dependence, and command-obedience are complementary responses. The Jewish complementary system might be called nurturing-deference. Nurturing is the good deed—*mitzvah*—of all parents, elders, wealthy, wise and learned men toward the children, the younger generation, the poor, and the still unschooled. In interpersonal relations these latter respond to the former with deference, "respect," but not with *mitzvah*. One never is rewarded in a coin of the same currency by one's vis-à-vis, either concurrently with the act or in the future. Parents provide for all their children's needs, but the obligation of the child to the parent does not include support of his aged parents when he is grown, and the saying is: "Better to beg one's bread from door to door than to be dependent on one's son." The aged parent feels this dependence to be humiliating, and this is in strongest contrast to the non-Jews of Poland, for instance, among whom parents can publicly humiliate their children by complaining of nonsupport. Among the Jews, a child's obligation to his parents is discharged by acting toward his own children, when he is grown, as his parents acted toward him. His aged parents are cared for, not by a son in his role as a son, but in his role as a wealthy man, contributing to the poor. Such impersonal benefactions are not humiliating to either party.

The swaddling situation is easily drawn into this Jewish system of complementary relations. The personnel involved in swaddling is necessarily complementary; it includes the binder and the bound. The bound will never reciprocate by binding the binder, and the Jewish binder conceives herself as performing a necessary act of nurturing, out of which she expects the child to experience primarily warmth and comfort; she is rather sorry for the accompanying confinement but she regards random mobility as a sign of the baby's being uncomfortable. She is not, like the Polish mother, "hardening" the baby or preventing indecencies, or like the Russian mother, taking precautions against its destroying itself. She is starting the baby in a way of life where there is a lack of guilt and aggression in being the active partner in all complementary relationships and security in being the passive partner.

REINHOLD NIEBUHR:

"Racial bigots bring all kinds of charges against the Jewish minority; but these charges are rationalizations of a profounder prejudice." (1946)

Reinhold Niebuhr, theologian and philosopher, was born in Missouri in 1892. After graduation from Eden Theological Seminary at St. Louis in 1913, Niebuhr studied at the Yale Divinity School. A pastor for thirteen years in Detroit, Niebuhr in 1928 became an associate professor of the

From Reinhold Niebuhr, *The Children of Light and the Children of Darkness* (New York: Charles Scribner's Sons, 1944; London: James Nisbet & Co. Ltd., 1945), pp. 141–145; copyright 1944 by Charles Scribner's Sons.

philosophy of religion at Union Theological Seminary in New York. Two years later he was appointed professor of applied Christianity, a post which he held for thirty years until his retirement in June, 1960. The holder of numerous honorary degrees from universities in the United States and abroad, he is the author of more than fifteen books and many hundreds of articles.

The selection here reprinted is from *The Children of Light and the Children of Darkness* (1946).

The case of the Jews presents an equally difficult problem for modern democratic society. It must be admitted that bourgeois liberalism did emancipate Jewish life from the restraints of the medieval ghetto. By creating an impersonal society in which money and credit relations became more important than organic ties it laid the foundations for ethnic pluralism. But the hope that the liberties derived from this situation would be infinitely extensible has proved to be mistaken. While fascist mania and fury have aggravated anti-Semitism and while some of the noxious fruits of race prejudice which have recently been harvested in the democratic world must be attributed to seeds scattered by the Nazis, we should be blind to attribute this evil altogether to this one specific cause. The Nazis have accentuated but they did not create racial pride. The ideals of democracy do contradict this pride; but it is an illusion of idealistic children of light to imagine that we can destroy evil merely by avowing ideals. The ideal of racial brotherhood is the "law of God" in which we delight "after the inward man"; but racial arrogance is "the law in our members which wars against the law that is in our mind."

Racial bigots bring all kinds of charges against the Jewish minority; but these charges are rationalizations of a profounder prejudice. The real sin of the Jews is twofold. They are first of all a nation scattered among the nations; and therefore they cannot afford to become completely assimilated within the nations; for that would mean the sacrifice of their ethnic existence. Secondly, they are a group which affronts us by diverging doubly from the dominant type, both ethnically and culturally. It is idle to speculate on whether the primary source of anti-Semitism is racial or religious; for the power of the prejudice is derived from the double divergence. If the Jews were only a religious and not an ethnic group, as some of them claim to be, they would arouse some prejudice by their cultural uniqueness. If they were only a unique ethnic group with the same religion as the majority they would also arouse prejudice. But in either case the prejudice would be more moderate. They are actually an ethnic group with a universalistic religious faith which transcends the values of a single people but which they are forced to use as an instrument of survival in an alien world.

There is no simple solution for a problem of such complexity. No democratic society can afford to capitulate to the pride of dominant groups. The final end of such appeasement is the primitivistic homogeneity of Nazism. On the other hand it is foolish to regard race pride as a mere vestige of barbarism when it is in fact a perpetual source of conflict in human life.

A democratic society must use every strategem of education and every resource of religion to generate appreciation of the virtues and good intentions of minority groups, which diverge from the type of the majority, and to prompt humility and charity in the life of the majority. It must seek to establish contacts between the groups and prevent the aggravation of prejudice through segregation. It must uncover the peculiar hazards to right judgment which reveal themselves in inter-group relations. A democratic society must, in other words, seek proximate solutions for this problem in indeterminate creative ventures. But the solutions will be more, rather than less, creative if democratic idealists understand the depth of the problem with which they are dealing.

Without this understanding the humility necessary for the achievement of democratic good-will is lacking. The foolish children of light are always seeking to mitigate race prejudice merely by championing the minority groups and by seeking to prove that they are not as bad as their detractors claim them to be. This procedure preserves the proud illusion of the majority that its "mind" is the final bar of judgment before which all nations and peoples must be brought. It would be more helpful if we began with the truer assumption that there is no unprejudiced mind and no judgment which is not, at least partially, corrupted by pride. The assumption must include the mind and the judgment of the pure idealists who imagine themselves emancipated of all prejudice in their benevolent condescension.

Upon the basis of such a presupposition we could work indeterminately on many proximate solutions for the problem of ethnic pluralism. Our knowledge that there is no complete solution for the problem would save us from resting in some proximate solution under the illusion that it is an ultimate one.

CHANDLER BROSSARD:

"There is a new Alienated Man around.
He is the Gentile intellectual in New York
City." (1950)

Chandler Brossard is the author of three novels, *Who Walk in Darkness, The Bold Saboteurs,* and, more recently, *The Double View.* He has been involved in magazine publishing and editorial work for a number of years, and at one time was executive editor of *The American Mercury.*
 Brossard's "Plaint of a Gentile Intellectual," here reprinted, first appeared as a *Commentary* article in 1950.

There is a new Alienated Man around. He is the Gentile intellectual in New York City. Hopelessly outnumbered by his Jewish colleagues on the New York intellectual scene, of late he has begun to feel that his back is against the wall.

It is tough enough for the Gentile born in New York, who is at least geographically, if not spiritually, acclimated, but it is at least five times that tough for the Gentile intellectual who immigrated here from some distant city. When he begins to acquire friends he finds, after a while, that somehow most of them are Jewish. (Somewhere in the process the few Gentiles were passed over.) Most, not some, of the smartest people he knows are Jews, and he soon begins to believe that the Jewish intellectual is the only intellectual who is really "hip," that is, in the know, and that the Gentile is "square," or naïve.

So what does he do? The Gentile simultaneously accepts and rejects. Partly consciously, partly unconsciously, he starts assuming some of the wise style of the Jewish intellectual, to overcome what he thinks is his own naïveté, in order to become part of the group surrounding him. The implications of this are almost infinite.

Strange things happen. His vocabulary becomes spiced with Jewish inflections and expressions (his friends teach him the correct pronunciations: he has an increasingly strong tendency to say "nu?" instead of "so?"). His gestures become sensual, curvilinear, and an elaborate and necessary part of his communication. His humor becomes less mirthful—so long, Mark Twain!—and more ironic, twisted, oblique, and gaggy. (If he is a writer this gag quality finally gags him insofar as his originality is concerned.) He cannot remember the last time he told a joke that did not involve a Jew or the Jewish point of view. He becomes much talkier than he ever was, and finds—sometimes with a helpless confusion, even distaste—that part of his enjoyment of any experience, often one of extreme privacy, is talking about it, exploiting it verbally. His own tradition was to withhold, to keep things to himself, not to make everything communal.

He feels, in effect, a kind of clown. His confusion is not helped by the fact that for the first time in his life he is now a member of a minority. It almost seems that he is a kind of extravagance of his Jewish circle; like an extra movie over the weekly ration, uptown and complete with vaudeville. He wonders whether he is ever really being accepted; he feels that his Jewish friends do certain things for each other that they do not do for him. Is he at the center or the periphery?

There was a lot of conversation and suddenly he looks up and sees that his friends have gone off to have a pastrami sandwich.

All this makes him re-examine what he thought were his friendships. He discovers that he has been misled by his Jewish friends' social ease. It was so painless for him to establish what he thought was real rapport: the Jews were so immediately warm and gracious and understanding, so intime, that he felt after a short while as if he had known them for years. He felt this way partly because it actually did take almost years sometimes to reach this same degree of relaxedness and confidence with another Gentile. And when it was reached with a Gentile, after a long and bruising feeling-out period, they had developed in the process a real friendship, and were committed to each other. So he experiences considerable shock when his Jewish friends, whom he mistakenly thinks have been with him through almost everything, suddenly treat him with the casualness of an acquaintance. But it is his own fault, he soon realizes: his friends had never signed a blood pact with him, he just thought they had.

It is only after a long groping period that he begins to understand his Jewish intellectual friends in New York. Particularly those in Greenwich Village.

Never before, for instance, has he seen so much concern with an individual style, so much intensive self-conscious development of a "personality."

He sees the young Jewish poet who wants to seem like an underworld character, talking and thinking out of the corner of his mouth, his every public move calculated to encourage this personality myth. While the other person in this cultivated schizophrenia is the soft, boy-faced poet protectedly experiencing his baroque emotional reactions to life unseen by the gullible public. And he looks on with suspended judgment as this poet shows him the way to turn an image into a gimmick.

He watches the under-thirty Jewish writer of Kafkaesque fiction who seems to have trouble choosing between the role of an American cowboy with blue denim pants and checked shirt, slouch-walking as best he can, prairie-swept, or on the other hand the avuncular academician from Minsk, with accents and gestures and style so rich and convincing you will almost swear he offered you a sip from that steaming glass of tea you are sure he was holding. And our friend the goy, remembering one story that sounded like a translation from the German, reads something else by this man that extends the confusion even further because it sounds like Ring Lardner.

Another of his friends wants to be known as an athlete, and is constantly proposing a boxing match at the gym, or a swimming race under water, or a run around the mile track, or a tennis match on an equatorial day. Actually he is quite frail, and is shy about being a painter.

The Gentile at first takes all this seriously. It is—or was—his habit to play it straight, to maintain a personality and behavior consonant with what he believes to be his real or true self. He then gets the feeling that his Jewish friends are smiling at him because he is so straight. What happens? He often winds up playing straight man to his friends at a nearly all-Jewish party. All those true words said in jest. . . .

After a while he stumbles into certain back corners of the lives of his Jewish friends.

He visits Coney Island. Here he sees the blurred shifting faces of his Jewish friends as they grew up. The whole place is one vast objective correlative—the Castles in the sand, the continually moving juxtaposition of youth and age and group sexual pursuit and sightseeing and shrieking on the boardwalk, the shooting galleries where the dead ducks flip alive at the next turn, the three-for-a-quarter reproductions of posed absurdity, the hot dogs with sauerkraut and onions and India relish, the sudden strength that rings a bell on a tall pole, the giant laughing woman being endlessly tickled by a machine.

He comes away wiser than he was, linking a gesture on the boardwalk to a line in a lyric, a certain quick scene to a gibe he had heard two weeks ago at a party, a barker's spiel to a book reviewer's technique. He taps his pocket to see if his passport is still there.

Then he visits a home in Brooklyn. The front living room with the brand-new-looking furniture (the caul still protecting the lampshade) stiffly arranged as if waiting for the principal speaker of the evening. The strong, loving, almost masculine mother who still hovers around her son even though he is now in his late twenties. (Where was that caul? Over the lampshade?) He senses with increasing uneasiness that the Jewish mother would like to stroke him too as he sits there. He listens to his friend's continual reminiscences about his childhood and his schooldays. His finest years. And the combination of Bubbe and cookies turns up with the regularity of a creditor. He, the goy, feels the compulsion to keep these objects and areas in his already finished past. Perhaps because they were so depressing, so full of unexpressed rage and unlove.

Now, perhaps, he understands the situation somewhat better. He sees the Jewish intellectual in New York as a person actually very different from himself, in cultural tradition almost opposed, and then, perhaps for the first time, he discovers himself for what he is traditionally. (His circle of intellectual friends has indirectly told him he is actually the bourgeois, playing around intellectualism "for kicks"—though they say this with envy.) He has the choice now of recognizing his background and origins, his differences, and living accordingly, or of denying them and reshaping himself with the help, or proximity, of his Jewish friends. The temptation to submit to reshaping is strong; it is hard to be different in these surroundings.

But if the Gentile submits, then his ambivalence becomes acute, and he thinks his helpmates are patronizingly corrupting him, and where once he may have considered himself, jokingly, as the All-American Goy, he now thinks of himself as the Inauthentic Goy. But even this new alienation of his seems a Jewish literary brand of alienation, not his own raw brand.

If, on the other hand, he rejects the influences around him, his reaction is often stronger than is necessary, his behavior more separate, and he hears his friends remark that something is wrong with him lately, he is acting so strange. Those Gentile neurotics, they're so wild. He wonders if he even knows how to be properly neurotic. (Once he dreamed he had been turned into a goat and was about to be dispatched into the wilderness of his Jewish friends.)

What can he do? He does not intend to leave New York. (Everybody knows you can't go back home.) Paris? Who wants to go to Paris? He cannot afford, yet, to be psychoanalyzed. His friends kid him about the possibility of changing his name. One of them even suggested that maybe the American Jewish Committee would eventually set up a fund for the investigation of his dilemma. Meanwhile, here he is at *Commentary*.

EDMUND WILSON:

*"Thus if the outlook of Judaism seems
somewhat bleak, if its observances—to a
non-Jew—mean little, some contact with it
is nonetheless bracing. We are living with
God in an empty room—in a room without
pictures: the synagogue, where the only
things displayed on the walls are
words." (1956)*

Edmund Wilson, critic and novelist, was born in 1895. Following graduation from Princeton in 1916, he became a reporter for the New York *Evening Sun*. In 1920–1921, he was managing editor of *Vanity Fair,* and in 1926 he was appointed book review editor of *The New Republic*. He was associate editor of *The New Republic* when he resigned from the magazine in 1931 to devote more time to writing. Since 1944 Wilson has served as literary critic for *The New Yorker*. His numerous books include *Axel's Castle* (1931), a volume of literary criticism, and *To the Finland Station* (1940), a study of the Marxist revolutionary movement which culminated, in 1917, with Lenin's trip across Germany to the Finland Station in St. Petersburg (now Leningrad).

I have had, in the course of my reading, three somewhat similar experiences. It happened that I had never read Voltaire till after I already knew well the work of a number of writers—Stendhal, Flaubert, Anatole France—who owed a good deal to his spirit and tone. These are all, in their various fashions, deliberately artistic writers in a way that Voltaire was not. They are predominantly novelists and aphorists, whereas Voltaire was a fast-producing journalist, with a style based on conversation. In Voltaire, the bright mocking attack is something so completely natural that ironic effects do not need to be built up; the witticisms are never planted:

Edmund Wilson, "The Jews," in *A Piece of My Mind: Reflections at Sixty* (New York: Farrar, Straus & Cudahy), pp. 85–107, © 1956 by Edmund Wilson, © 1956 by the American Jewish Committee. A part of this selection was originally published in *Commentary*.

they are spontaneous and over in a flash, like the quick striking of a match, almost before the reader knows it. One realized that here was the essence—in its free original form—of an element one had only encountered as the leaven in substantial loaves.

When, later on, I came to read Pushkin, I recognized that here was the artistic model as well as the humane spirit that had dominated Russian literature. The foreigner who does not know this model is likely to remain unaware of certain of the admirable qualities that make the Russian writers he does know effective. It has been usual for Western readers to assume in the case of Turgenev that he must owe his perfect balance and his nice sense of form, his restraint and his ironic portraiture, to imitation of Western models. But all this is to be found in Pushkin, and nothing could be more misleading than the belief, so prevalent abroad, that it is typical of Russian literature to be formless, prolix and hysterical. The reader of translations from the Russian can know nothing of Russian poetry, which has never lost Pushkin's mold: a classical regularity and a concise epigrammatic turn that make the quatrains of A. E. Housman peculiarly congenial to Russians. In fiction, the Western critic—who has concluded from Constance Garnett's translations that Russian novelists all write very much alike—pushes Turgenev aside as an exception; takes Gogol as a gross farceur, a kind of prose Russian Rowlandson; regards Tolstoy as the lavish compiler of an uneven and fatiguing epic and Dostoevsky as an inspired madman. Henry James's strictures on the Russians are typical of the Western attitude: Tolstoy and Dostoevsky are "fluid puddings, though not tasteless . . . thanks to the strong rank quality of their genius and their experience . . . we see how great a vice is their lack of composition, their defiance of economy and architecture"; "I have been reading over Tolstoy's interminable *War and Peace*. . . . He doesn't *do* to read over, and that exactly is the answer to those who idiotically proclaim the impunity of such formless shape, such flopping looseness and such a denial of composition, selection and style." Yet *War and Peace*, which was several times rewritten and from which Tolstoy eliminated about a third of the original material, is a masterpiece of economy and organization. Like the prose and verse tales of Pushkin and his miniature dramas in verse, each one of Tolstoy's little episodes exactly makes its picture, its point, and none of them is allowed to go on too long. In the balance of personalities that provides the system of stresses and strains on which the novel rests, Tolstoy also follows the Pushkinian tradition—established in *Evgeni Onegin*—which gives its structure to Turgenev's work. The devotion and sobriety of Princess Marie set off the electric vitality and the reckless self-abandonment of Natasha; the three men—Pierre, Prince André and Nikolai Rostov—maintain a steady equilibrium between three fundamental types: the idealist inept at life, the serious and responsible aristocrat and the nonintellectual natural man. There is, also, in Tolstoy as in Pushkin, a detached and ironical point of view that is closer to the comic than the tragic, and which even the self-righteous moralizing that commences in *Anna Karenina* can never entirely destroy. Dostoevsky *is* really diffuse, a creator through whom his creation is rushing to get itself down; but his work is not in the least, as Hugh Walpole, in reply to the complaints above, called it in a letter to Henry James, a "mad jumble that flings things down in a heap." You have also in Dostoevsky the balance of personalities: Myshkin and Rogozhin in *The Idiot*, the three brothers Karamazov, representing a different trinity from Tolstoy's; and you have also a dramatization which seems to me much more objective, rather closer to the ideal of comedy than to the traditional pattern of tragedy—in spite of the horrors involved— than even many Russians grant. I felt this in Dostoevsky before I had ever read Pushkin; but the reading of Pushkin confirmed it and enabled me to appreciate, in general, the classicism of Russian literature: the clear observation, the matching of opponents, the coolness of resolution.

A similar revelation comes out of the Hebrew Bible. The Hebrew religious conceptions, the imagery of the Hebrew scriptures have been an element of literature in English from the King James translation on. This is, of course, especially strong in Milton, who knew Hebrew at first hand; but the pregnant phrases of the Bible, its apocalyptic visions, are a part of the texture of our language. The culture of no other Western people seems so deeply to have been influenced by these: something in the English character, something mystical, tough and fierce, has a special affinity to Hebrew. Yet the strong Hebrew strain in English is to some extent at variance with the influence of the Greek and Roman tradition. In proportion as one inclines toward this latter, one is likely to resent the other. In my own case, I followed, in my youth, the line of reaction then common against old-fashioned Bible-worship, the recoil from the rigors of Calvinism. Yet my grandfather on my father's side was a Presbyterian minister, though a very moderate one, and when my parents went to church on Sunday, they would leave me with my formidable grandmother, who undertook my instruction in the Scriptures. These bleak and severe Sunday mornings, though they left me with a respect for the Bible, had the effect of antagonizing me against it, and this attitude was tacitly encouraged by the moral sabotage of my mother, whose family, once rigorous New Englanders, had scrapped the old-time religion and still retained a certain animus toward it. At college, I was enchanted by classical Greek, and, though I made a point of reading through the Gospels, I told myself how immeasurably much I preferred Socrates to Jesus. Later on, I elected the second half of a course in Old Testament literature. I already admired Ecclesiastes, and—though finding Ezekiel tedious—I tried to do justice to the Prophets. It was not till much later, in my fifties, that I acquired a little Hebrew, and, for a third time, I had the experience of finding myself in contact with something in its pure and original form that I had previously only known in compounds or adaptations. The strangeness of this element in English became a good deal more comprehensible when one was able to take account, not only of the structural differences between the Semitic languages and the Teutonic and Latin ones, but also of the difference from ours of the oriental way of apprehending the world that these structural divergences reflected. I have written about this elsewhere at length, so I merely want here to note that an acquaintance with the Hebrew Bible is at once to make the Biblical narratives sound a good deal more simple and natural— the archaic Jacobean English still today partly screens them from us—and to compel one to pay attention to certain fundamental discrepancies between the Hebrew way of thinking and ours. The language of Jehovah and his worshippers, which seems in English grandiose and mysterious, may not, even in Gesenius' dictionary, become to us readily intelligible and render itself in familiar terms; but here at least we can meet at first hand this vocabulary and these locutions, try to form some idea of their meaning to the men who first coined and employed them to deal with their objective and subjective worlds—or rather, with the moral continuum that embraced the phenomena of both. It is useful to approach the Bible with a scholarly dictionary and commentary—for otherwise it is bound, more or less, to remain an esoteric text, a repository of tales for children, a dream book, a compendium of incantations. The Jews—who have lost touch with the original text—have been interpreting it for a couple of thousand years in ever more far-fetched and fantastic ways. The Christians have been equally fantastic—beginning with the extravagances of Justin Martyr—in reading back into it the coming of Christ; and the old lady who was infinitely grateful for that blessed word *Mesopotamia* was only an extreme case of the Christian dependence on Scripture for this sort of consolation. Some of the oddest features of the Bible, as we get it through our Jacobean version, are simply due to mistranslations. So Joseph's coat of many colors was in reality a coat with long sleeves; so Moses had sprouting from his head, not horns, but rays of light. Yet the horns of Moses and the many-colored coat are as hard to get out of one's head, unless one sees what they are in the original, as the images in nursery rhymes. Many mysteries, of course, remain. Some are puzzles of vocabulary or grammar: there are, in the text of the Bible, something like five hundred words that do not occur anywhere else, and the copyists have made mistakes. But it is difficult, also, to adjust oneself to certain fundamental features of the Hebrew way of looking at things, and, though there is constant speculation on these matters, they are now so remote from our habits of thought that some scholars believe we must give them up. In any case, we find here—with the language they have minted—the religio-legal codes and the lofty prophetic poetry, the wisdom derived from experience and the permanently significant legends, the influence of which, refracted by the organisms of other mentalities, have reached distant countries and distant times. Here it is, that old tongue, with its clang and its flavor, sometimes rank, sometimes sweet, sometimes bitter; here it is in its concise solid stamp. Other cultures have felt its impact, and none—in the West, at least—seems quite to accommodate it. Yet we find we have been living with it all our lives.

Thus the Gentile of American Puritan stock who puts himself in contact with the Hebrew culture finds something at once so alien that he has to make a special effort in order to adjust himself to it, and something that is perfectly familiar. The Puritanism of New

England was a kind of new Judaism, a Judaism transposed into Anglo-Saxon terms. These Protestants, in returning to the text of the Bible, had concentrated on the Old Testament, and some had tried to take it as literally as any Orthodox Jew. The Judaic observances in New England were reduced to honoring the Sabbath on Sunday, but the attendance at the house of worship and the cessation from work on this day approached in their rigor the Jewish practice; and in England "certain extremists," says Mr. Cecil Roth, in his *History of the Jews in England,* had "regarded the 'old' dispensation as binding, and even reverted to its practices of circumcision and the observance of the seventh-day Sabbath. In 1600, the Bishop of Exeter complained of the prevalence of 'Jewism' in his diocese, and such views were comparatively common in London and the Eastern counties. Numerous persons were prosecuted here for holding what were termed 'Judaistic' opinions, based on the literal interpretations of the Old Testament. As late as 1612, two so-called Arians died at the stake (the last persons to suffer capital punishment in England purely for their religion) for teaching views regarding the nature of God which approximated to those of Judaism. The followers of the Puritan extremist, John Traske, went so far on the path of literalism that they were imprisoned in 1618-20 on a charge of Judaizing. In this case, the accusation was so far from being exaggerated that a number of them settled in Amsterdam and formally joined the synagogue."

When the Puritans came to America, they identified George III with Pharaoh and themselves with the Israelites in search of the Promised Land. They called their new country Canaan and talked continually of the Covenant they had made with God. Winthrop and Bradford were Moses and Joshua; Anne Hutchinson was pilloried as Jezebel. "The Christian church so-called," said a preacher in New Marlborough, Massachusetts, "is only a continuation and extension of the Jewish church." "If we keep this covenant," said Winthrop, "we shall finde then the God of Israel is among us." The Hebrew language, later on in New England, was to be taught as a major subject, not merely in the colleges but even in the schools.

All this, of course, is well enough known. There is an interesting chapter on the subject, to which I am indebted for the facts above—in a volume by various hands called *The Hebrew Impact on Western Civilization—Hebraic Foundations of American Democracy* by

Abraham I. Katsh. Yet we tend to forget how close our original relationship was to the Old Testament Jewish tradition. Our conception itself of America as a country with a mission in the world comes down to us from our Mosaic ancestors. We are told by Harriet Beecher Stowe that she had always felt in her childhood, after reading Cotton Mather's *Magnolia*, that "the very ground I stood on [in New England] was consecrated by some special dealing of God's providence"; and, even in our own time, Santayana, in *The Last Puritan*, has made one of his New England characters say: "We were always a circumcised people, consecrated to great expectations." The Gentile American however, is no longer aware of this in his attitude toward Judaism, and the American Jew does not recognize in what is left of the Puritan tradition a Gentile imitation of Judaism. I have recently been collecting examples of the persistence through the nineteenth century of the New Englander's deep-rooted conviction that the Jews are a special people selected for a unique role by God, and that New England somehow shares this destiny.

Perhaps the most curious of these is the rabbinical metamorphosis of the Hebrew scholar Calvin Ellis Stowe, the husband of Harriet Beecher. That Harriet was herself very close to the Pilgrims' self-identification with Israel is indicated not merely by the passage above but again and again elsewhere in her writings. She will, for example, open a chapter of *Poganuc People* with the statement that "Zeph Higgins was a good Jew." This does not mean that the pious Connecticut farmer was literally of Jewish blood, but simply that he tried to conform to the New England version of the Jewish code. "Zephaniah Pennel," she writes, in *The Pearl of Orr's Island*, "was what might be called a Hebrew of the Hebrews. New England, in her earlier days, founding her institutions on the Hebrew Scriptures, bred better Jews than Moses could, because she read Moses with the amendments of Christ. The state of society in some of the districts of Maine, in these days, much resembled in its spirit that which Moses labored to produce in ruder ages. It was entirely democratic, simple, grave, hearty and sincere—solemn and religious in its daily tone, and yet, as to all material good, full of wholesome thrift and prosperity." And again, in *Old Town Folks:* "I think no New Englander, brought up under the regime established by the Puritans could really estimate how much of himself had actually been formed by this constant face-to-face intimacy with Hebrew literature. . . . My grandfather [at family prayers] always prayed standing, and the image of his mild, silvery head, leaning over the top of the high-backed chair, always rises before me as I think of early days. There was no great warmth or fervor in those daily exercises, but rather a serious and decorous propriety. They were Hebraistic in their form; they spoke of Zion and Jerusalem, of the God of Israel, the God of Jacob, as much as if my grandfather had been a veritable Jew; and except for the closing phrase, 'for the sake of Thy Son, our Savior,' might all have been uttered in Palestine by a well-trained Jew in the time of David." Now, Calvin Stowe, in his Hebraic studies, went on from the Bible to the Talmud, and he prepared a pioneering study of this later difficult work, in which Harriet attempted in vain to interest the *Atlantic Monthly.* He allowed his beard and his hair to grow and wore habitually a rabbinical skullcap, and, with his spectacles, he presents in his photographs an appearance that would have adorned any synagogue. He liked to pose with a New Testament—in some curious unbooklike form, perhaps masquerading as a Torah scroll—held up before him like Moses' Tablets. His wife was in the habit of referring to him as "my old rabbi" or simply "Old Rab." It may be that, in the case of Calvin Stowe, his Judaizing was a parallel development to that which eventually led Harriet to become an Episcopalian. Harriet had arrived by that time at a full and outspoken revolt against the Calvinist doctrines of Original Sin and salvation through Election; and it may be that Calvin, in a quieter way—he had to teach in Calvinist seminaries—was exemplifying a similar tendency. In Judaism, the Protestant of the Puritan tradition finds the spiritual austerity he already knows, but not bedevilled—the word is exact—by the fear of a despotic Deity who seems to favor or condemn by whim. The Jewish God may be retributory and terrible but he is not preoccupied with torment, not a perpetrator of nasty surprises as the Calvinist God was.

The most extreme case, however, of an atavistic obsession with the Jews on the part of a well-educated New Englander is that of James Russell Lowell. His mania on this subject is mentioned, in a letter to Charles Eliot Norton, by his English friend Leslie Stephen. "He was so delighted," says Stephen, "with his ingenuity in discovering that everybody was in some way descended from the Jews because he had some Jewish feature, or a Jewish name, or a Gentile name such as the Jews were in the habit of assuming, or because he was connected with one of the departments of business or the geographical regions in which Jews are generally to be found, that it was scarcely possible to mention any distinguished man who could not be conclusively proved to be connected with the chosen race. The logic sometimes seemed to his hearers to have trifling defects; but that was all the greater proof of a sagacity which could dispense with strict methods of proof. To say the truth, this was the only subject upon which I could conceive Lowell approaching within measurable distance of boring." And an anonymous reporter, in the *Atlantic Monthly*, of "Conversations with Mr. Lowell"—quoted in the biography of Lowell by Horace Elisha Scudder—describes in detail such a disquisition.

"At the mention of some medieval Jew," he says, "Lowell at once began to talk of the Jews, a subject which turned out to be almost a monomania with him. He detected a Jew in every hiding place and under every disguise, even when the fugitive had no suspicion of himself. To begin with nomenclature: all persons named for countries or towns are Jews; all with fantastic, compound names, such as Lilienthal, Morgenroth; all with names derived from colors, trades, animals, vegetables, minerals; all with Biblical names, except Puritan first names; all patronymics ending in son, sohn, sen, or any other versions; all Russels, originally so called from red-haired Israelites; all Walters, by long-descended derivation from wolves and foxes in some ancient tongue; the Caecilii, therefore Cecilia Metella, no doubt St. Cecilia, too, consequently the Cecils, including Lord Burleigh and Lord Salisbury; he cited some old chronicle in which he had cornered one Robert de Caecilia and exposed him as an English Jew. He gave examples and instances of these various classes with amazing readiness and precision, but I will not pretend that I have set down even these correctly. Of course there was Jewish blood in many royal houses and in most noble ones, notably in Spain. In short, it appeared that this insidious race had penetrated and permeated the human family more universally than any other influence except original sin. He spoke of their talent and versatility, and of the numbers who had been illustrious in literature, the learned professions, art, science, and even war, until by degrees, from being shut out of society and every honorable and desirable pursuit, they had gained the prominent positions everywhere.

"Then he began his classifications again: all bankers were Jews, likewise brokers, most of the great financiers,—and that was to be expected; the majority of barons, also baronets; they had got possession of the press, they were getting into politics; they had forced their entrance into the army and navy; they had made their way into the cabinets of Europe and become prime ministers; they had slipped into diplomacy and become ambassadors. But a short time ago they were packed into the Ghetto: and now they inhabited palaces, the most aristocratic quarters, and were members of the most exclusive clubs. A few years ago they could not own land; they were acquiring it by purchase and mortgage in every part of Europe, and buying so many old estates in England that they owned the larger part of several counties.

"Mr. Lowell said more, much more, to illustrate the ubiquity, the universal ability of the Hebrew, and gave examples and statistics for every statement, however astonishing, drawn from his inexhaustible information. He was conscious of the sort of infatuation which possessed him, and his dissertation alternated between earnestness and drollery; but whenever a burst of laughter greeted some new development of his theme, although he joined in it, he immediately returned to the charge with abundant proof of his paradoxes. Finally he came to a stop, but not to a conclusion, and as no one else spoke, I said, 'And when the Jews have got absolute control of finance, the army and navy, the press, diplomacy, society, titles, the government, and the earth's surface, what do you suppose they will do with them and with us?' 'That,' he answered, turning towards me, and in a whisper audible to the whole table, 'that is the question which will eventually drive me mad.'"

Though Lowell admired the Jews, he conceived them as a power so formidable that they seemed on the verge of becoming a menace. In this vision of a world run entirely by Jews there is something of morbid suspicion, something of the state of mind that leads people to believe in the *Protocols of Zion*, in a Jewish international conspiracy to dominate the civilized world.

But, before trying to get to the sources from which this delusion springs, let me give another example of New England Pan-Judaic doctrine. It might be thought that Barrett Wendell of Harvard was the perfect type of old-fashioned snob in regard to every kind of American not of strictly Anglo-Saxon origins, yet we find him—on October 18, 1891—writing to his father as follows: "I heard a queer theory the other day about the Yankee Puritans, whose religious views were so strongly Hebraic. They came chiefly, it seems, from Norfolk and Lincolnshire. These counties, some two or three centuries before the Reformation, had been the chief strongholds of the English Jews, who were finally expelled from the kingdom by one of the Plantagenet kings. At the time of the expulsion, many changed their faith and remained to be absorbed in the native population. It is wholly possible, then, that the Yankee Puritan, with all his Old Testament feeling, was really, without knowing it, largely Jewish in blood. There is in the Yankee nature much that would give color to the theory; but of course it is very far from being a proved fact. . . ." Is there any actual evidence for this or have we here simply a recrudescence of the Judaizing tendency of the Puritan?

I have noted that Lowell's prophecy of a universal Jewish dominance seems to skirt the state of mind of those who believe in the *Protocols of Zion*. It is possible to cite examples of a glorification of the Jews that has passed suddenly into a neurotic anti-Semitism. Such an example was the late John Jay Chapman. He was a mixture of New York and New England, but the New England strain in him was very strong. His grandmother had been a lieutenant of William Lloyd Garrison, whom (Garrison) Chapman very much admired and about whom he wrote a book. Especially in this connection his relations with the Jews are significant. "There is a depth of human feeling in the Jew," he wrote in a memorandum of 1897, "that no other race ever possessed. We do no more than imitate it and follow it. David, for instance, and his conduct about Uriah's wife and the child that died—and Absalom—and Jonathan. Compare the Greek— the Chinese, the Roman. These Jews are more human than any other men. It is the cause of the spread of their religion—for we are all adopted into Judah. The heart of the world is Jewish. There is the same spirit in the Old Testament as in the New. What monstrous perversion—that we should worship their God and despise themselves! We admire the Pyramids and the Egyptians, but the history of the Jews is the most remarkable, the most notable thing, on the

globe. Their sacred books and chronicles and traditions and history
make the annals of every other nation mere rubbish—and I feel this
same power in the Jews I know. They are the most humane and
the strongest people morally, mentally and physically. They persist.
I'm glad I'm a Jew. I believe that's the reason why this paper-faced
civilization impresses me so little. Take Habakkuk," etc. (It was
true that Chapman looked rather Jewish, and he wore an impressive
beard in a period when beards had ceased to be fashionable; but
neither Chapman himself in his memoirs, nor his biographer, Mr.
M. A. deWolfe Howe, records that he had Jewish blood.)

This pro-Semitism was unquestionably to some extent due to
Chapman's political dependence on a devoted Jewish friend, Mr.
Isaac H. Klein of New York, who worked with him in his efforts
at reform. "The Jews have in my experience," he writes in a letter
dated from Wall Street, a little later in 1897, "more faith than the
Christians. They have clever heads, better hearts and more belief
in the power of good every way. They gave to the world all the
religion it has got and are themselves the most religious people in
it. I work with them day and night and most of the time is spent
in prying up some Christian to do a half day's work."

But between the eighteen nineties and the nineteen twenties,
Chapman's attitude toward the Jews underwent an astonishing
change. One gets the impression from a letter, written from Atlantic
City, of December, 1919, that his disillusion may have begun with
the spectacle of crowds of vacationing Jews who did not strike him
as being the equals of Habakkuk and Isaac Klein: "They are uncritical," he now writes. "Life is a simple matter to them: a bank
account and the larder. No, they will never rule the world. They
are too easily deflected—absorbed and satisfied. It is foolish to rule
the world and the Jew knows it. They are crumbling material for
the hands of their leaders, and ropes of sand. They have too much
sense—and will go for the glittering garments and not murder
Progress. They strike me as an inferior race, in spite of their great
advantages. . . . But to return to the Jews, my long acquaintance
with Klein and his club makes me at home with them—but I'm glad
I haven't *more* Jewish blood in me than I have. I don't want any
more. These people don't know anything. They have no religion, no
customs except eating and drinking."

Note here again the specter of Jewish power. As Chapman

watches a crowd of Jews behaving in a perfectly natural way, he
concludes that they will not "rule the world." Why should he have
expected them to?—and why should he be surprised that these citizens from New York and Philadelphia show an interest in their
larders and their bank accounts? Do Americans of other stocks not
give evidence of similar interests? Later on, he went even further
and began to link the Jews with the Catholics in his attacks on the
Catholic church. He actually got to the point of publishing in an
organ of the Ku Klux Klan—the *National Kourier* of May 29, 1925—
the following queer anti-Semitic sonnet:

CAPE COD, ROME AND JERUSALEM

How restful is it to survey the sea
From some low, windswept, silvery, sandy dune,
And watch the eternal climbing of the moon
Full-orbed, above the shore's complacency;
Wondering the while if Asian plains there be,
Or rock-walled valleys, never shined upon—
Save by the perpendicular sun at noon—
So safe, so guarded, so remote as we.
But see, a sail!—nay more—from every land
They cloud the ocean, convoyed by a crew
Of Master Pirates who have work in hand:
Old Europe's nation-wreckers heave in view!
And lo, to aid them, on our margin stand
Our citizens—the Jesuit and the Jew.

There is, I think, involved in Chapman's case, as perhaps in
Lowell's also, a special relation to the Judaic element in the Puritan
New England tradition. This tradition came to life again—after a
partial eclipse during the early eighteen hundreds—in the Abolitionist crusade against slavery that inspired so much of the ardor of the
Federal forces in the Civil War. *The Battle Hymn of the Republic*
comes straight out of the Biblical Prophets, and the Jehovah of the
Old Testament takes the field again at the head of the Federal
armies. In the period before the war, Lowell had been stirred by
this fervor—under the influence, it is said, of his first wife—and had
worked for the Abolitionist cause; John Jay Chapman, who was
proud of his grandmother, and had relived the Abolitionist movement in writing his book about Garrison, had once travelled to a

Pennsylvania town where a Negro had been burned alive to hold an expiatory meeting—a meeting at which he was the only speaker and to which only two people came. Both Lowell and Chapman, in their later years, more or less dropped crusading, somewhat lapsed in their faith. The former, ambassador to the Court of St. James, became an official figure; the latter, having married a well-to-do wife, became the proprietor of a country estate and a somewhat petulant critic of everyone in literature and politics who was playing a more active part than he. Both, perhaps, had a bad conscience. In Lowell's case he seems half to hope, half to fear, that the Puritan-Jewish Jehovah is going to take over the world; in Chapman's case, he seems—not admitting it—to be gnawed by a sense of guilt toward the moral inspiration of the Jews in which he has felt he shared: he accuses lest he stand condemned.

But there is something else, too, in this curious shift from a faith in the Jews to a fear of them. The basic thing here, I believe, is that the Jews have been all too successful in convincing the rest of the world of their privileged relations with God. They have made it all too easy for visionary people—that is, people like themselves—to assume that there is something supernatural about them. What Chapman, who has idealized the Jews on the evidence of the Bible and of his friend Mr. Klein, was so startled one day to realize, on the boardwalk at Atlantic City, was that German or Russian or Polish or Lithuanian Jewish Americans were human beings like everyone else. And yet for a certain type of mind—the apocalyptical kind—it is difficult to accept this conclusion. For such a mind, an awe of the Jews persists but it takes on a different aspect. It may turn to the extreme anti-Semitism of Hitler and Henry Ford—both idealistic cranks—which, as Waldo Frank has said in his study *The Jew in Our Day,* is a department of demonology. Or it may merely— as in Lowell's case—survive as a superstition, an uneasiness in the presence of something unknown, an uncomfortable apprehension. These people, unique in their cohesiveness, their inbreeding, their self-isolation, so impressive in their sureness of their contact with God, is there not something queer about them? Do they not possess special powers? May they not be masters of a magic that enables them to intrigue against us, to demoralize, subvert, destroy us? Nor is it, I think, out of the question that we ourselves, deep in our "psyches," may consider it correct that we should thus be destroyed

THE JEW IN AMERICA

in punishment for our own apostasy, our apostasy toward, precisely, the Jewish God—that apostasy of which the two Testaments have combined, at the basis of our moral training, to implant in us the sense of danger?

An odd non-American example of this tendency to credit the Jews with supernatural powers is to be found in the novels of George du Maurier. I have not been able to discover in any of the biographical material about him that du Maurier himself had a Jewish strain; but in each of his three novels a rather unexpected Jewish theme plays a more or less important role. In the first of these, *Peter Ibbetson,* we are told of the mother of Colonel Ibbetson that she "had been the only child and heiress of an immensely rich pawnbroker, by name Mendoza; a Portuguese Jew, with a dash of colored blood in his veins, besides, it was said." But Peter himself is a nephew of the Colonel's on the latter's *paternal* side, and the Jewish character here is the villain. In *The Martian,* on the other hand, the third of the series, a woman with Jewish blood is the heroine. We are told of Leah Gibson that "her mother . . . was a Spanish Jewess—a most magnificent and beautiful old person in splendid attire, tall and straight, with white hair and thick black eyebrows, and large eyes as black as night. In Leah the high Sephardic Jewish type was more marked than in Mrs. Gibson. . . . It is a type that sometimes, just now and again, can be so pathetically noble and beautiful in a woman, so suggestive of chastity and the most passionate love combined—love conjugal and filial and maternal—love that implies all the big practical obligations and responsibilities of human life, that the mere term 'Jewess' (and especially its French equivalent) brings to my mind some vague, mysterious, exotically poetic image of all I love best in woman." But in the intermediate *Trilby,* du Maurier's conception of the Jew is developed in a major and a very strange way. We are told, in the first place, of Little Billee, one of the three British art students in Paris about whom the story centers, that "in his winning and handsome face there was just a faint suggestion of some possible very remote Jewish ancestor—just a tinge of that strong, sturdy, irrepressible, indomitable, indelible blood which is of such priceless value in diluted homeopathic doses, like the dry white Spanish wine called Montijo, which is not meant to be taken pure; but without a judicious admixture of which no sherry can go round the world and keep its flavor intact; or like the famous bull-dog strain, which is not beautiful in itself; and yet just for lacking a little of the same no greyhound can ever be a champion." Little Billee is thus the only one of the three companions who is shown to possess any genuine talent. But the great Jewish character in *Trilby* is, of course, the German Jewish Svengali: the fabulous musician who cannot sing but who, by hypnotizing the tone-deaf Trilby and exploiting her wonderful voice, makes of her a great artist. Svengali, in other connections, is always represented as everything that these gentlemanly Britishers most abhor: he is dirty, insulting, boastful, mendacious, malicious, quarrelsome; they have constantly to put him in his place. Yet Trilby, in spite of her voice, has not only no ear whatever for music, no range of emotion or expression which would be adequate, even if she had one, to achieve the astounding effects which Svengali is able to teach her by turning her into a simple automaton. The concert—described at great length—at which Trilby so triumphantly sings, is "the apotheosis of voice and virtuosity"; she sounds like a combination of Adelina Patti and Yvette Guilbert. Yet—except for the voice itself—the whole thing is an emanation of Svengali's musical soul; and if this is true, the horrid Svengali must have, after all, as Bernard Shaw says, "better grounds for [his] egotism than anybody else in the book except Little Billee and Trilby." But from whence does all this subtlety and innocence, this tenderness and joy and sorrow, arise in the Svengali we know? There is no explanation of this: the character, in human terms, is not in any deep sense created. What is really behind Svengali is the notion, again, that the Jew, even in his squalidest form, is a mouthpiece of our Judaico-Christian God, whose voice he has, in this case, transferred, ventriloquially, to the throat of Trilby. There is always in these novels of du Maurier's—binational, bilingual as he was—a certain light playing-off of French civilization against English; but the picture is further complicated—it is one of the things that make them interesting—by this dual role of the Jew, who appears—in Colonel Ibbetson, Svengali in his ordinary relations— now as a malignant devil, whose malignancy is hardly accounted for; now—in Leah, Little Billee and the Svengali who animates Trilby—as a spirit from an alien world who carries with it an uncanny prestige, who may speak in a divine tongue.

In the meantime, for the Jew—or for many Jews—it must become

almost as embarrassing to be taken for a Hebrew prophet on con-
fidential terms with God as for a diabolical demiurge who is out
to "murder Progress"—whatever Chapman meant by that. I remember a clear illustration of this in a story told of himself by Dr. Paul
Tillich of Union Theological Seminary in a discussion after one of
his seminars. Dr. Tillich explained that he had never at first approved of the Zionist movement. He had thought it a good thing
that a group—the Jews—should survive in the modern world to represent a religious faith independent of patriotism, whose kingdom—
since they had no country—could not be of this world. But it was
then pointed out to him by a Jewish friend that he was being quite
unfair to "the petty bourgeois Cohens and Levis," who could hardly
be expected to be Moseses and Isaiahs, and who ought not to be
restricted to the status of aliens in countries in which they were
still not accepted on quite the same basis as other natives and which
were liable to anti-Semitic panics. Dr. Tillich was so struck by the
justice of this that he at once joined a Zionist organization.

To look into, to contemplate Judaism after living with Christianity
is to feel at first a certain emptiness. But it is something of a relief,
also, to get rid of the Christian mythology. The half-human figure
of the Savior is likely to introduce a disquieting personal element.
The Christian must refer himself to Jesus. What would Jesus have
done? What does He want me to do? How should a Christian be-
have? Or—in the case of a more fervent person—he may go further
and identify himself with Christ: struggle with temptations, endure
ordeals, offer himself to martyrdoms. There is always an emotional
relationship to another half-human being, and—since this being is
the Son of God—through him, to a Heavenly Father who is bound to
be more or less anthropomorphic. But the God of the Jews is remote: one cannot speak or write his name. He has no go-between
but the prophets, and these are human beings, whose words one
uses in praying but to whom one does not pray. In the Calvinist
church, to be sure, Jesus Christ played a minor role, could hardly,
in some cases, be said to figure; yet, in contrast to this kind of
"Christianity," too, the theology of Judaism affords a relief: no worry
about being Elected, no preoccupation with Hell.

Thus if the outlook of Judaism seems somewhat bleak, if its
observances—to a non-Jew—mean little, some contact with it is

nonetheless bracing. We are living with God in an empty room—in a room without pictures: the synagogue, where the only things displayed on the walls are words. These words declare the power of the Spirit, the authority of the moral sense. The source of this power and authority gains dignity from not being seen, from not being given a name, from being communicated with—not through the bread and wine of Christ's flesh and blood—but only through thought and prayer. There is only the conviction of its eternal reality, and sometimes of its actual presence.

EPILOGUE

Harold D. Lasswell

In the millennia covered by this volume Jews have been perceived by non-Jews as players of nearly every conceivable role and as possessors of every imaginable trait. The statements in the anthology are presented, not analytically according to a system chosen and applied by the editor, but historically and geographically; and within this capacious plan utterances are selected for representativeness or originality, with regard to diversity and prominence of source. The reader is faced with highly articulate formulations of practically every assertion that can be made by anyone about anybody.

In the arena of power Jews have been seen as friendly allies, correct neutrals, or threatening enemies. In the market place Jews have been valued customers and suppliers, or resented as clannish monopolists and cutthroat competitors. In matters related to skill they have been acclaimed for the excellence of their contribution to many fields, such as psychology and mathematics, or reviled for clumsiness in manual arts and infertility in music and the higher arts. In terms of enlightenment they have been hailed for cosmological conceptions which enrich civilization, or derided for lack of philosophic depth. In the sphere of friendship and intimacy Jews have been loved for lively warmth of personality and family devotion, or rejected for supposed incapacity for affections uncontaminated by cupidity and suspiciousness. In reference to bodily and mental health and innate capacity Jews have been highly regarded for whatever genetic factors may account for their hardiness, or their racial constitution has been stigmatized for alleged malformation and degeneracy. In regard to social class Jews have been perceived as natural aristocrats, or dismissed with contempt as a nation of upstart shopkeepers and pawnbrokers. Most persistently, they have been acknowledged as an instrument chosen by God to further the divine plan of salvation, or assailed for arrogance and obstinacy in refusing to recognize the true religion.

Impressive as this enumeration is, it barely hints at the diverse perceptions of Jews, collectively or individually, that have been attested by their Gentile environment. It is reasonable to affirm two propositions: *Jews have been perceived by non-Jews as all things to all men; some Jews have in fact been all things to all men.* In the arena of power Jews have at one time or another been somebody's ally; they have observed correct neutrality; they have been someone's enemy. In the market place Jews have in fact under various circumstances been valued customers and suppliers, or clannish monopolists and cutthroat competitors. And so on through the roles referred to in the previous paragraph. Diversity of perception, yes; diversity of fact, yes.

But the two do not invariably or even typically coincide. The "conventional" image of a particular time and place is not necessarily congruent with the image of the facts as established over the years by scholarly and scientific research. Conventional images of Jews have this in common with all perceptions of a configuration in which one feature is held constant: images can be both true and false.

The genuinely interesting question, then, becomes: What factors determine the degree of realism or distortion in conventional images of Jews? The working test of "the facts" must always be the best available description obtainable from scholars and scientists who have applied their methods of investigation to relevant situations. Granted, such "functional" images are subject to human error; they are self-correcting in the sense that they are subject to disciplined procedures that check and recheck against error.

In accounting for realism or distortion two sets of factors can be usefully distinguished: current intelligence; predispositions regarding intelligence. General Grant may have been the victim of false information in the instance reported in this book; if so, he would not be the first or last commanding officer who has succumbed to bad information and dubious estimates of the future. But General Grant may have been self-victimized. He may have entered the situation with predispositions that prepared him to act uncritically in the press of affairs.

Predispositions, in turn, fall conveniently into two categories for purposes of analysis. To some extent predispositions are shaped by exposure to group environments. In some measure they depend upon the structure of individual personality. The anti-Semitism of Hitler owed something to his exposure to the ideology of Lueger's politically successful Christian socialist movement in Vienna. But millions of human beings were exposed to Lueger's propaganda and record. After allowing for group exposures, it is apparent that other factors must be considered if we are to comprehend fanaticism. These are personality factors; they include harmonies and conflicts within the whole man, and mechanisms whereby inner components are more or less smoothly met. Modern psychiatric knowledge provides us with many keys to unlock the significance of behavior of the kind.

The foregoing factors are pertinent to the analysis of perceptual images and the broad conditions under which they achieve realism or fall short of it. Undoubtedly one merit of the vast panorama of Gentile conceptions of the Jew unfolded in the present anthology is that it provides a formidable body of material that invites critical examination in terms of reality. Many selections are themselves convincing contributions to this appraisal.

Undoubtedly, however, the significance of the volume is greater than the foregoing paragraphs suggest. Speaking as a non-Jew I believe that its primary contribution is in the realm of future policy. Since we can neither undo nor redo the past, we are limited to the events of today and tomorrow. In this domain the simple fact of coexistence in the same local, national, and world community is enough to guarantee that we cannot refrain from having some effect, large or small, upon Gentile-Jewish relations. What shall these effects be?

I am deliberately raising the policy problems involved in Gentile-Jewish relations. Comprehensive examination of any policy question calls for the performance of the intellectual tasks inseparable from any problem-solving method. The tasks are briefly indicated by these questions: What are my goals in Gentile-Jewish relations? What are the historical trends in this country and abroad in the extent to which these goals are effectively realized? What factors condition the degree of realization at various times and places?

What is the probable course of future developments? What policies if adopted and applied in various circumstances will increase the likelihood that future events will coincide with desired events and do so at least cost in terms of all human values?

It is beyond the province of this epilogue to cover policy questions of such depth and range. The discussion is therefore limited to a suggested procedure for realizing at least some of the potential importance of this volume for future policy. As a groundwork for the proposal I give some attention to the first task enumerated above, the clarification of goal.

My reply is that I associate myself with all those who affirm that Gentile-Jewish relations should contribute to the theory and practice of human dignity. The basic goal finds partial expression in the Universal Declaration of Human Rights, a statement initiated and endorsed by individuals and organizations of many religious and philosophical traditions.

Within this frame of reference policies appropriate to claims advanced in the name of the Jews depend upon which Jewish identity is involved, as well as upon the nature of the claim, the characteristics of the claimant, the justifications proposed, and the predispositions of the community decision makers who are called upon to act. If Jews are identified as a religious body in a controversy that comes before a national or international tribunal, it is obviously compatible with the goal of human dignity to protect freedom of worship. When decision makers act within this frame they determine whether a claim put forward in the name of religion is to be accepted by the larger community as appropriate to religion. Since the recognition of Israel as a nation state, claims are made in many cases which identify the claimant as a member of the new body politic. Community decision makers must make up their minds whether a claim is acceptable to the larger community in terms of prevailing expectations regarding members of nation states. In free countries many controversies involve self-styled Jews who use the symbol in asserting a vaguely "cultural" rather than religious or political identity. The decision maker who acts for the community as a whole must decide whether the objectives pursued and the methods used are appropriate to public policy regarding cultural groups.

We know that much is made of the multiplicity and ambiguity of the identities that cluster around the key symbol of the Jew. Many public and private controversies will undoubtedly continue to reflect these confusions in the mind and usage of Gentile and Jew. However, in the context of legal and civic policy, these controversies are less than novel. They involve similar uncertainties regarding the multiple identities of any number of non-Jewish groups. So far as the existing body of formal principle and procedure is concerned, categorical novelties are not to be anticipated in Jewish-Gentile relationships; claims are properly disposed of according to norms common to all parties.

It is not implied that formal principles and procedures are so firmly entrenched within the public order of the world community or even of free commonwealths that they will control in all circumstances involving Jews and Gentiles during coming years. Social process is always anchored in past predisposition; but it is perennially restructured in situations where anchors are dragged or lost. In conformance with the maximization principle we affirm that Gentile-Jewish relations will be harmonious or inharmonious to the degree that one relation or the other is expected by the active participants to yield the greatest net advantage, taking all value outcomes and effects into consideration. It is not difficult to anticipate circumstances in which negative tensions will cumulate; for instance, imagine the situation if Israel ever joins an enemy coalition. The formal position of Americans who identify themselves with one or more of the several identities of the Jewish symbol is already clear; the future weight of informal factors cannot be so easily assessed.

When we consider the disorganized state of the world community, and the legacy of predispositions adversely directed against all who are identified as Jews, it is obvious that the struggle for the minds and muscles of men needs to be prosecuted with increasing vigor and skill. During moments of intense crisis the responsibility of political leaders is overwhelming. But their freedom of policy is limited by the pattern of predisposition with which they and the people around them enter the crisis. At such critical moments predispositions favorable to human dignity most obviously "pay off." By the same test predispositions destructive of human personality exercise their most sinister impact, with the result that men of good will are often trapped and nullified.

Among measures in anticipation of crisis are plans to inject into the turmoil as assistants of key decision makers qualified persons who are cognizant of the corrosive effect of crisis upon personal relationships and are also able to raise calm and realistic voices when overburdened leaders near the limit of self-control. We are learning how to do these things in some of the vast organized structures of modern society; the process can be accelerated.

A truism is that the time to prepare for the worst is when times are best. During intercrisis periods the educational facilities of the community have the possibility of remolding the perspectives and altering the behavior of vast numbers of human beings of every age and condition. As more men and women are made capable of living up to the challenge of decency the chances are improved that the pattern of predisposition prevailing in positions of strength in future crises can be favorably affected.

Now an abiding difficulty of paragraphs like the foregoing is that they appear to preach; and in contemporary society we often complain of too much reaffirmation of the goodness of the good. In any case I do not intend to let the present occasion pass without dealing more directly with the problem of implementing good intentions. I assume that the number of readers of this anthology who regard themselves as morally perfect is small, and that most readers are willing to consider procedures by which they may gain more insight into themselves and better understanding of others. Properly used, the present book is an excellent instrument of enlightenment.

Let us not confuse the issue by labeling the objective or the method "psychoanalytic," for this is a well established term of art for the specific ideas and procedures initiated by Sigmund Freud and his followers for the study and treatment of disordered personalities. The traditional method proceeds by the technique of free association, punctuated by interpretations proposed by the psychoanalytic interviewer.

What we have in mind does have something in common with the goals of psychoanalysis and with the methods by which they are sought. For what we propose, however, a psychoanalyst is not necessary, even though one aim is to enable the reader to get beneath his own defenses—his defenses of himself to himself. For this purpose a degree of intellectual and emotional involvement is necessary;

but involvement needs to be accompanied by a special frame of mind.

The relatively long and often colorful selections in this anthology enable the reader to become genuinely absorbed in what is said, whether he responds with anger or applause. But simple involvement is not enough; self-discovery calls for an open, permissive, inquiring posture of self-observation.

The symposium provides an opportunity to confront the self with specific statements which were made at particular times by identifiable communicators who were addressing definite audiences—and throughout several hundred pages everyone is talking about the same key symbol of identification.

An advantage of being exposed to such specificity about an important and recurring feature of social reality is that it can be taken advantage of by the reader to examine covert as well as overt resonances within himself, resonances triggered by explicit symbols clustering around the central figure of the Jew. In recent times we have learned that minute investigations are essential if we are to disclose preconscious and unconscious processes to full waking attention. In this rather laborious way the individual's freedom of choice is actually enlarged, since hitherto unnoticed though influential components of the self are brought into the open and made subject to the discipline of examination in the setting of the total context of present aims and circumstances, and future contingencies.

Psychoanalytic experience has convincingly shown that not all pertinent clues to the self are deeply embedded within the well-nigh inaccessible depths of the unconscious system. On the contrary the profile of marginally accessible components is a jagged coast line. Hence it is no futile exercise to strike a permissive posture toward the self, and to note the flow of expectations, demands, and identifications, or accompanying feeling tones and intensities.

The first suggestion, then, regarding a procedure by which the impact of the present book can be enhanced is this: *Permit the mind to imagine and recall freely,* with minimum direction, as new statements are read, whether the manifest content of a statement is acceptable or not.

This frame of mind is in contrast with the argumentative stance so prominent in our civilization. The quick defensiveness of the argumentative posture excludes from attention the full admission of possible discrepancies between the norms that we profess and intimate thoughts, words and deeds.

Part of the flow of subjectivity that we experience as we read or reread these selections will be composed of reminiscences of past events, events of feeling, thinking, communicating, behaving; or events in which we listened to or observed the behavior of others. Each reminiscence is an eligible point of possible departure for a great many inquiries pertinent to the penetration of the social reality comprising ourselves and others.

If the objective of the exercise were primarily psychoanalytic in the traditional sense reminiscences would be associated to and interpreted for the purpose of exposing the deepest drives and mechanisms of personality. Such is not the aim of the present proposal which can be engaged in productively by persons who either have, or have not, experienced brief or protracted psychoanalysis. Persons who have undergone psychoanalysis have not necessarily become acquainted with the structure of the social reality to which they were originally exposed or the probable nature of the situations awaiting them in the future. Often the psychoanalytic experience seems to possess a distinctive reality of its own that attributes to the specific history of the individual ego, or to the principal figures in the early environment, attributes of uniqueness that leave a distorted map of the historical and social context in which the primary circle was interactive, and which may continue to be significant for the destiny of the person. By linking the intimate sequence of subjective and behavioral events with the larger social context the individual achieves an enrichment of perspective that affects his policy impact upon future individuals and groups. By breaking out of the caissons of private events and perceiving the ego event, with its fluctuating lines of identification with other egos, its demanded outcomes and assumptions of fact about past and future, the person is able to discover the universe of events and to transcend the alienation generated by exaggerated notions of uniqueness. In the modern world we have been learning the significance of perceiving our past and future career lines as sequences of events, subjective and non-subjective, within the challenging and as yet barely plumbed universe of events. Insofar as our subjectivities can be explained, they are at present explicable by referring to categories of factors present in every human situation. The events that we identify as our own appear to be outcomes of specific sequences in the ever shifting constellation of these factors.

Such questions as the following are pertinent to our "semifree" commentary as we read the anthology, especially if we are in temporary seclusion with our subjectivities and willingly undergo a private epidemic of candor. The questions ask "what" and "why"? *What* do I identify as my matter-of-fact assumptions about Jews in general or a particular Jew? What do I discover to be my feeling tones—of affectionate warmth, of alert suspiciousness, of distaste, of vague anxiety, or what not—at the thought of Jews, or a Jew? What do I discern to be my evaluative criteria (and applications)? For instance, am I thinking and feeling in terms of physical attractiveness or repugnance? Of ethical probity? What do I find are my urgencies to action regarding Jews in general and in particular? For example, has the symbol become so multicolored in reference that I have long since ceased to experience other than matter-of-fact subjectives when the term is used, or when I perceive that X is regarded as a Jew by Y or by himself? And *why* are my responses and initiatives what they are? How long have they been like this and why did they change or stay the same? In what situations do they differ and why?

These queries have been phrased in terms of "I," "me." It is evident that many of our reminiscences of recent and not so recent events will refer to other people who have said something about, or done something about, Jews. Then, too, there were persons and references in communication media who *were* Jews. With little verbal legerdemain the questions can be reformulated to raise parallel queries to those which have been asked about the primary ego of the reader.

Since an important aim of the present proposal is to call attention to the context of social reality at times or places that illuminate the manifold of events in which we live, suggestions will be offered about categories that may prove helpful. I take as a point of departure a simple reminiscence of my own. While reading a selection in the symposium I called to mind a contrast between professed norm and performance that was brought home to me and to fellow members of a social fraternity many years ago, when a fraternity brother whose articulated morality was unexceptionable suddenly broke off his engagement with a girl when he found that her mother was Jewish. He came from a Middle Western family of modest industrialists who were proud of their Prussian, though unillustrious ancestry; and his renunciation was abetted, not only by family upbringing, but by paternal threat to leave him no factories. Well, we asked one another, would we have the guts to act differently? And besides, may it not be that marriage is too serious to be left to love alone?

I dismiss at once the impact of the episode upon my own ways of thinking and doing in regard to Jews. The impact was minimal, save for some measure of indignation that my fraternity brother allowed himself to be influenced by family hostility and unacknowledged bias. But there are important questions regarding predispositions toward Jews in America at a recent cross section through history. As a convenience I frame these questions in six categories which, though they cannot receive exhaustive treatment here, may aid in clarifying the proposed procedure.

First, how representative was the incident of the predispositions that prevailed among young men in the early 1920's who had been exposed to a family environment provided by parents reared in a Prussian small town, who had come to a small city in the Middle West where there were many other German families? The general category here is *culture*, in the sense of a pattern of community life; and the cultures involved were Prussian, rural, and urban Middle Western America. It is impossible on the basis of existing research to provide a detailed reply to the question. However, many relevant data can be obtained from histories of the assimilation of Germans in the United States, from community studies in the Middle West, and from the results of sample surveys and related work. Trends in the dissipation or reenforcement of pro- or anti-Jewish syndromes can be described more fully as we come down to date.

Second, how typical was the pattern for young men currently or previously exposed to an upper-, middle- or lower-class environment? One of the principal emphases in recent decades in American sociology has been upon the empirical study of class perceptions, in the sense of who, in a given community, sees himself as occupying a higher, lower, or equal social position with other particular persons. In this way the perceived structure of social class—at least in the sense of respect groupings—is brought to light. The family of my fraternity brother was moving rapidly into an upper-class status in the local community; and there is evidence that the parents had experienced few challenges to the perspectives regarding Jews which they carried over from their upbringing as prosperous peasants abroad. The son, however, had been exposed to high school and later college (though not fraternity) mates, many of whom were Jews and with whom he was on a casually friendly footing. He was conscious of no advantages of any kind from acting, talking, or thinking of these individuals in any disparaging terms related to their religious or ethnic identification. We know that researches conducted in this country have located "pockets" of Jewish-awareness, often coupled with degrees of rejection, in various social strata.

Third, we can narrow the consideration of social environments to *interest* groups; that is, to groupings that may not include all members of a class, or which cut across class lines. My fraternity brother was active in athletic and in church affairs; also he was acquiring specialized skills in order to widen the range of business possibilities. In the several groups in which he participated Jews were sometimes allies and colleagues, sometimes rivals; but there were no crystallized alignments of which he was aware. We know, of course, that crystallized alignments of interest are ubiquitous and that a pro- or anti-Jewish posture may influence individual success or failure in many circumstances.

Fourth, we do not overlook the relatively stable value orientations which, together with preferred mechanisms of self-regulation, comprise a total *personality*. My friend had no doubt about his major social value: he wanted money. He also valued the respect, the political power, the opportunities for physical gratification, and other values that money seemed to make possible. He was in search of the sense of security that he felt was synonymous with great wealth. Today we have no hesitation in recognizing the relatively rigid mechanisms upon which he relied to keep himself in order. In modern behavioral research a recurring theme is the propensity of rigid personality systems to generate inner tensions that often flare out destructively.

Fifth, in this sequence, we speak of level of *crisis*. Strictly speaking, each of the preceding four categories might be reviewed in order to bring out the special significance of crisis level, since we previously assumed a "normal" condition. Here I shall refer to but one crisis: World War I and its aftermath. The incident described was to a degree an expression of World War I and the ideological disturbances connected with the defeat of Germany and the occurrence of the Bolshevik Revolution. My fraternity brother was affected by the exacerbation of anti-Jewish sentiment that accompanied these events. Many Americans of Prussian antecedents openly or covertly blamed the Jews for conniving at the defeat of Germany, the overthrow of the Hohenzollern dynasty, and the Russian terror.

Sixth, what *values* did my fraternity brother seek to maximize in situations in which Jews or Jewish symbols were involved? The reference here is to the maximization postulate as a dynamic principle. In simplest form it holds that we do what we expect will be to our net advantage. Hence we perceive and evaluate or act toward Jews as we do because we expect to be better off than by adopting another pattern. In this naked form the principle does not necessarily convey a sense of its potential importance. By the word "advantage" is not meant money alone, or power, or affection, or any single category of preferred events. Advantages refer to valued outcomes and effects of all kinds. Of some expectations we are fully aware. Other expectations may not be clearly recognized at the time, though when asked we have no difficulty in recalling that we were marginally conscious of them. We have also learned that unconscious processes include expectations, demanded values, and symbols of the self or of others.

For present purposes it is enough to recall that among the predispositions of my fraternity brother several conscious value goals were in intense conflict: affection, respect from one set of intimates, self-approval in terms of many ethical norms, self-assertion against domineering parents—all were ranged on one side; wealth, affection, and respect from important family figures, self-approval in terms of obedience to the family code—these, at least, were on the other.

The six questions are appropriate to the examination of groups as well as individuals. I refer only to the last question. This anthology provides a rich store of pertinent cases in which many values have played an obvious role in orienting group policy for or against the Jews. I shall not take the time to review the values of our college fraternity; they were, however, very relevant to the conflict I have been describing.

The procedure which I have outlined relies only to a limited extent upon the permissive, semifree technique of association that was mentioned first. Having no authority such as the psychoanalyst presents to propose interpretations (explanations) of reminiscences or other phenomena, the reader must rely mainly upon his own hypotheses, and also upon his own intensity of motivation to follow up questions and hypotheses by independent investigation. Undertakings of this kind readily lend themselves to self-selected study groups composed of members who share the common value of enlightenment.

All in all, the proposal is a simple one. It suggests that elements which are widely present in everybody's experience shall be given more articulate shape as a procedure of psychosocio-analysis. The aim is in no sense hostile to individual or group psychotherapy; in fact, there are grounds for predicting that many therapeutic processes would benefit by including psychosocio-analytic methods at some point. In a day of multiple experimentation with many strategies of education and therapy it is probable that many approximations have been made to this modest—in this case non-Swiftian—proposal.

To accept the discipline of psychosocio-analysis will probably have several consequences for the policy orientation of the participant. It will be borne in upon him that the existing institutions upon which we rely for comprehensive, accurate, and timely intelligence about social reality leave much to be desired. The consideration of Jewish-Gentile relations in a context that embraces all of history will inspire the suggestion that further anthologies are needed which can be of no less pertinence to the task of mutual perception and common definition of policy, as the future moves into the present. Besides the Jews, many other entities have kept their identity for long periods, and have been the target of enormously diverse perceptions which are apt objects of inquiry by methods that include psychosocio-analysis.

From the standpoint of policy goals and possibilities the present anthology can provide a renewal of dedication to the task of building a global community in harmony with the ethical aspirations which received such permanent and pervasive expression in the most truly universal part of the Jewish tradition. From the standpoint of non-Jews the urgency and magnitude of the task is great; and it is to be taken for granted that the process as a whole requires the full participation of insightful human beings, Gentiles and Jews.